Collected

Bodhi Leaves

Publications

Volume I

Numbers 1 to 30

BPE

BPS Pariyatti Editions

BPS Pariyatti Editions
An imprint of Pariyatti Publishing
www.pariyatti.org

Published with the consent of the original publisher.

First BPS Pariyatti Edition, 2017
ISBN: 978-1-68172-514-7 (hardback)
ISBN: 978-1-68172-330-3 (paperback)
ISBN: 978-1-68172-075-3 (PDF)
ISBN: 978-1-68172-073-9 (ePub)
ISBN: 978-1-68172-074-6 (Mobi)
LCCN: 2017910765

Typeset in Palatino Pali

Triple bodhi leaf cover image used with permission from Keith Carver Photography: www.keithcarverphotography.com

KEY TO ABBREVIATIONS

A	Aṅguttara Nikāya	Paṭis	Paṭisambhidamagga
Ap	Apadāna	Peṭ	Peṭakopadesa
Bv	Buddhavaṃsa	S	Saṃyutta Nikāya
Cp	Cariyāpiṭaka	Sn	Suttanipāta
D	Dīgha Nikāya	Th	Theragātha
Dhp	Dhammapada	Thī	Therigātha
Dhs	Dhammasaṅgaṇī	Ud	Udāna
It	Itivuttaka	Vibh	Vibhaṅga
Ja	Jātaka verses and commentary	Vin	Vinaya-piṭaka
Khp	Khuddakapāṭha	Vism	Visuddhimagga
M	Majjhima Nikāya	Vism-mhṭ	Visuddhimagga Sub-commentary
Mil	Milindapañha	Vv	Vimānavatthu
Nett	Nettipakaraṇa		
Nidd	Niddesa		

The above is the abbreviation scheme of the Pali Text Society (PTS) as given in the *Dictionary of Pali* by Margaret Cone.

The commentaries, *aṭṭhakathā*, are abbreviated by using a hyphen and an "a" ("-a") following the abbreviation of the text, e.g., *Dīgha Nikāya Aṭṭhakathā* = D-a. Likewise the sub-commentaries are abbreviated by a "ṭ" ("-ṭ") following the abbreviation of the text.

The sutta reference abbreviation system for the four Nikāyas, as is used in Bhikkhu Bodhi's translations is:

AN	Aṅguttara Nikāya	DN	Dīgha Nikāya
MN	Majjhima Nikāya	SN	Saṃyutta Nikāya
J	Jātaka story		
Mv	Mahāvagga (Vinaya Piṭaka)		
Cv	Cullavagga (Vinaya Piṭaka)		
SVibh	Suttavibhaṅga (Vinaya Piṭaka)		

Contents

Dhammacakkappavattana Sutta

(The Wheel of Law)

With the Pāli Text

Translation and Introduction by

Soma Thera

Bodhi Leaves No. 1

First published: 1960

INTRODUCTION

On the Fullmoon of Esala (July) every year, the Buddhist world celebrates the Festival of Isipatana, which marks the anniversary of the proclamation of the Noble Eightfold Path to the world by the Perfect One. For the Buddhist who appreciates the path of the Blessed One, and for all who have learned to think clearly on matters concerned with inner development and the enrichment of the mental life of mankind, the discovery of the Path and its promulgation constitute landmarks in the history of spirituality.

For seven weeks after the enlightenment, the Buddha, staying near the Bodhi Tree, thought over the implications of the discovery he had made, and its bearing upon the destiny of beings. He had seen life truly as it is; that is, as an arising and a passing away; he knew that when there is an arising, there is only the arising of ill, and when there is a ceasing, only a ceasing of ill. His compassion urged him to pass this knowledge on to the world for the benefit of living beings.

So, after much thought upon the way of presenting the doctrine to the world, he decided to seek out his old companions in struggle, the group of five ascetics, Koṇḍañña, Bhaddiya, Vappa, Mahānāma, and Assaji, who, next to two great teachers, Āḷāra Kālāma and Uddaka Rāmaputta, now dead, had been of greatest assistance to him in his quest. These five were then staying at Isipatana, the Sages' Resort, in the deer sanctuary near Benares, where, according to an ancient tradition, Enlightened Ones first make known their discovery of the freeing truth to mankind. And thither the Buddha went.

Earlier, at the end of the seventh week after enlightenment, while staying under the Goatherd's Banyan in the vicinity of the Tree, the Master had also thought thus, "The truth I have come at is deep, hard to meet with, hard to be awakened to, peaceful, sublime, outside the scope of speculation, subtle, and to be known by the wise. This generation, however, likes attachment, is gladdened by attachment, and delights in attachment. For this generation liking attachment, gladdened by attachment, delighting in attachment, it is hard to meet with this fact, namely, definite conditionality, dependent origination; this too, is a fact hard to meet with, namely the quiescence of all formations, the relinquishing of all essential support, the exhaustion of craving, unstaining, ceasing, extinction. Were I to teach the truth, and were others not to understand me, the fatigue would be to me: the weariness would be to me." But, after seeing that there were at least a few who were capable of developing insight, and after understanding the sufferings of beings, and wishing to relieve them of their burden, he, out of compassion for the many, wished to devote himself to the dissemination of the truth he had found.

Poets have movingly written of the journey of the Blessed One to give the gift of the teaching to his old friends. In the poetic accounts, it is said that trees were full of their flowery dower, cool winds were laden with blossom-scents, and in the fragrant air, birds' music floated throughout the fine pleasant days around the time of the full moon of Āsāḷha: it was as if nature in the country from Buddhagaya to Benares had got into a festive mood to observe the great occasion of the Setting in Motion of the Wheel by the World-honoured One.

The Buddha did not go far along the main road from the Bodhi Tree before he met a stranger, the ājīvaka (naked ascetic) Upaka, who was struck by the serene personality of the Buddha. Upaka addressing the Buddha said: "Pleasant and fully clear, friend, are your faculties of sense; your complexion is completely pure and bright. With whom have you gone forth? Or who is your teacher? Of whose teaching do you admit? On that, the Blessed One spoke to Upaka the ājīvaka in verse,

I am one who has overcome all, who cognises all, in all states uncleaving,
Who has abandoned all, and who has been released, having by my self understood.
Whom should I acknowledge? I have no teacher; one like me is not.
In the world with its deities there is not my counterpart:
I indeed am the arhat in the world; I, the teacher with no peer,

I am the rightly all-enlightened one; I am one become cooled, extinct.
To set in motion the wheel of truth I go to the Kasi's town;
In the world of blind beings I shall beat the drum of the deathless.
Upaka: By the manner in which you declare yourself, you are an infinite conqueror.
Buddha: Like me are conquerors whose cankers have been exhausted.
Conquered by me are evil states, so Upaka, I am a conqueror.

When these words had been spoken, Upaka the ājīvaka, said, "May it be so," moved his head back and forth, and, taking another road, went away.

After meeting with Upaka, the Master, according to one tradition, by easy stages came to the hilly country of Gaya, Rohithavastu, Uruvilvakala and Anala; from there he went to Sarathipura and finally to the shores of Ganges. At the last place the ferryman asked money of him to row him across. The Buddha said that he had no money; then by supernormal power he is said to have passed to the other side of the river. It appears that when Seniya Bimbisara heard about this, he ordered that bhikkhus should be ferried free, henceforth, in his kingdom.

When the Buddha reached Benares he went begging for food; and after his meal went to the Sages' Resort in the sanctuary of the deer. The five when they saw him at a distance were not keen in welcoming him, thinking that he was a slacker because he had given up self-torture. But when he came to their dwelling-place they rose from their seats and paid their respects to him.

Of Koṇḍañña it is said that he was not in mind averse to welcoming the Buddha from the start. The five knew not that the Buddha had attained enlightenment and would not believe at first that the Master had reached the goal. Later, the Buddha was able to convince them that he had. Then he taught them the middle path, and set in motion the Wheel of the Law (Dhammacakka).

That Wheel which was set in motion twenty-five centuries ago is in movement still in the universe of men's minds. It is a movement that increases with the growth of knowledge, of understanding, of wisdom, and the more the peoples of the world rise in culture, the greater are the chances for the continuance and prosperity of the Buddha-dhamma. The Dhamma will disappear from the world only when humanity reverts again to barbarism, savagery, and mutual destruction, through irrationalism, debased conduct, or stupid fanaticism. Then alone will it be time for a fresh setting in motion of the wheel by a new Buddha; but there is no need to pass through that dark night of the law, if we are tolerant and patient of each other, and wise to live without hurting and harming one another. Let it be the thought of every Buddhist by day, and his dream by night, to extend the frontiers of the Kingdom of Righteousness founded by the Buddha. We can extend the influence of that kingdom and preserve its power in the world for a long time only by following the principles that govern that kingdom; these principles are easy to practise if one straightens one's views and obeys the dictates of the good, the true, and the pure, the perfectly selfless ones, the arhats, of whom the Blessed One is the chief.

Dhammacakkappavattana Sutta

Thus have I heard.

Once when the Blessed One was staying in the pleasance of Isipatana, the deer sanctuary near Benares, he spoke to the group of five bhikkhus:

These two extremes, bhikkhus, should not be followed by one who has gone forth from worldly life: sensual indulgence, low, coarse, vulgar, ignoble, unprofitable, and self-torture, painful, ignoble, unprofitable.

Bhikkhus, the middle way, understood by the Tathāgata, after he had avoided the extremes, produces vision, produces knowledge, and leads to calm, penetration, enlightenment, Nibbāna.

What middle way, bhikkhus, understood by the Tathāgata, produces vision, produces knowledge and leads to calm. penetration, enlightenment, Nibbāna ?

Only this Noble Eightfold Path, namely,

Right Understanding—*Sammā Diṭṭhi*
Right Thought—*Sammā Saṅkappa*
Right Speech—*Samma Vācā*
Right Action—*Sammā Kammanta*

Right Livelihood—*Sammā Ājīva*
Right Effort—*Samma Vāyāma*
Right Mindfulness—*Samma Sati*
Right Concentration—*Samma Samādhi*

Truly bhikkhus, this middle way understood by the Tathāgata produces vision, produces knowledge, and leads to calm, penetration, enlightenment, Nibbāna.

This, bhikkhus, is the noble truth of ill: birth is ill, decay is ill, disease is ill, death is ill, association with the unloved is ill, separation from the loved is ill, not to get what one wants is ill, in short the five aggregates of grasping are ill.

This, bhikkhus, is the noble truth of the source of ill: the craving which causes rebirth is accompanied by passionate pleasure, and takes delight in this and that object, namely sensuous craving, craving for existence and craving for annihilation.

This, bhikkhus, is the noble truth of the cessation of ill: the complete cessation, giving up, abandonment of that craving, complete release from that craving and complete detachment from it.

This, bhikkhus is the noble truth of the way leading to the cessation of ill; only this Noble Eightfold Path namely, right understanding, right thought, right speech, right action, right livelihood, right effort, right mindfulness and right concentration.

With the thought: 'This is the noble truth of ill,' there arose in me, bhikkhus, vision, knowledge, insight, wisdom, light, concerning things unknown before.

With the thought, 'This is the noble truth of ill, and this ill has to be understood,' there arose in me, bhikkhus, vision, knowledge, insight, wisdom, light, concerning things unknown before.

With the thought, 'This is the noble truth of ill, and this ill has been understood,' there arose in me, bhikkhus, vision, knowledge, insight, wisdom, light, concerning things unknown before.

With the thought, 'This is the noble truth of the source of ill,' there arose in me, bhikkhus, vision, knowledge, insight, wisdom, light, concerning things unknown before.

With the thought, 'This is the noble truth of the source of ill, and this source of ill has to be abandoned,' there arose in me, bhikkhus, vision, knowledge, insight, wisdom, light, concerning things unknown before.

With the thought, 'This is the noble truth of the source of ill, and this source of ill has been abandoned,' there arose in me, bhikkhus, vision, knowledge, insight, wisdom, light, concerning things unknown before.

With the thought, 'This is the noble truth of the cessation of ill,' there arose in me bhikkhus, vision, knowledge, insight, wisdom, light, concerning things unknown before.

With the thought, 'This is the noble truth of the cessation of ill, and this cessation of ill has to be realised,' there arose in me, bhikkhus, vision, knowledge, insight, wisdom, light, concerning things unknown before.

With the thought, 'This is the noble truth of ill, and this cessation of ill has been realised,' there arose in me, bhikkhus, vision, knowledge, insight, wisdom, light, concerning things unknown before.

With the thought, 'This is the noble truth of the way leading to the cessation of ill,' there arose in me, bhikkhus, vision, knowledge, insight, wisdom, light, concerning things unknown before.

With the thought, 'This is the noble truth of the way leading to the cessation of ill, and this way has to be developed,' there arose in me, bhikkhus, vision, knowledge, insight, wisdom, light, concerning things unknown before.

With the thought, `This is the noble truth of the way leading to the cessation of ill, and this way has been developed,' there arose in me bhikkhus, vision, knowledge, insight, wisdom, light, concerning things unknown before.

So long, bhikkhus, as my knowledge, and vision of reality regarding these four noble truths, in three phases and twelve ways, was not fully clear to me, I did not declare to the world with its devas and māras, to the mass of beings with its devas and humans, that I understood incomparable, perfect enlightenment.

But when, bhikkhus, as my knowledge, and vision of reality regarding these four noble truths, in three phases and twelve ways, was fully clear to me, I declared to the world with its devas and māras, to the mass of beings with its devas and humans that I understood incomparable, perfect enlightenment.

Knowledge and vision arose in me. Unshakable is the deliverance of my mind; this is the last birth, now there will be no birth.

Thus spoke the Blessed One and the group of five bhikkhus glad at heart approved of the words of the Blessed One.

As this exposition was proceeding the passionfree stainless view of truth appeared to the Venerable Koṇḍañña, and he knew 'Everything that has the nature of arising, has the nature of ceasing.'

When the Blessed One set in motion the Wheel of Dhamma, the Bhummattha devas proclaimed with one voice: 'The incomparable Wheel of Dhamma is turned by the Blessed One at Isipatana, the deer sanctuary near Benares, and no recluse, brahmin, deva, Māra, Brahma, or other being in the world can stop it.'

The Cātummahārājika devas having heard what the Bhummattha devas said, proclaimed with one voice, 'The incomparable Wheel of Dhamma is turned by the Blessed One at Isipatana, the deer sanctuary near Benares, and no recluse, brahmin, deva, Māra, Brahma, or other being in the world can stop it.'

This utterance was echoed and re-echoed in the upper realms and from Cātummahārājika, it was proclaimed in Tāvatiṃsa, Yāma, thence to Tusita, Nimmānaratī and to Paranimmitavasavattī. The Brahmakāyika devas, having heard what the Paranimmitavasavattī devas said, proclaimed in one voice, 'The incomparable Wheel of Dhamma is turned by the Blessed One at Isipatana, the deer sanctuary near Benares, and no recluse, brahmin, deva, Māra, Brahma, or other being in the world can stop it.'

Thus in a moment, an instant, a flash, word of the Turning of the Wheel of Dhamma went forth up to the World of Brahma and the system of ten thousand worlds trembled and quaked and shook. A boundless, sublime radiance, surpassing the power of devas, appeared on earth.

Then the Blessed One made the utterance, 'Truly Koṇḍañña has understood, Koṇḍañña has understood.'

Thus it was that the Venerable Koṇḍañña got the name Koṇḍañña the wise.

Dhammacakkappavattana Sutta

Evaṃ me sutaṃ:

Ekaṃ samayaṃ Bhagavā Bārāṇasiyaṃ viharati Isipatane Migadāye. Tatra kho Bhagavā pañcavaggiye bhikkhū āmantesi—

Dve'me, bhikkhave, antā pabbajitena na sevitabbā:

i. Yo cāyaṃ kāmesu kāmasukhallikānuyogo—hīno, gammo, pothujjaniko, anariyo anatthasaṃhito;

ii. Yo cāyaṃ attakilamathānuyogo—dukkho, anariyo anatthasaṃhito, ete te, bhikkhave, ubho ante anupagamma majjhimā paṭipadā Tathāgatena abhisambuddhā cakkhukaraṇī, ñāṇakaraṇī, upasamāya, abhiññāya, sambodhāya, nibbānāya saṃvaṭṭati.

Katamā ca sā, bhikkhave, majjhimāpaṭipadā Tathāgatena abhisambuddhā—cakkhukaraṇī ñāṇakaraṇī, upasamāya, abhiññāya, sambodhāya, nibbānāya saṃvaṭṭati?

Ayam'eva ariyo aṭṭhaṅgiko maggo—seyyathidaṃ:—

Sammā diṭṭhi, sammā saṅkappo, sammā vācā, sammā kammanto, sammā ājīvo, sammā vāyāmo, sammā sati, sammā samādhi.

Ayaṃ kho sā, bhikkhave, majjhimā paṭipadā Tathāgatena abhisambuddhā—cakkhukaraṇī, ñāṇakaraṇī, upasamāya, abhiññāya, sambodhāya, nibbānāya saṃvaṭṭati.

Idaṃ kho pana, bhikkhave, dukkhaṃ ariyasaccaṃ:—

Jāti'pi dukkhā, jarā'pi dukkhā, vyādhi'pi dukkhā, maraṇam'pi dukkham, appiyehi sampayogo dukkho, piyehi vippayogo dukkho, yamp'icchaṃ na labhati tam'pi dukkhaṃ, saṅkhittena pañcupadānakkhandhā dukkhā.

Idaṃ kho pana, bhikkhave, dukkha-samudayaṃ ariya saccaṃ:-

Yāyaṃ taṇhā ponobhavikā nandirāgasahagatā tatratatrābhinandinī—seyyathidaṃ:—kāmataṇhā, bhavataṇhā, vibhavataṇhā.

Idaṃ kho pana, bhikkhave, dukkhanirodhaṃ ariyasaccaṃ:

Yo tassā yeva taṇhāya asesa-virāga-nirodho, cāgo, paṭinissaggo, mutti, anālayo.

ldaṃ kho pana, bhikkhave, dukkhanirodhagāminī paṭipadā ariyasaccaṃ:—

Ayameva ariyo aṭṭhaṅgiko maggo—seyyathidaṃ:—sammā diṭṭhi, sammā saṅkappo, sammā vācā, sammā kammanto, sammā ājīvo, sammā vāyāmo, sammā sati, sammā samādhi.

1 (i) *Idaṃ dukkhaṃ ariyasaccan'ti me, bhikkhave, pubbe ananussutesu dhammesu cakkhuṃ udapādi, ñāṇaṃ udapādi, paññā udapādi, vijjā udapādi, āloko udapādi.*

(ii) *Taṃ kho pan'idaṃ dukkhaṃ ariyasaccaṃ pariññeyyan'ti me, bhikkhave, pubbe ananussutesu dhammesu cakkhuṃ udapādi, ñāṇaṃ udapādi, paññā, udapādi, vijjā udapādi, āloko udapādi.*

(iii) *Taṃ kho pan'idaṃ dukkhaṃ ariyasaccaṃ pariññātan'ti me, bhikkhave, pubbe ananussutesu dhammesu cakkhuṃ udapādi, ñāṇaṃ udapādi, paññā udapādi, vijjā udapādi, āloko udapādi.*

2 (i) *Idaṃ dukkhasamudayaṃ. ariyasaccan'ti me, bhikkhave, pubbe ananussutesu dhammesu cakkhuṃ udapādi, ñāṇaṃ udapādi paññā udapādi, vijjā udapādi, āloko udapādi.*

(ii) *Taṃ kho pan'idaṃ dukkhasamudayaṃ ariya saccaṃ pahātabban'ti me, bhikkhave, pubbe ananussutesu dhammesu cakkhuṃ udapādi, ñāṇaṃ udapādi paññā udapādi. vijjā udapādi, āloko udapādi.*

(iii) *Taṃ kho pan'idaṃ, dukkhasamudayo ariyasaccaṃ pahīnan'ti me, bhikkhave, pubbe ananussutesu dhammesu cakkhuṃ udapādi, ñāṇaṃ udapādi, paññā udapādi, vijjā udapādi, āloko udapādi.*

3 (i) *Idaṃ dukkhanirodhaṃ ariyasaccan'ti me, bhikkhave, pubbe ananussutesu dhammesu cakkhuṃ udapādi, ñāṇaṃ udapādi, paññā udapādi, vijjā udapādi, āloko udapādi,*

(ii) *Taṃ kho pan'idaṃ dukkhanirodhaṃ ariyasaccaṃ sacchikātabban'ti me, bhikkhave, pubbe ananussutesu dhammesu cakkhuṃ udapādi, ñāṇaṃ udapādi, paññā udapādi, vijjā udapādi, āloko udapādi.*

(iii) *Taṃ kho pan'idaṃ dukkhanirodhaṃ ariyasaccaṃ sacchikatan'ti me, bhikkhave, pubbe ananussutesu dhammesu cakkhuṃ udapādi, ñāṇaṃ udapādi, paññā udapādi, vijjā udapādi, āloko udapādi,*

4 (i) *Idaṃ dukkhanirodhagāmini paṭipadā ariyasaccan'ti me, bhikkhave, pubbe ananussutesu dhammesu cakkhuṃ udapādi, ñāṇaṃ udapādi, paññā udapādi, vijjā udapādi, āloko udapādi.*

(ii) *Taṃ kho pan'idaṃ dukkhanirodhagāminī paṭipāda ariyasaccaṃ bhāvetabban'ti me, bhikkhave, pubbe ananussutesu dhammesu cakkhuṃ udapādi, ñāṇaṃ udapādi, paññā udapādi, vijja udapādi, āloko udapādi.*

(iii) *Taṃ kho pan'idaṃ, dukkhanirodhagāminī paṭipadā ariyasaccaṃ bhāvitan'ti me, bhikkhave, pubbe ananussutesu dhammesu cakkhuṃ udapādi, ñāṇaṃ udapādi, paññā udapādi, vijjā udapādi, āloko udapādi,*

Yāvakīvañ-ca me, bhikkhave, imesu catūsu ariyasaccesu evaṃ tiparivaṭṭaṃ dvādasākāraṃ yathābhutaṃ ñāṇadassanam. na suvisuddhaṃ ahosi, n'eva tāv'āhaṃ, bhikkhave, sadevake loke samārake sabrahmake sassamaṇabrāhmaṇiyā pajāya sadevamanussāya anuttaraṃ sammā sambodhiṃ abhisambuddho paccaññāsiṃ.

Yato ca kho me, bhikkhave, imesu catūsu ariyasaccesu evaṃ tiparivaṭṭaṃ dvādasākāraṃ yathābhūtaṃ ñāṇadassanaṃ suvisuddhaṃ ahosi, ath'āham, bhikkhave, sadevake loke samārake sabrāhmaniyā pajāya sadevamanussāya anuttaraṃ sammā sambodhiṃ abhisambuddho paccaññāsiṃ.

Nāṇañ ca pana me dassanaṃ udapādi, akuppā me cetovimutti ayaṃ antimā jāti, natthi' dāni punabbhavo'ti.

Idaṃ avoca Bhagavā. Attamanā pañcavaggiyā bhikkhū Bhagavato bhāsitaṃ abhinandun'ti..

Imasmiñ-ca pana veyyākaraṇasmiṃ bhaññamāne āyasmato Koṇḍaññassa virajaṃ vītamalaṃ dhammacakkhuṃ udapādi—yaṃ kiñci samudayadhammaṃ sabbaṃ taṃ nirodhadhamman'ti,

Pavattite ca pana Bhagavatā dhammacakke bhummā devā saddam-anussāvesuṃ: Etaṃ Bhagavatā Bārāṇasiyaṃ Isipatane Migadāye anuttaraṃ dhammacakkaṃ pavattitaṃ appativattiyaṃ samaṇena vā brāhmaṇena vā devena vā mārena vā brahmunā vā kenaci vā lokasmin'ti.

Bhummānaṃ devānaṃ saddaṃ sutvā Cātummahārājikā devā saddam-anussāvesuṃ ....

Cātummahārājikānaṃ devānaṃ saddaṃ sutvā Tāvatiṃsā devā— Yāmā devā— Tusitā devā. —Nimmānaratī deva— Paranimmitavasavattī devā —Brahmakāyikā devā saddam-anussāvesum:—Etaṃ Bhagavatā Bārāṇasiyaṃ Isipatane Migadāye anuttaraṃ dhammacakkaṃ pavattitaṃ appativattiyaṃ samaṇena vā brāhmaṇena vā devena vā mārena vā brahmunā vā kenaci vā lokasmin'ti.

Itiha tena khaṇena tena muhuttena yāva brahmalokā saddo abbhūggañchi. Ayañca dasasahassī lokadhātu saṅkampi sampakampi sampavedhi. Appamāṇo vā uḷāro obhāso loke pāturahosi atikkamma devānaṃ devānubhāvaṃ

Atha kho Bhagavā udānaṃ udānesi:—

Aññāsi vata bho Kondañño, aññāsi vata bho Koṇḍañño'ti.

Iti h'idaṃ āyasmato Koṇḍaññassa Aññā Kondañño t'v'eva nāmaṃ ahosi'ti.

— §§§ —

The Simpler Side of the Buddhist Doctrine

Kassapa Thera

Bodhi Leaves No. 2

First published: 1960

The Simpler Side of Buddhist Doctrine

When Prince Siddhattha, over 2500 years ago, finally achieved his quest and, under the Bodhi Tree at Buddhgayā, gained full enlightenment, becoming a Sammā Sambuddha, his first thought was that so high an attainment as this would be beyond the capacity of mankind, and that any attempt to teach others would only involve him in weariness of body. At the Temple of Rammaka the Brahmin, speaking to the bhikkhus, he said:[1]

"The thought came to me, O bhikkhus: 'This doctrine to which I have attained is profound, hard to understand, difficult to explain, rare, precious, not to be reached by mere reasoning, subtle, to be grasped only by the wise.

But mankind is seized, entranced, spell-bound by its greeds. Thus seized, entranced, spellbound by its greeds, this race of men will find it hard to understand the arising of all things through causes, and in dependence upon causes. And it is also difficult for them to understand how all the constituents of being can be made to subside—the doing away of all the bases of being, the quenching of craving, dispassion, cessation, Nibbāna. And now, should I teach this doctrine and others fail to understand, it would only result in trouble and weariness for me.'"

But looking over the world with the eye of a Buddha, the Exalted One saw that "Just as in a pond where lotuses are growing, blue, red and white, some of the plants, which have sprung up and grown in the water, do not reach the surface but grow under the water, while some reach the surface of the water, and others yet, standing clear of the water, are not touched by it, so, looking over the world with the eye of Enlightenment, I perceived beings of all kinds, lightly stained and deeply stained, intelligent and dull,

1 Majjhima Nikāya, 26.

good and bad, keen-witted and stupid, and some also who saw the terrors of the afterworld and the results of ill deeds."

> *So the Buddha decided to teach the doctrine, and breathed forth the words:*
>
> *"Open are the doors of the Deathless to those who have ears: let them repose trust."*

It is a common aspiration among Buddhists today to desire rebirth, as men, in the lifetime of the next Buddha, Metteyya; and there were large numbers of men and women who, making such aspiration in ages past, and working strenuously to deserve it, were reborn during the lifetime of the Buddha Gotama. Those were the lotus buds, unstained by the water, and standing clear of it, who waited but for the rising sun to open their petals in the glory of full bloom. Those were the first to "repose trust," listen to the Master and pass through "the doors of the Deathless," and there were thousands of arahants in the world.

But what of the great mass of humanity, those lotuses not yet ready for the dawn of the morrow's sun, those whose promise of bloom was even yet embedded deep in the mud of saṃsāra's slime? It is for such as these that the Arahants of the First Great Convocation, immediately after the Master's final passing away, patiently rehearsed the whole of the Dhamma, thereafter known as the Tipiṭaka which, till today, has been so carefully treasured in this Sri Lanka, in Ceylon.

The goal, achieved by the arahants of the Master's lifetime, and for hundreds of years since, may not be immediately within our reach today. But in this vast collection of teaching, our greatest heritage, there abound poems and parables, compassionate advice and direct simple appeal such as would touch any heart open to truth's simple message.

It is this that has brought countless millions to the feet of the Peerless One throughout all these centuries, and even today, more than 2500 years after that Dhamma was first revealed, yet commands the allegiance of a third of humanity. It is the simpler side of this Dhamma, the unchanging eternal law, whether Buddhas appear or not—well declared by the Blessed One, difficult to grasp even by the wise but not beyond the understanding and appreciation of the meanest intellect, that the majority of Buddhists follows today.

Strong limbs may dare the rugged road which storms,
Soaring and perilous, the mountain's breast;
The weak must wind from lower ledge to ledge,
With many a place of rest.

So is the Eightfold Path which brings to peace;
By lower or by upper heights it goes.
The firm soul hastes, the feeble tarries.
All will reach the sunlit snows.[2]

There are many Suttas in our books wherein the Dhammassāmi, the Lord of Truth, outlines the qualities to be acquired by the humble follower who would strive to lead a good life. But one chooses here an incident, recorded in the Aṅguttara,[3] that is a very poem of joy and domestic felicity.

The Blessed One was dwelling in the Deer-park near Suṃsumāragira, and he visited his followers, "the parents of Nakula." It is curious that nowhere are these delightful people mentioned by their own names: the commentary gives no help and, perforce, only as "parents of Nakula" may we know them. Both came to where the Teacher was seated, made obeisance to the Exalted One, and Nakulapitā spoke thus:

"Bhante, ever since Nakulamātā as a girl, was brought home to me, a youth, never have I known any transgression on her part, even in thought, much less in deed. We wish, Bhante, in this life to rejoice with each other, and also to rejoice with each other in the next world."

Then Nakulamātā spoke thus:

"Bhante, ever since I, as a girl, was taken home to Nakulapitā, a youth, never have I known any transgression on his part, even in thought, much less in deed. We wish, Bhante, in this life to rejoice with each other, and also to rejoice with each other in the next world." And, to these two, the Teacher speaks:

2 *The Light of Asia*, Edwin Arnold.
3 Catukka Nipāta, Vagga VI, Sutta 5.

"If, householders, both wife and husband should plan to rejoice with each other in this life and also in the next, then indeed should both be equally *saddhāvanta* (have trustful confidence in the Triple Gem), equally virtuous, equally generous, and equally wise.

Then, truly, will they rejoice with each other not only in this life but also in the next."

Here then is a teaching all can easily grasp—simple and straightforward. Sow together, and similarly, and you will reap together. If the sowing be of a high order, the reaping will also be of a high order.

As long as human nature remains what it is, men and women will marry; and marriage should be the closest companionship possible. No two others may aid or mar each other's progress in the sea of life as a married couple may. They can be beneficent friends (*kalyāṇa-mittā*); and, of such friendship, when once[4] the Thera Ānanda asked the Master, "Is it not a half of the holy life?" the Buddha replied: "Not so Ānanda! Not so. Beneficent friendship is the whole of the holy life."

The Exalted One himself is, naturally, the best "beneficent friend" a being may obtain, and next to him, in due order, come his disciples. But in the ideal marriage that everybody desires, the ordinary average man can visualize a happy couple, beneficent friends to each other, and aiding each other's progress not only in this life, but in life after life to come till, at last, each aids the other to the summum bonum of deliverance from all suffering.

In the Holy Books are many sermons, long and short, full of advice to the average layman. Notable amongst these is the Sigālovāda Suttanta, known as "the Layman's Vinaya" which details correct behaviour for the good layman. Excellent though all such sermons are, none can surpass the brief simple appeal of the words to Nakula's parents, which advise the cultivation of four things: *Saddhā*, Virtue, Generosity and Wisdom.

1. ***SADDHĀ*** is a difficult word to translate. It connotes so much more than "faith," which is the usual English rendering, that it is best left untranslated. The simplest form of *saddhā* is that which is

---

4 Saṃyutta Nikāya, Kosala Vagga.

seen in a child reverencing the Blessed One through his symbols, the relic-enshrining Dagoba, the Bo-tree that sheltered him when he became a Buddha, and the image that tries to picture him to our eyes. The child's *saddhā* in the Triple Gem of Buddha, Dhamma and Sangha, is due to its trust in its parents who thus far have guided it safely. It approximates the average man's "faith" in such matters as the North Pole, the electron and quantum theory, none of which he is likely to prove for himself in this life. The *saddhā* of the adult Buddhist is on a higher plane. It is the essential characteristic of Buddhist devotion, so conspicuous in the crowds that adoringly move from shrine to shrine in any Buddhist land on a Vesak full-moon day. Strangers, visiting Sri Lanka, may be surprised at the sight of this devotion, so like the attitude of the worshipping theist, in adherents of Buddha-dhamma which acknowledges no "creator," and demands cold reasoning and keen investigation.

What then is the meaning of this intense devotion, this earnest adoration? It is evidence of true Buddhist *saddhā*. Can we analyse this *saddhā*? Yes; and a powerful element in it is grateful love. It is this love that makes *saddhā* so sublime; it is utterly selfless; it expects nothing in return, for the Peerless One has "gone beyond" and can no longer aid any cosmic being personally again. In this devotion there is naught of the fear that may move a theist, no supplication. There is only love, selfless grateful love.

This love is the main moving element of *saddhā*, but its essential element is trust that becomes more and more confident as the devotee progresses in study, practice and realization, till, at last, it becomes the supreme unshakable assurance of one who knows, the arahant.

Both these factors, the Dhamma tells us, are worth cultivating. Their driving power is supreme. There is nothing to equal this unique thing, Buddhist *saddhā*. It is the spark that, tended with care, will one day burn up all impurity. And it is directed towards a man and his teaching, not towards a god. A man, who was once a man like ourselves, but whose heart blazed with a compassion, for all that suffer, such as we puny ones can scarce conceive. It was such a compassion as drove him on, sacrificing all that men hold dear, sacrificing life itself, time and again, so that he may, some day, snatch from life the solution of this riddle of an endless chain of deaths and suffering. Perfecting himself, life after life for countless aeons, he at last succeeded in his search. Under the Bodhi Tree at Uruvelā he sat, in that last struggle, with steeled determination—"Let my flesh and blood dry up, my skin, ligaments and very bones, but from this seat I rise not till Perfect Enlightenment is attained!"

He won, and, in winning that last fight, Prince Siddhattha became a Buddha, a fully enlightened one, an omniscient and incomparable one.

On that very Vesak Full-moon night, attaining the deepest 'one-pointedness" of mind, the Prince acquired in succession: "memory of past existences," "divine sight"—by which he saw beings dying and being reborn again—and knowledge of the "Wheel of Life"—the chain of causes and effects that makes up existence. "Then, O bhikkhus," said he, "Myself subject to birth, growth and decay, disease, death, sorrow and stain, but perceiving the wretchedness of things subject to birth, growth and decay, disease, death, sorrow and stain, and seeking after the incomparable security of Nibbāna the birthless, the free from growth and decay, the free from disease, the deathless, sorrowless and stainless—to that incomparable security I attained—even to Nibbāna the birthless, the free from growth and decay, the free from disease, the deathless, sorrowless and stainless.

Then I saw and knew—'Assured am I of deliverance, this is my final birth, never more shall I return hither!"[5]

For 45 years thereafter the Peerless One—compassionate, tireless, and patient—taught all who have ears and would repose *saddhā*, and his last words were:

"Look now, O bhikkhus, I urge you. Transient innately are all compounds. With zeal work out your aim."[6]

And we, ordinary average followers of that flower of humanity bow down at his shrines today, in that specially Buddhist form of devotion, *saddhā*, which is not faith indeed, so far as faith is blind, unreasoning, and based on no principle or fact in life. *Saddhā* is

---

5 Ariyapariyesana Sutta, Majjhima Nikāya.

6 Mahāparinibbāna Sutta, Dīgha Nikāya.

rather the maturer love and confidence, the true heart's adoration that comes in the train of understanding, when we have gained a little of self-mastery and begin to understand the value of self-sacrifice; when we begin to gain some glimpse of the meaning of that infinite love that has for us resulted in some slight knowledge of the law, our treasure.

So we heap piles of scented flowers, offer incense and lights before our teacher's shrine, and preface all our acts of worship and meditation with the well-known formula:—

> *Namo Tassa Bhagavato. Arahato, Sammā-Sambuddhassa !*
> "Glory unto Him, the Exalted Lord, the Holy One, the Utterly Awakened!"

So long as the self looms great in each of us, it seems derogatory to its vanity that one should kneel in adoration of any being, though he be the greatest on this our Earth or in the heavens beyond; it appears of little value that another should have given all his life, all of many lives, for the sake of helping life at large to find security. But as we learn to understand that craving desires, the cause of all our sufferings, spring from this same thought of self, and how difficult each poor act of self-renunciation is, we begin to see the value of our teacher's long quest. Setting our puny efforts beside our knowledge of the sacrifice which this discovery of the eternal law involved for one, the greatest and most perfect of men, we turn with shame from the thought of our paltry efforts, so mean do they appear.

Thus we see our true place, as compared with the heights of selflessness and attainment won by the holy and exalted. Our hearts are filled with wonder and love as we chant the ancient, beautiful Pali Hymn:

The Buddhas of the ages past,
The Buddhas that are yet to come,
The Buddhas of the present age,
Lowly, I each day, adore !

No other refuge do I seek,
Buddha is my matchless refuge:
By might of truth in these my words,
May joyous victory be mine!

This then is *saddhā*—a devotion, a love and a confidence that helps us onward. Without it, we can never win the fire, the power and earnestness that alone can forward our high aim. As the mists of "self" roll aside, bright and brighter yet glows the Buddha-beacon. "Once has one achieved, and still, on Earth, his glory shines over the dark floods of life's ocean, marking the path that each must cross to win the peace." By understanding the doctrine he revealed, we may surely guide our barque straight to that other shore, but the motive power, to drive our ships, is born from *saddhā*. Therefore, it is not children alone who need to kneel before the master's shrine and offer lowly gifts of light, flower and scent. We all need it, for the mental power it alone can yield—for none of us has finally escaped the fangs of self, and *saddhā* is the antidote to its poison.

We too need the act of homage though its adoration is directed, not to a person—for in truth all personality is a dream— but to our hearts' ideal. Thus may we ever find fresh strength and build a shrine of our own lives, cleansing our hearts till they are worthy to bear that image in an innermost sanctuary of love. Upon that altar all of us need to offer gifts daily, gifts, not of dying lights, fading flowers and evanescent scents, but of deeds of love, of sacrifice, and selflessness towards those about us.

These should be the Buddhist's daily offering in worship of the Perfect One. Striving to be his followers not merely in name alone, but in our hearts and lives proving that our Ideal has yet the power to call us and to guide.

And the cleansing power of *saddhā* will surely lead us upward, and towards our goal. For this we have the master's own assurance. In a sermon preached at the Jetavana Monastery, in Sāvatthī, known as 'The Parable of the Snake,'[7] an extremely instructive discourse to the bhikkhus, after assuring the Saints of the Four Grades of the absolute certainty of their deliverance, the Lord of Truth continues:

"Thus, O bhikkhus, the Dhamma has been well taught by me, made known, revealed, elucidated, free from shoddiness. And, O bhikkhus, in the Dhamma thus well taught by me, made known, revealed, elucidated, free from shoddiness—whatsoever bhikkhus

7 Alagaddupama Sutta, Majjhima Nikāya 22.

conform to the Dhamma, follow with *saddhā*, all these are destined to full awakening." It is true that the commentary, referring to this section, says: "The Theras of yore termed such bhikkhus 'Baby Sotāpannas"—possibly alluding to those who have reached the seventh and last "purity's" dawn, yogis of high attainment, but not yet "Ariya"—who also are termed "Cūla Sotāpanna." But I prefer the Commentator's earlier description of these bhikkhus as "Discerning people, who see there is no other Ariya Dhamma."

But that is not the end of the Sutta; for, our teacher concludes—and one cannot help but quote the very words of the All-seeing, so heartening are they:

"And, O bhikkhus, in the Dhamma thus well taught by me, made known, revealed, elucidated, free from shoddiness, whosoever turn to me merely with trust and love—all these are destined to heavens." So spoke the Blessed One. After such a clear and cheering assurance as this, there is no need to stress the value of *saddhā* to each and every ordinary average lay-woman and man.

2. **VIRTUE**—The next thing to cultivate is Virtue (*sīla*).

A striking thing in the Buddha-dhamma is that here we find naught of "Thou shalt" or "Thou shalt not." When once it is realized that selfishness and self-indulgence cause all our woe, then a wise one strives for self mastery. *Sīla* is the mastery of speech and action. Of his own free will, the Buddhist "pledges to observe" this precept of virtue, and that. The minimum number of such precepts of virtue that the good Buddhist should observe is five: (1) I undertake to observe the precept to abstain from destroying the life of beings; (2) from taking things not given; (3) from sexual misconduct; (4) from false speech, and (5) from liquor that causes intoxication and heedlessness.

On holy days, the earnest Buddhist observes eight precepts. In this list, instead of undertaking to abstain from only sexual misconduct, one substitutes 'all unchastity.' And the added three precepts pledge to abstain from taking food between midday and the next day's dawn; from dancing, singing, music, unseemly shows, the use of garlands, perfumes, beauty creams, and things intended to beautify and adorn; and lastly, from using grandiose and luxurious beds and seats.

All these precepts, from the layman's minimum five to the bhikkhu's numerous observances of virtue, are intended to purify speech and deed, to aid self-restraint and self-mastery. Non-Buddhists, at times, find fault with these precepts of virtue, calling them "negative." This is due partly to ignorance of Buddhist ideals, and partly to an innate selfish tendency to interfere in other beings' affairs which is a very common trait, both in individuals and nations. Great nations like to take up weak nations' burdens—at a reasonable profit. The ideal of plain living and high thinking is gradually becoming obsolete. The new model is to 'improve the standard of living,' a slogan of individuals and nations who have much to sell and want others to buy. The fashionable tailor would like even a bhikkhu to clothe himself stylishly. If the majority of us adopted Eastern dress, it would be a bleak outlook for the fashionable tailor. It is not universal love that prompts us to help a lame dog over a stile. We are not eager to aid a maimed snake or centipede over anything, except perhaps a passage into the next world. The dog protects us and our possessions, and yet, when our self interest demands it, we deliver even the dog to the vivisectionist.

The Buddhist wants to dominate his senses. Every one of the five senses clamours to be fed with what it likes—the eye clamours for beautiful sights, the ear for sweet music, the nose for pleasing odours, the tongue for delightful food and drink, the body for sensuous and even sensual contacts. Long have the senses done this, and long have they been pampered, till their insistence has become dominant and arrogant. And what, like an overworked tired servant, must serve these five lordly senses? It is mind. Mind, the true king, has been deposed, and mind's servants, the five senses, have usurped its place. The Buddhist would restore to mind its sovereignty. For mind is the sole weapon wherewith we may carve our way. The worldling's mind is exhausted by its labours, devising ways and means to serve the usurping senses. It has no breathing space to see things as they really are, because, forsooth, the taste sense may even addle it moreover, and blunt its keenness, with intoxicating drinks.

Sīla begins to remedy all this, and helps mind to study other things and to understand. The more one understands, the more one realizes the value of this *sīla* discipline. "As hand washes hand,

and foot washes foot, so right conduct aids right understanding, and right understanding aids right conduct."

With regard to the Buddhist precepts being "only negative virtues"—although one is tempted to ask what the positive aspect is of some of them, it is well to state here that Buddhist psychology does not share that view. Although the dominant "volitional" factor in each thought moment of determination to refrain from killing is the factor of "abstinence," a number of other factors, powerful amongst them being the positive factors of liberality, selfless love, and compassion, crowd around that leading factor of abstinence, making it easy for the strict observer of the first precept to practise the positive Buddhist meditations on universal compassion and universal love. So it is with each precept. *Sīla,* moreover, is not the whole tale of Buddhist effort at perfection. Every Buddhist must strive to perfect ten "highest states" (*pāramī*). Without perfection in these, he cannot hope to "enter the stream" of *pāramī,* of alms-giving, energetic activity, truthfulness, resolution and love, to such an extent of awe-inspiring completeness as would make the hair of even the most ardent admirer of "positive virtue" stand on end.

How would such an one, for instance like to "give alms" of his own body to a starving tigress? How far will he succeed in extending love towards a man who is lopping off his limbs the while he himself is bleeding to death? One who knows, knows that Buddhist doctrine inculcates the practice of the highest positive virtues to the highest extent possible.

And again, will the admirer of "positive virtues" prefer to live with murderers, thieves, lechers, liars and drunkards as his neighbours, or with Buddhists who abstain from all these things? He will naturally prefer the Buddhists. Why? Because with the Buddhists he will never have cause for fear. In other words, the virtuous Buddhist gives him *abhaya dāna,* the positive virtue of the gift of freedom from fear. And virtuous Buddhists, wherever they live, are constantly and freely giving *abhaya dāna* to all around them.

To a Buddhist, "Contentment is the greatest wealth." He aims at reducing his needs, not multiplying them; at controlling his senses, not indulging them. The five senses have combined to soil the lamp of mind to such an extent that, ordinarily, its light is dim and murky and things cannot be seen as they really are. *Sīla* is designed to cleanse that lamp, to purify the fouled oil, to renew the clogged wick, and wipe away the soot and dirt on the chimney, so that the lamp may glow brightly and throw light all around. Mind is the lamp, and Virtue is the cleansing process.

3. **GENEROSITY**—The next quality that the Buddha advised Nakula's parents to cultivate is Generosity (*cāga*).

The Pāli word *cāga* means "giving up," renunciation, generosity, munificence.

Cāga, with *saddhā, sīla* and *paññā* (wisdom) form the four blessings (*sampadā*) or accomplishments, pregnant with promise of early deliverance from all ill. And these same four—*saddhā, sīla, cāga* and *paññā*—are characteristic of the *kalyāṇa mitta*, the beneficent friend who will aid one to attain all good. The Teacher tells us[8] that "he who has *sīla* and *saddhā* excels all stingy people in generosity (*cāga*)."

The world thinks that treasure is acquired by hoarding and accumulating. The Buddhist ideal is just the opposite, and "*cāga paribhāvita citta*, a heart bent on giving," is one of the Seven Noble Treasures (*satta ariya dhana*).

Saddhā and *sīla* are two others of these "Seven Noble Treasures," and *paññā* (wisdom), which we have yet to consider, is another.

Beings burn with the fires of greed, hatred and ignorance. It is only with the extinguishing (*nibbuto*) of these fires, through not feeding them (*aggi anāhāro*), that it is possible to achieve the bliss of Nibbāna.

Note how, again, it is those five insatiable senses that cause all this world's woe. It is through the sateless greed of these five that even hatred springs up and all earth's quarrels, wars and endless strife. In the Mahā Nidāna Suttanta,[9] the Awakened One tells us how this comes to pass:

"Thus it is, Ānanda, that through sensations (*vedanā*) comes craving (*taṇhā*); through craving, comes chasing after (*pariyesanā*); through chasing after, comes acquisition of possessions (*lābha*);

8 Aṅguttara Nikāya 3:34.
9 Dīgha Nikāya.

through acquisition, comes deciding what to do with these gains (*vinicchaya*); because of decision, comes the excitement of desire (*chandarāga*); because of the excitement of desire, comes cleaving to these possessions (*ajjhosāna*), because of cleaving, comes enclosing with boundary walls and fences (*pariggaha*); because of enclosing, comes miserly avarice (*macchariya*); because of avarice comes a need for keeping watch and ward over possessions (*ārakkha*); and because of this watch and ward, there come to be the laying hold of cudgel and weapon, blows, wounds, dispute, disunion, strife and quarrel, slander, lies and many another unskilful things."

Again the Master says: "Ānanda, were there no craving of any sort or kind whatsoever, by anyone, for anything—that is to say, no craving for sights, sounds, odours, tastes, contacts, or ideas—then, there being no craving whatsoever, would there, with such cessation of craving, be any appearance of clinging?"

"There would not, Bhante."

"And sensations cause craving. Ānanda, were there no sensations of any sort whatsoever, in anyone, for anything—that is to say, no sensations born of stimuli received by way of sight, hearing, smell, taste, touch and imagination—then, there being no sensation whatsoever, would there, with such cessation of sensation, be any appearance of craving?"

"There would not, Bhante."

"Wherefore, Ānanda, just that is the origin, the cause of craving, to wit, sensation."

So one has to be ever watchful with these same clamouring senses, and when we experience their insistent calls, take care that craving greed does not arise from them. Such right mindfulness is the key to the whole course of Buddhist meditation, and ultimately opens the door to Nibbāna.

Cāga— generosity and giving up—opposes the thoughts of greed. Each one of us must learn to cultivate this "heart bent on giving." We must learn to give, to give promptly, before that ancient greed's after-thoughts rush in to prevent meritorious actions, whenever the urge arises. The urge arises in one's heart mainly from two kinds of beautiful thoughts—thoughts of compassion (*karuṇā*), and thoughts of reverential offering (*pūjā*). Thus arises all true greedless volition (*alobha cetanā*). He who gives a little with the aim of gaining much, in this very journeying of life, is only a practiser of usury. His heart is bent on accumulating, not on giving up.

Compassion prompts when we see a poor man in urgent need. Thoughts of reverential offering (*pūjā*) prompt when we see the greatly wise, the virtuous, the other-worldly and holy. The much misunderstood Buddhist practice of reverentially offering food-*pūjā* before the master's image is of the latter kind. The image does not eat food. The Exalted One himself has "gone Beyond" and needs food no more. Yet, were he here, how greatly would we like to offer him such humble p*ūjā* and because he has "gone beyond," our heart's urge prompts us to reverentially make such offerings before his image. It is a pure and greedless volition, and highly meritorious.

The hospitality of people in Buddhist lands is well known. In some lands folk may say—"There's a foreigner, heave a brick at him"—but not thus does the Buddhist treat a stranger—even after the strain of long years of exploitation and disappointment.

So long as he has aught to give, the Buddhist gives with an open hand. *Mitampacayā*, a 'measuring cook,' one who measures just enough of the rice he cooks for guests, is the old Sinhala term of obloquy for a niggardly person. Greatness of heart in giving, and greatness of heart in accepting a gift—these are things illustrated again and again in our books.

Once the Peerless One was going on his round for alms, and a slave-girl offered him all she had—plain poor cakes made of waste rice powder. She thought, "Alas! It is all I had. Will the Lord deign to eat such coarse food, he who so often is served by Mahārājās and Seṭṭhīs?" And the Buddha, seating himself by the roadside there, ate those cakes, in her presence and to her unutterable joy.

Once, the noble Arahant Mahā Kassapa, on his alms-round, stood before a forlorn leper.

"Will he really accept food from such as I?" wondered the leper, who, yet wondering, gave of the food in his own begging bowl. As he emptied the poor food into the Great Thera's bowl, a leprous finger, that had rotted to near self-amputation, dropped with the food into the Thera's bowl. "Woe is me!" thought the leper, "now he will never partake of this food !" But the mighty-hearted Arahant, carefully placing that fetid finger on one side, there and then serenely ate that tainted food.

Such are the marks of real culture. Mankind today is prating much of a "new world order." Can there be a "new order" in hearts that yet nurture the old, old poisons of greed, hate and ignorance? The only "new order" possible is for mankind to open its eyes to actuality, to see the truth of the Buddha-revelation and, adopting it, bring about that revolutionary change of heart that once made the glory of Dhammāsoka reign so great that its echoes still resound in world-history.

4. **WISDOM**—The last noble quality, mentioned by the Master to Nakula's parents, was the cultivation of Wisdom (*paññā*). And, with *paññā*, we ordinary average folk find that we gradually leave the simpler side of Buddhist doctrine and go towards the abstruse.

Yet, even here, there is much that, even to the less fortunate Buddhists of today, is clear and straightforward.

The Buddhist has no impossible postulates; he tries to see, as his teacher taught, "things as they really are." He looks at the world around him and sees that all, all is transitory there. He sees that what is transitory is bound to be sad. All that we love is passing away, and such parting from the loved is suffering. And we, we too are part of the passing show—with greying hair, falling and decaying teeth, disease and death looming ahead—it is all sad. The Buddhist sees that, to what is transient and sad, one clings in vain, and in all this we can see naught of which he can say—with assurance as to the permanent value of such statement—"This is me, this is mine, this is a soul."

Right here, one must pause to say that too many people in this world think that the world about them really is what they wish it to be; that happiness is round the corner, even if it is not too evident in the immediate environment. Thought is too undisciplined and vague. We refuse to pursue a train of thought that seems to lead to unpleasant conclusions, or even unfamiliar conclusions—like the woman who, seeing a giraffe for the first time in her life, exclaimed,

"I refuse to believe it !" We allow old usage, vested worldly interests and immediate convenience to dominate our freedom of thought. We shrink from facing facts—and yet, this is precisely what we must inflexibly do. The Buddha reveals facts. To him there were no theories. He, the "Teacher of Gods and men," knew.

In the Saṃyutta Nikāya[10] we are told how, long years after the meeting already related, the aged Nakulapitā visits the Buddha once again. No mention is made of Nakulamātā who, perhaps, has died.

"The fairest things have fleetest end, their scent survives their close: but the rose's scent is bitterness to him that loved the rose."

The old gentleman is broken-down, sick and ailing. He feels lonely and complains that rarely does he see the Exalted One:

"Let the Exalted One cheer and comfort me," he mourns, "so that it may be a profit and a blessing to me for many a long day."

To him the Lord gently replied:

"True true is it, gahapati; disease-harassed is the body, weak and encumbered. For one, householder, hauling this body about; to acknowledge even a moment's health—what is this but folly?

Therefore thus, say I should thou train thyself:

'Sick of body though I be, mind shall be healthy'—thus should thou train thyself.'

That was all. And Nakulapitā, feeling that he had been "sprinkled with nectar," gladly welcomed these words and, rising, saluted the Exalted One and departed.

How then is one to cultivate this "healthy mind" that remains serene in spite of all? The Buddha teaches us how.

He teaches us how to sow, so that we may reap happily. Though the Highest is not immediately open to everyone, the directions are clear. The Buddha wants us to see clearly, to see things as they really are—not as we imagine or wish them to be. He tells us to

10 Khanda Saṃyutta, Nakulapitu Vagga I.

objectify even ourselves—this body, these senses, all experiences, and even mind itself.

Close investigation on these lines alone can reveal the truth that nothing cosmic lasts, that nothing cosmic affords true happiness, that nothing cosmic has an unchanging core, a soul.

Then, at long last, one SEES—one sees the worthlessness, the filth and horror of the cosmic. One flings it away and, in the very flinging—at that instant—one intuits the HYPERCOSMIC, the permanent, the truly happy.

And that is what is termed "Nibbāna"—the goal.

— §§§ —

Earnestness

Vappo Thera

Bodhi Leaves No. 3

First published: 1960

Earnestness

Handa dāni bhikkhave āmantayāmi vo:
Vayadhammā saṅkhārā, appamādena sampādethā ti.

"Verily, I say unto you now O monks:
All things are transient, work out your deliverance with earnestness!"

These were the last words of the Buddha: for us, a reminder not to give up the struggle against the fetters of greed, hate and ignorance (binding us to existence), in order to escape the misery of saṃsāra.

A great satisfaction is given us by the master's solemn assurance that we do possess the power to overcome all evil things in us and to develop all good things. Just as the overcoming of evil, so also the begetting of good things in us, will bring us joy and happiness.

Therefore the Buddha said: "The evil and unwholesome things you should abandon, and arouse in you the wholesome." If this were impossible, the Buddha never would have advised us of putting forth all our energy and effort, and never would have said: "I am a teacher of endeavour, of energy."

Training must be done, will must be exercised, exertion must be made; there must be no turning back, there must be ardour, there must be perseverance, there must be mindfulness, there must be right understanding, there must be earnestness.

Whenever anyone accuses the Buddha of being a denier, a suppressor, a scorner, having no regard, etc., he should be answered thus: "Truly, regardless is the Buddha because all regard to visual objects, sounds, smells, tastes, bodily impressions and mental objects is utterly abolished in the Blessed One.

"Without love is the Buddha, because all love for visual objects, sounds, smells, bodily impressions and mental objects is utterly destroyed in him.

"Inactivity teaches the Buddha, because he teaches not to be active in doing evil by thoughts, words and deeds.

"Annihilation teaches the Buddha, the annihilation of greed, anger and delusion. A scorner is the Buddha because he scorns all bad actions in thoughts, words and deeds. A denier is the Buddha because he denies all greed, hate and ignorance and all the other unwholesome things.

"A suppressor is the Buddha because he teaches us to suppress all evil and unwholesome things, and to suppress all bad action, in thoughts, words and deeds. And one who has completely suppressed all these things is called a suppressor. An outcast is Buddha because has been cast out from saṃsāra and excluded from further rebirth." (AN 8:11)

> *Earnestness leads to the Deathless,*
> *Heedlessness is the road to death;*
> *The earnest men will never die,*
> *The heedless seem already dead.* (Dhp 21)

"What many monks and laymen have attained—why should I not attain this? I am healthy, full of faith, am not a hypocrite, not a pretender or boaster, but I have willpower and understand that all sense objects are transient, subject to pain and suffering, an ulcer, a thorn, a misery, a burden, an enemy, a disturbance, empty and void of an ego. Why should I not hope for deliverance and Nibbāna?"

In the Mahāvacchagotta Sutta, the Blessed One said that not only monks and nuns attained Nibbāna, but that even many laymen and laywomen, remaining in the world and living a chaste life free from fetters and hindrances of mind, had attained Anāgāmiship—i.e. the third state of the "Non-returner," so called as he after death never will again return to this world.

Just now, in this present materialistic age, such words of the Buddha should have a stimulating and encouraging effect, because many people are labouring under the delusion that in this modern time of aeroplanes and auto cars, the present generation, despite their best intentions, could not find time and leisure to cultivate higher mental faculties.

Over and over again the Buddha assures: "You can rouse your will, you can act, you can change your character by certain lines of efforts and attain deliverance!"

He who wills success, is half way to it. Where there is a will, there is a way! The will is the root of all things, not only of vice and suffering, but also of virtue.

Negation of the will for demeritorious action is taught by the Blessed One.

"*Chanden'eva chandaṃ pajahati*: through will willing can be conquered." Having attained holiness through will, the will for holiness has been stilled.

In the Iddhipāda-Saṃyutta (SN 51) the brahmin Unnabha asks the Venerable Ānanda: "What is the purpose of the holy life as explained by the ascetic Gotama?"

"To give up one's will, therefore one practises the holy life under the Exalted One."

"Is there a way, a path, to give up one's will?"

"There is, Brāhmana, a way, a path, to give up one's will." "What is now, Venerable Ānanda, the way, the path, to give up this will?"

"Herein a monk develops the four roads to power: concentration and effort of will, of energy, of mind and of investigation. This, Brāhmaṇa, is the way, the path, to give up one's will."

"This being so, Venerable Ānanda, there will be only an endlessness: but no end of the actions of willing. That through will, the will may be dissolved—such a thing is not possible."

"So I shall put you a question, Brāhmaṇa, and you may answer it as you please.

"What do you think, Brāhmaṇa, did not arise in you first the will to go to the monastery, did the will then not come to an end?"

"Yes, O Lord."

"It is just the same with the monk who, holy, freed from greed, perfect, who has accomplished his task, thrown off the burden, attained deliverance through wisdom. Whatever such a one formerly possessed of will, energy, mind and investigation with regard to the attainment holiness, having become holy—such energy, such mind and such investigation has ceased.

"What you think now, Brāhmaṇa, if so is there an end or endlessness of willing?"

"Certainly, Venerable Ānanda, if it is so, then there is an end of willing and no endlessness."

"The will (*cetanā*)," says the Buddha, "I declare as the (karma): for through the will one performs actions in thoughts, words and bodily deed." The will is the action, and nobody can pull back the decision one has taken. Only he who earnestly strives for developing higher mental faculties can accomplish what the multitude thinks impossible.

"You will became truth, if you love the truth. You will become earthly, if you love the earthly." The faith of every man comes out of his innermost: what he loves he is, and what he is he loves, and he believes it too and will be united with it; because every thought attracts its thought object.

He who does his work as in duty bound, will attain Nibbāna by following the Holy Eightfold Path, consisting in Right Understanding, Right Thinking, Right Speech, Right Action, Right Living, Right Effort, Right Attentiveness and Right Concentration, be it in this life, be it in the next life, be it in any other future life.

Therein take your refuge, therein see your sovereign remedy, and with all your heart strive for it; then will peace develop into everlasting bliss.

To know the whole truth, not merely by words, but to know it from actual inner experience, this is the greatest need of life.

"To know is to do": without carrying out in practice, there is no true knowledge in mind. Take it and make it the guide of your life! But the proof of the pudding is in the eating.

A true Buddhist lay devotee always strives for wisdom, trying to know the world in its outer and inner manifestation, to penetrate to the conditional arising of all mental and physical phenomena. He will reach that high and lofty realm of freedom; because of his self-control he will get to know the wholesome and unwholesome influxes of his mind.

Therefore, he is always alert and mindful, gets his livelihood by a right way of living, abstains from alcohol, narcotics and stimulants, refrains from food after noon at least once a month, leads a retired life; he avoids harsh language and abstains from quarrelling, suppresses all demeritorious things arising in his mind, remains always even-tempered when despised, passes no judgment about others as he knows that by doing so he will harm himself.

In short, he is always clearly aware of all his actions in thoughts, words and deeds, utters always the right word, at the right time, on the right spot.

Thus he lives for his own welfare, for the welfare of the whole world. In spite of all ignorance, of all greed, anger and delusion, mankind is connected by an invisible tie, a tie of goodwill, loving-kindness, compassion and sympathetic joy, a tie which binds us together as the same kind of beings of nature. It is not an empty dream but a truth. The destination of mankind is to attain to highest wisdom, Enlightenment and Nibbāna, and every one can reach this goal if he fulfils the necessary conditions.

Whether one lives the life of a householder, or whether one becomes a monk, when there is wrong living it is impossible to attain deliverance of mind; but if the mode of life is according to the Holy Eightfold Path, one is sure to attain the goal of holiness, Nibbāna.

In gradual progress the holy path leads man along, from the mundane to the supermundane; such a being, following the holy path, becomes a superman compared with the worldling; but its highest perfection is reached by the Enlightened One.

To work for enlightenment and deliverance of mind is everywhere possible for one who has heard the teachings of the Buddha and puts them into practice.

At what epoch, in which era, is it possible to attain enlightenment and deliverance of mind? It is not limited to any epoch or era. As long as there are men willing to develop the Holy Eightfold Path, and are absorbed in meditation on the Buddha, Dhamma and

Sangha, delighted in the growth of moral and mental faculties, for so long the attainment of the highest goal of final emancipation will be possible.

Hence the truth proclaimed by the Blessed One depends on no special period of time. It is the visible truth leading to Nibbāna, but it can be penetrated and realized only by a wise man, through his own experience.

"Enraptured with lust, enraged with anger, blinded by delusion, with mind ensnared, man aims at his own ruin, at the other's ruin, at the ruin of both, and he experiences mental pain and grief." But as soon as lust, anger and delusion are given up, then all mental pain, grief and sufferings are destroyed and one has reached "the Everlasting." Such is the teaching of the Holy One, the timeless and visible truth leading to Nibbāna, which is intelligible only to a wise man through his own experience.

So long as there are monks who are filled with living faith in the Buddha, Dhamma and Sangha and live together in harmony and feel it their duty to follow the Holy Eightfold Path, and live untiring in developing meritorious actions, and detest slothfulness, for so long will the Dhamma, the universal law, continue.

Thus it rests with us to decide whether the Dhamma should continue for the good of many or whether the demon in human shape should gain power.

The "will" manifested in our good and bad actions decides about our future and our whole destiny. Only he who understands the whole truth, and nothing but the truth, furnishes the conditions for a long duration of the Dhamma; whilst those with a wrong understanding will ruin the Dhamma in no time.

The truth has one great obstacle to face—delusion, which constantly opposes it. Not the common sceptic is the greatest adversary of the Dhamma, but the man with great enthusiasm and little knowledge; the clever hair-splitter who adheres to his system as the one and only refuge, the pious man who follows blindly tradition and faith, who is afraid to give any opinion of his own but only what he has learnt in school, and the fanatic with his narrow mind—all those are the real enemies of truth.

It seems nearly impossible to carry the torch of truth through the crowd without scorching it. Now, what may be the cause that there are only so few people in our present time that attains deliverance of mind, though the path to liberation is clearly shown? The cause is that the mass of the people are not walking on the Holy Eightfold Path, and that they do not like to exercise control over their minds. They will perhaps say:

Well, what can the world bestow on me?
"Thou shouldst renounce, renounce."
That's the constant song that ever in our ears resounds.
And all our life we hear that irksome song!

"Why, truth, didst thou come to worry us before our time and bring so much affliction?" Thus the ignorant talk without rhyme or reason. They feel bored, and at that time they shun to delve into their own minds. Often it is also politics that swallows up all desire for developing higher faculties of the mind which would enable man to perceive clearly and distinctly the world in which he lives in its true light.

The noble disciple of the Buddha, however, considers this world as a labyrinth of errors, as a dreadful desert, as a morass of infamy, as a dwelling place of wild beasts, as a land of ill-luck, as a source of sorrow, as an ocean of misery, as a false joy, as an endless suffering, as greed, anger and delusion beyond measure, as thirst never stilled, as a skeleton at the feast, as a laugh on the wrong side of the mouth, as a stink in the nostrils, as a delicious drink mixed with poison, as a place too burning hot for staying on, as a mirage, as a den of vice, as a constant disharmony, as a pitiless war, as the breath of death, as a hell for the living, as an endless funeral, as a pompous illusion, as an arrogant misery, as a deplorable luck, as an apothecary's shop full of bitter though gilded pills.

For that reason, the noble disciple has no longer the desire to build up this world but to get rid of it. He knows that no thing in it is worth to be attached to. All bodily forms, feelings, perceptions, mental formations, and consciousness he regards as transient, subject to pain and suffering and void of an ego. Having thus attained insight into these five groups of existence, the noble disciple will attain deliverance of mind in due course and will reach happiness supreme.

Hence, how can one say that the following of the Holy Eightfold Path be equal to self-torment and pessimism, while it is the unfolding of inner serenity accompanied by unhemmed moral courage—the only worthy endeavour in life. This is the solace the Buddha gives in which our heart always delights and which guides us from worldly illusions into the realm of truth. From the restless struggle for existence to everlasting peace.

It is a delusive idea to regard this world as the best that is imaginable; behind the laughing mask of nature other things hide than mere mirth and jubilation. Take away the mask and you will find such things as cannibalism, child murder, sanctioned killing in many forms, slavery and bondage, theft and robbery, oppressing and torturing of old and helpless people and prisoners, disregard for the life of others. Massacre and attack from enemies shedding blood like water, taking delight in ferocious deeds, shamelessness and sexual perversion of every sort; and there is egotism without limits. Thus the silent thinker beholds the world and life which multitudes welcome and love so dearly.

"Don't trouble me with your Mother Nature," told Prof. Naegeli to a student who in his thesis bestowed great praise upon nature.

He said: "If Mother Nature had been as kind-hearted as the common run of people say, she would never allow the cat playing with the mice so cruelly, and the red-backed shrike piercing the insect in such a horrid and dreadful way. Who else did put such horrid instincts into these animals but your glorified mother nature?

"She certainly disposes over wonderful instruments and arrangements by which she is of great use to us today, but she will destroy us tomorrow.

"Don't try to find compassion in nature! Amongst men you may find compassion. We must compel nature to hand over to us her instruments to our interest."

For evaluating life correctly it is necessary to plunge into a deep contemplation of all that is alive and astir on this earth. There the "Ecce vita" will, as a plastic picture, reveal to our mind's eye that Gorgon's head whose looks turn the beholder to stone.

Generally, most people dislike to see the true facts of life. They like to lull themselves in security by sweet dreams and imaginations, taking the shadow for the substance; but whenever they see for one moment things in their true nature, they turn away in a shudder and say: "My dear Sir, don't think about those things so deeply."

Such people succeed in deceiving themselves more thoroughly by their false pretences, subterfuges and evasions, than often the philosopher does by speculating on "self" or "soul."

In the air, as on earth and in water, all living beings are engaged in a permanent struggle for existence, in the unending battle of life. "*Aññamaññakhādikā ettha vattati*—Devouring each other is the practice here," says the Buddha.

Due to greed, anger and delusion, man is always at war with his neighbour, trying through tricks, dodges and devices, to live at the expense of others; like Cain, to kill his brother, rob him or make him his slave. And the more man becomes civilized, the more dreadful is the struggle for existence—sounds of merciless savagery, anguished shrieks of mortal fear and horrible yells of death cry to heaven for vengeance.

With shuddering, we behold the gruesome scenes of crime, of war and plague, with their havoc, devastation and misery. With our mind's eyes we can read in the human heart the torturing thoughts of guilt, of repentance and accusation, "Oh, have pity, your gloomy ghosts of guilt." But they have not. Threateningly they appear before the guilty conscience: pictures of judgment run through the mind that is in mortal fear.

Numberless like the stars in the sky, man's prayers rise to heaven, but there is no response.

> *They never will be heard in heaven*
> *If heaven does not enter us.*
> *And only there the prayers ripen,*
> *Where love and mercy fill our heart;*
>
> *There will the ever rising sorrows calm down,*
> *there in that heart alone,*
> *That, free from fear and unrest, firmly*
> *Is fixed on Buddha's Holy Law.*

Through steadily following the Holy Eightfold Path, and by training the heart in noble effort and patience, it is possible even for the worst evil-doer to bring gradually the liberation of his heart to highest perfection and so partake of happiness sublime.

Thus one can rightly say that the teaching of the Buddha bestows the highest happiness, even in this present life. It fulfils all our higher aspirations and makes the sun of righteousness shine in our heart. It satisfies all that can rightly be expected from a life that is impermanent, and gives us a deep sense of imperturbable calm. It does not allow us to fall into error and guilt again and again, and cleanses us gradually from all greed, anger and delusion. It frees us for ever from all evil and suffering by bestowing the incomparable ultimate security of Nibbāna.

Even our good acts and our sacrifices for the welfare of others, be they ever so great and noble, even they are transient, and will not protect us for ever against the torments of suffering. But the Four Noble Truths proclaimed by the Buddha are immutable, indestructible and everlasting.

And that generation is the happiest where these four holy truths are well established and well understood. For that reason, one should not miss such rare opportunity which our present age still affords, but rouse one's will to realize these truths and reach enlightenment.

That is why the Buddha said at the time of his death: "All things are impermanent, work out your deliverance with earnestness!"

Adhigataṃ idaṃ bahūhi amataṃ,
Ajjāpi ca labhanīyaṃ idaṃ,
Yo yoniso payuñjati
Na ca sakā aghaṭamānena.

"Attained has been this deathlessness by many,
And still today this state can be obtained by him who strives in earnestness,
But none will reach it without effort."

Therīgāthā 513

— §§§ —

Of Gods and Men

Francis Story

BODHI LEAVES NO. 4

First published: 1960

Of Gods and Men

We are all familiar with the fact that man in former days readily believed in the existence of an unseen world, a world of ghosts, demons, nature-spirits which were worshipped as gods, and a host of other supernatural beings. This world lay all about him and in some respects was more real to him than the physical world. It was his belief in it, and in the power of the forces it contained, that gave birth first to primitive magic and later to religion.

Even today, vast numbers of people all over the world, and not merely among savage tribes or backward peasantry, but in advanced and educated communities, particularly in Asia, still believe in this mysterious realm and in various classes of beings that inhabit it, to an extent that would surprise most Westerners apart from those who have made a study of the subject. To the Asian mind it is equally surprising that Westerners, with the exception of spiritualists, are sceptical regarding it.

Since this widespread belief cannot be attributed to ignorance or to any collective infirmity of mind, there must be another reason for it. If it is a reason that the average Englishman, American or Australian finds difficult of acceptance, the obstruction may be in his own mental attitude. We are all conditioned by past habits of thought, the mental climate of our environment and concepts, those "idols of the market place and of the theatre"[11] which we take to be established truths without having troubled to question them. Before dismissing the ideas of a considerable portion of the human race as mere fantasy we should do well to examine first the background of our own thinking.

For many years past, science has been exploring the physical world and laying bare its secrets. In order to do so, scientists have worked on the assumption that for every visible phenomenon there must be a physical explanation, and this axiom has had to be taken as a

11 Two of Bacon's classifications, adopted by him from Giordano Bruno.

fundamental principle of scientific method. It must always be so, in regard to the substance and laws of this tangible world in which we live and receive our ordinary sense-impressions, for once it were admitted that a certain phenomenon was not to be explained by any but supernatural means, all systematic investigation of it would come to a stop at whatever point the investigator found himself baffled. It always has to be believed that if the answer to a particular problem is not at present available within the limits of scientific knowledge, it will ultimately become known through an extension of the methods already in use. This may quite legitimately be called the scientist's creed; it states his faith in the *rationale* of the principles on which he works.

The remarkable success of the method has given the ordinary layman a picture of the universe that appears to leave no place whatever for any laws or forces apart from those the scientist knows and employs in his work. But as knowledge increases and the scientist develops a philosophic mind his own picture of the world changes. He knows, better than the reader of popular science literature, how limited scientific knowledge is when it is confronted with the ultimate questions of man's being. So we get Sir James Jeans with his concept of a universe which, although it excludes God, nevertheless bears all the marks of a mental construction; Bertrand Russell with his opinion that it is unreasonable to suppose that man is necessarily the most highly developed form of life in the universe; Max Loewenthal showing on physiological and dialectical principles that the mind must be something independent of the brain cells; and a number of other eminent scientific thinkers who are not afraid to admit that knowledge gained on the material level, while it can show us the way in which physical processes take place, has brought us no nearer to a revelation of their underlying causes.

But the non-technical man-in-the-street who sees only the astonishing success of scientific research has come to hold the mistaken view that the principle which calls for a material explanation of all phenomena must mean that there cannot, *ipso facto*, be any other laws or phenomena apart from the physical. In other words, he mistakes the principle adopted as the necessary basis of a certain method for a final verdict on the nature of existence. That in itself is an unscientific view, for science does not deliver any final verdicts on any question, least of all on those beyond its present scope. The materialist who adopts a dogma to that extent is departing from true scientific principles. If, as a scientist, he tries to make his discoveries conform to his dogma, he is betraying the first rule of his calling.

Fortunately, that does not happen where scientists are still free men, and the horizons of scientific thought are now being expanded to include phenomena that cannot be classed as material. We now have not only biologists who are seemingly on the verge of discovering how non-living matter becomes transformed into living organisms, but also workers in the field of parapsychology who are intensively studying a range of hitherto neglected phenomena connected with the mind itself. Their findings, surprising and sometimes disturbing as they are, do not come before the general public to the same extent as do those of scientists whose work has a more immediately applicable function, such as that of the nuclear physicists. But these discoveries, nevertheless, may prove ultimately to be of greater value to mankind than the more sensational work of the scientists who are giving us new, and potentially dangerous, sources of power.

Parapsychology is the term used to denote all forms of extrasensory perception (E.S.P); it has given scientific respectability to the study of a variety of mental phenomena whose existence has always been known to non-scientific peoples, such as clairvoyance, telepathy and trance-mediumship. One reason for the fact that it has not yet received universal recognition is that no absolutely satisfactory scientific methodology has so far been devised for investigating these faculties, since obviously the formulas of physical experiment and verification cannot be applied. So far, the investigators have been able to present the results of experiments in telepathy, telekinesis, clairvoyance and clairaudience which show the existence of such extrasensory faculties in certain persons, but they cannot yet offer a scientifically-formulated account of the laws or conditions under which they operate. This is the case at present with the work of the numerous Societies for Psychical Research and that of Dr. J. B. Rhine of Duke University, California, Prof. Thouless of Cambridge and a number of other independent investigators. They are having to formulate tentative principles as they go along, which is not a simple task when dealing with a realm of intangible and highly variable phenomena. It is complicated by the fact that the faculties in question manifest themselves in the same person to different degrees at different times, and appear to be intimately connected with emotional states.

At present the evidence for E.S.P. is mostly statistical. Nevertheless, considerable advance has been made in the application of scientific method to the study, using sophisticated techniques for the detection of fraud and an increasingly rigid control of experiments to eliminate bias on the part of the observer. There is already an extensive literature on the subject, from which anyone who is interested may form his own theories. It is important if only for the light it sheds on the religious and mystical experiences, to say nothing of the miraculous element in religion, that man from the earliest times has believed in. Since the so-called "supernatural" has always been a part of man's universal experience, it obviously does not "prove" the truth of any particular religion. It only proves that there are indeed realms outside our normal range of perception, and faculties that are not subject to the limitations of the physical sense-organs. But this we already know from physical science itself, for it has shown that the world we perceive is something quite different from the actual world; so different that it is in fact impossible to establish a convincing relationship between them. No one has yet succeeded in showing how the subjective world can be made to tally with an objective reality. This constitutes the major stumbling-block of modern philosophy.

The European tradition of materialistic thinking goes a long way back. Even in an age when "philosophy" still meant the natural sciences, it was necessary for Hamlet to remind Horatio that "there are more things in heaven and earth than are dreamt of in your philosophy," with the accent on the last word. Yet still quite a large number of people in the West continue to believe in ghosts, or "entities on the Other Side," as some spiritualists prefer to call them. The persistence of the belief among rational and practical-minded people can be accounted for only on the assumption that there is some objective basis for it, or at least that it represents some aspect of experience which they, in common with people in more primitive societies, have known. If this were not the case it must surely have been eradicated completely by the centuries of realistic thinking that lie behind us.

There is scarcely any need, then, to explain away the fact that Buddhism does not confine its view of life to the world of our immediate sensory experience. On the contrary, as a system of thought claiming to embrace every aspect of man's experience it would be incomplete and seriously defective if it did so. Realms of existence other than the human may not be strictly necessary for the working-out of the all-important Buddhist principle of moral cause and effect; but if Buddhism denied them, as it categorically rejects the theory of a Creator-God and an immortal soul, it would be denying something that may one day be proved as a scientific truth; something, moreover, which is already accepted by some on the basis of logical inference and by many others through direct experience.

Although Buddhism lays all the emphasis on the importance of the human plane of existence, since it is here, and here alone, that there is freedom of choice between good and bad action, the Buddhist texts mention other spheres of being, some below and some above the human realm. In particular, there are many references to devas and the various spheres they inhabit. The devas, or "shining ones," are beings born in higher realms as the result of good kamma (= karma in Sanskrit) generated in previous lives as human personalities. They are of various grades and enjoy the appropriate results of their past meritorious deeds, but their condition is not permanent; they are not "enjoying the bliss of heaven" for all eternity. When the force of the good kamma has expended itself in results, they pass away and the current of their life-continuum finds a new manifestation elsewhere; they are reborn as the consequence of some residual kamma, good or bad, from previous lives, which has not hitherto taken effect. All beings have an undetermined store of such kamma, technically known as *katatta-kamma,* which comes into operation in the absence of any fresh kamma from the immediately-past life.[12]

12 This comes about because some kinds of kamma are of greater moral consequence than others. An action of heavy moral significance produces its results before one that is of lesser importance and so delays the results of the latter. Furthermore, the results of kamma have to wait upon the arising of suitable conditions to bring them about. The interplay of counteractive forces in the good and bad kamma of an individual is the factor that makes kammic operations incalculable.

Thus, although the word *deva* is usually translated "god," these beings are not in any sense gods as the term is generally understood. They are not considered to have any power over human actions or destiny—nor even necessarily superior knowledge. One of the titles given to the Buddha is that of *satthā deva-manussānaṃ,* the "Teacher of gods and men," because in the Pali scriptures it is said that the devas themselves came to him for instruction in the Dhamma. Their place, therefore, is below that of the highest human being, the All-Enlightened One, who is also a *visuddhi-deva,* or "god by (self-) purification."

Beings who are reborn in the higher realms carry with them the beliefs they held when they were living on the human plane, so that "revelations" from other worlds do not necessarily carry any more truth than those that have a human origin. But the devas who have understood the Buddha-dhamma, themselves pay respect to the human world, as being the most suitable sphere for moral endeavour and for the attainment of Nirvana. Alone among the realms of existence, it is the human plane whereon Buddhas manifest themselves; so it is said that the god Sakka, after his conversion to Buddhism, daily saluted the direction in which the human world lay.

At the same time, the devas have a claim to the respect of human beings, for it was by the practice of virtue, and by deeds of supreme merit, that they attained to their present condition. The reverence paid to them by Buddhists on this account is of a quite different order from the worship given to gods who are believed to be controllers of human destiny.

In this sense it is true to say that Buddhism is non-theistic; the worship of gods for favours or forgiveness of sins has no part in it. To this extent it is not very important whether a Buddhist believes in the existence of higher states of being or not. But it is important for the appreciation of Buddhist philosophy to have a clear understanding that whatever other realms of existence there may be, they are all subject, like our own, to the law of cause and effect. Since cause and effect belong to the natural order, even though they may operate in ways that are non-physical, as in the case of the mental faculties of extra-sensory perception, the realms of the devas are not supernatural worlds; it is more accurate to regard them as extra-physical. The distinction may not be at once apparent; but if our own world of sense-data is a mental construction, as Yogācāra philosophy and Berkeleyan immaterialism maintain that it is, there is no reason why there should not be other realms of being constructed on the same basis. We know for a fact that the world as it appears to us is something quite distinct from the world of physics, and that understanding alone should make us chary of accepting it at its face value. Our familiar world of objects that appear to be substantial and real is nothing more than the interpretation we give to a something that is quite other than our senses report to us—a world of atomic energy, with scarcely anything substantial in it. The true nature of that world still remains a matter for metaphysical speculation, with which the Buddha was not concerned. He taught that the reality could be known only through insight developed in meditation, and that the secret lay not outside but within ourselves: "Within this fathom-long body, O bhikkhus, equipped with the mental faculties of sensation, perception, volition and consciousness, I declare to you is the world, the origin of the world, its cessation and the Path leading to its cessation."

Aldous Huxley, in his two brilliant essays, "The Doors of Perception" and "Heaven and Hell" (1956), cites Bergson's theory that the function of the brain, nervous system and sense organs is in the main *eliminative* and not productive. According to this view, the area of individual awareness is practically infinite and extends to modes of being outside those commonly experienced; but with such an awareness continually present, life in the ordinary sense would not be possible. There has to be a "reducing valve" (Huxley's term) which filters this multiple complex down to the essentials of consciousness that are required for biological survival. The reducing valve is the brain and nervous system, which isolate us in the sphere of individual consciousness formed by our sense-impressions and concepts. If for some reason the efficiency of the reducing valve is lowered, other material flows in, material which is not necessary for biological survival and may even be inimical to it, by lessening the seeming importance of ordinary life. From this come the trance experiences of mystics and the visionary entry into other worlds that has been the common property of mankind in all ages. Huxley's conclusion is that these experiences have a validity of their own which is independent of the means used to obtain them.

I quote the final paragraph of his "Heaven and Hell," the second of the two essays on his experiences under the influence of mescaline:

> "My own guess is that modern spiritualism and ancient tradition are both correct. There is a posthumous state of the kind described in Sir Oliver Lodge's book, *Raymond;* but there is also a heaven of blissful visionary experience; there is also a hell of the same kind of appalling visionary experience as is suffered here by schizophrenics and some of those who take mescaline; and there is also an experience, beyond time, of union with the divine Ground."

Huxley's "divine Ground," since it is not a personal God and is free from attributes, functions and any remnant of personal selfhood, appears to be of the same nature as the highest Brahma realms of Buddhism, if it is not that complete cessation of becoming which is the final goal of all, Nirvana.

All beings live in worlds created by their own kamma; the nature of the being creates the peculiar features of the world it inhabits. But in Buddhist doctrine there is no abiding ego-entity, no immortal and unchanging essence of selfhood. When it speaks of rebirth it does not mean the transmigration of a soul from one body or state to another. It means that a new being is created as the result of the volitional activities, the kamma, of one that has lived before. So long as desire remains unextinguished, and with it the will-to-live, the stream of cause and effect continues to project itself into the future, giving rise to one being after another in the causally-related sequence. Their identification with one another lies solely in the fact of each belonging to the same current of kamma generated by desire, so that what each one inherits from its predecessors is only a complex of tendencies that have been set in motion by the act of willing and doing.

In this connection even the word "birth" has to be understood in a peculiarly Buddhist sense, as meaning "arising" (*jāti*), or coming into existence, and not merely in the sense of physical generation. It also stands for the moment-to-moment coming into existence of mental impulses or units of consciousness in the ordinary course of life. The stream of consciousness is made up of a series of such momentary births and deaths. In sleep and unconsciousness the current still flows on in the form of the subconscious life-continuum. And at death the last moment of the series is immediately followed by the first of a new sequence, in perhaps a different form and under entirely different conditions of birth. In Pali, the language of the Buddhist texts, another word, *punabbhava,* is used to denote this renewed existence after death. The old personality, being a psycho-physical compound and therefore unstable and impermanent, has passed away, but a new one arises from the mental impulses it had generated. In this way the kamma of a human being may bring about renewed existence below or above the human level, in a being of a quite different order.

The question of identity between any two beings belonging to the same sequence is not in any way different from the same question as it relates to different stages in the life of an individual. In the ordinary course of life we find that the nature of some persons alters radically for better or worse with the passage of time, while that of others remains fairly constant. Change is sometimes slow and imperceptible; sometimes it comes with dramatic suddenness; but change is continually and inevitably taking place. Birth and death—or death and rebirth—are merely points of more complete psycho-physical transition in the continuous flow of "becoming." The new being may inherit many characteristics, both mental and physical, from the previous one, or it may differ in everything except the predominant characteristic developed in the last life. The deciding factor is the nature and strength of the kamma of the human being, and more especially the kamma present in the consciousness at the last moment before death.[13]

Impermanence, suffering and absence of any enduring self-essence: these are the three characteristics of all life. Whatever

13 Death-proximate kamma, consisting of a mental reflex (*nimitta*) symbolizing some act, or aggregate of actions, performed in the past life. This arises in the last moment of consciousness and forms the basis, good or bad, for the consciousness-moment that immediately follows it. The last consciousness-moment therefore gives the key-signature to the next existence. Death in unconsciousness or in sleep also has its death-proximate kamma; this occurs on the dream level and does not manifest outwardly. Those who die in full or semi-consciousness frequently show, by their happy or fearful state of mind, the kind of death-proximate kamma that is coming into operation. Huxley makes some interesting observations on this in his references to the *Tibetan Book of the Dead* in the two essays mentioned previously.

sentient beings there may be in the cosmos besides man and the animals, they are all marked by these three characteristics. They are all subject to decay and dissolution. When we come to realise this we cease to concern ourselves with heavenly states or with metaphysical speculations connected with them. All that is left is the urgent need to gain release from the delusions and attachments that bind us to the incessant round of renewed existences. It is only in the attainment of Nirvana, the Unconditioned and Absolute, that eternal peace is to be found. The Buddha, supreme Teacher of Gods and Men, discovered the Way, and out of his compassion for suffering beings revealed it to all. But, having found it, he could be no more than a guide and instructor to others. Each of us has to tread the path for himself, working out his own deliverance. Worlds may be infinite in number, but the same law prevails everywhere and gods must again become men to fulfil their destiny. Like the deeds that caused them, rewards and punishments—man's interpretation of the universal law of action and reaction—pass away. There have been men, like Alexander the Great, deified by priests while they were yet alive; but it is not by bloodshed that gods are made; it is not by ceremonies that men are sanctified. The humblest man living, if he has all his mental faculties intact, can forge for himself a higher destiny than these. In the law of change lies opportunity. Piled up, the bodies of our dead selves would raise a mountain loftier than the peak of Sumeru.[14] And the man who has made his own mountain should try to climb it. Who knows where it might lead him? Perhaps to the abode of the gods—or Beyond.

— §§§ —

14 Mount Meru, the mythological home of the gods; the Indian Olympus.

The Lesser Discourse of the Buddha on the Elephant-Footprint Simile

(27th Sutta of the Majjhima Nikāya)

The first exposition of the Dhamma in Ceylon Translation and Historical Introduction

Soma Thera

Bodhi Leaves No. 5

First published: 1960

Introduction

How the Buddha's Teaching Was Established in Ceylon
(According to Pāli Narrative)

The Meeting of the King and the Arahant on the Missaka Hill

Among the festivals of the Sinhala people, one that has been observed from very early times falls on the day of the full moon of Poson. This festival had royal sanction, as our chronicles show. On this feast-day the King Devānampiyatissa is said to have made a realm-wide proclamation, "Let the people play the games of the day of the Poson festival," and commanded the townsfolk of Anuradhapura "to amuse themselves with festal water-sports." Meanwhile he went to the forest at Mihintale to enjoy the pleasures of the chase with forty thousand men, arriving soon after the Arahant Elder Mahinda[15] and his companions had reached the top of Missaka hill to propagate the teaching of the Buddha in Lanka.[16]

This feast of the full moon of Poson was an astral festival of the Sinhalese before the Dhamma was brought to Ceylon. It was after the coming of the Elder Mahinda that the festival lost its astral significance and became the great national festival of the first sowing of the seeds of the Good Law in Sinhaladvīpa. The first mention of the celebration of Vesak is connected with King Duṭṭhagamini, who reigned one hundred and fifty years after Devānampiyatissa.

---

15 The Arahant Elder Mahinda, son of King Dhammasoka, was appointed missionary to Tambapanni Island (Ceylon) by the Arahant Elder Moggaliputta Tissa, president of the Third Buddhist Council, at the end of its sessions held at Patna under the aegis of King Dhammasoka. (Ed.)

16 Ceylon.

The astral festival of Poson was an occasion for the people to amuse themselves with sports usually played on that feast-day. The Elder Mahinda had knowledge of this national festival of the Sinhalese and he chose that very day to come here, as he wanted the king and the people to be in a happy mood favourable for receiving the noble message of the Buddha, which makes for the good fortune and prosperity of living beings here and hereafter.

When Devānampiyatissa, who was on pleasure bent, came to the foot of the Missaka hill, the tutelary deity there, who wanted the Elders to be seen by the king, wandered near him taking the form of an elk-stag that appeared to be eating grass and leaves. Having seen the deer, the king twanged his bow-string not wishing to take the animal unawares. The animal fled along the path to the hill, and the king went behind the quarry, which disappeared not far from the place in which the Elders were.

Having seen the king coming towards him the Elder Mahinda wished thus, "Let the king see only me and not the others," and said, "Tissa, Tissa, come hither."

The king, having heard the Elder's words, thought, "No one in this island is able to address me by name, saying, 'Tissa.' Is this person with a shaven head, who is wearing garments made of torn cloth stitched together and dyed yellow, a human being or a non-human?" The Elder, having made the others of his company visible to the king and his followers, who surrounded the Elder and the king, said:

"Great king, we are monks,
Hearers of the king of truth.
Just out of compassion for you,
Have we from Jambudīpa[17] arrived here."

On hearing these words of the Elder, the king was freed of fear, as he remembered then the message from his unseen friend, the great king of India, Dhammāsoka, who had informed Devānampiyatissa of his taking refuge in the Three Jewels, and had advised the king of Lanka too to go for refuge to the Buddha, the Dhamma, and the Sangha. Then through his being convinced that those who

17 India.

were before him were really monks, the king laid aside his bow and arrow, went up to the Elder, exchanged greetings with him, and sat down at one side. "When did these come?" asked the king." They came with me, great king," said the Elder. "Are there in Jambudīpa, other monks like these?"—"There are, great king. At the moment, Jambudīpa is gleaming with yellow robes, and is pervaded by the atmosphere born of the movement of the robes and bodies of bhikkhus.

Many are the hearers of the Buddha who have gained
The threefold lore and supernormal powers,
And who are clever in reading others' minds,
And consummate ones whose cankers have run out."

"Venerable sir, by what way have you come here?"—"Not by sea nor by land, great king." The king understood that they had come through the sky. Then the Elder, in order to find out whether the king was possessed of wisdom, questioned him about a mango tree that was nearby, "Great king, what is the name of this tree?"—"Venerable sir, this is a mango tree."—"Great king, besides this mango is there another mango or not?"—"There are, venerable sir, many other mango trees."—'"Besides this mango and the other mangoes, are there, great king, still other trees?"—"There are, venerable sir, but they are not mango trees."—"Besides the other mangoes, and the trees that are not mangoes, is there indeed another tree?"—"There is, venerable sir, this very tree."—"Very good, great king, you are wise."—"Have you relatives, great king?"—"Venerable sir, there are many."—"Great king, besides the many, are there any others who are not related to you?"—"Venerable Sir, more than my relatives are those who are not relatives of mine."—"Great king, besides those who are your relatives and those who are not your relatives, is there still any one?"—"There is still myself, venerable sir."—"Very good, great king, self is not called one who is a relative or one who is not a relative of self." Then the Elder thought, "The king is wise; he will be able to understand the Dhamma."

After the Arahant Elder Mahinda had satisfied himself regarding the fitness of Devānampiyatissa to receive the doctrine, he explained to the king the teaching of the Buddha contained in the 27th Sutta of the Majjhima Nikāya, The Lesser Discourse of the Buddha on the Elephant-footprint Simile, *Cūla Hatthipadopama Sutta.* In this sutta the master tells the brahmin Jāṇussoṇi how the disciple of the Noble Ones, the Buddhas, comes to the conviction that the Blessed One is all-enlightened, that his doctrine is revealed well, and that his disciples have reached the good path. At the end of the explanation of the sutta by the great thera, "the king with forty thousand living beings" says the chronicler, was established in the Three Refuges. At that very moment, food was brought for the king. While listening to the thera's exposition of doctrine, the king understood, "To these, food is improper at this time of the day." Having thought even without inquiring that it was not right for bhikkhus to eat then, the King said to the venerable thera, "Venerable sir, will you eat?" The thera said, "Mahāraja, it is not proper for us to eat now." The king: "At what time is it proper?" The thera: "From dawn till noon." The king: "Let us proceed to the city." The thera: "It is not necessary, Mahārāja. We shall remain here." The king: "Venerable sir, if you remain here, let this young one come." The thera: "The young one has attained to the fruit of non-return. He is one who is endowed with a correct knowledge of the master's teaching. He will now go forth." The king: "Since the matter is so, I shall send the carriage tomorrow. You may get into it and come." After saying that the king departed from the hill.

The Lesser Discourse of the Buddha on the Elephant-Footprint Simile

Jāṇussoṇi, to whom this discourse was delivered by the Master, was a very rich brahmin of high rank in Sāvatthī. He is said to have been the equal of such brahmins as Cankī, Tārukkha, Pokkharasāti, and Todeyya.

Jāṇussoṇi was not the name given to him by his parents, but the name of the office he held as king's chaplain in the Kosala government. He used to perform an auspicious drive round Sāvatthī every six months. For that drive he used an all-white carriage of state, arrayed himself in white, and had a retinue also clad in white. The carriage of state of those days was long and broad. It could accommodate a parasol-bearer, a fan-bearer, and in all about eight or ten persons. These could stand, sit, or sleep in the carriage. The wheels, body, pole, and the rest of the brahmin's carriage was of silver. Its decorations and accessories were white. The whisk that was used in the carriage too was white. The four mares which drew the carriage were white and their harness was of silver. The reins were cased in silver and silver was the goad.

At the time of the drive, the brahmin was dressed in a white garment, and white were his upper garment, turban, and sandals, as were also the parasol held over him, and the unguent with which he was anointed. He wore silver earrings, silver rings on all his fingers, and adorned himself with white flowers. His vast retinue of brahmins, ten thousand in number it is said, was also dressed in white, anointed with a white unguent, and adorned with white flowers.

Before the performance of the auspicious drive of the brahmin it was usual for an announcement to be made thus, "In so many days from now the auspicious drive round the city will be performed." On hearing that, people who were not leaving the city did not want to leave it, and those who were leaving the city returned to it saying, "We shall see the good fortune of the meritorious one."

On the day of the auspicious drive the streets were swept and sanded, quite early in morning. Flowers and roasted paddy were strewn on them. Along the streets pots filled with water and decorated with flowers were placed, banana trees planted, flags hoisted, and incense burnt throughout the city.

Early on the day of the drive, the brahmin bathed his head and breakfasted, and having dressed himself in white and adorned himself, left his dwelling and entered his carriage. Then his retinue of brahmins, clad in white, followed his carriage, bearing white parasols. In order to bring the people together, young girls scattered fruits, and after that *māsaka* coins and at last *kahāpana* coins. Then people assembled, and there were shouts of joy and waving of cloths. Then the brahmin, while such as those who utter what is lucky and those who wish well performed their work, drove round the city clothed with magnificence.

During the auspicious drive people went to the upper storeys of their houses and, having opened the windows, watched the procession, while the brahmin, having driven up to the southern gate of the city, stood before it, flooding, as it were, the city with the splendor of his high position and good fortune.

The brahmin was engaged in performing the auspicious drive round the city when he met the wanderer Pilotika on the road, at the entrance to Sāvatthi, and had the following conversation with him. The conversation became a reason for Jāṇussoṇi's visit to the Buddha and for the Master's discourse to the brahmin on the simile.

The Conversation Near the Gate of Sāvatthī

Jāṇussoṇi: "Now, from where does the revered Vacchāyana[18] come at noon?"

Pilotika: "Revered sir, I come from the monk Gotama's presence."

Jāṇusoṇi: "What does the revered Vacchāyana think of the monk Gotama's skill in wisdom? Does he think that he is an expert?"

Pilotika: "Revered sir, who am I? How shall I know the monk Gotama's skill in wisdom? Who would know the monk Gotama's skill in wisdom should certainly be one like him."

Jāṇussoṇi: "Surely, it is with high praise that the revered Vacchāyana praises the monk Gotama."

Pilotika: "Revered sir, who am I? How shall I praise the monk Gotama? The monk Gotama has been praised indeed by those who have been praised themselves. He is the highest for both deities and human beings."

Jāṇussoṇi: "Beholding what particularly good reason does the revered Vacchāyana believe thus in the monk Gotama?"

The Four Footprints of the Blessed One According to Pilotika

Pilotika: "Revered sir, in whatsoever way were a tracker of elephants to enter an elephant forest and to see a big footprint of an elephant, long in length, and broad in breadth, he might conclude, 'Truly, a big bull elephant!' Even so, revered sir, when I saw the four footprints of Gotama the monk, I concluded, 'The Blessed One is all-enlightened, rightly. The doctrine has been

18 Ven. Pilotika's clan name.

revealed well by the Blessed One. The community of disciples of the Blessed One has reached the good path well.' What are the four?

"Here I see learned, clever nobles, who have experience in disputing others' theses, and are like archers skilled in splitting a horse's hair,[19] wander destroying, methinks, with the force of their wisdom others' subtly false views. These learned, clever ones hear that the monk Gotama will be visiting such and such a village or township, and prepare a question, thinking, 'Having approached the monk Gotama, we shall put this question to him. If he is questioned by us thus, he will make answer thus. Then we shall confute him thus. If he is questioned by us thus, he will make answer thus. Then we shall confute him thus.' When these hear that the monk Gotama has arrived at such and such a village or township, they go up to the place in which the monk Gotama happens to be, and the monk Gotama, with a talk, instructs them in the doctrine, makes them to accept it, has them filled with ardour for it, and gladdens them. And when they have been instructed in the doctrine, made to accept it, filled with ardour for it, and gladdened by the monk Gotama, they do not put their question to him. How then should they confute him? Rather they become his disciples. Revered sir, when I saw this first footprint of the monk Gotama, I concluded, 'The Blessed One is all-enlightened. The doctrine has been revealed well by the Blessed One. The community of disciples of the Blessed One has reached the good path.'

"Again, revered sir, I see learned, clever brahmins who have experience in disputing others' theses and are like archers skilled in splitting a horse's hair ... become his disciples. Revered sir, when I saw this second footprint of the monk Gotama I concluded, 'The Blessed One is all-enlightened. The doctrine has been revealed well by the Blessed One. The community of disciples of the Blessed One has reached the good path.'

"Again, revered sir, I see learned, clever householders, who have experience in disputing others' theses, and are like archers skilled

19 This refers to an archer who from a distance of about 100 bow-lengths shoots and splits a horse's hair from which is suspended a small fruit with the help of which he takes aim.

in splitting a horse's hair … become his disciples. Revered sir, when I saw this third foot-print of the monk Gotama I concluded, 'The Blessed One is all-enlightened. The doctrine has been revealed well by the Blessed One. The community of disciples of the Blessed One has reached the good path.'

"Again, revered sir, I see learned, clever monks, who have experience in disputing others' theses, and are like archers skilled in splitting a horse's hair, wander destroying methinks, with the force of their wisdom others' subtly false views. These learned, clever ones hear that the monk Gotama will be visiting such and such a village or township, and prepare a question thinking, 'Having approached the monk Gotama, we shall put this question to him. If he is questioned by us thus, he will make answer thus. Then we shall confute him thus. If he is questioned thus, he will make answer thus. Then we shall confute him thus.' When these hear that the monk Gotama has arrived at such and such a village or township, they go up to the place in which he happens to be, and he with a talk instructs them in the doctrine, makes them to accept it, has them filled with ardour for it, and gladdens them. And when they have been instructed in the doctrine, made to accept it, filled with ardour for it, and gladdened by the monk Gotama, they do not put their question to him. How then should they confute him? Rather, they beg permission of the monk Gotama to go forth from home to homelessness. The monk Gotama makes them go forth, and has them given full admission to his dispensation.

"Those who have gone forth in the dispensation and living alone, secluded, diligent, devoted to exertion, and endowed with resolve, they, in no long time, dwell having, here and now, by their own profound knowledge realised and attained the acme of celibacy for the sake of which sons of good family truly go forth from home to homelessness.

"They said thus: 'Revered ones, we were almost finished, we were almost quite finished, since formerly, we being no monks, called ourselves monks; being no brahmins, we called ourselves brahmins; being no consummate ones, we called ourselves consummate ones: Now, indeed, we are monks; now, we are brahmins; now, we are consummate ones.'

"Revered sir, when I saw this fourth footprint of the monk Gotama, I concluded, 'The Blessed One is all-enlightened. The doctrine has been revealed well by the Blessed One. The community of disciples of the Blessed One has reached the good path. Since I saw these four footprints of the monk Gotama, revered sir, I concluded, 'The Blessed One is all-enlightened. The doctrine has been revealed well by the Blessed One. The community of disciples of the Blessed One has reached the good path.'"

Thereupon, the brahmin Jāṇussoṇi alighted from his carriage, which was entirely white and drawn by white mares, draped the upper garment over his left shoulder while keeping his right bare, bowed with raised joined hands towards the place where the Buddha was, and gave utterance to his feeling of joy thus, "Homage to the Blessed One, the Consummate One, the All-enlightened One! Homage to the Blessed One, the Consummate One, the All-enlightened One! Homage to the Blessed One, the Consummate One, the All-enlightened One! Were I to be with the revered Gotama some time, it would be good. It would be good if there should be some satisfying, friendly speech on meeting him."

Then the brahmin Jāṇussoṇi proceeded to the Blessed One, and when he had come to the Blessed One's presence he exchanged friendly greetings with the Blessed One, sat at one side, and detailed the talk he had with Pilotika.

Elephants in an Elephant Forest

The Blessed One: "Brahmin, a tracker of elephants might enter an elephant forest and see a big elephant's footprint. But a clever tracker would not yet conclude, 'Truly, this is a big bull elephant's footprint.' Why? Because in an elephant forest there are cow elephants called dwarfs, whose footprints are big. Thinking, 'This may be a footprint of one of them,' he follows that. Following that, he sees in the elephant forest a big elephant's footprint, long in length, and broad in breadth, and places resorted to for allaying the itch, high up on the trees. But a clever tracker does not yet conclude, 'Truly, this is a big bull elephant.' Why? Because in an elephant forest there are cow elephants called the tall whose footprints are big. Thinking, 'This may be a footprint of one of them,' he follows that. Following that, he sees in the elephant forest a big elephant's footprint, long in length, and broad in breadth, and places resorted to for allaying the itch, and places gashed with tusks, high up in the trees. But a clever tracker does not yet conclude, 'Truly, this is a big bull elephant.' Why? Because in an elephant forest there are cow elephants called the tall with prominent tusks whose footprints are big. Thinking 'This may be a footprint of one of them,' he follows that. Following that, he sees in the elephant forest a big elephant's footprint, long in length, broad in breadth, and places resorted to for allaying the itch, places gashed with tusks, and places with branches torn off, high up on the trees: he too sees the elephant walking, standing, sitting, or sleeping, at the root of a tree or in the open. Then he concludes, 'This indeed is a big bull elephant.'

Appearance of a Perfect One in the World

"Even so, brahmin, there appears in the world a Perfect One, consummate, all-enlightened, endowed with true knowledge and flawless conduct; sublime, knower of the world, matchless guide of men to be tamed, teacher of divine and human beings, enlightened, blessed. He makes known to others this world with its deities, Māras, and Brahmas, and the human race with its monks and brahmins and its princes and peoples, which he has by himself, through supernormal knowledge realised. He sets forth the doctrine, which is good at the beginning, in the middle and at the close, with the letter and meaning and absolutely perfect. He proclaims the celibacy that is purified quite.

Going Forth

"A householder or a householder's son or one born in a different kind of family, hears that doctrine. Having heard the doctrine, he comes to have faith in the Perfect One. Possessed of that faith, he thinks thus, 'Full of distress is dwelling in a home, which is passion's (dusty) way; like an open-air life is going forth. It is not easy for one dwelling in a home to practise celibacy that is wholly perfect, wholly pure, and polished like a conch. So, it would be good, were I to get rid of hair and beard, put on brown-red garments, and go forth from home to homelessness.' Later, giving up a small or a large amount of property and a small or a large number of relatives, he gets rid of his hair and beard, puts on red-brown garments, and goes forth from home to homelessness.

Training and the Life Common to Bhikkhus

"Being gone forth thus, he, having reached training and the life common to bhikkhus, gives up the killing of living beings and becomes one who refrains from killing living beings. And being one who has laid aside the cudgel and the knife and who is modest and merciful, he dwells wishing well to and compassionate for all that lives.

"Giving up taking what is not given, he becomes one who refrains from taking what is not given. And he dwells, taking what is given, desiring what is given, personally pure through not stealing.

"Giving up non-celibacy, he becomes a celibate, who lives aloof, refraining from lust, which is characteristic of the commonality.

"Giving up lying, he becomes one who refrains from lying, speaks the truth, links truth to truth, is single of speech, is trustworthy, and deceives not the world.

"Giving up traducing speech, he becomes one who refrains from traducing speech. What he has heard here he does not repeat elsewhere to cause a breach with these, nor does he repeat what he has heard elsewhere to these to cause a breach with those. Thus he becomes one who unites the divided, encourages those who are friends, enjoys concord, delights in concord, cleaves to concord, rejoices in concord, and speaks words that make for concord.

"Giving up harsh talk, he refrains from harsh talk. He speaks such words as are innocent, pleasing to the ear, amiable, going to the heart gently, urbane, agreeable to many, and pleasant to many.

"Giving up trivial talk, he refrains from trivial talk. Speaking what is seasonable, true, meaningful, connected with the doctrine, and connected with the discipline, he becomes a speaker, at the right time, with illustrations, of sober, purposeful words, worthy of being garnered in the heart.

"He becomes one who refrains from injuring seeds and plants. He becomes one who eats during one definite portion of the day, giving up eating at night, and refraining from eating at an unprescribed time. He becomes one who refrains from dancing, singing, music, and unseemly shows. He becomes one who refrains from the use of garlands, perfumes, unguents, ornaments, what adorns, and what beautifies. He becomes one who refrains from using high and luxurious beds. He becomes one who refrains from accepting gold and silver. He becomes one who refrains from accepting raw grain... raw meat... women and girls... bondsmen and bondswomen ... sheep and goats... poultry and pigs... elephants, cattle, horses, and mares... fields and lands.

"He becomes one who refrains from carrying messages for laymen and from going on errands.

"He becomes one who refrains from buying and selling. He becomes one who refrains from defrauding with scales, defrauding with bronze (by passing off inferior metal as gold), and defrauding with measures. He becomes one who refrains from the crooked acts of bribery, trickery, and deception. He becomes one who refrains from cutting, killing, putting in bonds, robbing, plundering, and violence.

Contentment of the Virtuous Bhikkhu

"He becomes one who is content with robes for keeping his body, and with almsfood for keeping his belly; wherever he goes; he takes even all with him and goes. As a bird with wings, wherever it flies, flies only with the burden of its wings, so the bhikkhu becomes one who is content with the robes for keeping his body, and with almsfood for keeping his belly; wherever he goes he takes even all with him and goes. And endowed with this fund of virtue of the Noble Ones, he experiences within himself blameless bliss.

Restraint of Faculties of the Noble

"On seeing a form with the eye, he becomes one who neither clings to the signs nor the particulars.

"He engages himself in restraining that by which evil, unprofitable states of covetousness and grief might stream into him who dwells with the eye faculty unrestrained. He watches the eye faculty; he reaches restraint in the eye faculty.

"On hearing a sound with the ear ... On smelling an odour with the nose ... On tasting a flavour with the tongue ... On touching what is tangible with the body ... On cognizing a mental state with the mind, he becomes one who neither clings to the signs nor the particulars. He engages himself in restraining that by which evil, unprofitable states of covetousness and grief might stream into him who dwells with the mind faculty unrestrained. He watches the mind faculty; he reaches restraint in the mind faculty. And endowed with this restraint of faculties of the Noble Ones he experiences within himself unadulterated bliss.

Mindfulness and Full Awareness of the Noble

"He becomes one who practises full awareness in going forwards and in returning. He becomes one who practises full awareness in looking at the direction before him and away from it. He becomes one who practises full awareness in bending and in stretching. He becomes one who practises full awareness in carrying the bowl, wearing the outer double robe, and the upper and under robes. He becomes one who practises full awareness in eating, drinking, chewing, and tasting. He becomes one who practises full awareness in easing nature. He becomes one who practises full awareness in walking, standing, sitting, going to sleep, waking, speaking, and being silent.

"Endowed with this fund of virtue of the Noble Ones, this restraint of faculties of the Noble Ones, and this mindfulness and full awareness of the Noble Ones, he resorts to a sequestered dwelling: a forest, the root of a tree, a rock, a mountain cleft, a mountain cave, a charnel ground, a remote thicket, a wide open space, or a heap of straw.

Elimination of Hindrances

"After meal time on stopping the wandering for almsfood, he sits down cross legged, keeps his body erect, brings mindfulness to bear on the subject of meditation before him, gives up covetousness for the world, dwells with mind free from covetousness, and purifies his mind of covetousness. He gives up the fault of ill will, dwells with his mind free from ill will, and wishing well to and compassionate for, all that lives, he purifies his mind of the fault of ill will. He gives, up rigidity and torpor, dwells free from rigidity and torpor, as one perceiving light, mindful and fully aware, and purifies his mind of rigidity and torpor. He gives up agitation and anxiety, dwells unagitated, with his mind pacified within, and purifies his mind of agitation and anxiety. He gives up uncertainty, dwells free from uncertainty, and not doubting about what are wholesome states of mind, purifies his mind of uncertainty.

The Four Meditations

"He gives up these five hindrances, the mental defilements that spoil understanding. Then, aloof from sense-desires and unwholesome mental states, he attains to, and abides in, the first meditation (*jhāna*), which is with initial and sustained thought, and has happiness and bliss that spring from solitude.

"This, brahmin, is truly called a footprint of the Perfect One, what has been resorted to by the Perfect One, what has been gashed by the Perfect One. But, indeed, the disciple of the Noble Ones does still not conclude, 'The Blessed One is all-enlightened. The doctrine has been revealed well by the Blessed One. The community of disciples of the Blessed One has reached the good path.'

"Again, with the subsidence of initial and sustained thought, the bhikkhu attains to, and abides in, the second meditation, which produces full serenity within, has unification of mind, is without initial and sustained thought and has happiness and bliss born of concentration.

"This, brahmin, is truly called a footprint of the Perfect One, what has been resorted to by the Perfect One, what has been gashed by the Perfect One. But, indeed, the disciple of the Noble Ones does still not conclude, 'The Blessed One is all-enlightened. The doctrine has been revealed well by the Blessed One. The community of disciples of the Blessed One has reached the good path.'

Again, by detachment from happiness, the bhikkhu abides with equanimity, mindful and fully aware, and experiences bodily bliss. He attains to and abides in the third meditation, about the one who abides in which the Noble Ones say, 'He has equanimity, has mindfulness, and has the abiding that is blissful.'

"This, brahmin, is truly called a footprint of the Perfect One, what has been resorted to by the Perfect One, what has been gashed by the Perfect One. But, indeed, the disciple of the Noble Ones does still not conclude, 'The Blessed One is all-enlightened. The doctrine has been revealed well by the Blessed One. The community of disciples of the Blessed One has reached the good path.'

"Again, by the giving up of bodily pleasure and pain, and by the prior disappearance of joy and grief, he attains to and abides in the fourth meditation, which is neither painful nor pleasant, and has mindfulness that is purified by equanimity. This, brahmin, is truly called a footprint of the Perfect One, what has been resorted to by the Perfect One, what has been gashed by the Perfect One. But, indeed, the disciple of the Noble Ones does still not conclude, 'The Blessed One is all-enlightened. The doctrine has been revealed well by the Blessed One. The community of disciples of the Blessed One has reached the good path.'

Knowledge of Past Lives

"When his mind has thus come to be serene, purified, cleansed, spotless, freed of defilements, pliable, workable, steadfast, imperturbable, he bends his mind to the knowledge of the recollection of past life. He recollects his manifold past existence ... With indication,[20] and aspect,[21] he recollects his manifold past existences.

"This, brahmin, is also called, the footprint of the Perfect One, what is resorted to by the Perfect One, and what is gashed by the Perfect One. But the disciple of the Noble Ones does still not conclude, 'The Blessed One is all-enlightened. The doctrine of the Blessed One is revealed well. The community of disciples of the Blessed One has reached the good path.'

Knowledge of the Passing Away and Arising of Beings

"When his mind has thus come to be serene, purified, cleansed, spotless, freed of defilements, pliable, workable, steadfast, imperturbable, he bends it to the knowledge of passing away and the arising of beings ... With divine vision purified and surpassing that of men, he sees beings passing away and arising. He understands the low, the lofty, the comely, the uncomely, the fortunate and the ill-fated, the beings faring on according to their actions.

"This, brahmin, is also called the footprint of the Perfect One, what is resorted to by the Perfect One, and what is gashed by the Perfect

20 With name, family, etc.

21 With appearance, etc.

One. But the disciple of the Noble Ones does still not conclude, 'The Blessed One is all-enlightened. The doctrine of the Blessed One has been revealed well. The community of disciples of the Blessed One has reached the good path.'

Knowledge of Exhaustion of Cankers

"When his mind has thus come to be serene, purified, cleansed, spotless, freed of defilements, pliable, workable, steadfast, and imperturbable, he bends it to the knowledge of the exhaustion of the cankers. He understands really, 'This is ill.' He understands really, 'This is the origin of ill.' He understands really, 'This is the cessation of ill.' He understands really, 'This path leading to the cessation of ill.' He understands really, 'These are cankers.' He understands really, 'This is the origin of cankers.'

"He understands really, 'This is the cessation of cankers.' And he understands really, 'This is the path leading to the cessation of cankers.'

"This, brahmin, also is called a footprint of the Perfect One, what is resorted to by the Perfect One, and what is gashed by the Perfect One. But the disciple of the Noble Ones does still not conclude. 'The Blessed One is all-enlightened. The doctrine of the Blessed One has been revealed well. The community of the disciples of the Blessed One has reached the good path.

"In him who knows thus, who sees thus, the mind is released from the canker of sense-desire, from the canker of being, and from the canker of ignorance, and when it has been released there is the knowledge, 'It has been released,' and he understands, thus, 'Birth has been destroyed, the celibate life has been lived, what ought to be done has been done, and of this there is nothing more to come.'

"This, brahmin, is also a footprint of the Perfect One, what has been resorted to by the Perfect One, and what has been gashed by the Perfect One. By this much, indeed, does the disciple of the Noble Ones become one who has concluded, 'The Blessed One is all-enlightened. The doctrine has been revealed well by the Blessed One. The community of disciples of the Blessed One has reached the good path.'"

Jāṇussoṇi: "Marvellous, revered Gotama, marvellous, revered Gotama! As if, revered Gotama, a person were to turn face upwards what is upside down, or were to uncover the concealed, or were to point the way to one who is lost or were to carry a lamp in the darkness, thinking, 'Those who have eyes will see forms,' so has the doctrine been set forth in many ways by the revered Gotama. I go to the revered Gotama for refuge, and to the doctrine and the community of bhikkhus. May the revered Gotama regard me as a follower who has gone for refuge from today for life."

— §§§ —

Buddhist Aids to Daily Conduct

Edward Greenly

Bodhi Leaves No. 6

First published: 1961

Buddhist Aids to Daily Conduct

To arrive at a proper understanding of any ethical system, there are many aspects of it that need to be considered. We may inquire into its theory concerning the origin of ethical ideas in general, into its relationships or indebtedness to other systems, into the validity of the sanctions that it attaches to them.

That which will be considered in the following pages is the Buddhist motives and aids to conduct, the machinery by which Buddhism endeavours to ensure the conversion of its precepts into practice. Taking as granted the Buddhist code, assuming as valid the Buddhist ideas, the question will be: What follows as to conduct? Nor is this a matter of interest that is merely academic. For, suppose any of the considerations turn out sound and valid, then, clearly, they have an interest that is practical enough— applicable here or now or anywhere, they must have an immediate bearing on our own lives, on how we are to think and act this very day, whether we use the Buddhist name or not.

The first thing to be observed is that Buddhism does not make what we may perhaps call a "frontal attack" upon evil. There is in it no "commandment," no "thou shalt" or "thou shalt not," but merely an "it is good to" or "it is not good to:" and that always for the reason "such and such a thing helps or hinders sorrow's ceasing."

Again, the system being not faith but knowledge, evil is, in its eyes, not "wickedness," but a "not-understanding," a mental blindness, a failure to see things as they really are. The remedy, then, evidently, must be "right understanding," sane and unclouded mental vision, a coming to see things as they really are.

We all know only too well (who is there that does not?) the inner moral conflict, the cry of the aspiring heart in all ages, "The good that I would I do not, the evil that I would not, that I do." Whence this terrible internal conflict, this division of the mental house against itself? Again, it is Right Understanding that is wanted: the mind has come (by mere precept) to see some things rightly, but it sees other things wrongly; and so there arises a conflict between two wholly inconsistent views of things. "See all things rightly all round," says Buddhism, "you are as one awaking from a dream; some things you see as in the wakened world, but some you still see as in the dream world; the trouble can only be ended by waking up altogether."

And what is this Right Understanding, this undistorted view of life, this Buddhist picture of the truth of things? It is general ideas or principles which at first sight may appear to us to have little, if any, bearing upon ethical matters at all, except, indeed, in so far as they are rather dreaded than otherwise by the exponents of the ethical system that is most prevalent among us in the West.

In their briefest form, these are what are known as the great signs, the characteristics of all existence, combined with the principle of universal causation, which is in reality implicit in them. The three signs are: (1) *anicca*, that is, impermanence or "momentariness"; (2) *dukkha*, sorrow, or, better, dissatisfaction; and (3) *anattā*, the absence of abiding substance, especially of psychic substance (called 'soul' or 'self'). The sources of evil, Buddhism places, for practical purposes, under three heads: (1) *lobha*, or craving, (2) *dosa*, or ill-will; (3) *moha*, or illusion, especially the self illusion. In both of the groups the several members are not independent, but interdependent, each being more or less involved in the other two principles. These, then, are the things whereof a comprehension is the Right Understanding that we seek. And how are they applied?

Well, each of the three great sources of evil is taken separately, in the order in which they are given above, and to it, for its cure, is made a special, direct, application of the corresponding member, again in the same order, of the group of the three signs.

There are also what we may call intercrossing applications, so that it is possible to construct a sort of "graphic" representation of the more important lines of remedy thus:

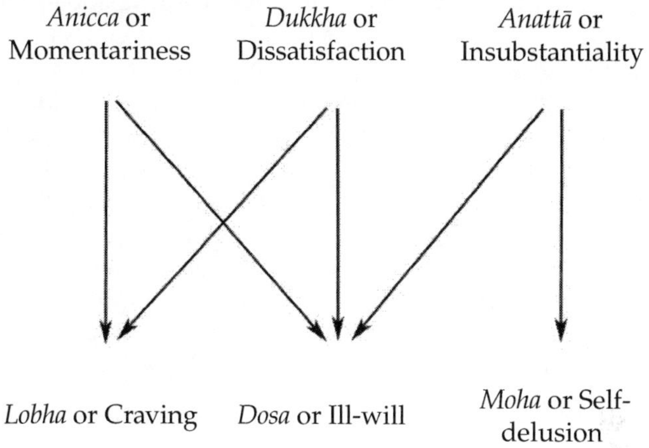

We will take the direct applications first. A man is smitten with a craving for wealth or one or other of the many much-hankered-after things of life. Moral precept comes and says, "You ought not to grasp after that." "Why should I not, when I can get it?" he will perhaps say; or possibly, "I know I ought not, but I cannot help hankering" And then Buddhism comes to him and says, "No, you can never, though you think it, grasp that thing. Anicca! All things are ever changing. That after which you hanker is changing while you grasp at it: the hand which you stretch out towards it is changing while it grasps. An ever-changing flux without, an ever-changing flux within the mind. How can the flowing grasp the flowing?" And then to the, perhaps, disillusioned and embittered mind it further whispers, "There is a satisfaction after all, but it is not in grasping. Look for it in sorrow's ceasing, and sorrow ceases when you see things as they really are." And so, finding that there is really no such thing as getting, the mind begins to look for satisfaction elsewhere.

To ill-will, aversion, hatred, anger, or any of the many forms of *dosa*, Buddhism applies its second sign of *dukkha*—that most unpopular of all its doctrines in the West. Orthodox and heretic alike alternately scout or fear this doctrine, yet in it is to be found that which is a solvent for all the bitterness of *dosa* (ill-will). Nowhere, moreover, is the ethic of mere precept more apt to fail than here, as is, indeed, very generally admitted. "Love your enemies." Maybe;

but the world is full of very unkind, unpleasant people; people who are always in the way, people whose very presence is a source of irritation to us. And they are so complacent, these people, so self-satisfied, sometimes even prosperous as well, flourishing like the green bay-tree of the Hebrew psalmist? Well, if the experience of the readers of this article is at all like that of the writer of it, they will by this time have sadly found that all the precepts in the world, and all the resolutions to obey them, have never succeeded in getting them to love these people. Civilization can restrain the angry hand; precept and training may restrain the angry tongue; virtue may even prompt external acts of kindness; but hostile feeling still remains, the inner attitude has not been changed.

Nor does example effect the change we need. It is, indeed, a powerful stimulus to effort. We may be roused thereby to emulate the Buddha, who, alone of the world's teachers, appears to have succeeded in this matter. We shall but discover before very long, that to live as he lived, there is nothing for it but to see as he saw! And the vision so seen—what is that? It is no other than this same Dukkha sign, this same unwelcome "Holy Truth of Suffering." Looking through the Buddha-eyes, we see all these unkind, unlovely people suffering. Behind the thick mask of prosperity and pride, transparent to the rays of Buddha-sight, goes on dissatisfaction always, always striving after what they have not, are not; never an hour of satisfaction with what they have or are. For that is life's conditioning; "Man never is, but always to be blest," and so the never-ceasing chase goes on, while the face grows hard or worn or ennui-weary, until, with life's meaning still unlearnt, the inevitable passing comes.

And the seer of the vision, what of him? Why, though he could not love, though even now he cannot like, yet at sight of sorrow he can pity, nay more, he cannot help but pity. And, where compassion is, there is no room for hatred, nor room for any of the minor forms of Dosa, indignation, anger, even "righteous anger;" all these disappear in presence of compassion. And so this feared and scouted sorrow-doctrine brings peace and light where all precepts and commandments fail. It is a cure, too, for what we may call the negative forms of Dosa, the callous indifference to our fellow beings that refined and cultured minds are so addicted to. A crowd, an unsavoury, prosaic mob, how we draw back our phylacteries almost at the very thought of it; the horses up and down the street, we give them, save when they are badly beaten, scarcely a single passing thought. Yet once see all these as, by life's very inner nature, suffering, and, instead of indifference, pity comes at once. And so, where all precepts and commandments fail, this sorrow-doctrine can make possible the full practice of the "golden rule," and lead our feet into the path of peace.

Moha, the Self-illusion, is for Buddhism the root of all evil, the parent both of craving and ill-will; so that whatever be the remedy for it cuts really at the root of them as well. Still, there are special ills that arise immediately out of this illusion, and to them the sign of signs, as we may call it, of Anattā, has immediate and direct application. Self-esteem, self-importance, pride, the troubles that come of these, are a commonplace of moralisers, and a perennial perplexity to whom falls in any way leadership or management of the affairs of men. And not the least part of the trouble is that, granted the ordinary view of life, these things positively have logic on their side! Mere vanity, of course, the baseless foible of the foolish and light-headed, needs no discussion; but the knowledge of just merit, from which arises "that last infirmity of noble mind," that is very far from baseless. A good mechanic knows his work is good; a master in painting knows that he can paint; one that is born a leader is quite aware that he can lead. Sometimes, defying modesty, one such will say so. "It cannot be done better," wrote D rer, they say, to Raphael, sending him a drawing.

Now, if in each of us there be a "soul," then obviously and logically enough, as the deeds, so the soul is. What, then, if I know my deed is good? Why, of course, I cannot help but know my soul is good. If I have thought a clever thought, I cannot fail to be aware I have, or am, a clever soul! With manifest danger to my morals. That genius often is modest proves nothing but that, in so far it holds, or thinks it holds, a soul or/and creed, it is illogical. Apply the Anattā principle, however, and what follows? This that I am, it is compound, it is conditioned by Kamma; by the arising of such-and-such it has come to be; heredity, teaching, environment, a hundred things unknown, untold, have helped to make it what it is, in no wise a substance, thing or space, it is rather to be likened to a mathematical point, itself without parts and without magnitude, a meeting-plane of intercrossing lines of cause, coming together from we know not where, to radiate at once we know not whither. Or we might compare it with a line, the locus of a point, moving in the resultant of these interacting lines of force. What room, in the light of such a concept, is there left for self-esteem?

Of the innumerable cross-applications, only one or two can be touched on here. The bearing of Dukkha on craving, for example, is plain enough. For he who knows that the tempting "pleasure" cannot bring him satisfaction, will he crave like other men? And he who sees his fellows as Anattā, void of self, will he hate? For him there exists no such evil, wicked soul; those that trouble, they too are, like himself, Anattā, component, cause-driven; what is there in that to hate? We are not angry when we clearly discern the causing of some evil, such as an earthquake or storm.

That which sets up the real Dosa-feeling in us, the real anger, is the supposed self-originatedly hateful "soul"; embodiment (or rather enpsychment), of malignity; out of its own free and evil will bringing uncaused hurtfulness to birth.

One most important bearing of transience upon conduct, however, is so often overlooked, that it is well worth pointing out. Obvious enough in its external, general aspects, it is far more deeply penetrative than at first appears. Perhaps a sharp unkind word passes; perhaps a kindly act is left undone; for a moment we regret, and then we think, "Ah, we will set that right another day." And then, perhaps, that day comes, and we forget again, and yet again; perhaps half subconsciously we even reckon on that "future life," that "all eternity"[22] in which to set it right. With what result? Is there anyone, at any rate anyone past his early youth, who knows not that bitterest of all reflections, "O, to have done this or left undone that, to have said this or left unsaid that—but now the beloved is gone, the rest is silence. O, for that chance back again!" Transience, however, is something far more than a reflection concerning three-score-years-and-ten and then a passing; it is the knowledge that the life is always passing: it is more than transience, it is momentariness, a far more subtle, penetrating thing. There is a remarkable passage in the Visuddhi

22 Probably the world will never know the price it has paid, and still pays, for that 'optimistic' doctrine, in little kind acts left undone.

Magga: "The duration of the life of a being is strictly speaking, extremely brief, lasting only while a thought lasts."

If this be so, however, what follows as to conduct? Why, manifestly, this—that, just as to the longer life we crudely think of can good be done only while it lasts, so also to life considered thus. Would we do good to those we love, to anyone? Then we must do it now, there is no other time. Yesterday's sufferings, longings, fears, are not today's; tomorrow's will be different again. Let pass the ever-slipping opportunity, and not all the trusted-in tomorrows, not all the immortal paradises that man ever dreamed of, can bring that opportunity again. Not in the past is the life, it is not in the future, it is nowhere but in the present, passing, fleeting thought, and only in that thought moment can we do the good we would.

Such are some of the considerations by which Buddhism converts its fundamental, highly philosophical ideas into aids for daily conduct.

But for a thought to be effective, it must become habitual. These thoughts are wanted, not now and then or here and there, but all day long, and on all manner of occasions, unexpected almost always too. They are of little use if put off to those occasions. He that would save his life by swimming does not wait until he falls into the water; he learns the art, and practises and practises, until to float is more instinctive than to sink. So with these life-saving thoughts. They must be practised, and practised assiduously, when they are not wanted, until they become a mental habit, and come uppermost when they are wanted.

For this purpose, what are generally called "meditations" are generally recommended; introduced by the old Buddhist masters, and through long ages of experience proved of value. There are many of them and endless variations can be made of them.[23]

For instance, we may take the several root-ideas, these three signs, with Kamma and the others, day by day throughout a week; and applying them each especially to our characteristic hindrances of temperament or circumstance, practise looking at life that way.

---

23 Thoughts and texts suitable for such meditations can be found in Wheel No. 20: *The Three Signata,* by Prof. O.H. de A. Wijesekera. [Ed.]

Or we may review the episodes of each day in order backwards, asking concerning each of them "Was this good to have been done: was it well done?" (Never "Did I do well?") "Was therein it any doing, separately activating soul, or was it wholly Kamma action? Did it contain any element of Dukkha, of suffering for myself, for others or for both?" Few things are more profitable than this very simple-seeming exercise, because from it we learn the real nature of the life-process almost better than by any other means.[24] It bears much the same relation to the study of Buddhist theory as does laboratory work to the reading of a text book. Anattā, Dukkha and the like we have demonstrated, no doubt, to our complete satisfaction, and so, indeed, we ought to do. But to discover by direct introspection that every episode that makes up life is of these very elements compact—that makes of the conviction a seen and vivid thing, like the visit to a foreign country that we have only known from books. After six months of it, indeed, Life appears in very different guise. The disturbing heats of craving die away; through the cool, clear, transparent air of truth we begin to "see things as they really are."

Yet it is but a beginning. For deep has been the sleep, and tremendous is the Buddha vision, dawning but gradually on the mind.

Hour after hour, we lapse back into the dream-land, dreaming, indeed, at first for far longer than we wake; and what we believe "to be awake" is too often a mere half awakeness. As we see things, however, so we live; and therefore, while those minutes of awakening last, the conduct problem solves itself. And in them are the first foretastes of the final peace.

— §§§ —

24 Better still, indeed, is that continuous mindfulness that has got past the need of a day's-end review.

One's Own Good—And Another's

David Maurice

Bodhi Leaves No. 7

First published: 1961

One's Own Good—And Another's

This is not an article about kamma and rebirth, but, in order to explain the Buddhist attitude to life and "social welfare," an introductory explanation is necessary.

Quite often friends who are not Buddhists, and even those who are but have either newly come to realize the truth of the Buddha's teaching or are Buddhists mainly because their fathers were, find their greatest difficulty in understanding the "long view" of Buddhism; and that what the Buddha discovered and taught to men was a complete cure for the disease of life and not a mere palliative.

It is largely because they do not accept the truth of kamma and rebirth, or only half accept it.

It is in the nature of things that kamma and rebirth should be so difficult of conscious acceptance. There are those who accept it because it was taught in early childhood and yet bury it below their level of conscious thought, together with half-formed fears and doubts that have arisen. There are those who will resist any seeming proof of kamma and rebirth since they find it so totally different to all they have heretofore been told. They will accept the most absurd and impossible things as dogma, things that are not at all susceptible of proof and can but remain dogma, rather than give the slightest credence to the idea of rebirth.

Yet, taking it just for the sake of argument as a working hypothesis: it has never been disproved and cannot be disproved, and is so far the only hypothesis put forward that completely explains the facts. And it is, at least, the best working hypothesis there is for an understanding of man and his place in the universe.

There are those who know that kamma and rebirth are true but either find it impossible to say how they came by that knowledge, and therefore stand convicted in the eyes of the clever worldlings of self-hypnosis and 'leaky credulity,' or whose knowledge, memory of previous existences, is at most valid only for themselves and still susceptible to the worldlings' view that it is self-hypnosis and imagination.

But first, perhaps, I should explain the sense in which I am using the word kamma, since it is a word that has been much misused. It is the same as the Sanskrit "karma" and I cannot do better than quote from the *Buddhist Dictionary* of the Venerable Nyanatiloka: "*karma* (Skr.), Pali *kamma*: action, correctly speaking denotes the wholesome and unwholesome Volitions and their concomitant mental factors, causing rebirth and shaping the destiny of beings. These karmic volitions become manifest as wholesome or unwholesome actions by body, speech and mind. Thus the Buddhist term "karma" by no means signifies the result of actions, and quite certainly not the fate of man, or perhaps even of whole nations (the so-called wholesale or mass-karma), which misconceptions through the influence of theosophy have become widely spread in the West."

It is in the sense of this meaning, and as a convenient shorthand, that I use the term. There have been other booklets in the "Wheel" series dealing with kamma and with rebirth, and these give an idea of the Buddhist placement of value, and should be studied by those who find it difficult to understand "the long view."[25]

This long view we see as man, as every man and woman, as you, for instance, living not one life but millions: struggling in a vortex made by craving, by craving to have and craving not to have, by hate and ill will, by delusion and ignorance. In this, all beings, all men and women, you also, are conditioned by past deeds, by deeds of bodily action, deeds of speech, deeds of thought; and conditioned by present deeds as well; never for one moment the same being, never from one moment to another, another being. Indeed the changes in your "self" are so rapid that you can almost visualize the process as a sort of flowing "now."

Against this terrible background of an infinity of suffering, ranging from unease to anguish, is a "way out" to something that is all that this vortex is not, and that we call simply, "Nibbāna."

---

25 Wheel No. 9: *Karma and Rebirth*, by Nyanatiloka Mahāthera; Wheel No. 12/13: *The Case for Rebirth* by Francis Story.

So when a cultured Western lady asks, in all sincerity, and after surveying for a year or two the Asian scene, "Why are devout Buddhist laymen not so interested in social welfare as their Christian counterparts in Western countries?"; or on another level, with not so much opportunity of "surveying the scene," a Western air-pilot asks: "Isn't it bad to escape in "meditation," to save oneself when there is so much good needing to be done in the world?"; or, on still another level, a pushing Western association of "good" men tries to bring Buddhist monks into social welfare work: the difference between a palliative and a cure must be stressed, and there must be some attempt to bridge the wide and difficult gulf of different outlook.

First of all, however, it must be stressed that there is nothing in the Buddha's teaching against social welfare, but very much the reverse. It must also be stressed that there are many devout Buddhist laymen actively and physically interesting themselves and engaging themselves in social welfare, and making a good job of it.

That is not always immediately apparent to the Western visitor, who sees so much to be done and expects to see people running round "organizing" things and other people. In Asia, generally, a great deal is being done, perhaps a little less noisily than it is done in some other places.

So much remains to be done in Asia, in all of Asia, not only in the Buddhist countries, because all of Asia had been disorganized by military or economic penetration, where it was not by both. But that is quite another story. The clock cannot be put back, nor can it, all circumstances considered, be speeded up too drastically, too quickly, without risking disaster. Those who know the circumstance see a very great deal being done while those who do not know, think nothing is happening. The digression is necessary lest you should get a wrong idea from what follows.

It must be mentioned also that it is the Buddhist feeling of mettā (loving-kindness to all) that in truly Buddhist countries has ensured that there is a degree of social welfare right "from the grass roots" and springing from the heart, and ending in practical help that, because it is unregimented and unorganized, is not always so apparent to the casual onlooker. This is not at all to say that more of it is not needed or that it would not be better if a little better organized. But that also is another story.

Buddhist Bhikkhus and Their Noble Work

Before going on to consider the Buddhist outlook that colours all of the way of life of bhikkhus and laymen, we should think of the duties and responsibilities entrusted to the bhikkhus by the Buddha. There were two, *dve dhurāni,* two burdens or responsibilities: *ganthadhura* and *vipassanādhura.*

The first of these is the responsibility of study in order to learn the teaching and be able to transmit and keep alive the teaching.

The second is the responsibility of practising mental development for insight-knowledge so that the teaching may be the better kept alive, so that the influence of one himself wholly freed may be to the benefit of many.

For the Buddha had said in the Eighteenth Discourse of the Majjhima Nikāya:

"But, Cunda, that one who himself is in the mire should pull out of the mire another sunk therein—this, verily, is an unheard-of thing.

"But that one himself clear of the slough should be able to lift out of the slough another foundered therein—such a thing may well be. And that one who himself is not subdued, not disciplined, has not attained to the extinction of delusion, should cause others to become subdued, and disciplined, to attain to the extinction of delusion—such a thing has never been known. But that one, himself controlled, trained delivered from delusion, should lead others to become controlled and trained, lead them to deliverance it on delusion—such a thing may very well be."

And he had also pointed out the advantage of helping the many, to a critic who thought that such a practice conduced but to welfare of oneself:

"Now, master Gotama, he who goes forth as wanderer from this or that family, from the home to the homeless life, tames only the single self, calms only the single self; leads to Nibbāna only the single self. So what I say is, thus he is proficient in practice of merit that affects only one person, as a result of his going forth."

"Well, brahmin, as to that I will question you. Answer as you think fit. Now what think you, brahmin? In this connexion a Tathāgata arises in the world, an arahant who is a fully enlightened one, perfect in knowledge and practice, well-farer, world-knower, incomparable charioteer of men to be tamed, teacher of devas and mankind, a Buddha, an exalted one. He says thus: 'Come! this is the way, this the practice, proficient in which I make known that incomparable bliss which is steeped in the holy life, by my own powers of comprehension realizing it. Come you also! Practise so that you too may be proficient therein, so that you too by your own powers of comprehension may realize it and abide therein.'

"Thus this teacher teaches Dhamma and others too practise to attain that end. Moreover there are many hundreds, many thousands, many hundreds of thousands of such. Now what think you, brahmin? Since this is so, is it a practice of merit affecting only one person or many persons; that is, the result of going forth?"

It will be readily understood that there is a set responsibility for a bhikkhu, and it is for this that the yellow robe is donned. This is the highest possible service to mankind.

The first nine of the "twenty-one wrong kinds of occupation for a bhikkhu" deal, seven of them with administering medical treatment of one sort or another and two with going on errands or performing duties at the behest of laymen, and naturally this precludes the type of social service envisaged by the good organization referred to above.

It may be asked in one of those hypothetical questions that some folk love to ask: "If a bhikkhu saw a man dying, should he not pause and save him if he could?" The answer is, of course, in the affirmative as the rules were not made, as some modern rites are, to be enforced against reason and loving-kindness.

The Buddha once pointed out to a group of monks who in their intentness on gaining the "higher things" were neglecting one of their number who was seriously ill, that they should look after each other in such respects. He was very emphatic about this.

However, if a bhikkhu has it in his heart to go round tending the sick as an occupation, that is a totally different matter. His rules and common sense alike demand that he disrobe and do the noblest work a layman can.

Palliative or Cure?

The position of the devout Buddhist layman is different. He may, and very certainly where possible should, do as much in public service and social welfare as he can until he feels that he can do something better. Then he will—very likely, though not necessarily—become a bhikkhu.

But even here there is a difference in outlook from that of the average Western man of good-will.

Nothing so highlights the difference in thinking of the pure materialist, the devout theist, and the Buddhist, as the outlook in respect of suffering.

A very recent controversy in England widely reported in the world press helps to make the relative positions and viewpoints clearer.

A certain doctor reported that he gave a fatal dose of drugs, at the request of the patient, to a woman suffering from incurable cancer.

The pure materialists said: "Quite right, saves the State a great deal of wasted effort and puts her out of her misery."

The theists were rather divided about it all. One Christian church had three views: one of its leaders applauded the doctor's action; another disagreed and said that drugs should not be used to end life; a spokesman for the church said there was no "official" view and that "any attempt to make one would be keenly contested."

Other theists had other views. "If it were not God's will that she should suffer" said one, "she would not suffer, and one should not interfere with God's will."

The logical conclusion to this seems to be that even were the cancer curable, it should not be cured; although there are others who would regard themselves as "God's informants" to cure suffering. The same view extended can "justify" those who regarded themselves as God's instruments to burn heretics at the stake.

Of the pure materialist and the theist, it is the former who is logical. If he postulates this life ends entirely at death, then the materialist position is the only logical and correct one. Its extension to the killing of, whether they wish it or not, of badly injured, extremely weak and very old people, is also correct and logical.

The theist finds it hard to be consistent because nowhere ever has "God," any god, clearly and unequivocally expressed his will in such matters.

The cancer patient, in the case in question, was stated to have "made her peace with God" and was presumably satisfied that she would go to "heaven." According to her light, and those of the doctor if he is a fellow believer, her position and his are logical and correct.

There are billions of thought-moments in the time it takes to blink one's eyes, so fantastically rapid is the stream of thought, and if her last thought-moment was one of peace and set on a "heaven state" she would, indeed enter that state temporarily. But as to her last thought-moment, only the being she has since become would know that, possibly, but not surely, for at that time it is rare for memory to be strong.

Take another angle. A recent conference on family planning in a thickly populated Asian country concluded that there must be birth control. A report of this in an Asian magazine featured several photographs of participating Westerners. It can hardly be by coincidence that they all looked very unhappy people, though one could hardly decide whether they were unhappy because they were advocating Asian birth control or were advocating Asian birth control because they are unhappy.

It seems though that one must ask "*Cui bono*"—whose good?

The biologists, the more cynical among them, are already saying that Asians of the intellectual classes are accepting some measure of birth control, and that those of the less advanced classes refuse it. They argue that this will produce a lowering of the intellectual population and the less intellectual will increase still. That is yet another story.

The doctors for a research in population problems of an American university say: "At the beginning of what is called the atomic age our world has approximately 2,850 billion people. If population were to continue to increase at the 1958 rate of 1.8 percent it would amount to nearly six billion at the end of the present century. In about eight centuries from now there would be one person per square foot of the world's area, including its deserts, mountains and oceans. This of course would be an impossible situation."[26]

Another alternative that has been suggested, but which nobody has dared to emphasize, is to "dispose of eugenically" and "put out of their misery" all people who reach a certain age. Indeed it has only been suggested as a possibility, a necessary possibility, of the future.

In all countries men are frantically working on problems of nutrition, and of irrigating deserts and, in the Arctic, clearing laneways through ice-bound seas to make possible easier food transport and open up new country for the production of food.

Men are beginning to see that without waiting for the eight centuries to pass, without waiting even for the end of this century, sufficient food for all is going to be a problem calling for solution either by a wholesale massacre, by a world government outlawing unlicensed birth, or by a concerted effort to produce more food including synthetics that take up smaller space; and the conditioning of mankind to a smaller intake, i.e. to the digestion and efficient metabolism of a smaller bulk to maintain life. In such cases there would arise again problems that would make today's "good" the "bad" of tomorrow. One, for instance, could visualize the world government overriding the "reactionary religious scruples" of a large portion of India's population and demanding the slaughter of all cows (except those permitted to zoos) as unwieldy and inefficient wasters of food and cumberers of the earth's surface, since synthetics could be used so much better than meat, butter and milk.

This is but a digression and this is very serious: one cannot arrive at a conception of good without "looking before and after." It introduces the question of palliative or cure.

---

26 *Control by Fate or Foresight,* Pascal K. Whelpton.

The Long View

What do you believe really? Do you really and sincerely and consistently believe "with your whole heart" that merely by a fortuitous set of circumstances and without any volition on your part, at any time in the past, you have come to be what you are now? And are you consistent enough to believe, without any doubts, that therefore, when you die, maybe before you have finished reading this or maybe shortly after, there is nothing left behind but your rather small impact on infinity?

Or do you believe that what you are now has been due partly to your own volition and power since birth? If so, from what age? If you believe this, what percentage of your present personality is due to "You"? If "You" is not a flux that changes moment by moment, what is it?

If you believe in the coming-to-be of "you" by chance accidents (such a very different you, if you look at yourself in the mirror, than the "you" at birth) and that therefore you owe nothing to the past as far as "you" are concerned, and that on the death of the "you" (such a different "you" if you live a few years longer, than the present "you") there will be nothing left of "YOU," why are you worried enough to read this?

Communists, as well as quite a few people who are certainly not communists, make much of the idea of "the good of the world," and of "posterity"—but there was a very great deal of truth actually in the exclamation of Sir Boyle Roche: "Posterity! Why should we consider posterity? What has posterity done for us?"

That is of course in relation to the purely materialist idea. If one postulates "a loving father in heaven" and "brotherhood of man," with the loving, and only occasionally angry, father keeping an eye on his sons from time to time, one may have a different idea. Here one must be consistent and admit that even if one postulates such a father, and the very word shows the origin and the wish, one must consider that, even granted the independent existence of a father, there are two things that follow:

(a) the "father" must also be a changing flux, since the minds of men that "know him," even the minds at their peak, the minds of the mystics in supramundaue trance, are themselves a flux;

(b) it is these minds that do most of the creating, and that in any case colour all they contact, so that even if the mind of man has not "created God in its own image," it has at least draped all the attributes on a very bare skeleton. One can see this from the fact that by all accounts the father has, like the best of men short of the arahants, a divided mind and so is slightly schizophrenic. As Goethe was constrained to write: "*Nemo Contra Deum nisi Deus ipse*"—"There is nobody against God unless it be God himself."

So whatever extreme view you take, either of there being nothing beyond this life, or of an omnipotent creator who has made all things, you are unable to find any sure cure for your own ills, let alone for those of the world; and you may as easily as not do harm in your attempts to do good.

For a man who cannot swim at all to jump into the deep sea to save another who is drowning, is not an act of bravery but an act of foolishness. If he can swim a little and takes the calculated risk of being drowned himself but takes the risk because he has at least a chance of upholding the drowning man for a brief period until coming help arrives, he is acting bravely and wisely.

There is a story told by Voltaire of a young traveller who fell in with a strange old man as travelling companion. One evening they were charitably taken in by a poor widow who gave them lodging and fed them without charge from her scanty store. Her hospitality extended to sending her only son, a boy who would support her in her old age, as guide for part of the way.

When they came to a bridge across a rocky and swift-flowing stream, the strange old man suddenly seized the boy and pushed him off the bridge into the raging torrent below where he was dashed against the rocks and killed.

The young man exclaimed in horror and thought his old companion was a devil, but the old man then appeared as a deva and told the young man that he had repaid the widow for her kindness and hospitality by saving her from heartbreak and a horrible death, as the young boy, had he lived, would have stolen and got her into serious trouble, finally murdering her.

The reverse of this moral is that much of the good we do has evil results and it behoves us to get wisdom first. To do this, we must find out what we are. That does not at all mean that we should let our thoughts run round in circles. That way lies no release, as the Buddha pointed out:

"And of his foolishness he ponders thus: 'Have I verily been in bygone times or have I not been? What have I been in those bygone times? How have I been in bygone times? What was I before I became what I was in the far distant past? Shall I verily be in far-off days to come or shall I not be? What shall I be in those far-off days to come? How shall I be in the far-off days to come? What shall I be before I become what I shall be in the far distant future?' The present also supplies him with matter for doubt, and he asks himself: 'Am I now or am I not? and if I am, what am I and in what way? This present being—whence has it come and whither is it going?'

"And with such cognitions he arrives at one or other of the following six views, the which becomes his solemn and settled conviction: either the view, 'I have a self,' or else the view, 'I have not a self,' or the view, 'by self I apprehend self,' or the view, 'by self I apprehend non-self,' or else the view, 'by non-self I apprehend self.' Or perhaps he adopts the view: 'This identical self of mine, I maintain, is veritably to be found, now here, now there, reaping the fruits of its good and of its evil deeds; and this, my self, is a thing permanent, constant, eternal, not subject to change, and so abides for ever.' But this, bhikkhu, is a walking in mere opinion, a resorting to mere views; a barren waste of views; an empty display of views. All this is merely to writhe, caught in the toils of views. Held thus fast to the bonds of views the uninstructed man of the world remains unfreed from birth, growth, decay, and death; is not delivered from sorrow, lamentation, pain, grief, and despair; in brief, he obtains no release from suffering."

The first thing to find is that we are not "I" or "you," and that can be found by realizing, by fully realizing, Impermanence.

"Just as, brethren, of all starry bodies whatsoever, the radiance does not equal one-sixteenth part of the moon's radiance, just as the moon is reckoned chief of them; even so is it with the perceiving of impermanence. Just as, brethren, in the autumn season, when the sky is opened up and cleared of clouds, the sun, leaping up into the firmament, drives away all darkness from the heavens, and shines and burns and flashes forth; even so, brethren, the perceiving of impermanence, if practised and enlarged, wears out all sensual lust, wears out all lust for body, all desire for rebirth, all ignorance, wears out, tears out, all conceit of 'I am.'

"And in what way, brethren, does it so wear them out?

"It is by seeing: 'Such is body, such is the arising of body, such is the ceasing of body, such is feeling, perception, the activities, such is consciousness, its arising and its ceasing.'

"Even thus practised and enlarged, brethren, does the perceiving of impermanence wear out all sensual lust, all lust for body, all desire for rebirth, all ignorance, wears out all conceit of 'I am.'"

But let us see how long is the long view. The Buddha pointed out more than two thousand five hundred years ago that there exist countless galaxies with their suns and planets and moons and stars, lying in every direction round this universe. This, which was "fanciful" to the West a hundred years ago, modern science is now learning how to prove, having seen that it is sober fact.

As for time, no better picture of its duration can be shown than the one given by the Buddha. "Just as if there were a mighty mountain crag four leagues in length, breadth, and height, without a crack or cranny, not hollowed out, one solid mass of rock, and a man should come at the end of every century, and, with a fine cloth of Benares, should once on each occasion stroke that rock; sooner would that mighty mountain crag be worn away by this method, sooner be used up, than the aeon.

"Thus long is the aeon: of aeons thus long many an aeon has passed away, many hundred aeons, many a thousand aeons, many a hundred thousand aeons."

The Buddhist Layman and "Social Service"

Let us try to pull the threads together. We have seen that the work of a Buddhist bhikkhu is more noble and more necessary than social service but that social service is a noble and necessary occupation from the Buddhist standpoint for a dedicated layman.

A layman may be both in the world and of it. He can, and should, also, be strenuous in attempting to leave the world behind. If he is set entirely upon the higher life, he may become a bhikkhu, just as a bhikkhu who feels a greater necessity to perform social service than to do those things for which the noble Order was instituted, may become a good and devout layman.

A devout Buddhist layman will first of all keep the five precepts. Even by just doing that, he is setting an example to others visibly, and in more subtle ways, an example that is never without influence for good. "They also serve who only stand and wait."

By going further, by practising the four brahma vihāras—the active, intense, radiation of loving-kindness, compassion, joy in the achievements and gains of others, and tranquillity, tranquillity for himself and others—he is influencing many for good, in perhaps too subtle a way to be realized in full even by himself.

By going further still and practising *vipassanā bhāvanā*, mental development for insight-wisdom, he is influencing all of existence.

This practice is by no means "escapist." The man who lulls himself with alcohol, tobacco or even good books, good paintings and good music, is thereby escaping, in some degree, from reality; but the man who is facing reality, and that is the beginning of the practice, is doing the very opposite. It is the first who is negative, and the second who takes the positive approach really. In this way, always bearing in mind the long view, a man is doing more than he could ever do in his endeavours to be "his brother's keeper."

That does not at all mean that he should not do all that he can to help all sentient beings, physically and materially as well as in other ways. The Buddha, as usual, put it in a clear and rational way. On a certain occasion the Exalted One was staying among theSumbha, at Desaka, a district of Sumbhā.

On that occasion the Exalted One addressed the monks, saying:

"Once upon a time, monks, a bamboo acrobat set up his pole and called to his pupil, Medakathālikā, saying:

"'Now, you climb the pole and stand on my shoulder.'

"'All right, master,' replied the pupil to the bamboo acrobat and climbed the pole and stood on the master's shoulder.

"Then said the master to his pupil: 'Now, Medakathālikā you watch me and I'll watch you. Thus watched and warded by each other, we'll show our trick, get a good fee and come down safe from the bamboo pole.'

"At these words Medakathālikā the pupil replied:

"'No, no! That won't do, master! You look after yourself and I'll look after myself. Thus watched and warded, each by himself, we'll show our trick, get a good fee and come down safe from the bamboo pole. That's the way to do it."'

Then said the Exalted One; "Now monks, just as Medakathālikā the pupil said to the master: 'I'll look after myself' so ought ye to observe the station of mindfulness which means 'I'll ward myself,' likewise that which means 'we'll ward another.' By warding oneself, monks, one wards another. By warding another one wards himself.

"And how, monks, by warding oneself does one ward another? "It is by following after, by cultivating, by making much of him.

"And how, monks by warding another does one ward himself? "It is by forbearance, by harmlessness, by goodwill, by compassion towards him. That, monks, is how he wards himself. "Monks, ye must observe the station of mindfulness which means: 'I ward another.' It is by warding self, monks, that one wards another.

"It is by warding another that one wards himself."

It should perhaps be explained that these bamboo-acrobats perform various feats, such as the master balancing the pupil on his chest and the pupil climbing the pole and balancing on the top. Were one to neglect for a moment the business in hand, his own side of it, it might easily spell disaster to both.

By protecting oneself well, taking the long view and the moral outlook, the knowledge and wisdom to realize that morality and loving-kindness are the best way of guarding oneself, one guards others, influencing the world even if one is far from the world.

If one takes the long view and lives a purely moral life with sustained loving-kindness to all, one thereby protects oneself in the best possible way, and guards others in the best possible way, influencing the world for good even if "far from the madding crowd's ignoble strife."

This can perhaps be better understood if one thinks of the times when impending danger to a loved one has been "felt" though divided by distance.

All but the most extreme extroverts have had such an experience, at least faintly. Mental development (*bhāvanā*) strengthens that bond, extends it, and enables one to influence for good all that lives and breathes. One then, in every way, physically where possible, as well as mentally, protects and guards others. This is the surest way to protect and guard oneself, as even the extreme extroverts are beginning to see, in this shrinking world which daily becomes more vulnerable to terrible destruction.

This article has necessarily been somewhat discursive but may help you to formulate some thoughts on the real and lasting goal of yourself and others, and of the Buddhist teaching thereon.

— §§§ —

The Four Sacred Shrines

Piyadassi Thera

Bodhi Leaves No. 8

First published: 1961

The Four Sacred Shrines

While staying in the Sal Grove at Kusināra, a few hours before he attained Parinibbāna the Supreme Buddha, at the ripe age of eighty, addressing the Venerable Ānanda, his most dutiful and beloved attendant, said: "There are four places, Ānanda, which the devotee should visit with feelings of inspiration (*saṃvega*): the place at which he can say 'Here the Tathāgata was born,' 'Here the Tathāgata attained Supreme and Perfect Enlightenment,' 'Here the Tathāgata set in motion the incomparable Wheel of the Dhamma,' 'Here the Tathāgata finally attained Parinibbāna, the Deathless.' And there will come, Ānanda, to these places, pious Brethren and Sisters of the Holy Order, and devout men and women."

It is significant and interesting to note that the being bent on Enlightenment or Buddhahood was born under trees in a park, practised self-mortification in quest of Enlightenment in the open under trees. He attained Buddhahood under a tree, delivered his first sermon to the five ascetics under trees in the Deer Park, and finally passed away to the Deathless under the twin sala trees in an open park.

I

Lumbinī, or Rummindei, the local name by which it is now known, is the birth place of Prince Siddhattha Gotama.[27] It is one hundred miles north of Benares and within full sight of the snow-crowned Himalayas. Siddhattha Gotama, the Buddha, the Enlightened One, is the founder of the 'religion' called Buddhism. His father, Suddhodana Gotama, the *Kshatriya* (warrior clan) king, was ruling at Kapilavatthu over the land of the Sakyans on the Nepal frontier. Mahāmāyā, a princess of the Koliyas, was his queen.

On the full moon of May (Vesākha) Queen Mahāmāyā was travelling in state from Kapilavatthu to Devadaha, her parental

27 In Sanskrit: *Siddhārtha,* the Bodhisatta's personal name, and Gotama, his family name.

home, according to the custom of the times, to give birth to her child. But that was not to be; for halfway between the two cities in the beautiful Lumbinī Grove, under the shade of a flowering Sal tree, she brought forth a son.

The discovery and identification of the Lumbinī park in 1896 CE is attributed to that renowned archaeologist, General Alexander Cunningham, owing to whose indefatigable effort and perseverance many a hidden Buddhist holy spot, and the sacred body relics of the two chief disciples Venerable Sāriputta and Venerable Mahā Moggallāna, were brought to light.

At Lumbinī what attracts the attention of the pilgrim or the tourist most is the mighty Asoka stone pillar erected some 2210 years ago. History records that Emperor Asoka, after he became a Buddhist, gave up *Dig-vijaya* (conquest of the world) and established *Dharma-vijaya* (conquest by righteousness) and state pilgrimages. The course of the state pilgrimages, which Asoka instituted in place of royal hunting parties, and the holy places of Buddhism which he visited, were marked by memorials in the form of imperial standards *(dhvaja-stambhas)*, splendidly wrought in stone and inscribed with Asoka's edicts or inscriptions recording the Emperor's visit. Many of these still exist in a more or less perfect condition.[28]

Asoka went in procession to Lumbinī with the Venerable Upagupta, his teacher and adviser. The latter pointed out the birthplace of Prince Siddhattha Gotama, saying, "Here, Great King, the Venerable One was born." Asoka then paid homage to the holy spot and ordered a column of stone to be erected there to mark this first station of his pilgrimage. This pillar, "as crisp as the day when it was cut," had been struck by lightning, when Hiuen Tsiang, the Chinese pilgrim saw it towards the middle of the seventh century CE. The inscription engraved on the pillar in five lines consisting of 93 Asokan characters reads:

1. *Devāna piyena Piyadasina lājina vīsati-vasābhisitena,*
2. *atana āgācha mahīyita hida Budhe jāte Sakyamunī ti,*
3. *silā vigadabhī chā kālāpita silāthabhe chā usapāpite,*
4. *hida Bhagavaṃ jāte ti Lummini-game yubalike kate,*
5. *atha-bhāgiye cha.*

28 *The History of Aryan Rule in India*, E. B. Havell, p. 96.

"The king Devānampiya-Piyadassi, when he was twenty-years-anointed, did (this place) the honours of coming (here) in person. Due to the fact the Buddha, the Sakya saint, was born here, he caused a stone surrounding and screening wall to be made[29] and a stone pillar to be set up. Also, he made the village of Lumbinī free of rent and entitled to the king's eight share of the grain."[30]

II

Buddhagayā , or Bodh-Gayā as the Indians call it, is the most sacred place to the Buddhists the world over. For it was here that the Master at the age of thirty-five attained Supreme Enlightenment *(anuttaraṃ sammā sambodhiṃ).* It is recorded in the Buddhist texts that the Prince Gotama, at the age of twenty-nine, renounced wife and child, his father and a crown that held the promises of power and glory, and in the garb of an ascetic retreated into the solitude of the forest in quest of the eternal verities of life. Accompanied by five other ascetics he practised severe asceticism on the bank of the Nerañjarā at Uruvelā near Gayā. Strenuously and zealously struggling for six long years, he came to death's very door. But self-mortification could not lead him to the desired goal. Abandoning asceticism and extreme fasting, he partook of food. His five companions, disappointed, forsook him. Then, un-aided by any teacher, save fixed determination, unflinching energy, and complete faith in his own purity and power, and accompanied by none, the Bodhisatta resolved to make his final quest in complete solitude. Cross-legged he sat under the Bodhi tree at Uruvelā—"a pleasant spot, soothing to the senses and stimulating to the mind"—making the final effort with the inflexible resolution: "Though only my skin, sinews and bones remain, and my blood and flesh dry up and wither away, yet never from this seat will I stir, until I have attained full enlightenment *sammā-sam-bodhi."* So indefatigable in effort, so unflagging in his devotion was he, and so resolute to realize the Truth.

On a full moon day of May exactly 2551 years ago as the sun rose in a glowing Eastern sky, and the Vesākha (Vesak) full moon

29 Or "he caused a stone and brick wall to be made" as Fleet suggested later in JRAS, July, 1903, p. 832.

30 "The Rummindei inscription and the conversion of Asoka to Buddhism", by F.J. Fleet, JRAS, April, 1908.

set slowly in the West, Bodhisatta Gotama solved the riddle of becoming, unravelled the mystery of being by comprehending in all its fullness, the Four Noble Truths, the Eternal Verities: Sorrow, the Cause of Sorrow, the Cessation of Sorrow, and the Path leading to the Cessation of Sorrow. Because of its sacred associations Gayā came to be known as *Buddha Gayā,* and the tree under which he sat and meditated as the Bodhi Tree, 'The Tree of Wisdom.'

Thus did he become one whose *saṃsāra,* continued existence, had finally ended. He thought thus: "My mind is free from the corruption of the craving for repeated existence. Birth is destroyed, the noble life has been perfected, done all that there was to be done, for me there is no more rebirth. Knowledge and vision arose in me. Unshakable is my deliverance, this is my last birth."[31]

It was here under the Bodhi Tree that the Enlightened One reflected on the *paṭicca samuppāda* (dependent origination); the central conception of his Teaching, in direct and reverse order thus: "When this exists, this is; with the arising of this cause, this effect arises; when this cause does not exist, this effect is not; with the cessation of this cause, this effect ceases."

The present Bodhi tree is one of the successors of the original Bodhi Tree. It is well-known that Saṅghamittā, the daughter of Emperor Asoka, brought with her the south branch of the original tree and planted it at Anuradhapura in Sri Lanka. It still flourishes and is the oldest known tree in the world.

According to the records of the Chinese pilgrims Fa-Hien and Hiuen Tsiang, Emperor Asoka was in the habit of visiting the Mahā Bodhi often. The story of the Bodhi Tree and Asoka's visit are represented on the sculpture of Sāñchī. It is said that Asoka erected a shrine on the spot where the Master attained Enlightenment and enclosed the Bodhi Tree with a magnificent stone railing. However, no remains of Asoka's shrine have survived. "The existing temple of Bodh-Gayā can hardly be dated earlier than the first century before Christ, but there is good reason to believe that it reproduces the design of the original temple which Asoka built on the same site."[32]

---

31 MN 25

32 *Aryan Rule in India*, E. B. Havell, p. 112.

There is a cultural link between Buddha-Gayā and Sri Lanka, for during the time of Samudragupta in India, Meghavaṇṇa, the reigning king of Sri Lanka, sent an embassy with costly presents to Samudragupta which led to the founding of a monastery at Buddha-Gayā for the residence of the monks from Sri Lanka, at the request of Meghavaṇṇa. Hiuen Tsiang writes vividly about this monastery which he visited towards the middle of the 7th century CE.

"This was the first Sinhala Saṅghārāma erected in Northern India but certainly not the first monastic foundation of Sri Lanka in India, for we learn from the Nāgarjunakonda inscription of Virapurisadatta that a spacious monastery called Sinhala-Vihara was built on the bank of the river Krsan in South India at least a century earlier. The foundation of the Mahābodhi Saṅghārāma still exists just outside the northern entrance of the Bodhgayā temple, defying the ravages wrought by time and in spite of the neglect of centuries."[33]

III

Next we come to Isipatana, modern Sārnāth, where the Master set in motion the Wheel of the Dhamma (Dhammacakkappavattana).

Barely two months had passed since his enlightenment when the Buddha left Gayā for far away Benares, walking a distance of not less than a hundred and fifty miles, to make known the Truth to those five ascetics, his erstwhile companions, still steeped in the unmeaning rigours of extreme asceticism.

Travelling in stages, the Blessed One reached the deer sanctuary at Isipatana and met the five ascetics, and said: "The Tathāgata (an epithet of the Buddha, one of the meanings of which is 'One attained to Truth'), monks, is an Arahant, an Accomplished One, a Supremely Enlightened One is he (*Sammā-sambuddha*). Give ear, monks, the Deathless has been attained. I shall instruct you. I shall teach you the doctrine. Following my teaching you will know and realize for yourselves, even in this life time, that supreme goal of purity for the sake of which clansmen retire from 'home to follow the homeless life.'"

---

33 *Ceylon Lectures*, B. M. Barua, p. 18.

Thereupon the five ascetics said: "Friend Gotama, even with the stern austerities, penances and self-torture you practised, you failed to attain the superhuman vision and insight. Now that you are living a life of luxury, self-indulgence and have given up the struggle, how could you have reached superhuman vision and insight?"

Then replied the Blessed One: "The Tathāgata has not ceased from effort and reverted to a life of luxury and abundance. The Tathāgata is a supremely Enlightened One. Give ear, monks, the Deathless has been attained. I shall instruct you. I shall teach you the Dhamma." A second time the monks said the same thing to the Buddha who gave the same answer a second time. A third time did they repeat the same question. Then the Master asked, "Monks, did you ever hear me speak in this-wise before?" "Nay, indeed, Lord," was their answer. Overcome and convinced by his utterance the monks indicated their readiness to listen to him.

Now, on a full moon day of July (Āsāḷhā), at eventide, in the shady Deer Park at Isipatana in Benares, addressing the five ascetics the Buddha said: "There are two extremes, monks, which ought not to be cultivated by the recluse. What two? Gross sensuality which is low, worldly and conducive to harm; and self-mortification which is painful, low and conducive to harm. The Middle Path, monks, discovered by the Tathāgata, avoids these extremes and gives vision, gives knowledge and leads to peace, to insight, to enlightenment and Nibbāna.

> "What, monks, is that Middle Path? It is this Noble Eightfold Path itself, namely:
>
> Right Understanding
> Right Thoughts
> Right Speech
> Right Action
> Right Livelihood
> Right Effort
> Right Mindfulness
> Right Concentration."

Then the Blessed One explained to them the Four Noble Truths: the Noble Truth of Dukkha (Suffering), the Noble Truth of the Cause of Dukkha, the Noble Truth of the Cessation of Dukkha, and the Noble Truth of the Path leading to the Cessation of Dukkha.[34]

Sārnāth which is situated five miles to the north of Varanasi marks the birth place of the Dhamma, the Teaching of the Buddha, and the Sangha, those taught by the Buddha. For it was here that the Enlightened One proclaimed the Dhamma for the first time, and sent forth his first sixty disciples with the words:

"Released am I, O bhikkhus, from ties both human and divine. You also are delivered from fetters human and divine. Wander for the welfare and happiness of many, out of compassion for the world, for the gain, for the welfare and happiness of gods and men. Proclaim the Dhamma, excellent in the beginning, excellent in the middle and excellent in the end, in the spirit and in the letter. Proclaim you the life of consummate purity. I shall go to Uruvelā, to Senānigama, to teach the Dhamma."[35]

Thus did the Supreme Buddha commence his *dhammadūta* work, his ministry, which lasted to the end of his life.

Asoka the Great came on pilgrimage to this holy spot and caused a series of monuments and a pillar with the lion capital to be erected. The lion capital which is given the pride of place in the excellent Museum at Sārnāth is today the official crest of free India. The pillar with the Asokan inscription reads "… the Sangha cannot be torn asunder by anyone whatsoever. Whoever, monk or nun, breaks up the Sangha must be made to wear white garments and to take up abode in a place other than a monastery."

Shri Nehru writes in his *Discovery of India* (p. 44), "At Sārnāth I would almost see the Buddha preaching his first sermon, and some of his recorded words would come like a distant echo to me through two thousand five hundred years. Asoka's pillars of stone with their inscriptions would speak to me in their magnificent language and tell me of a man who, though not an emperor, was greater than any king or emperor."

About Asoka's pillars, H.G. Rawlinson writes in *India* (p. 84): "These pillars are burnished till the surface is almost like glass, and

34 SN V 420 Dhammacakkappavattana Sutta.

35 Vinaya Mahāvagga, Khandaka.

their high polish so deceived later travellers that they thought they were made of metal. They were surmounted with a bell-capital, an abacus and a symbolic figure, usually a lion. The most striking of these capitals is the one found at Sārnāth, with its four magnificent lions upholding a *dharma-cakra* or "Wheel of the Law," which was set in motion at this spot. The abacus is decorated with realistic figures." John Marshall speaks with profound admiration of "the masterful strength of the crowning lions, with their swelling veins and tense muscular development," and goes so far as to declare that both bell and capital are "masterpieces in point of both style and technique—the finest carvings, indeed, that India has yet produced, and unsurpassed by anything of the kind in the ancient world."

IV

From Sārnāth we come to Kusinārā or Kusināra as it is now called. It is in the Uttar Pradesh about 120 miles north-east of Varanasi. This being the scene of Buddha Gotama's Mahā-Parinibbāna, devout Buddhists all over the world visit this holy spot with feelings of inspiration. The Blessed One had now reached the ripe age of eighty. His two chief disciples, Sāriputta and Mahā Moggallāna, had passed away three months earlier. Pajāpatī Gotamī, the foster-mother of the Master and head of the Order of Nuns, Yasodharā and Rāhula were also no more.

The Buddha was now at Vesāli, and the rainy season having come, he went together with a great company of monks to Beluva to spend there the period of the rains. There a severe sickness fell upon him, causing him much pain and agony, but being mindful and self-possessed, bore it patiently. He was on the verge of death; but he felt he should not pass away without taking leave of the Sangha, the Order. So with a great effort of will he suppressed that illness, and kept his hold on life. His sickness gradually abated and when quite recovered he journeyed from Beluva to the Mahāvana. Worn out with sickness, with feeble limbs, the Buddha now journeyed on with much difficulty followed by the Venerable Ānanda and a great company of monks. Even in this last, long, wearisome journey of his, the Master never failed in his attention to others.

The Blessed One now reached the Sāla Grove of the Mallas at Kusināra—the journey's end. Knowing that here would be his last resting place, he told the Venerable Ānanda, "I am weary, Ānanda, and would lie down. Spread over for me the couch with its head to the north between the twin Sāla trees." He then laid himself on his right side, composed and mindful, with one leg resting on the other. Speaking now to the monks the Buddha instructed them on many an important point which are recorded in the Mahāparinibbāna

Suttanta or the discourse on the passing away of the Buddha, the longest discourse of the Buddhist canon. All the events that occurred during the closing years of his life also are recorded in this discourse. It is indeed a discourse that not only the devout Buddhist, but the students of Buddhism too, should read, for it is replete with important sayings and the instructive utterances of the Master.

The Buddha made his final exhortation to those who wished to follow his Teaching now and in the future in these memorable words:

> *Vayadhammā saṅkhārā. Appamādena sampādetha.*
>
> "Transient are all compounded things. With heedfulness work out your deliverance."

With these last words the master passed away. He attained *parinibbāna* that is free from any substratum of further becoming.

At Kusināra the main objects of interest are the Matha Kunwarka Kot, the shrine with the recumbent image of the Master, the Mahāparinibbāna Stupa immediately behind the image house, and the Aṅgāra Cetiya about six furlongs from the stupa, built at the spot where the remains of the Tathāgata were cremated. The Cetiya, of course, is in ruin and the restoration work has already commenced. When A. C. Carlyle discovered the image in 1833, it was in fragments, but he ably restored it. This colossal reclining image of the Tathāgata, 20 feet in length, lying on his right side with the head towards north, evokes nothing but *saṃvega*—a noble inspiration and feelings of reverence in the pious pilgrim, and hardly any visitor leaves this shrine without being moved by the glance of the Buddha.

An inscription carved on the stone couch on which the image is placed, in characters of the 5th century CE, reveals the name of the donor and sculptor:

> *Deyadharmoyaṃ mahā-vihārasvāmino haribālasya pratimāceyaṃ ghatitā dine … māthurena.*
>
> "This is the religious gift of Haribāla Svāmi of the Mahā Vihāra. This image is made by Dina of Mathura."[36]

The Mahāparinibbāna Stupa indicates the spot where the All Compassionate Master breathed his last and attained Mahāparinibbāna. The identity of the place with the site of Parinibbāna was settled beyond doubt by the discovery of inscriptions referring to the Parinibbāna Caitya.

History tells us that Asoka, having paid homage to this holy spot, caused a stupa to be built, but this has not been brought to light. "The Parinirvāna Caitya, to which the inscriptions refer, dates from the Gupta period and it is not impossible that the Asoka stupa lies buried underneath the later construction."

— §§§ —

36 *Buddhist Shrines in India,* D. Vahsingha, p. 41.

How to Teach Buddhism to Children

Dr. Helmuth Klar
of Heidelberg, Germany

Bodhi Leaves No. 9

First published: 1961

How to Teach Buddhism to Children

The Problem

The problem means in particular: How can Buddhist parents best teach their own children Buddhism? since they will seldom have the opportunity to teach it to other children, let alone the children of non-Buddhist parents. As I do not wish to theorize, I shall speak only from practical experience with my own children, and so of Western children in general. It is moreover particularly the Western child which is exposed to a Christian or materialistic environment, and hence is in need of a carefully considered Buddhist education. In a Buddhist country, steeped in its centuries-old Buddhist tradition, the position of a Buddhist child is (or should be) far easier. In such a favourable environment a good and effective Buddhist educational system may have developed. But even if it had it would be a great mistake for us, as Westerners, to copy it without due consideration.

We live in entirely different conditions and so cannot take such an important problem as Buddhist education too lightly. Our Great Teacher, the Buddha himself, has taught us to see for ourselves, to examine and draw our own conclusions, and not to believe blindly in others. Just as everyone must work out his own salvation so must we evolve a Buddhist educational system suitable for Western conditions. Naturally any advice or suggestions which other countries can give will be thankfully accepted. We hope to receive many such proposals and to hear of other people's experiences.

Imitation

The educational programme depends very much on the age of the child, or children. The good example of the parents is the most important part of any education and if the parents live in accordance with the Dhamma this will be the surest guide to the children, whatever their age. Children develop the faculty of observation to a high degree and imitation is with them an important factor. We should not neglect this fact. Everything depends on how much the parents themselves succeed in realizing the Dhamma in their everyday life, in making Buddhism a living thing, and not just something to talk about.

Externals Help

Together with imitation, externals play an important role during childhood. No Buddhist household should therefore be without a Buddha-rūpa (image), or at least a picture of the Enlightened One. It is a good idea to let each child have a small Buddha-rūpa of its own before which it can offer regularly flowers, incense and light (the "lights" are, in India, little coconut oil lamps, sometimes in coloured paper shades, sometimes candles). But it is vital that we see to it that the child does not come to worship the image itself, but that it pays devotion to the Buddha as the greatest teacher of mankind. For although we must not develop any system of rites, we must not neglect the fact that a simple ceremony such as this brings Buddhism closer to the hearts of children. To adult Buddhists rites are more a fetter than a help, in so far as they are apt to make us think that we have achieved something merely by the performing of them. The philosophical aspects of Buddhism, although essential for adults, are generally too deep for children to grasp. But as externals help our children towards the Buddhist way of life we may make use of some simple ceremony. Children love the spectacular, and the regular offering of flowers, incense and lights, helps to develop such good habits as veneration and respect.

The Use of Festivals

Children always enjoy festivals, and since non-Buddhist children have so many, Buddhist children may be allowed their Uposatha-day once or twice every month. This day should be made quite different from an ordinary day, different even from an ordinary Sunday. As it is not always possible in Western countries to keep the new or full-moon day itself, parents may choose the Sunday nearest to it and make that day a festival. Workaday life must stop on this Uposatha-day, and everyone should be intent on observing the *sīlas*.

Teaching the Dhamma

Parents should teach their children the Dhamma or influence them in that way. Now how can this best be done?

As already pointed out, this depends very much on the age of the children. In this article I will speak of children aged about ten years, as my two boys are now this age. Parents with younger children may simplify what follows, and those with older children can expound the Dhamma a little more deeply. A lot depends on the children's abilities and their perceptive faculties. (A translation of the Dhammapada and such little collections as Bhikkhu Sīlācāra's *Lotus Blossoms* will prove inspiring sources from which to study).

From time to time the father can read one of the Buddhist legends or a story from the Jātakas, the tales of rebirth. There is no reason why these beautiful tales should be neglected so long as the moral of the story be stressed and the amoralities carefully explained away. Since children have to learn so much about Greek mythology in school and the cruel fighting between the Greek gods and other gods, why should we avoid telling our children the Jātakas? These stories will introduce them into the Indian way of thinking and the concepts of kamma and rebirth will find a natural place in their minds. And since an understanding of kamma and rebirth requires a minimum of intellectual reasoning, the ideas can be taught even to children. In fact the whole teaching of the Buddha could be taught to children if only we could present it in the right way. To abstain from teaching our children Buddhism is a great mistake, and it is incongruous that some Buddhists put much stress on such a thing as vegetarianism, while neglecting to give their own children a Buddhist upbringing.

Buddhist Education a Duty

In any other religion the education of children in that belief is quite self-evident and takes a predominant place. So why should it be otherwise with Buddhism? It may be answered that Buddhism is more of a philosophy than a religion. But is not Buddhism also a way of living? And it is just this way of living which we have to impart to our children. If the position of Buddhism in the modern world is not so good as it was in former times, this is due to the fact that we have neglected the education of our children. What I should especially like to stress in this article is that a Buddhist education in Western countries is possible, and since it can be done it must be done. I am fully aware that we are far from the establishment of a Buddhist educational system, but a start has to be made, and this article is a contribution to the problem, which is already being discussed in many Buddhist communities.

But there is another reason why we should try to make Buddhist education a reality. In Oriental countries a Buddhist enters monkhood, the Sangha, not only to "work out his own salvation" but also "for the continuance of the Dhamma." But as in most of the Western countries, there are no regular Buddhist missions from the East, we lay-Buddhists of the West must give our share towards upholding the Dhamma here. To teach our children Buddhism is part of that duty. It would be unfair to hold Eastern countries responsible for not giving us Buddhist education. It would mean waiting until such missions were not only established in all Western countries but had learned the western languages thoroughly and understood the problems peculiar to Westerners. Until this time we must help ourselves as best as we can in the most efficient way that we can.

Buddhist History

In addition to the Jātakas already mentioned, we should tell our children about the life of the people during the time of the Buddha, their social structure, the historical background of early Buddhism, the history of Buddhism in general, and how the "Wheel of the Dhamma" rolled over the whole of India and beyond.

Explaining the Dhamma

The children's mind will gradually grow into the spirit of Dhamma, while developing an understanding of the basic doctrines of Buddhism. The parents can then read some easy Suttas to the children, e. g., those concerning the basic five sīlas and what a lay-Buddhist ought to do and ought not to do, more particularly the discourses of the Aṅguttara, the "layman's Nikāya." This is all within the grasp of children. In addition, some easy stanzas from the Dhammapada may be read:

"All tremble before punishments, all fear death.
Comparing others with oneself, kill not; neither cause to kill." (Dhp 129)
"To refrain from all evil, to cultivate the good,
To purify one's thoughts—this is the Teaching of the Buddhas." (Dhp 183)

Buddhism is not as complicated as some of us are apt to think, and furthermore we are right to presume that a child of Buddhist parents had kammic tendencies which caused it to be born as a child of such parents, and so there is every reason why it should be given a Buddhist education.

Learning by Heart

As children learn things easily by heart we can give them the five sīlas and the Triple Refuge to learn, perhaps even in Pali. It is a good idea for the children to learn some of the stanzas of the Dhammapada in their mother-tongue, such for example, as:

"He abused me, beat me, overpowered me, robbed me—in those who harbour such thoughts hatred will never cease" (Dhp 3) and the two following stanzas.
"This is an old rule—not just a rule of today—they blame him who sits silent. They blame him who speaks much, they even blame him who speaks little. "There is none in the world who escapes blame." (Dhp 227) Also Dhp 228.
Dhp 129 (already quoted), and the four following stanzas.

The more a child learns by heart from the Pali Canon the more it will profit from this knowledge when it can understand the deeper meaning. This does not mean that a child should learn sentences which it does not understand at all, but the knowing of such simple things as the above will stand it in good stead as it grows up.

Uposatha-Day

Uposatha-days are the days par excellence for the children to recite the stanzas they have learnt, and for the parents to explain the Teaching of the Buddha. But we must be careful not to over-exert the children, especially on such occasions as this, for the capability of children to pay attention for any length of time is very limited. The Uposatha-day should be on the contrary a festival to which they eagerly look forward. We should therefore take them for a walk, or even an excursion, and not hesitate to play with them. While walking happily through fields and woods we may teach them to observe nature and see life as it really is. When Prince Siddhattha drove out of his palace garden he saw an old man, a sick person, a corpse, and on the last occasion a monk. In a similar manner we should take the children out from the safe and narrow confines of our household, out into the troubled world.

Buddhist children should not be brought up in a world corresponding to the walled palace-garden in which Gotama grew up. Such excursions into nature will give ample opportunity for our children to see what life is really like. They will see that nature is "red in tooth and claw," each animal fighting and eating the weaker. They will see too how hard the living conditions of most people are. Children are generally not aware what it means to be old, sick or dying. We should give them, little by little, a proper understanding of these things. We should teach them at the same time to practise mettā and compassion towards our fellow-sufferers. Smaller children are often cruel to animals because they do not realise what they are doing. Here everything depends on the parents noticing such things early enough and making the children understand what they are doing. Buddhist parents should be very careful that their children avoid all cruelty to animals. The Buddhist child should always respect an animal as a living-being and not merely as a source of food. On our excursions into the countryside we should have many opportunities to show children how to be sympathetic and full of loving-kindness towards both man and animal, and this not only by words, but what is more essential, by deeds.

Like a good scout our child should be taught to help an old woman to carry a basket or to push a hand-cart. He or she should save an ant that has fallen into a puddle, or carry some fish to the deep water which are dying in a far too small pond where they have been left by high water. There are so many opportunities where even a child can show that it is practising Buddhism in following the example of its parents. It is of the utmost importance for Buddhists always to bear in mind that knowledge is not enough. Only knowledge and conduct can assure us of the fruit of Nibbāna.

Buddhism—the Religion of Compassion

Buddhism is moreover the religion of compassion, and we should never forget to present it to our children as such. The Buddha taught the Dhamma out of compassion for the world. Just as the All-Compassionate One made *karuṇā* a central part of his Teaching, so we should not neglect this fact by making discussion the main part. If we only succeed in teaching our children *mettā* (friendliness, active interest in others), *karuṇā* (compassion) and *mudita* (sympathy) we shall have succeeded in doing what we can best do. *Upekkhā* (equanimity) is also important, but rather difficult for children to grasp.

The Buddha as Our Model

We should not make the path for our children too difficult, for this will discourage them. Everything depends on the psychological sensitivity of the parents. They themselves must know how far they can go. The Buddha always knew just how to address people—he spoke to the ordinary person in a different way than to the philosopher, and we can learn much from his example. He was the greatest psychologist as well as the greatest philosopher. How could it be otherwise with a Fully-Enlightened One? Therefore we who wish to teach Buddhism must first learn it thoroughly ourselves. This is of course an indispensable condition which is so evident that I had nearly forgotten to mention it.

Study Your Children's Character

The Buddha taught the Dhamma to kings and beggars, to landowners and peasants, to warriors and merchants, to free men and slaves to philosophers and courtesans. He knew thoroughly the sociological structure and the problems of his country as well as the character of every different type of person. In the same way we should try to study the character of our own children in order that we may teach them the Dhamma in the most effective way. Being reborn in our family they are under our trusteeship as it were. Although they are separate independent beings we are responsible for them. They were not given under our trusteeship by some divine power but have put themselves under our trusteeship. They are reborn in our family because of our similarities to them. This makes it easier for us to understand their characters, an indispensability in the teaching of Buddhism. Therefore it should not be too difficult for the parents to make their children acquainted with the Teaching of the Buddha and this fact should encourage all Buddhist parents. If the parents cannot teach their children Buddhism, who else can succeed in this most important task? For, as already pointed out, there is no better gift we can give our children than this gift of Dhamma. As the Buddha himself said: *Sabbadānaṃ Dhammadānaṃ jināti,* "The gift of the Dhamma excels all other gifts" (Dhp 354).

Immunity Against Christianity and Materialism

In order to keep the minds of our children open to the light of the Dhamma we must pay careful attention that they are not drawn into the nets of materialism or into the belief in an omnipotent God. Since European Buddhist children are growing up in an environment of the two extremes, materialism and Christian faith, we must explain to them the difference between Buddhism and Christianity in particular, and Buddhism and any other kind of philosophy in general. We must point out the singularity of the Teaching of the Buddha as the middle way between the two extremes, and so make our children immune to outside influences. As Christianity and materialism are the two main influences in the West we should point out the fallacies of materialism and acquaint the children with the basic teaching of Christianity. This would include a knowledge of the Christian churches, Christian rites and ceremonies, choral singing and so on. Otherwise, as the children grow up, and especially during the romantic period of puberty, such things may make a greater and more dangerous impression on them. It is therefore better that they should already be acquainted with these things than that they should discover them by their own initiative. Musically inclined children should be introduced very early to worldly singing so that they may not be fascinated too much later on by hearing choral singing and church music. In this and many other ways we have to consider the psychological environment of school children. In Germany for instance, Christmas plays a very important part in family life, even among non-Christian families. Buddhist children will naturally ask: "Why haven't we such a nice festival?" Actually Christmas is more of a family festival (the ancient German Yule), celebrating the shortest day of the year and the beginning of the sun's ascendancy. Originally the festival of Yule had nothing to do with Christianity, and it is in this way that it is still celebrated by many Germans, and thus it should be explained to our Buddhist children.

Self-Responsibility

Self-responsibility is a focal point of Buddhism and we must stress its importance over and over again, for the unbiased mind of the child will understand it. Every evening when other children are praying to "God," Buddhist children should spend a little time in meditation and in reflecting over the things they have done that day. If they find they have not thought, spoken and acted in conformity with the Teaching they should see how to avoid this mistake another time. If they find they cannot get rid of some bad thought or action, then their parents should help them so that they can go to sleep with the resolution to do better on the morrow. In the morning they can begin the new day by reflecting again over their resolution. In this way the children will be able to develop the powers of their own mind, purifying them by the cultivation of "good" or skilful thoughts, words and deeds. So, even at an early age, they will grow beyond the Christian dogma of purification by the grace of an all-forgiving God or through one of his priests. The law of kamma will show the children more clearly than anything else that every thought, word and deed carries within itself both the seed and the fruit and the only thing we can do to rectify "wrong" or unskilful conduct is to do better in future while trying to avoid that which we have done wrong in the past. Complete self-responsibility is the mark of the mature mind, and when our children develop this quality in themselves it will prove their surest and safest guide through life and will prove a natural bulwark against faith— religions on the one hand and the shallow philosophy of materialism on the other.

There are many other things which have to be considered by Buddhist parents in relation to their children. At meal times, for example, when Christian children thank a Creator God for their food, Buddhist children can reflect on the fact that there are many people who have not so much and such good food as they have.

They should never be allowed to be critical of their food: their "tastes" should never be mentioned so that prejudices are not stimulated. Lay people should eat what is on the table in the same way as bhikkhus eat whatever is put in their bowl, merely to nourish the body. But as children grow they must not have any dietetic restrictions in essential foodstuffs.

In this article I have been able only to give a small outline of Buddhist education. Actually each section needs an article to itself. I hope I have succeeded in showing Buddhist parents the dangers of educational indifference towards their children. If so, I shall not hear again the inexcusable opinion of some Buddhist parents: "Our child can choose its religion later on, just as we did: we have no right to influence it." "Later on?" After the influences of Christianity and materialism have worked on the child unopposed, it may, when it grows up, no longer have a free intellectual choice! How can we expect the child to find the Way by itself? Buddhas are awake to the Dhamma without external help; but all other people need guidance and instruction. This is why the Buddha said to his disciples: "Go ye, O bhikkhus, and wander forth for the gain of the many, for the welfare of the many, in compassion for the world, for the good, for the gain, for the welfare of gods and men. Proclaim, O bhikkhus, the glorious Doctrine, preach ye a life of holiness, perfect and pure." (Vinaya Mahāvagga). We are fully aware that laymen are no bhikkhus, but since there are so seldom any bhikkhus in the West, laymen can play their part in proclaiming the Dhamma. Buddhist parents have not merely the right to influence their children in the Buddhist way of thinking, but it is their duty so to do, and that thoroughly and thoughtfully. The best gift for the world is the gift of the Dhamma. What Buddhist parents would take the responsibility for depriving their own children of this gift?

Sabbadānaṃ Dhammadānaṃ jināti!

— §§§ —

Rabindranath Tagore and Buddhist Culture

Sudhansu Bimal Barua

BODHI LEAVES NO. 10

First published: 1961

Rabindranath Tagore and Buddhist Culture

Rabindranath Tagore, whose birth centenary is being celebrated this year (1961), went through all the vital stages of Indian culture. Beginning from the Vedic age, he went through the Buddhist period, the age of the great epics Rāmayana and Mahābharata, and the age of the mystic saints of the Middle Ages. Even the most distinctive thoughts of resurgent India stirred him and found expression in his writings. He is the symbol of the true spirit of Indian thought throughout the ages. The inner voice and vision of ancient India manifested and found exalted expression in Gautama the Buddha and his exponent, King Asoka the Great. The poet was very much impressed by the glory of the Buddha and Buddhist India.

Eclipse and Revival of Buddhism

At certain times the Buddha was almost eclipsed in the land of his birth due to Brahminical, social, and political opposition. Buddhism had to face many difficulties in India due to the ascendency of Hindu religious leaders like Shankara and Kumaril Bhatta on one side, and the Muslim invasion on the other. In one of the chapters of the Rāmāyaṇa, it is stated:

> *Yathahi cora sa tathāni Buddhas*
> *tathāgatam nāstikamatra biddhi.*[37]

> Buddha is like a thief.
> Know Tathāgata [Buddha] to be an atheist.

The so-called "moderate Vaishnavas" of the Middle Ages went some steps further. The famous Vaishnava epic *Chaitaniya Bhagavat* of Vrindavan Das bears evidence of it:

37 *Valmiki: Rāmayana, Ayodhyakanda.*

> *Tave Nityananda gela Bauddher bhavan,*
> *dekhilen prabhū basi ache Bauddhagan,*
> *jigjnashen prabhū keho uttar na Kare,*
> *Kruddha hai prabhū lathi marilen shire.*

> Then Lord Nityananda, disciple of Chaitaniya, went to the house of the Buddhists. He asked them but they did not reply [out of fear]. Being enraged, the Lord [Nityananda] kicked on their heads.[38]

But this tendency against Buddhism could not last long. Towards the end of the nineteenth century, with the reawakening of our national life, the greatness of the Buddha and Buddhist culture that hitherto had guided the destiny of India in the right direction emerged from the ashes like the Phoenix. Buddhism in retrospect blossomed forth in Girish Chandra Ghose's *Baddhadev Charita (*1292 Bengali Era), Nabinchandra Sen's *Amitava Kabya* (1302 Bengali Era), Satyendranath Datta's *Buddha Baran* and *Buddha Purnilna* and Satyendranath Tagore's *Bauddha Dharma* (1308 Bengali Era). It was his family that influenced the religious trend of Tagore's mind towards Buddhism and this is discernible in the work *Bauddha Dharma* of Satyendranath Tagore, elder brother of the poet.

Buddhism in Tagore's Work

Examples of Tagore's devotion to Buddhist culture is found through his various works. In his critical appreciation of the *Dhammapada* he says: "As the preceptor of the Geeta has endowed in it Indian thought with a precise religious shape, so in the *Dhammapada* a picture of the mental make-up of India has been delineated."

He further says in this connection:

> Materials of different shades of Indian thought and culture are confined in Buddhist literature and due to the lack of intimacy with them the entire history of India remains unfulfilled. Being convinced of it, cannot a few youths of our country dedicate themselves for the restoration of the Buddhist heritage and make it a mission in life?

38 *Chaitanya Bhagavat*, Part I.

At that time Tagore introduced Buddhism as a special course of study for the students of Santiniketan. To widen the knowledge of Buddhism he deputed Prof. Nitai Benode Goswami to go to Ceylon, the bastion of Buddhism.

The centre of Buddhist studies augmented by Tagore at Santiniketan is today one of the greatest symposiums of Buddhist culture.

Apart from Indians, there are today a good many scholars from Ceylon, Cambodia, Thailand, Japan, China etc. deeply interested in Buddhism. To quote Thomson, "He [Rabindranath Tagore] is almost more Buddhist than he is in sympathy with many forms of Hinduism that are most popular in his native Bengal."

On the occasion of the consecration of the Mulagandha Kuti Vihara at Sarnath, where the Buddha preached his first sermon, Tagore's poem on the Buddha reads:

> *Bring to this country once again the blessed name*
> *Which made the land of thy birth sacred to all distant lands!*
> *Let thy great awakening under the Bodhi-tree be fulfilled.*
> *Sweeping away the veil of unreason and let,*
> *at the end of an oblivious night,*
> *Freshly blossom out in India thy remembrance!*[39]

Never did words reveal themselves better as are expressed in these lines. The message of love of the Lord Buddha in a world which is wild with "the delirium of hatred" cannot but be quoted:

> *All creatures are crying for a new birth of thine.*
> *Oh, thou of boundless life,*
> *save them, rouse thine eternal voice of hope.*
> *Let love's lotus with its inexhaustible treasure of honey*
> *open its petals in thy light.*
> *O Serene, O Free*
> *in thine immeasurable mercy and goodness*
> *wipe away all dark stains from the heart of this earth.*[40]

On 8th May, 1935, the Buddha Purnima Day, in his presidential homage to the Blessed One, Tagore says:

---

39 *Parisesh*, poem 37.

40 *Natir Puja*, poem 84.

On this full-moon day of Vaisaka I have come to join in the birthday celebrations of the Lord Buddha, and to bow my head in reverence to him whom I regard in my inmost being as the greatest man ever born on this earth. This is no formal demonstration of adoration on my part, befitting the occasion. I offer him here, today the homage I have offered him again and again in the deep privacy of my soul.

Buddha Gaya and Borobudur

Tagore fostered a very high respect for Buddha Gaya, Saraṇath, and other Buddhist holy places. He expressed it with deep emotion: "I am a disciple of the Buddha. But when I present myself before those holy places where the relics and foot-prints of the Buddha are found I come in touch with him to a great extent."[41]

With reference to Tagore's visit to Buddha Gaya, Mr. Krishna Kripalani writes: "Only once in his life, said Rabindranath, did he feel like prostrating himself before an image, and that was when he saw the Buddha at Gaya."[42] Through the mighty pen of Tagore, his homage to the Buddha (the living image of Indian culture) in Java, Bali, Siam, Burma, Japan, China, and other places abroad, has been perennial, undimmed by the lapse of time. On the occasion of his visit to the famous Borobudur temple in Java he observes:

Man today has no peace,
his heart arid with pride
He clamours for an ever-increasing speed in a fury of chase,
for objects that ceaselessly run, but never reach a meaning.
And now is the time when he must
Come groping at last to the sacred silence,
which stands still in the midst of surging centuries of noise,
till he feels assured
that in an immeasurable love dwells the final meaning of freedom,
whose prayer is: 'Let Buddha be my refuge.'[43]

---

41 *Samalochana*, 1888.

42 *Visva Bharathi Quarterly*, April 1943.

43 *Parisesh*.

Pilgrim in Siam

When the poet went to Siam as a "pilgrim" he expressed his great satisfaction on observing Buddhist culture and civilization. Finding a real manifestation of Indian culture in Siam he exclaims: "If one likes to know the real wealth of India one should go overseas—the field of our gift. The picture of India as we see it here is rough atmosphere; a more distinct and glazing form of eternal India may we find from outside."

Greater India

Lord Buddha liberated mankind from the different forms of ritualism and superstitions and destroyed racial barriers between man and man. Here his reasoning, message of compassion, and ideal of non-violence, won over all. He made vehement objection to outward conventionalism:

Kim te jaṭāhi dummedha, kith te ajinasāṭiyā
abbhantaram te gahanam bāhiram parunajjasi.

"O thou witless man, what avails thy matted hair and deerskin? Within all is darkness in thee, while outwardly thou cleanest thyself!"[44]

On the other hand Lord Buddha proclaimed the gospel of an immeasurable love for all beings:

Sabbe sattā bhavantu sukhitattā

"How broad is this address of good-will. How deep is this love!"

Mātā yathā niyam puttam
āyusā ekaputtam anurakkhe
evam pi sabba bhūtesu
mānasam bhāvaye aparimānam

"Just as with her own life
a mother shields from hurt
her own, her only child,
let all-embracing thoughts
for all that lives be thine."[45]

---

44 Brāhmaṇa-vagga, Dhammapada
45 Mettā Sutta, Sutta Nipāta.

Non-Violence and Renunciation

This non-violence and compassion have had inimitable expressions in the works of Tagore. So the poet prays for a new birth of the Blessed One in this world which is now "wild with the delirium of hatred." Even the animal sacrifice that mortally pained the poet is vividly reflected in his works, specially in *Rajarshi* (a novel) and *Visarjan* (a play). Animal slaughter is strictly prohibited within the precincts of Santiniketan.

Sacrifice is co-related with non-violence and compassion. Tagore's oft quoted line *tena tyakteno bhūnjatha* (enjoy him through sacrifice) from the Upanishads is the key-note of his life. So the poet sings in obeisance:

Thou giver of immortal gifts
Give us the power of renunciation
and claim from us our pride.

O Serene, O Free

The historical background of his work entitled *Katha* (a collection of verses based on mostly Buddhist stories) represents a model of renunciation. In Srestha-Bhiksha, Mastakbikray, Nāgarlaksmi, Mulyaprapti, Pujarini, etc., the glory of renunciation as depicted in the verses inspired by the ideal of Lord Buddha has no parallel in the history of the world. Here we see that a poor girl can dedicate her only piece of cloth to the Buddha and a mighty king wearing the clothes of a beggar becomes a recluse. Inspired by this ideal of renunciation, the dancing girl Sreemati can defy the royal scepter of King Ajatashatru and sacrifice her life for worship at the feet of Lord Buddha. Tagore gleaned all of these historical events of Buddhist India.

Universal Love

Universal love in Buddhism has taken deep root in India. So we find after abandoning the royal pleasures, the prince and the princess of a mighty monarch went to Ceylon for the propagation of Buddhism.

And the old and invalid Atisa Dipankara crossed the insurmountable Himalayas and lighted the lamp of Buddhism in Tibet.

Tagore, who travelled all over the world many times with the message of universal good, had in him the main object of universal love. This is exactly what the Lord Buddha propagated 2,500 years ago and handed over to posterity. So the poet naturally discovered an affinity of mission and declares with all the emphasis he commands:

> Buddhism was the first spiritual force known to us in history which drew close together such a large number of races separated by most difficult barriers of distance, by differences of language and custom, by various degrees and divergent types of civilization. It had its motive power not in international commerce, nor in empire-building, nor in scientific curiosity, nor in a migratory impulse to occupy fresh territory. It was a purely disinterested effort to help mankind forward to its final goal.[46]

The laws of harmony of all human beings is at the root of this universal brotherhood. Lord Buddha tied the whole world by the bond of unity and it touched the inner depth of the poet's heart. In Siam the poet discerned the power of a single-pointed devotion to one Dhamma, one Sangha and one immortal Teacher. India had accepted all men as kin. India ignored none and, therefore, remained unacknowledged by none. The barriers of race and country were swept away by the flood of truth, and India's message reached men of all races in every land.[47]

The theme of the build-up of an indivisible unity lies at the root of Tagore's devotion to literature and culture. The most unique efflorescence of this prowess of cohesion is to be seen from the constructive activities of the Buddhist Sangha:

> *When the thunder-voiced prayer of the Three Refuges*
> *rang from sky to sky across deserts and hills and distant shores*
> *the awakened countries poured their rejoicings*
> *in great deeds, and noble temples,*
> *in the rapture of self-dedication, in mighty words,*
> *in the breaking of the bond of self.*[48]

---

46 *Buddha and Buddhism* 1.

47 *Buddhadev*, p. 6.

48 *To Siam.*

Peaceful Conquest

The Buddhist power of concentration has no parallel in the annals of the world. In this conquest there was no bloodshed as in the battles of Ohod and Badar, and no inhuman torture as in the crusades. Buddhism has a bloodless record in the history of the world. In this expedition for the propagation of Buddhism, Asoka the Great, Guṇavarman, Kasyapmataṅga, Kumarājīva, Dīpaṅkara, Mahendra and Saṅghamittā, and the Chinese monks Fa-hsien, Yuan Chwang, and I-Tsing were at the head. Great empires of Caesar, Napoleon, Hannibal, and the Nazi dictator Hitler sank into oblivion, but the empire of love of the Buddha and his followers shines for ever.

Some think that Buddhism is merely a religion for one who has relinquished all. But Tagore knew that this religion is not an object of illusion and delusion. This religion is not meant for the weak—it is based upon strength. Tagore observes: "The spread of industry, science, commerce and imperial power was never so prominent in this country as it was during the rise and under the influence of Buddhism."[49] Therefore, it is quite natural that Tagore should have great reverence for the Buddha who is the source of inspiration of this great power.

Caste System

The course of the caste-system, colour bar, and untouchability in the social life of the country pained him deeply. Sacrilege under the veil of religion, malpractices in the name of scripture, and profligacy under the garb of convention, retard progress in every sphere of social life. "The cruel stupidity of wicked racial discriminations and caste and colour bars, parading as religion, has stained the earth with blood; mutual hatred, more deadly than mutual violence, outrages humanity at every step."[50]

The poet also accuses the Indian brahmins who erected artificial walls of difference between man and man. In India, Buddhism has liberated men from the slavery of Brahminical religion. Lord Buddha proclaims:

---

49 *Jattar Purbapatra Pather Sanchay.*

50 *Buddhadev*, p. 7.

One does not become a brahmin by birth.
One does not become an outcaste by birth.
One becomes a brahmin by act,
One becomes an outcaste by act.[51]

So the poet paid homage to the Blessed One who placed supremacy of action above the so-called aristocracy of birth.

Tagore glorified the eternal virtues of Buddhism through the *Malini*, *Chandalika*, and *Natir Puja*, three dramas based on Buddhist stories. In the *Malini*, universal Buddhist toleration is established against narrow sectarianism of the Brahmanical religion. In the *Chandalika*, the revolutionary spirit of Tagore is manifest through the character of Prakriti, a chandala girl low-born and untouchable. She bursts out "Many chandalas abound in the country in the houses of brahmins; I cannot be a chandala."

In the *Natir Puja*, when Princess Ratnavali ironically expressed her disregard for Bhikkhu Upāli, born of the barber Sunanda (a son of a milk man) and Sunita (an untouchable), the nun Uppalavaṇṇa, replied: "Oh Princess! They are all equal in caste; you have no knowledge of the yard-stick of the aristocracy."

Here the inner self of Tagore reveals itself.

In reply to the witty expressions of Ratnavali, queen Lokeswari tauntingly said: "Oh! the follower of this dancing girl! You will cause that to happen and that religion is apprehended in which the fallen will come with the gospel of emancipation."

By the touch of the Great Emancipator a good number of fallen women attained salvation, paved the way, and shed the lustre of emancipation to many others.

Buddhist Humanism

Buddhism has restored human rights to the deprived, to those who were trampled under feet by the so-called high-ups of society.

This humanism is what deeply impressed Tagore, who is himself a great exponent of humanity. Today the world is very much injured

51 Vasala Sutta, Sutta Nipata.

with violence: humanity is narrow-minded. So the poet implores the Buddha to wipe "all dark stains" from the heart of this earth:

> *Man's heart is anguished with the fever of unrest,*
> *with the poison of self-seeking,*
> *with a thirst that knows no end.*
>
> *Countries far and wide flaunt on their*
> *foreheads the blood-red mark of hatred.*
> *Touch them with thy right hand,*
> *make them one in spirit,*
> *bring harmony into their lives,*
> *bring rhythm of beauty.*[52]

A deep and expansive analytical exposition of the glory of the Buddha-dhamma and Buddhist culture by Tagore is an invaluable treasure in Bengali literature and, as a matter of fact, in any literature of the world.

Tagore has once again deeply ingrained within us the impact of the Buddha-dhamma and Buddhist culture, which pervaded the length and breadth of India as the sun pervades the earth and every grain upon it.

— §§§ —

52 *Natir Puja.*

Buddhist Ideals of Government

Gunaseela Vitanage

Bodhi Leaves No. 11

First published: 1961

"Our ancient kings considered hitherto the practice of virtue as their only duty; they knew how to rule without being severe and honoured the Three Jewels; they governed and helped the world, and were happy if men practised righteousness. For myself I desire respectfully, in concert with the son of heaven, to magnify the Good Law in order to save beings from the evil of continued existence (in *saṃsāra*)."

Letter sent to the Chinese emperor by King Mānasam of Ceylon in 423 A.D

Buddhist Ideals of Government

Buddhism, like any other religion, lays emphasis on spiritual values rather than on material ones; on detachment from things of the world rather than on attachment to them; on the religious side of life rather than on the secular side of it. Buddhism does not, however, neglect the material, the secular and the worldly aspects of life altogether. In fact, there is a discourse in the Buddhist scriptures, that has been called the Gihi Vinaya or Code of Discipline for Laymen, wholly devoted to the householder's life.[53] It sets out in detail the layman's duties towards his neighbours and also the methods of disciplining himself to be a good and useful citizen. The Buddhist scriptures also set out certain norms of conduct for rulers as well as for subjects. They also contain references to various forms of government prevailing in India at the time, and, significantly, the Buddha's own words expressing his preference for the democratic form of government.

It must be remembered that the Buddha was born into a society which, comparatively speaking, was politically advanced, and which through the ages had developed certain very sound ideals of government. In the *Manu Neeti* or the Code of Manu, the Hindus already had laws hallowed by time to guide them in their civic duties. Incidentally, Manu, like Moses of the Bible, was the mythical lawgiver of the Indian people. These laws discussed not only the rights of the rulers, but also their duties towards their subjects. They also discussed the obligations of the subjects towards the rulers and also their rights. It is, therefore, necessary to have some idea about the Hindu views of government if we are to appreciate the Buddhist ideals of government.

Matsya Nyāya

The Hindu ideas of government were based on a theory called the *matsya nyāya*, literally meaning the "law of fish".

53 Sigālovāda Sutta: translated in *Everyman's Ethics*, Wheel No. 14.

The term *matsya nyāya* can be more appropriately rendered into English by the expression the "law of the jungle"—"Why should there be governments in the world at all?" "Why should there be some men to rule over other men?" "Why should there be laws which men were required to obey on pain of punishment?" The Hindu thinkers answered these questions by pinpointing a fundamental law of nature: "The Matsya Nyāya," the law whereby the small fish becomes the prey of the big fish. Government, rulers and laws are necessary to prevent this natural law from operating in human society. Remove the government, remove the rulers and remove the laws, and human society will degenerate into a state of anarchy in which the stronger will destroy the weak. "If there is no rule of law," says the Manu Saṃhita, "the strong would devour the weak like fishes." "If there is no ruler to wield punishment on earth" says the Mahabharata, "the strong would devour the weak like fishes in water. It is related that in the days of old people were ruined through sovereignlessness, devouring one another like the stronger fish preying upon the feebler."

It will be seen that this Hindu theory of government was based on a belief in the innate depravity of man. If there is no strong authority to keep men under control, the stronger would destroy the weaker, just as the big fish destroy the small fish in the sea. Government, rulers and laws become necessary to prevent this *matsya nyāya* operating in human society.

This theory of government naturally led to the corollary that there must be a controlling authority, and that authority must be vested with power to inflict punishment, or *daṇḍa*.

The Hindu monarch was thus enjoined to adopt *caturopāya* or the four-fold policy in ruling over the people: *sama, dāna, daṇḍa, bheda. Sama* means peace: the wise ruler must maintain peace among his subjects. *Dāna* means charity: the wise ruler must be charitable. *Daṇḍa* means punishment: the wise ruler must punish the wrong done according to the gravity of the crime. *Bheda* means creating division where necessary: the wise ruler must bring about differences among his subjects in order to make his position secure. In other words, he must adopt the "divide and rule" policy.

Amity

The Buddha differed radically from the Hindu view that *matsya nyāya* is the basic law of nature. He certainly saw the struggle for existence that was so evident in life but this he attributed to man's ignorance rather than to his innate depravity. The Blessed One also saw that man was ever ready to live in peace and amity with his fellow beings, to co-operate with his fellow beings, and even to sacrifice himself for the sake of his fellow beings, provided he was properly guided. In the Buddha's view it was not discipline imposed from above or external authority that was necessary to control man, but self-understanding and inward discipline.

The law of the jungle was certainly not universal even in the jungle. There was amity and co-operation even among the animals in the jungle—as the Buddha points out in several Jātaka stories.

Owing to this fundamental difference in outlook between Hinduism and Buddhism, we see that Buddhism lays little or no emphasis on authority (*bala*) or punishment (*daṇḍa*). For example, we observe that instead of the *caturopāya* or the four-fold policy of *sama, dāna, daṇḍa, bheda* of the Hindus, the Buddhist scriptures speak of the *catus-saṅgraha vastu* (Pāli: *catu-saṅgaha-vatthu*), or the four ways of treating subjects. They are, *dāna* or charity; *priya-vacana* or kind speech; *artha cariya*, or the spirit of frugality and of service, and *samanātmatā* or equality.

Thus, according to Buddhism the virtuous king should practise *dāna* or charity. Charity here includes not only the alms given to the poor but also gifts given to those who serve the monarch loyally. The virtuous king also must practise *priyavacana*, or kind speech. He must on no account use unkindly or harsh words towards anyone.

The king also must cultivate *artha cariya*. The word *artha cariya* has been interpreted to mean the spirit of service as well as the practice of economy and living the simple life. The good king or ruler also must cultivate *samanātmatā* or equality. That is, while retaining the exalted position of the ruler, he must consider himself in no way superior to the least of his subjects, and he must also learn to dispense justice to his subjects without fear or favour. The righteous monarch must also learn to treat everyone equally.

Dasa Rāja Dharma

In the *dasa-rāja-dharma* or the ten royal virtues, the Buddhist ideal of kingship is further elaborated upon. The ten royal virtues are *dāna*, charity; *sīla*, morality; *pariccāga*, munificence; *ajjavan*, straightforwardness; *majjavan*, gentleness; *tapam*, restraint; *akkodho*, non-hatred; *avihiṃsā*, non-violence; *khanti*, patience; and *avirodhatā*, friendliness and amity.

Dana in this context means giving of alms to the needy. It is the duty of the king to look after the welfare of his needy subjects, and to give them food, clothing and other wherewithals.

Sīla here means morality. The monarch must so conduct himself in private and public life as to be a shining example to his subjects.

Pariccāga means the grant of gifts to those who serve the monarch loyally. By the grant of gifts not only does the monarch acknowledge their efficient and loyal service, but he also spurs them on to more efficient and more loyal service.

Ajjavan means that the monarch must be absolutely straightforward. The good king must never take recourse to any crooked or doubtful means to achieve his ends. His yea must be yea, and nay must be nay.

Majjavan means gentleness. The monarch's straight-forwardness and rectitude that often will require firmness, should be tempered with gentleness. His gentleness will keep his firmness from being over-harsh or even cruel, while his firmness will keep gentleness from turning into weakness. A harmonious balance of these two qualities is essential not only for a ruler but for all leaders of men.

Tapan means the restraint of senses. The ideal monarch is the one who keeps his five senses under strict control, shunning indulgence in sensual pleasures.

Akkodha means non-hatred. The good king must not harbour grievances against those who injured him, but must act with forbearance and love.

Avihiṃsā means non-violence. The monarch should not indulge in games where killing is resorted to, or cause injury to any being.

He must practise non-violence to the greatest possible extent that is reconcilable with the duties of a ruler.

Khanti means patience. The king must conduct himself with patience, courage and fortitude on all occasions. In joy and sorrow, in prosperity and in adversity, in victory and defeat, he must conduct himself with calmness and dignity without giving in to emotions.

Avirodhata means non-enmity, friendship. The king must cultivate the spirit of amity among his subjects, by himself acting always in a spirit of amity and benevolence. It will be seen that *avirodhata* is in this context opposed to *bheda*—the divide and rule policy in the Hindu statecraft.

The Buddha also laid emphasis on the fact that the evil and the good of the people depend on the behaviour of their rulers; and for the good of the people he set out these ten royal virtues to be practised by the rulers of men.

Simple though this looks to us, it must be viewed from the point of view of contemporary society where the brahmin hierarchy divided the society permanently into various castes, and gave religious sanction to that division. No doubt the Buddha had in mind the claims of the brahmins that they were a unique people being "twice-born" once in the natural way and again from the shoulder of the creator himself.

Equality

The Buddha's rejection of caste and class was not merely theoretical. He admitted men of all castes into the Order. Upāli, a former barber, Sunita a former outcaste, found honoured places in the Order.

The Buddha says: "Monks, just as all the great rivers, that is to say the Ganges, the Jammu, the Aciravati, the Sarabhu, the Mahi, on reaching the great ocean lose their former names and identities and are reckoned as the great ocean, similarly the Kshatriya, the Brahmana, the Vaisya and the Sudra, after entering this Sangha lose their former identities, and become the members of one Order."

The Chinese pilgrims Fa-Hien, Yuan Chang and I-Ttsing tell us that these democratic and equalitarian concepts were still fostered in India centuries after the great decease of the Buddha.

"Oriental" Despotism

The constant reference by Western writers to oriental despotism has created the impression in the English reader's mind that until the advent of the Europeans there was no good or popular government in Asian lands and that with rare exceptions like the reign of Asoka it was a case of despotic monarchs tyrannizing over a helpless people. The study of both Hindu and Buddhist literature shows that among the Indian rulers there were certainly not more (and probably less) pleasure-seeking despots than among their Western counterparts. Ancient Indian society was, no doubt, feudal—but it was also a co-operative society. The type of oppression of the peasant by the lord as was witnessed in France before the French Revolution was never seen within the boundaries of Hindu or Buddhist India.

Story of Ummadayantī

The story of Ummadayantī in the *Jātakamālā* illustrates this point very well.

The Bodhisattva was once born into the royal family of the Sibis and in due time became the king of the Sibis. One day while touring the city with his retinue he saw Ummadayantī, one of the most beautiful women among the Sibis, and fell in love with her at first sight. But to the chagrin of the king he learned that Ummadayantī was already married. He also learned that the husband was no other than Abhiparaga, one of the officers of the royal household itself.

The king felt quite ashamed of his sudden passion for a woman who was married, and kept the knowledge of it to himself, and tried his best to extinguish the flame of love which arose in his heart.

The king thus suffered in silence because of the love he had for Ummadayantī. Abhiparaga, however, came to know about the king's condition and the reason for it. One day he approached the king while he was alone and broached the subject in a most tactful way. Abhiparaga told the king that he was very well aware of the reason for the king's poor condition and suggested to the king most respectfully that the king accept Ummadayantī as his consort.

The king was confounded and was stricken with shame. The secret love that was gnawing his heart was now known to the husband of the very woman whom he loved. And, here he was himself offering her to him, his king, because of the love and devotion Abhiparaga had for him.

"No, no," said the king, "that may not be. I would lose my merit and would know myself to be immoral. Further my wicked deed would be known also to the public".

Abhiparaga argued again and again with the king with a view to convincing him that he was doing no wrong in accepting Ummadayantī from his hands.

The king finally said, "No doubt, it is your great affection for me that prompts you to the effort to promote my interest without considering what is right and wrong on your side. But this very consideration induces me the more to prevent you. Verily, indifference as to the censure of men cannot at any rate be approved".

The king continued, "The evil and good the people do depend on the behaviour of their rulers. For this reason, and taking into account the attachment of my subjects, I shall continue to love the path of the pious above all in conformity with my reputation.

"As the herd goes after the leading bull in any direction, whether the right one or the wrong one, following his steps in the very same manner, the subjects imitate the behaviour of their rulers without scruple and undauntedly.

"You must take also this into consideration.

"If I should lack the power of ruling my own self, say, into what condition would I bring this people who long for protection from my side.

"Thus considering and regardful of the good of my subjects, my own righteousness and my spotless fame, I do not allow myself to submit to my passion. I am the leader of my subjects, the bull of my herd."

The Buddha in this story showed how a king should conduct himself.

Firstly, he must put his private passions aside in the interest of the people.

Secondly, he must always pay heed to public opinion.

Thirdly, there must not be any divorce between his private life and his public life—both must be without blemish.

Fourthly, he must always be regardful of the good of the subjects.

Fifthly he must give the correct leadership in all matters to the people.

Elsewhere the Buddha says that whether a nation is just and good depends on the conduct of the rulers.

"Monks, when the ruler of a country is just and good, the ministers become just and good. When the ministers are just and good, the higher officials become just and good. When the higher officials become just and good, the rank and file become just and good. And, when the rank and file become just and good, the people become just and good."

It was a belief among the Buddhists that even rains came in due season when the rulers are just and good.

Democracy

Having said so much about the ideals of kingship in Buddhism, we must ask ourselves whether Buddhism considers monarchy itself as the ideal form of government. During the Buddha's time there were a number of great kingdoms, in India, such as Magadha and Kosala. There were also a number of democratic states at the time. The Buddha has definitely expressed himself in favour of the democratic form of government and also expressed the view that it was a form of government which was conducive to the stability of society.

Referring to the preparations made by King Ajatasattu to attack one of these democratic principalities—that of the Vajjians— the Buddha said:

"Ānanda, have you heard that the Vajjians regularly assemble together in large numbers?"

"I have heard so," said the Venerable Ānanda.

"Well Ānanda, so long as the Vajjians assemble regularly and in large numbers, just so long may the prosperity of the Vajjians be looked for and not their decay.

"So long, Ānanda, as the Vajjians assemble in harmony and disperse in harmony; so long as they conduct their business in harmony; so long as they introduce no revolutionary ordinance or break up no established ordinance, but abide by the law; so long as they honour, revere, esteem and worship the elders among the Vajjians and deem them worthy of listening to; so long as the women and maidens can go about, without being molested or abducted; so long as they honour, revere, esteem and worship the Vajjian shrines, both the inner and the outer; as long as they allow not the customary offerings given and performed, to be neglected; so long as customary watch and ward over the holy men that are among them is well kept, so that they may have free access to the realm and having entered may dwell pleasantly therein, just so long as they do these things, Ānanda, may the prosperity of the Vajjians be looked for and not their decay."

That Buddhism helped greatly in the evolution of democratic forms of government in ancient India is borne out by what the Marquess of Zetland, a former Viceroy of India, says in his introduction to the book *Legacy of India*. Lord Zetland says:

"We know indeed that political science—*Artha āstra* in Sanskrit— was a favourite subject with Indian scholars some centuries before the Christian Era. The social contract as the origin of kingship is discussed in the now famous work attributed to Kautilya, the chief minister of Emperor Chandragupta, about the year 300 BC. And it would seem that the people who contracted for a king in these early days did so in order that there should be some external authority capable of ensuring that the laws and regulations of the various corporate bodies which had come into existence, were respected.

'The king,' wrote Yājñavalkya, 'must discipline and establish again on the path of duty all such as have erred from their own laws, whether families, castes, guilds or associations …' It is notable that the tendency towards self-government evidenced by these various forms of corporate activity received fresh impetus from the Buddhist rejection of authority of the priesthood and further by the doctrine of equality as exemplified by its repudiation of caste. It is indeed to the Buddhist books that we have to turn for an account of the manner in which the affairs of these early examples of representative self-governing institutions were conducted. And it may come as a surprise to many to learn that in the assemblies of the Buddhists in India two thousand or more years ago are to be found the rudiments of our own parliamentary practice of the present day. The dignity of the assembly was preserved by the appointment of a special officer—the embryo of 'Mr. Speaker' in our House of Commons. A second officer was appointed whose duty it was to see that when necessary a quorum was secured, the prototype of the parliamentary chief whip in our own system. A member initiating business did so in the form of a motion which was then open to discussion. In some cases this was done once only, in others three times, thus anticipating the practice of parliament in requiring that a bill be read a third time before it became law. If discussion disclosed a difference of opinion the matter was decided by the vote of majority, the voting being by ballot."

In the context of the knowledge we now have about the democracies in ancient India, the Buddha's appreciative reference to the Vajjian Republic is most significant.

As Lord Zetland says, the Buddha's doctrine of equality made a profound impression on the social and political life of the Indian people—and the influence lasted for nearly 14 centuries. In the Sutta Nipāta, we find the following statement of the Buddha:

> "Vāseṭṭha" (he replied), "I will expound
> To you in gradual and very truth
> Division in the kind of living things.
> For kinds divide! Behold the grass and trees.
> They reason not, yet they possess the mark
> After their kind; for kinds, indeed divide.
> Consider then the beetles, moths and ants,

They after their kind too possess the mark.
And so four-footed creatures, great and small …
The reptiles, snakes, the long-backed animals,
Fish and pond-feeders, water-denizens,
Birds and the winged creatures, fowls of the air,
They after their kind all possess the mark;
For kinds divide. Each after his kind bears
His mark. In man it is not manifold.
Not in the hair, or head or ears or eyes,
Not in the mouth or nose or lips or brows,
Not in the throat, hips, belly or the back,
Not in the rump, sex organs or the breast,
Not in hands or feet, fingers or nails,
Not in the legs or thighs, colour or voice,
Is mark that forms his kind, as in all else.
Nothing unique is in men's bodies found;
The difference in men is nominal."

Twenty centuries before the revolutionaries of France raised the standard of "liberty, fraternity and equality," the Buddha had enunciated these very values as essentials of good government!

— §§§ —

Attitudes to Life

Ruth Walshe

Bodhi Leaves No. 12

First published: 1962

Attitudes to Life

In this essay I want to give you as little book-knowledge as possible. Yet, in order to underline my approach, let me start off with a quotation from Goethe's Faust:

Greift nur hinein ins volle Menschenleben!
Ein jeder lebt's—nicht vielen ist's bekannt.
Und wo Ihr's packt, da ist's interessant!

"Just dip into the fullness of life!
Everyone lives it, not many understand it.
But wherever you seize it, it's full of interest."

Now what I want to do is to introduce six real persons to you and try to examine their attitudes to life through Buddhist eyes. When I say *attitude to life,* I mean the way a person looks at life and accordingly re-acts to it. We Buddhists even go so far as to say that we only know life through our senses and elaborate these sense-impressions in our mind.

Therefore, whenever we speak about life, it is not life as it is— but only the mental image we have formed for ourselves. Of course, there must be as many mental images of life as there are people in this world of ours. For each one of us is quite different from the other. Yet we find that there are groups of people who look at their sense-impressions of life in a similar sort of pattern. We say they have a similar attitude to life.

Now I have taken six people of my own acquaintance—each of them representing such a group—and I have given them six different labels:

1. The philosopher,
2. The materialist,
3. The perfect mother,
4. The woman who is afraid of life,
5. The non-accepter of *dukkha* (frustration, suffering), and
6. The accepter of *dukkha*.

Let us first have a look at Albert, the philosopher. He is a well-known doctor, a highly intellectual and cultured man. The world calls him very successful, for he is admired and loved by his patients as well as by his family and friends. He has a very good income, owns a house and a car and he even writes books on medicine and psychology. When you meet Albert outside his consulting-room, he is most charming and interesting, though perhaps a little condescending at times. But when you get to know him better, you find that his way of thinking, though very sharp and logical, is rather abstract and schematic and he dearly loves a juicy argument—even before breakfast. Albert's favourite topics, besides his own subjects, are politics, economics and philosophy—in fact, anything created by man's intellect. He has a very good wit—but little sense of humour—strong opinions, conventional convictions and is a great lover of personalities and traditions …

Would you say there was anything fundamentally wrong with Albert? From the Buddhist point of view: decidedly yes. For Albert mistakes the intellect for life. Please don't think that I regard the intellect as a bar to spiritual development. To think that would be quite wrong. We certainly need all the intellect we can muster to understand Buddhism and its application to daily life. Without intellect we could never lift the thick cloud of delusion we all suffer from and understand the Eightfold Path so clearly laid out by Buddha. But once we start treading this path, our intellect alone is no longer sufficient. Through watching ourselves like an outsider in meditation and later throughout the day, we start developing an awareness of ourselves, our surroundings, other people—in fact, everything we call our life. This awareness is only dim in the beginning, but with perseverance and sincere effort it can become *so* sharp and one-pointed that it ceases to be awareness and becomes insight. It is then that we reach the point where we transcend the intellect. Briefly, I would like to sum up the difference between intellect and insight thus. Intellect is the sharpness of mind still ego-bound while insight is the sharpness of mind no longer ego-bound. It is universal and all-embracing.

But Albert does not want to admit—even to himself—the limitations of his intellect. Instead of using it, as I have just pointed out, to understand the first stage of his journey and then to be content to let insight take over—if only for a flash of a moment—

he uses it as a shield between himself and life. Between himself and his own sense-impressions of the outside world. Though outwardly successful, he suffers-like the rest of us—from the feeling of insecurity which arises by identifying himself with the ego. To ward off this unpleasant feeling he greatly welcomes his intellect. But what does he do? He only tells himself more and more that he is a permanent entity—that he must build up and protect that permanent entity. So his ego-belief gets stronger and consequently his feeling of insecurity increases too. He reasons it all out with his intellect and represses emotions and doubts as much as he can. He is what Jung calls a very strong thinking-type. He just hasn't got the courage to see life as it is—in the raw! He dare not lift the lid of his own dustbin too far. As a psychologist Albert has some idea of what might be popping up. So he has developed a strong subconscious warning system which sounds the alarm at the slightest threat to his carefully built-up intellectual world. And so he only buries his head yet deeper in the sand ...

Charles has the label materialist. He is a very common type in our 20th century and I'm sure most of you know one or two yourselves. Mine is rather a charming man, kind and very clever. When I first met him many years in Vienna, he was a student of German. Rather hard up—but already developing a taste for the pleasant things in life. A few years ago I met Charles again in London. He has now become a very prosperous business-man, rather thin on top, with a fat cheque-book and an enormous black stream-lined car. He is divorced—like so many rich men and film-stars—and has half a dozen girl-friends trailing after him. He eats as well as his body allows him, drinks more whisky than soda-water and smokes fat American cigars. I shocked him right to the core when I told him that I was a Buddhist.

"No," he said firmly, "no Buddhism for me, my girl! Why should I give up all my pleasures? Surely I have worked hard enough to get them."

"But you don't have to give them up," I replied demurely. "You would just gradually lose the taste for them."

Charles was horrified, "Worse still! What good would all my money be then!"

I chuckled, "You could give it to a Buddhist Society, since you would have no more use for it yourself!"

He shuddered. Since then Charles hardly dares to see me any more …

Do you think Charles is really happy? I can honestly say that he is not. In fact, he is a living example for me that craving and clinging only increases one's suffering. True enough, Charles has what we call a happy temperament and seems on the surface more or less content with his lot. He does not even crave for much more money any longer, since most of it would only go straight to the inspector of taxes. But he clings with all his might to all his possessions and defends them like a tigress her young! He's terribly restless and blasé, since he has tasted nearly everything his materialistic world can offer him. He has become a slave to his own sense-pleasures—for there seems to be very little else in his life. Mind you, Charles is not uncultured, he likes reading good books, for example. But, like Albert, he makes quite sure that these books don't become his world. He won't let anything penetrate his ego. Books are only there to give him an intellectual stimulus—in one word, they provide him with yet another sense-pleasure; that of the mind. His feeling of insecurity is even greater than in the case of Albert—for his world is mainly built on money. And—yet deep down in him he knows only too well that he is the great loser. All he craves for is ever-changing and impermanent. And so is his ego, of course. Only that which knows and understands—in fact, which is knowledge and understanding and truth all in one—exists.

Fortunately, I believe in karma and rebirth. For I'm still fond of Charles and I like to think that in time he too will free himself from all his ignorance and delusion and gain enlightenment. After all, Charles is kind and helpful. He once told me that he only has one philosophy: that of everyone being just a little kinder. He himself keeps to it for he does a lot of good deeds which, in spite of his obstinate belief in his ego, will in his many lives to come sure enough open the doors to Nibbāna more and more, that is, if Nibbāna has any doors.

And now we come to the fair ladies. The first I want to introduce to you is Winnie—the perfect mother. She is what you might call a homely type: very capable and friendly. You just can't help liking Winnie. When I first met her, her daughter Rosemary was about nine. I soon found out that Rosemary was the be-all and end-all of Winnie's life. Her entire conversation, interest and worries always centred round Rosemary. While her husband Peter usually sat in a corner, rather shy and absorbed, reading a book.

I should think most of you must have known such a Winnie at one time or other in your lives. And you must have been just as thoroughly bored by her as I used to be. But unfortunately the case of a possessive mother is much more serious and complicated than just the surface-boredom she inflicts on her friends. My Winnie nearly broke up her marriage over Rosemary and did her best to ruin the child into the bargain. For it didn't take Winnie long to turn Rosemary into a thoroughly spoilt little brat. The children at school disliked her and the teachers complained that she was difficult and conceited.

And what did Peter do? The poor man had very little say in the whole matter. So he withdrew more and more to his library. He started going out on his own and even during the summer holidays he went mountain-climbing in Switzerland while Winnie took Rosemary to Blackpool. She didn't seem to mind. Her whole life was Rosemary—to such an extent that her own seemed completely subservient to it. In fact, she almost became Rosemary with all her problems, worries and pleasures. She didn't seem to be interested any more in her marriage nor in her husband—such was the strength of her maternal instinct. Fortunately Peter was a very clever and understanding man, and being very fond of both his wife and child, he put up with the situation as well as he could and adjusted his life accordingly.

Quite a lot of people these days openly criticize the so-called "perfect" mother. They say her attitude is due to an excessive mother-instinct coupled with too much possessiveness. Quite right, true enough. But we Buddhists go much further than that. Why in fact Buddhism is often described as one of the most effective mental therapies is because it goes so much deeper than even the psychiatrists. It doesn't only touch the root of the trouble—but it lifts it right out. Now how would the Buddhists analyse poor old Winnie? We would say, together with the psychologists, that

Winnie has projected her ego onto her daughter Rosemary. So far, so good! But what exactly lies underneath this projection of the ego? Let us get to the root of the diagnosis, for only thus can we cure the disease. As a homeopath once explained to me: it is not enough to discover that the patient suffers from a cancer of the stomach—we must also find out what kind of mental state brought about this illness. In this particular case, he told me it is always due to some kind of frustration. Only when we successfully tackle the patient's frustration can we be sure that his cancer—though it might be cured by the physician—doesn't come again!

This impressed me very much, for I suddenly realized that Buddhism is doing exactly the same thing: it cures the mental state which brought about the disease. Now let us go back to Winnie again. Why has she all her life projected her own ego onto Rosemary? The first reason is obvious: because she has a specially strong maternal instinct which was by no means fully satisfied. She should have had at least half a dozen children! But surely this doesn't really explain why Winnie submerged her own personality into that of her child? She could have loved her dearly—even possessively—and still led her own life independently from that of Rosemary. But Winnie's feeling of insecurity is specially strong and so her own ego feels the need of extending even further—to that of her child. After all, she thinks like so many mothers, Rosemary is part of herself. But is that so? Again we Buddhists say: decidedly no! If you believe in karma and rebirth, you will look upon Rosemary as the outcome of all her own volitions, thoughts and deeds, good and bad, from the past and present. Buddhism even goes so far as to say, there isn't such a thing as mental inheritance, only physical. Perhaps you might now understand why Buddhists say that, before we can advise and help anyone else, we must first be able to understand and help ourselves. As a rule, we know little enough about what goes on within us—how much less we know about someone else's inner life?

Thus advice soon becomes interference and often does more harm than good. But, even when we are in a position, through mastering our own emotions to some extent, to understand another person's difficulties and shortcomings, we can't really give him much direct help. All we can do is to lead him on very gently where he can help himself. That is, in fact, all a good teacher can do. Now to live your child's life on top of yours, so to speak, is quite ridiculous. I said right at the beginning that what we call life is only the mental image of our sense-impressions. How can we therefore have a mental image of someone else's sense-impressions?

But the cause of Winnie's extreme possessiveness where Rosemary is concerned is not only due to insecurity and excessive maternal instinct. There is also a lot of greed and conceit behind it all. Actually conceit is always a form of greed: greed for the manifestation of the ego. And this automatically brings about clinging. The greedier we are, the more we crave for and cling to sense-objects. Hence Winnie's clinging to Rosemary! Her case, however, is so exaggerated, so subnormal that Winnie no longer craves for her own sense-objects—but mainly for those of her child. Her ego has almost swallowed up Rosemary's! I think there is a good deal of frustration at the back of all this too. What Winnie was not able to get and achieve in her life, she now endeavours to achieve through Rosemary. The child's life is still in the making—so Winnie can build up new hopes, ambitions and desires which she now identifies with Rosemary's.

Let me say this however. I have great admiration for some mothers who, unlike Winnie, are not possessive and gladly sacrifice their lives for their children. For this is certainly the purest form of all worldly love. But when you analyse even this kind of love in the Buddhist way, you will still see the element of desire at the back of it: the desire for the child's love in return for your own. It is because of this attitude of unemotional analysing that some people accuse Buddhists of not feeling enough love for their neighbours as the Christians do. But this certainly is not so. Only in Buddhism we distinguish, besides worldly love, between loving kindness, compassion and sympathetic joy: *mettā*, *karuṇā* and *muditā*. In all these three faculties the ego is not involved. Therefore they are universal, all-embracing—the same as insight-wisdom: *paññā*. In fact, *karuṇā* and *paññā* always work together. I would say: one faculty develops the other until they fill the whole being. This is the end-goal for any Buddhist: enlightenment!

Paula—the woman who is afraid of life—is a matron in a large hospital with plenty of scope for organisation and responsibility.

Perhaps you might find it difficult to imagine a woman in such close contact with life and suffering being afraid of it herself. But then she is not a physical coward. Her fear is much more subtle than that: she is afraid of mental suffering. What does she do? She surrounds herself with high brick-walls. Her attitude towards life is greatly limited.

Paula is prudish, sex-frustrated—but she tells herself that her work is far more important than husband and children. She is a genuinely righteous woman with a very high ethical code. But her code is narrow at the same time. She dare not face what Jung calls the shadow: neither her own nor even that of others. She has not a grain of humour—so she just could not take it. In order that she can be a thoroughly good woman all her life, she strictly avoids any temptations which might lead her into strange and dangerous waters. She makes herself look even plainer than she is and never gets any nearer to a man than she can possibly help in her career. Naturally, Paula is a strict vegetarian, non-smoker and teetotaller. She is the most uninteresting person I've ever met!

You might think that the Buddhists would, in some way or other, approve of Paula. After all, she hasn't got many sense-attachments, nor does she do harm to other people. In fact, she is a religious person who has trained herself to look within. But—and that's the trouble—only to a rather shallow degree. For, as I said before, she never allows the pendulum to swing the other way. Now Buddhism never believes in repression and frustration. It is the philosophy of letting go of going right through suffering to non-suffering. Only by courageously facing up to the shady side of ourselves without any excuse or judgement, can we ever hope to transcend it. When I say: without excuse or judgment, I mean just the watching again—the watching of an outsider. Thus we don't allow emotions to come up which, after all, only fortify the ego. Instead, knowledge will come up and knowledge is wisdom. If we don't recognize a thing for what it is, how can we deal with it? It is like polishing one side of a penny only. The other side, dark and filthy, is constantly buried in the sand. And yet it is all the time one and the same penny!

Mizzi—the non-accepter of dukkha—is quite a different woman altogether. You might almost call her Paula's opposite! When I first met her in Vienna she was extremely attractive and smart and very flirtatious. She was what we call a woman of the world, or may be of the demi-world—for she modelled woollen jumpers and knew quite a lot of the leading Viennese fashion-photographers rather intimately.

But then one day, when Mizzi was not quite so young anymore and seemed a little tired of woollies and photographers, of cocktails and dancing, she suddenly went out and got herself a religion. She went in mainly for dogmas and rituals. In a way the dogma was good for her, for she lacked self-discipline—but she became rather holy at the same time. That was a pity because it wasn't genuine, but only the holiness of her strong ego. You see, as the years went by, something in her which we might call the potential for enlightenment, tried to come up. But again and again the ego pushed it down, deeper and deeper, hiding it under its thick shadow. So poor Mizzi has been suffering from pulls and counter-pulls all the time, as in fact most of us do. But through Buddhism we, at least, learn how to by-pass or even drop the ego—if only for a little while during meditation or mindfulness. Yet all Mizzi's ego can do is to adopt holiness in order to pretend to herself and to others that all is well with her. Where she greatly differs from Paula, however, is that she can't avoid temptations for she is what the Buddhists call the *greedy type.* That is to say, her greed prevails over hatred and delusion—the other two unwholesome roots. Actually we have, of course, quite a bit of all three. The three wholesome roots are non-greed, non-hatred and non-delusion.

Though Mizzi is now a respectably married woman with children and grand-children, her ego hasn't changed all that much since her youth. She still has greedy emotions and always wants to be the centre of everything. She continuously pushes herself into the limelight—even at the expense of other people. Only when she has got what she wants for the moment, does she consider anyone else. Yet she manages to deceive herself all the time. She is—at least consciously—convinced that she is sweet and gentle and helpful all round. It is true, she can be all these things—but only, as I have just pointed out, when her ego is satisfied for the time being. She is still very religious, goes to church regularly, and says her prayers. But there again she mainly uses her religion to ease her conscience. The trouble with poor old Mizzi is that she always wants to *be* and never is!

I feel that our own egos are not all that much better than Mizzi's—but the main point I want to stress is the need to be honest with ourselves. Don't let us put a cloak of holiness over our shadow and pretend it isn't there! Only by facing up to it, are we in a position to accept dukkha, which is the direct result of our false identification with the ego.

Of all my six living examples, the one who comes nearest to accepting dukkha is Eth. Eth—short for Ethel, you know. Eth used to be my "daily"—or rather "weekly." When I first met her, she was in rags and her Cockney accent was so thick that it took me quite a while to understand her. Yet in spite of this, we soon became friends. She was of a refreshing naivety coupled with a lovely sense of humour. Her life-story was that of great genuine hardship. Already at an early age Eth had to stay away from school a lot in order to look after her family. Her mother was often ill and she happened to be the eldest of a great number of children. When she married, it only meant more hardship and work, for they were very poor and Eth bore one child after another. Her husband died comparatively young and then she had to struggle all alone to bring up her five children.

By the time I knew Eth, most of them were married—but she was still slaving away all day long. When she was not out working, she now had to mind her many grandchildren, while their mothers worked in factories. When you consider that poor thin little Eth had helped to bring up three generations in her sixty-odd years, you can't help admiring her. And she just accepts her hard lot as something unalterable. Neither is she envious of all the people round her who are better off than she is, nor does she ask herself how it comes about that life is so "unfair" to her. In fact, she is a thoroughly good Buddhist without knowing it. You might have thought she knew all about the doctrine of karma and rebirth. Actually, Eth is not particularly religious in one way or another. She nominally belongs to the Church of England—but never has time to go to church. Nor has she ever spoken about God to me.

Sometimes I ask myself whether Eth is very near to enlightenment. This is rather a *difficult* question to answer. I feel she is certainly a good deal nearer to it than I am, or than most of my acquaintances are. There seems no doubt whatsoever that spiritually she is a highly developed woman. If only her intellect were equally balanced, I feel, she could be almost there. She has little greed and little hatred—but there is quite a bit of delusion. For unfortunately, owing to her lack of education, her thinking is still rather primitive and illogical. Her mind needs to be trained and sharpened. On the other hand, through the very hardship of her present life and her great sense of humour and fun Eth has acquired a lot of common sense which in my opinion can be equated with the lower states of insight.

I feel Eth is a very interesting example for us Buddhists. Without knowing anything about Buddhism at all, she has chosen the right path and has courageously progressed a good deal towards enlightenment. In some ways it might be even a good thing that her intellect is not developed enough to understand the Buddhist teaching, for she is blissfully unaware of all the pitfalls of its wrong interpretation. On the other hand, I often want to comfort her by pointing out the value of the very *dukkhā* she has to go through. But then she doesn't seem to need any comfort: she is always cheerful and content!

Perhaps you are asking yourselves now what is the Buddhist attitude to attitudes to life? Well, what we are striving at throughout our life is to break that protective shell of ours that grows harder and absorbs more and more of the living tissue. This protective shell is, in fact, no other than our good old friend, the ego. Now you might ask, what is left after we have successfully smashed our protective shell? This is, indeed, a difficult question, for the answer can't really be given in words—in concepts. We Buddhists say that we are not a permanent entity as the ego wants us to believe: we are but a series of moments of consciousness. Once our protective shell, made up by our vast ignorance and delusion, is broken, our true nature—which never was "ours", but is part and parcel of the whole Universe—is realized. As I said before, the absolute can't be explained in words, nor understood by our intellect. But let me try to put it to you this way.

As long as we have the delusion of an ego, we will have all sorts of attitudes, convictions and views, which are all thought-created. In fact, instead of having a direct experience of life in the present, we live in a world of thoughts of either the past or the future. We live by our memories, speculations and fears.

We miss so much of life by reproducing it second-hand in our mind.

But once we have realized our true nature by breaking through our protective shell, we will live in the present moment. All our bare attention will be given to the act without the assumption of an ego outside the act. That moment will fill the whole of our action—the whole of our sense-impressions: the seeing, the hearing, the smelling, the touching, the tasting, the knowing.

As Buddha said to Bāhiya:

> "In the seeing, Bāhiya—there is just the seeing.
> In the hearing, Bāhiya—there is just the hearing.
> In the knowing, Bāhiya—there is just the knowing."

Udāna I 10

— §§§ —

An Old Debate on Self

Soma Thera

Bodhi Leaves No. 13

First published: 1962

An Old Debate on Self

One of the famous discussions mentioned in our books (MN 35) took place between the Buddha and Saccaka Niganthaputta, in the city of Vesāli, the capital of the Licchavi Republic, which formed a part of the Vajjian Confederacy in ancient India. Today Vesāli is represented by the ruins of Raja Biaal Ka Garb at Basarh and Bakhira in the Muzaffapur District of North Bihār, about twenty-seven miles northwest of Patna. In the 7th century of this era Yuan Chwang, the great Chinese monk and traveller, describes it as being 5000 li (a li is a third of an English mile) in circuit, that is to say, as a place of about ten or twelve square miles, and as a very fertile region abounding in mangoes, bananas, and other fruits. The foundations of the old city were 60 or 70 li in circuit and the walled part of it 4 or 5 li in circuit. At the time of the Chinese monk's visit to the city there were only a few bhikkhus there and of the hundreds of Buddhist monasteries that had been established in earlier times only three or four were not deserted or dilapidated. Yuan Chwang saw that the Dīgambara Jains were flourishing, that various sects were living promiscuously, and devas were worshipped at Vesālī.

Vesālī was the birthplace of Mahāvira, known also as Nigantha Nataputta, the great Jaina teacher, who spent twelve of the last forty-two rainy seasons of his life at Vesāli. The Buddha visited Vesāli many times. His first visit to the place was in the fifth year of his enlightenment, when he spent the rainy season there. This visit took place at the invitation of the Licchavi princes when Vesāli was afflicted by famine and disease during a severe drought. It was on this occasion that the Blessed One is said to have asked the Venerable Ānanda Thera to recite the Ratana Sutta, the Saying on the Jewels, to produce in the minds of the people of the city confidence in the Buddha, the Dhamma, and the Sangha.

Vesālī was full of scenic beauty. It had many lovely shrines. On his last visit to the city, shortly before his passing away, the Blessed One, while at the Cāpāla shrine, told the Venerable Ānanda Thera,

"Ānanda, fascinating is Vesālī, fascinating are the Udena shrine, the Gotamaka shrine, the Sattambaka shrine, the Bahuputta shrine, and the Sārandada shrine. Fascinating is the Cāpāla shrine."

The hall with the gabled house, Kūtāgārasālā, where the Buddha was residing when Saccaka visited him was in the Great Wood, Mahāvana, which was partly natural, and partly planted, outside the city.

The Licchavis were Khattiyas, men of the noble class, who had many good qualities. they were friendly, hospitable, and not generally given to self-indulgence. Though some of their young men were not free from rough Manners and were easily roused to anger and greedy, they have also been described as a diligent people, devoted to the service of the community, hardy, and very energetic. After asking for refuge in the Buddha they took enthusiastically to the practice of many good qualities. Their unity has been praised, though owing to the machinations of their enemies, perhaps, they in the end became divided and were destroyed by the Magadha king.

Saccaka, the son of a Jain woman, whose debate with the Buddha on the self is graphically told in the 35th Sutta of the Majjhima Nikāya described below, was a public disputant who claimed to be wise, and who was respected by the Licchavis of Vesāli for his success in astrological predictions, and as a teacher and a disciplinarian. His father and mother had been taught five hundred theses each: they had both arrived at Vesāli on the same day, and had been found to be equals in the art of controversy. The Licchavis offered them a house and the means of livelihood. They lived as husband and wife and had four daughters and a son. The daughters were taught a thousand theses and they wandered from place to place disputing with those who challenged them to debate and defeating them. These four used to go about with a Jambu[54] branch. On reaching a town or village they used to plant the branch, which they regarded as a flag, on a heap of sand, and made known to the people that anyone who threw down the branch should debate with them. Once they came to Savatthī and planted their Jambu branch at the entrance to the city. The Venerable Sāriputta

54 A tree that bears purple berries; in Sinhalese *madan*.

Thera having found out the reason for its being there from some children told them, "Pull out that Jambu branch." "Venerable Sir, we cannot do that," said the children. The Thera: "Why are you so frightened? Pull it out. When those women come, tell them, 'It was pulled out at the Venerable Sāriputta Thera's request.'" And he also told the children, "Send them to debate with me." The women went to the monastery, debated with the great master of the Law and were defeated. After that they became bhikkhunīs in the Blessed One's Community of Nuns.

Saccaka, whose family name was Aggivessana, the brother of the four bhikkhunīs, was more intelligent than his sisters. He knew much besides the one thousand theses taught by his parents. He lived at Vesāli, his birthplace, teaching and training the Licchavi princes in the various *sāstras* of the time. When he wandered in the city he used to wear an iron belt fearing that because of the excessive weight of his knowledge his belly might burst. And he used to say at meetings of the townsfolk, "I do not see any monk or brahmin, any leader of an order or group, or even one who makes out that he is a consummate one, perfectly enlightened, who, were I to dispute with him, should not shake, quake, and tremble, and sweat at the arm-pits. Were I to dispute with a dead post, even that would shake, quake, and tremble. Let alone a human being."

Two statements in the debate on the self that follows need explanation. The first statement is this, "The questioned one's head will fall to pieces." This is an old Indian way of warning a person of the dreadful, consequences, of denying, subverting, or not acknowledging, the truth. The second statement is the one about the dramatic figure of Vajirapāṇi, who is the instrument for bringing about the dreadful consequences of denying the truth. He is identified with Sakka and Indra in the Pali commentaries, and is the fierce aspect of the wielder of the thunderbolt. In non-Theravāda Buddhism he underwent many changes. In Werner's *A Dictionary of Chinese Mythology*, p. 451, Vajirapāṇi is described thus, "The thunderbolt-handed. A personification of force. In Northern Buddhist countries a powerful subduer of evil spirits. Also a ferocious emanation of Vajrahara. A product of Mahayana and Tantric schools." Vajirapāṇi stands for the force that compels a man to do what is right, when he is unwilling to do it. His introduction into the Saccaka debate emphasises the intellectual plight in which Saccaka was.

Early one morning when the Buddha was staying at Vesālī the Venerable Thera Assaji, having dressed himself, and taken his bowl and robe, entered Vesālī for alms. Saccaka, who was then taking a walk in the town, saw the Venerable Assaji Thera coming in the distance, went up to him, exchanged greetings with him and standing at one side said this: "How, Venerable Assaji Thera, does the monk Gotama train his disciples? What is the kind of instruction generally given to the disciples of the monk Gotama?"

Assaji Thera: "Aggivessana, the Blessed One trains his disciples, instructing them generally thus: 'Form is impermanent, feeling is impermanent, perception is impermanent, formations are impermanent and consciousness is impermanent. Form is not-self, feeling is not-self, perception is not-self, formations are not-self, and consciousness is not-self. All formations are impermanent, all states are not-self.'"

Saccaka: "Now we know that the monk Gotama is an utterer of what must not be heard. It would be good, were we to meet the monk Gotama some time, talk with him, and free him of his evil, wrong notion."

Just then five hundred Licchavis were met together on some business at the town hall, and Saccaka went there and said to them: "Come, good Licchavis, come. Today I am going to talk with the monk Gotama. In talking with me, if he stands by what Assaji, a well-known disciple of his, says, then as a sturdy man might tug, shove, and pull about, a fleecy ram by its fleece, or as a sturdy workman at a brewer's might put into a deep pool of water a malt-drying and holding it by its edge, tug, shove, and pull it about, I will, disputing with the monk Gotama, tug him, shove him, and pull him about; or as a sturdy tippler might jerk, and blow away, the dregs from toddy-straining bag, holding it by its edge, I will, disputing with the monk Gotama, jerk him, and blow him away; or as a royal sixty-year-old elephant might descend into a deep pond, and amuse himself with what is called the sport of `washing hemp,' I will, indeed, amuse myself 'hemp-washing' the monk Gotama. Come, good Licchavis, come. Today, I am going to talk with the monk Gotama."

Then some Licchavis said, "How will the monk Gotama be able to dispute Saccaka Niganthaputta's thesis? Saccaka Niganthaputta may well dispute the monk Gotama's thesis."

And other Licchavis said, "How will Saccaka Niganthaputta be able to dispute the monk Gotama's thesis? The monk Gotama may well dispute Saccaka Niganthaputta's thesis."

And Saccaka, attended by the five hundred Licchavis, went to that part of the Great Wood where the hall with the gabled house was. At that time many bhikkhus were pacing up and down in the open, and Saccaka, going up to one of them, said, "Where, Venerable one, is the Venerable one, is the Venerable Gotama at present? We wish to see him," and the Bhikkhu said, "The Blessed One, Aggivessana, is sitting under a tree in the Great Wood."

Then Saccaka, with his large following of five hundred Licchavis, entered the Great Wood, and coming to where the Blessed One was, exchanged greetings with him, and sat at one side. The Licchavis too sat at one side. Some of them did so after saluting the Blessed One; some after exchanging greetings with him; some, after showing respect towards him with raised joined palms; some, after announcing their family names; others, in silence.

And Saccaka said, "Were the Venerable Gotama to give me leave, I would ask a question regarding a certain point."

The Buddha: "Ask as you please, Aggivessana."

Saccaka: "How does the Venerable Gotama train his disciples? What is the kind of instruction generally given to the disciples of the Venerable Gotama?"

The Buddha: "Aggivessana, I train my disciples, instructing them generally thus: `Bhikkhus, form is impermanent, feeling is impermanent, perception is impermanent, formations are impermanent, and consciousness is impermanent. Form is not-self, feeling is not-self, perception is not-self, formations are not-self, and consciousness is not-self. All formations are impermanent; all states are not-self.'"

Saccaka: "A simile strikes me, Venerable Gotama." The Buddha: "Come out with it, Aggivessana."

Saccaka: "Venerable Gotama, as all seeds and plants which grow, develop, and thrive, depend on the earth, and have the earth for their base, and as the doing of manual work depends on and is based on the earth, so the human being produces merit and demerit, by taking form, feeling, perception, formations, and consciousness as self and having made form, feeling, perception, formations, and consciousness the base."

The Buddha: "Aggivessana, do you say, 'Form is my self; feeling is my self; perception is my self; formations are my self; consciousness is myself?"

Saccaka: "Precisely, Venerable Gotama. I do say, 'Form is my self; feeling is my self; perception is my self; formations are my self; consciousness is my self.' And that is what this large company too says."

The Buddha: "Aggivessana, what can this large company do for you? Go on, Aggivessana. Unravel just your own thesis."

Saccaka: "I do say, Venerable Gotama, that form is my self, feeling is my self, perception is my self, formations are my self, and consciousness is my self."

The Buddha: "Then, Aggivessana, I shall question you again. Say what pleases you in reply. Would the power of an anointed, noble king, of a king like Pasenadi of Kosala, or like Ajātasattu of Magadha, the son of the Videha princess, prevail in his realm in executing those deserving execution, fining those who deserve to be fined, and banishing those deserving banishment?"

Saccaka: "It would, Venerable Gotama. Even the power of such communities and groups as the Vajjis and the Mallas prevails in the realms of those communities and groups in executing those deserving execution, fining those who deserve to be fined, and banishing those deserving banishment. What should one say of the power of an anointed noble king, of a king like Pasenadi of Kosala or like Ajātasattu of Magadha, the son of the Videha princess? It would prevail, Venerable Gotama, and it is fit to prevail."

The Buddha: "Aggivessana, how about this? You said, `Form is my self.' Does your power prevail in form, when you say, 'Let my form be so; let it not be so?'"

Then Saccaka was silent.

The Blessed One repeated the question and again Saccaka was silent. Then the Blessed one said, "Speak out, Aggivessana. For you this is not the time to be silent. If one who is questioned about a fact by the Perfect One for the third time does not make answer, the questioned one's head will fall to pieces then and there. Thus it is said."

At that time the spirit Vajirapāṇi stood in the air above the head of Saccaka holding his fiery, glowing, blazing, iron weapon of might, thinking, "If to the factual question put by the Blessed One for the third time, he does not make answer, I will make this Saccaka Niganthaputta's head fall to pieces." And the spirit Vajirapāni was visible both to the Blessed One and to Saccaka.

Then Saccaka Niganthaputta, terror-struck, horrified, shocked, seeking the protection, shelter, refuge, of the Blessed One, said, "Question me, Venerable Gotama, I shall answer."

The Buddha: "How about this Aggivessana? You said form, feeling, perception, formations, and consciousness are the self. Does your power prevail in regard to these when you say 'Let my form, my feeling, my perception, my formations, or my consciousness be thus?'"

Saccaka: "It does not, Venerable Gotama."

The Buddha: "Ponder, Aggivessana, ponder and make answer. You are contradicting yourself. How about this, Aggivessana? Form, feeling, perception, formations, and consciousness, are they permanent or impermanent?"

Saccaka: "Impermanent, Venerable Gotama."

The Buddha: "Is what is impermanent pleasant or painful?" Saccaka: "Painful, Venerable Gotama."

The Buddha: "Is it sound to regard what is impermanent, painful, and changeable as 'mine,' 'I' or 'my self?'"

Saccaka: "It is not, Venerable Gotama."

The Buddha: "How about this, Aggivessana? Could one who has clung to what is painful, gone over to it, and attached himself to it, see what is painful as 'mine,' 'I,' or my self,' live understanding things by himself, and extinguish what is painful?"

Saccaka: "Could that indeed happen, Venerable Gotama?

Indeed that could not happen, Venerable Gotama."

The Buddha: "How about this, Aggivessana? In that case, could you have clung to, gone over to, attached yourself to, what is painful, see it as 'mine,' 'I,' or 'my self?'"

Saccaka: "How could that not be, Venerable Gotama? It should be indeed thus, Venerable Gotama."

The Buddha: "Aggivessana, were a man roaming in need of pith, looking for pith, seeking pith, on entering a forest with a sharp axe to see a great, straight, young, unflowered banana tree, lay axe to its root, and having laid it low, cut off the crown, and strip off the rind, he would not in stripping off the rind get even to sapwood. How should he get pith? In the same way, Aggivessana, when by me you were questioned on your assertion, made to establish yourself on your assertion, made to repeat your assertion, you showed yourself to be empty, inane, and defeated. Aggivessana, you declared at meetings of the townsfolk at Vesāli: "I do not see any monk or brahmin, any leader of an order or group, or even one who makes out that he is a consummate one who is perfectly enlightened, who, were I to dispute with him, should not shake, quake, and tremble, and sweat at the armpits. Were I to dispute with a dead stump, even that would shake, quake, and tremble, let alone a human being.' But, Aggivessana, some drops of your sweat passing through your upper cloth are on the floor. I, Aggivessana, have no sweat on my body."

Saying that the Blessed One in that assembly bared the upper part of his golden body. On that Saccaka Niganthaputta sat silent, depressed, bowed down, dejected, perplexed, and confused.

Then the Licchavi prince Dummukha, seeing Saccaka Niganthaputta sitting silent, depressed, bowed down, dejected, perplexed and confused, spoke to the Blessed One thus, "Blessed

One, a simile strikes me." And the Buddha said, "Tell it, Dummukha." Then the Licchavi prince said this: "Venerable Sir, it is just as if there were a crab in a pond near a village or market-town, and many boys and girls, having left that market town, were to approach that pond, get into it, lift the crab from the water, put it on dry land, and break and smash completely all the crab's claws, as it angrily puts forth claw after claw in succession, so that the crab, with all its claws smashed and broken would not be able to go into that pond as before, and should become the food of crows and cranes. Just in the same way has the Blessed One broken all wrong views of Saccaka Niganthaputta and made it impossible for him to argue any more with the Blessed One."

Saccaka stopped Dummukha from speaking further and, knowing that the Licchavi princes were wanting to ridicule him, turned the conversation to another direction and began asking from the Blessed One how he trained his disciples to carry out his teaching, to get beyond all doubt, and to abide in the teaching of the Master, without external support.

The Master explained to Saccaka the way of training in the principles of his teaching, which lead to the understanding that in none of the aggregates of form, feeling, perception, formations, or consciousness, is there naught of which it may be said, "this is mine, this am I, this is my self." And how, freed from all ill through that understanding the Blessed One's disciple reveres, honours, salutes, and esteems, only the Perfect One, saying:

"The Blessed One who has been enlightened teaches the Dhamma for producing enlightenment in others.

"The Blessed One who has been tamed teaches the Dhamma for producing the tamed state in others.

"The Blessed One who has become serene teaches the Dhamma for producing serenity in others

"The Blessed One who has crossed the ocean of suffering and reached safety teaches the Dhamma for making others cross that ocean and reach safety.

"And the Blessed One who has become completely extinct teaches the Dhamma, for producing complete extinction in others."

Then Saccaka said, "Venerable Gotama, in debating with you I have been daring, bold. A man trying to attack an elephant in rut may escape harm, or he may escape harm from a great devouring fire in which he is caught, or he may escape from the jaws of a venomous snake without harm, but there is no escape possible for a man who gets caught in a controversy with the Venerable Gotama."

In saying this Saccaka did not, according to the commentary to the Cūlasaccaka Sutta, praise the Buddha but his own self. Such praise as Saccaka's is comparable to a king's reference to the heroism, cleverness and great power of enemies he has slain in battle, made in order to extol his own prowess and not the qualities of his opponents. And Saccaka's comparisons were to show that he was learned, wise, and clever enough, to argue with one who was like an elephant in rut, a mighty fire, and a venomous snake.

The Buddha set forth his doctrine on another occasion too to this disputant of Vesālī, but he did not become a follower of his. The Buddha's object in teaching Saccaka was to help him to obtain enlightenment in a future life. And it is said that after the Buddha's passing away Saccaka, who had been born in a past life as Senaka, the pundit mentioned in the Mahā Ummagga Jātaka, was reborn in a deva world, and later in Ceylon. He entered the Sangha in this country, and became an arahant.

— §§§ —

Pride and Conceit

Essays by

Dr. Elizabeth Ashby
and
Brian Fawcett

Bodhi Leaves No. 14

First published: 1962

If one regards himself superior or equal or inferior by reason of the body that is impermanent, painful and subject to change, what else is it than not seeing reality? Or if one regards himself superior or equal or inferior by reason of feelings, perceptions, volitions or consciousness, what else is it than not seeing reality? If one does *not* regard himself superior or equal or inferior by reason of the body, the feelings, perceptions, volitions or consciousness, what else is it than seeing reality?

— SN 22:49

What Can Be Done About Conceit?

by Dr. Elizabeth Ashby

From *The Sangha, The Journal of the English Sangha Association*, V. III.11

In Christian literature of the lighter sort we sometimes come across the expression "Little Devil *Doubt*." This personage is not unknown to Buddhists, but another little devil can be still more devastating. He is an ugly little Māra, named *Conceit*. Conceit is a mean, slinking little devil, lurking in dark corners and always ready to rush out and nip our heels. Doubt is slain when the disciple wins the stream; conceit, being a manifestation of pride, remains a menace to the very end.

Pride in all its forms devolves from self-esteem, which is in reality "ego-worship." It stems, so they say, from Greed, the first of the Roots of Evil. The thought here is rather subtle: when the ordinary person thinks of greed he thinks first of what one puts into one's stomach—that second helping of plum-pudding, or eating a pound of candies in a single evening. The commentators of old were much more drastic. Greed is "delight in one's own possessions." Hence we can be greedy about anything to which we have affixed the label "mine." My car, my table, my cat, my best beloved. The greedy aspect of conceit is when we "take delight" in our own good qualities or capacities.

Conceit can arise from the most trivial cause. One completes a piece of work, and having made a good job of it, one is naturally pleased. There's no harm in that: we all know the difference between a worker whose only interest is his pay-packet, and the man who takes pride in his work. The trouble arises when we begin to make comparisons—"X couldn't have done it half as well." That may be quite true, but it is dangerous to think that just because one's skill is superior in this instance that one is therefore a better person. That is "superiority conceit," and it has its counterpart in the "inferiority conceit" of the unsuccessful person, and the "equality conceit" of the man who says "I'm as good as you" with the underlying implication "And a good deal better!"

A feeling of superiority is a very pleasant mental state, but it is essentially *akusala*—unhealthy and highly dangerous in its results.

Conceit is very prone to arise when one is praised for some particular work or mental quality. Within limits, praise from a knowledgeable person is stimulating and encouraging; some people who are modest or diffident by nature can only work well when they are appreciated. The trouble is that too much praise, particularly if it borders on flattery, stimulates the sense of "I"-ness. The ego sticks out its chest and feels two inches taller; it has a delicious feeling of security and believes itself to be invulnerable!

This is the nasty sort of pride that the ancient Greeks called *hubris;* it was looked upon as an insult to the gods, and when the gods on Olympus found a man suffering from it they unloosed Nemesis, the goddess of revenge, who brought him to death or destruction.

Any conceit that arises in connection with the practice of Dhamma is much to be deplored. This sometimes occurs when students are making good progress in their studies. Some queer experience or flash of "insight" is assumed to be a sign of virtue or an advance towards Higher Consciousness, and the student, instead of checking up on his experience with a wise teacher, jumps to the conclusion that he is half-way to being an arahant. We do well to remember that no two people have exactly the same experience in regard to meditation practice. This was recognized in the Buddha's own day: Sariputta was revered for his wisdom, and Moggallana for his psychic powers, but both were venerated as "Great Beings." The cultivation of humility is not easy; there's a temptation to indulge in mock-modesty and untruthfully disclaim any real achievement, and still worse to be conceited about not being conceited. It is wiser, I think, to tackle conceit at its first uprising; if one can do that, then humility will develop in the natural course of events.

For our comfort we find that much can be done to curb the activities of pride. This persistent Māra has been aptly described as the "giant weed." We may grub up a few roots in this life-span, but the thing has already gone to seed and will appear in the future. "One year's seeds, seven years' weeds," say the old gardeners.

Methods for Eradicating Conceit

If we acquire the habit of eradicating conceit in this life, the habit will travel on in our sankharas and bear good fruit in future lives.

1. Recognize conceit whenever he pops up and *name* him. This, as readers will remember, is the advice given by Nyanaponika Thera in his valuable articles in *Sangha*. Māra, like Satan, hates to be recognized. This practice is doubly effective because it "keeps one on one's toes," and induces a real dislike of the tendency.
2. Get back to the first two "steps" of the Noble Eightfold Path:
(a) Right Understanding of the mental quality or capacity involved: to see according to reality "This (quality) is not mine; I am not this; there is no self in it"; and (b) Right Aspiration towards the expunging of conceit. In the Discourse on Expunging (MN 1:8) we read "Now I say that the arising of thoughts is very helpful in regard to skilled states of mind. Therefore the thought should arise 'Others may be harmful; as to this we will not be harmful' and so on for all our evil propensities. 'Others may be conceited; but we as to this will not be conceited.'"
3. The method of analysis is also helpful. "I" am being praised for some real or imagined virtue, say generosity. Generosity is non-greed (*alobha*) one of the Good Roots, and as such appears in the list of dhammas given in the Abhidhamma philosophy. According to Mahayana "All dhammas are empty of own-being"—that is to say they are not independently existent. Therefore "I" am being praised for something which doesn't exist by itself. This is so absurd that it knocks the bottom out of my conceit.
4. Alternatively, "I" am the result of past kamma. My talents are not due to my own virtue, but have arisen on account of the skilled actions performed by vanished personalities whose kammic descendant "I" am. Therefore it is silly of me to be conceited about qualities which are not in any real sense "mine."

Again and again in the suttas we find the expression "Thus must you train…" This is Buddhist mental culture: it is Right or Supreme Effort to put down unskilled mental states and prevent them rising in the future, and furthermore to encourage the arising of skilled states.

A word of warning may not be out of place here. It is inadvisable to dwell too much on our so-obvious faults. By unwisely reflecting on them, we encourage them to root themselves still more firmly in our unconscious (i.e., our sankharas). Instead, remember the advice of Paul the Apostle "Whatsoever things are true, whatsoever things are honest… whatsoever things are lovely, whatsoever things are of good report; if there be any virtue, if there be any praise, think on these things." We as Buddhists have the Buddha-dhamma to think about—"lovely in the beginning, lovely in the middle, lovely in the ending." This as Dr. Henn Collins has pointed out is the true philosopher's stone whose alchemy will transmute the base metal of our ordinary consciousness into the gold of Enlightenment.

The Mastery of Pride

by Brian Fawcett

From *The Sangha, The Journal of the English Sangha Association*, V. I

Few of us are free from pride in one form or another. We know that in the interests of spiritual development it must be eradicated. We are taught as much, and accept the teaching without question. But the method by which pride may be eliminated is a problem not easy to solve, and the indirect, sweeping precepts of the sages are of little practical help to us. It is all very well saying: "Eradicate this, and eradicate that," but what we want to know is, "How may we go about it?"

In the first place: what *is* pride?

Let us call analogy to our aid. Regard pride as a weed, propagating itself with alarming fecundity in the garden of the mind. Its root is not visible, but the flowering shoots are in plain view. Cut down these shoots and either they grow again or the root puts out new ones. The only way to destroy it is to dig it up altogether. That root is *self-esteem*. From it grow the shoots of *conceit, boastfulness, ambition, jealousy, envy and intolerance*. There are others, but let us take these six manifestations for the sake of discussions. Unbiased, detached self-scrutiny will disclose what others may exist in one's own character, and it is unlikely that all will be found equally developed. There is cause for alarm when we discover them in ourselves. Pride is invariably despised when observed in others, yet we sometimes boast of possessing it—"I have my pride, you know," is a common assertion.

Beneath every manifestation of pride lies *self-esteem*. It is the conviction of superiority over others—the feeling that we are what they are not, or that we can do what they cannot do. Successes in early childhood may sow the seeds of it. The praise of relatives fosters it. Once planted, it grows, and not even the flattening criticism by one's own contemporaries in adolescence can stop it. By and by it becomes a habit to compare oneself with the people one meets or passes in the street, generally to their disadvantage. What we know of our own accomplishments is measured by what we presume they lack. We think we know our friends inside and out, and our judgments are based on a firm belief in the infallibility of our perception. There is a tendency to group those who are not obviously outstanding under the heading of "ordinary people," and sometimes to place them in the inferior category for no more reason than that they look as if they belong there. How often we hear the remark: "He seems so ordinary, but when you get to know him there's a lot in him!" We are surprised to see our spot judgment wrong—that there really is something in that very ordinary-looking person. Can we honestly claim to be free of this habit of automatically comparing others with our own ideas of ourselves? If so, then *self-esteem* is not present.

It would be bad enough if pride flourished in no more than *self-esteem*, but it must manifest itself in every way it can. It strives to show on the surface, which is perhaps just as well, for then it becomes obvious. *Conceit*, first shoot of the weed pride, is *self-esteem* manifesting in visible form. Not content with merely feeling superior to the people around us, we show it in our bearing. A glance from some passer-by of the opposite sex may be interpreted as a look of approval. The fine figure reflected in the shop window as we pass engenders a feeling of warm satisfaction. Smart clothes, we believe, do justice to our carriage. We may not be as tall as that person over yonder, but we have a more distinguished look. No one would pick out any one of them in a crowd, but all can see we are different. Crude, isn't it? But that is the way *conceit* affects us, and its crudity is indeed shocking when self-analysis brings us face to face with it. Inspired by a consciousness of a desire for Truth, our minds turn the searchlight of enquiry inwards upon our own characters, and then there dawns the realization that *conceit* has been part of us for as long as we remember. Formerly, we would have angrily denied the charge of being conceited. Now we see that it is well founded. Our "apartness," our treasured "individuality," is plainly one of its aspects.

Conceit has grown without its presence being suspected, and an even more dangerous and disgusting shoot has sprung up beside it. This is *boastfulness—self-esteem's* oral manifestation. One of our national conventions is the taboo on bragging, and the idea of voicing a plain, undisguised boast would shock us as much as it would disgust the conventional listener. A very admirable convention it is too—but it by no means eliminates *boastfulness*, for there are other ways of boasting, and as long as the *desire* to call attention to oneself exists, that particular ramification of pride is a danger. We can get others to boast for us. We can also impress them (particularly our relations) that they sing our praises to others. In this way we gain more than were it to come from ourselves, and run no risk of its incurring disagreeable criticism. We can seek publicity and, once gained, declaim it. We may artfully bring a conversation round to a point at which we "modestly" have to admit to something we are really proud of. It takes a certain amount of courage to probe one's own secret heart and bring to light some of the many ways in which we who sincerely believe ourselves to be guiltless can actually indulge in *boastfulness*. It is one of the most persistent shoots of the weed of pride, and the most dangerous because so frequently overlooked.

Ambition comes in two forms. There is *wrong ambition*, and *right ambition*. One is based on *self-esteem*; the other is free of any taint of it. *Wrong ambition* is the desire to excel or succeed in order to enhance one's standing—one's reputation. It is the urge to achieve with the object of "putting the other chap's eye out!" In its more socially acceptable and therefore more insidious aspect, it is the will to gain admiration and respect—to become, in fact, a worldly "success," which nearly always means a financial success. Confident of our great worth, we cannot be satisfied until repeated successes have called the attention of others to it. We feel that wealth is a concrete recognition of it.

Right Ambition, on the other hand, is above "self." It is the will to succeed, not for the gratification of self-esteem, but to further achievement for its own sake. The painter who strives to express adequately the idea inspiring him—the poet who seeks to express an emotion as it has never been expressed—the craftsman ever intent on bettering his achievement—all are followers of *right ambition.* Their "selves" are forgotten. They work as instruments, and they feel that in the expression of their art is little personal, but rather a universal power whose tools they are. Noblest ambition of all is the desire to achieve an objective of disinterested service to one's fellow creatures, whether human or animal. It is sometimes gratifying to learn how many of us have this objective.

Jealousy might be defined as the resentment felt against another for competing at the same level. Note that it is *at the same level* that competition begets jealousy. An admission of inferiority by the other will quickly banish the jealousy we may feel against him. Those we admit to be our superiors do not arouse our jealousy. It is a bestial emotion, but one that undoubtedly had its uses in our passage through the lives in the Instinctive Mind, for it was an aid to our survival. Carried over into the influence of Intellect it has no place, and puts a drag on our upward progress. He who is at one moment the object of our jealousy, is regarded with affection once that jealousy has been smothered. What may have served us for the conservation of the means of life when we existed in a lower condition is now no more than a vehicle for pride's manifestation, and its redundancy is obvious the moment the reason has torn Jealousy's red veil from the perception. We know it is useless, and we long to rid ourselves of it. We seem to succeed, and then conditions come about favourable to its reappearance, and the unwelcome pangs are felt again. Remember, then, that it is a shoot of *self-esteem* and until that root has been killed out the shoot may be beaten down only to blossom again.

Envy we joke about, and are inclined to look on it as less despicable than Jealousy, its near relative. Think about it—think over and around it—define it to yourself—get to know it. When the nature of an unpleasant thing is known, it is less to be dreaded. With all these ramifications of the weed of pride the same approach can be recommended. Define them to yourself. Figure out what they are and how much you are subject to their influence. *Envy* can be called the resentment felt against another for possessing that which one values and does not posses oneself. It may be only a gentle resentment sometimes, but is dangerous nevertheless, for it may become fierce. Underlying it is the feeling, "Why should he have it, and not I?" *Self-esteem* is outraged.

Then there is *intolerance*. Sometimes it is the only form of pride we are subject to. It is often the most robust shoot of the whole plant. It springs directly from *self-esteem*, for it is a refusal to accept anything that conflicts with our own ideas. It is to brand as wrong all that to us is not right. *Intolerance* causes us to condemn a person for doing that with which we disagree, but let him do just what we would do ourselves and—here is what is so unreasonable—a feeling of jealousy may be aroused. Pride sweeps us first one way, then another. There is no keeping our feet when once in its grasp. Don't expect pride to be in any way "reasonable," for it wilts and disappears in the light of reason, its greatest foe.

We are repeatedly being asked: "Why carry the burden of pride? Throw it aside! It is so much relief to rid yourselves of its weight and know the lightness of freedom!" We feel inclined to retort: "That's all very well, but *how* can we get rid of it? We know we must, but we don't know how to begin!"

The sickle which can cut down these shoots is reason—calm reflection—meditation. Make it your task for a few weeks to give up half an hour daily for reasoning it out, and the results may amaze you. Look at yourself, as it were, from outside. Be honest with yourself, in making a searching examination to determine how pride is manifesting through you, for fair self-analysis is in itself a powerful weapon to use against it. Classify those manifestations. Reason them out. Do they make sense? In your everyday life, try and form the habit of watching with interest to spot each of pride's several shoots as it appears, and once a week spend a meditation hour in asking yourself for a detailed report of every one noted. Form a picture in your mind of the perfect character, and compare your own character with it. For example, say to your self: "Now, I think there was an inclination to boast in my remark to Mrs So-and-so at tea yesterday. How would the Ideal Being have acted under the circumstances?" Or again: "Would the Ideal Being have considered himself superior in bearing to those ugly people I passed in such-and-such a street? Of course not! He would have been above that."

The power of standing apart from, and criticizing, the Ego who is subject to pride, allows you to find satisfaction in adverse criticism from others. Whereas formerly you felt bitter if ridiculed or put "in the wrong," it now amuses you, for you see what good medicine it is for the Self you desire to set free. When others treat you with intolerance, welcome it, for they are doing you a favour by striking direct at your own intolerance. Seek those things which formerly aroused in you the pangs of Envy or Jealousy. Find pleasure in feeling that other self hurt by them, knowing that the wounds are suffered by the false Ego—pride—and not by the real You. It will not be long before the pain is gone, and then you will have a good laugh at the memory of that squirming demon who fled surprised and vanquished.

We who are subject to conceit dread ridicule. Cease to dread it. When we see the wicked caricatures, or witness those vivid mimicries of ourselves, it is for us to welcome them, for they are aiding us materially in the conquest of pride. So also, to hear ourselves belittled is an antidote for Boastfulness. When we do, there is no need to hide a raging heart behind a sickly smile. Once we have learned the trick of standing apart from ourselves these things can no longer hurt.

But beat down the shoots of pride as we may, we cannot be free from the weed until the root has gone. It is right to prevent the shoots from thriving. Destroy them by all means. But pride will persist in making its appearance until *self-esteem* is rooted out—and to accomplish that is the hardest job of all!

Here is a tip that may perhaps be of service. Try and form the habit of supposing every passer-by on whom the thoughts rest to be possessed of at least one attribute superior to your own. Think to yourself: "This creature isn't much to look at, but I'll bet she is far more even-tempered than I am!" Look at that rather foppish young man whose appearance used to annoy you and think: "All the same, in a pinch he would show far greater physical courage than I." Cease to regard the large, loud-mouthed person as empty-headed and think instead: "He's probably far cleverer with his hands than I." We are all learning our lessons in life's school-room. Some are more advanced than us in one thing, and behind us in others. The person who cannot resist the temptation to gratify the senses may nevertheless be a good angel to others in need of help. The thief may be an actual hero. If we consistently regard others as possessing at least one of those desirable characteristics we ourselves are striving for, we are actually admitting our inferiority, and *self-esteem* suffers a staggering blow.

Remember that *self-esteem* is a habit, and just as a habit must be acquired, so may it be abandoned. We are not born with it. We cultivate it by regarding ourselves as superior to others in some particular thing—then in more things—ultimately in everything. Eradicate it by recognizing the superiority of others in some way. Credit them with that superiority, even though you don't know they possess it. *Self-esteem* will die for lack of nourishment, and one day will come the first joyful realization that there is no him nor her nor you, but that we are all one. You need not fear going too far and acquiring an "inferiority complex." Your eyes will be open, and what you will find is true humility.

— §§§ —

Buddhist Meditation

Francis Story
(Anāgārika Sugatananda)

Bodhi Leaves No. 15

First published: 1963

Buddhist Meditation

The mental exercise known as meditation is found in all religious systems. Prayer is a form of discursive meditation, and in Hinduism the reciting of slokas and mantras is employed to tranquillize the mind to a state of receptivity. In most of these systems the goal is identified with the particular psychic results that ensue, sometimes very quickly. The visions that come in the semi-trance state, or the sounds that are heard, are considered to be the end-result of the exercise. This is not the case in the forms of meditation practised in Buddhism.

There is still comparatively little known about the mind, its functions and its powers, and it is difficult for most people to distinguish between self-hypnosis, the development of mediumistic states, and the real process of mental clarification and direct perception which is the object of Buddhist mental concentration. The fact that mystics of every religion have induced in themselves states wherein they see visions and hear voices that are in accordance with their own religious beliefs indicates that their meditation has resulted only in bringing to the surface of the mind and objectifying the concepts already embedded in the deepest strata of their subconscious minds. The Christian sees and converses with the saints whom he already knows; the Hindu visualizes the gods of the Hindu pantheon, and so on. When Sri Rāmakrishna Paramahamsa, the Bengali mystic, began to turn his thoughts towards Christianity, he saw visions of Jesus in his meditations, in place of his former eidetic images of the Hindu Avatars.

The practised hypnotic subject becomes more and more readily able to surrender himself to the suggestions made to him by the hypnotiser, and anyone who has studied this subject is bound to see a connection between the mental state of compliance he has reached and the facility with which the mystic can induce whatever kind of experiences he wills himself to undergo. There is still another possibility latent in the practice of meditation; the development of mediumistic faculties by which the subject can actually see and hear beings on different planes of existence, the devalokas and the realm of the unhappy ghosts, for example. These worlds being nearest to our own are the more readily accessible, and this is the true explanation of the psychic phenomena of Western Spiritualism.

The object of Buddhist meditation, however, is none of these things. They arise as side-products, but not only are they not its goal, they are hindrances which have to be overcome. The Christian who has seen Jesus, or the Hindu who has conversed with Bhagavan Krishna may be quite satisfied that he has fulfilled the purpose of his religious life, but the Buddhist who sees a vision of the Buddha knows by that very fact that he has only succeeded in objectifying a concept in his own mind, for the Buddha after his Parinibbāna is, in his own words, no longer visible to gods or men.

There is an essential difference, then, between Buddhist meditation and concentration and that practised in other systems. The Buddhist embarking on a course of meditation does well to recognize this difference and to establish in his own conscious mind a clear idea of what it is he is trying to do.

The root-cause of rebirth and suffering is *avijjā* (ignorance) conjoined with and reacting upon *taṇhā* (desire). These two causes form a vicious circle; on the one hand, concepts, the result of ignorance, and on the other hand, desire arising from concepts. The world of phenomena has no meaning beyond the meaning given to it by our own interpretation.

When that interpretation is conditioned by *avijjā,* we are subject to the state known as *vipallāsa,* or hallucination. *Saññāvipallāsa,* hallucination of perception, *citta-vipallāsa,* hallucination of consciousness, and *diṭṭhi-vipallāsa,* hallucination of views, cause us to regard that which is impermanent *(anicca)* as permanent, that which is painful *(dukkha)* as a source of pleasure, and that which is unreal *(anattā),* or literally without any self existence, as being a real, self-existing entity. Consequently, we place a false interpretation on all the sensory experiences we gain through the six channels of cognition—that is, the eye, ear, nose, tongue, sense of touch and mind: *cakkhu, sota, ghana, jivhā, kāya* and *mano (āyatanā).* Physics, by showing that the realm of phenomena we know through these channels of cognition does not really correspond to the physical world known to science, has confirmed this Buddhist truth. We are deluded by our own senses. Pursuing what we imagine to be desirable, an object of pleasure, we are in reality only following a shadow, trying to grasp a mirage. It is *anicca, dukkha, anattā*—impermanent, associated with suffering, and insubstantial. Being so, it can only be the cause of impermanence, suffering and insubstantiality, since like begets like; and we ourselves, who chase the illusion, are also impermanent, subject to suffering and without any persistent ego-principle. It is a case of a shadow pursuing a shadow.

The purpose of Buddhist meditation, therefore, is to gain more than an intellectual understanding of this truth, to liberate ourselves from the delusion and thereby put an end to both ignorance and craving. If the meditation does not produce results tending to this consummation—results which are observable in the character and the whole attitude to life—it is clear that there is something wrong either with the system or with the method of employing it. It is not enough to see lights, to have visions or to experience ecstasy. These phenomena are too common to be impressive to the Buddhist who really understands the purpose of Buddhist meditation. There are actual dangers in them which are apparent to one who is also a student of psychopathology.

In the Buddha's great discourse on the practice of mindfulness, the *Mahā-satipaṭṭhāna Sutta*, both the object and the means of attaining it are clearly set forth. Attentiveness to the movements of the body, to the ever-changing states of the mind, is to be cultivated in order that their real nature should be known. Instead of identifying these physical and mental phenomena with the false concept of "self," we are to see them as they really are: movements of a physical body, an aggregate of the four elements *(mahābhūta),* subject to physical laws of causality on the one hand, and on the other, a flux of successive phases of consciousness arising and passing away in response to external stimuli. They are to be viewed objectively, as though they were processes not associated with ourselves but belonging to another order of phenomena.

From what can selfishness and egotism proceed if not from the concept of "self" *(sakkāyadiṭṭhi)*? If the practice of any form of meditation leaves selfishness or egotism unabated, it has not been successful. A tree is judged by its fruits and a man by his actions; there is no other criterion. Particularly this is true in Buddhist psychology, because the man *is* his actions. In the truest sense they, or the continuity of kamma and *vipāka* (consequence) which they represent, are the only claim he can make to any persistent identity, not only through the different phases of this life but also from one life to another. Attentiveness with regard to body and mind serves to break down the illusion of self; and not only that, it also cuts off craving and attachment to external objects, so that ultimately there is neither the "self" that craves nor any object of craving. It is a long and arduous discipline, and one that can only be undertaken in retirement from the world and its cares.

Yet even a temporary retirement, a temporary course of this discipline, can bear good results in that it establishes an attitude of mind which can be applied to some degree in the ordinary situations of life. Detachment, objectivity, is an invaluable aid to clear thinking; it enables a man to sum up a given situation without bias, personal or otherwise, and to act in that situation with courage and discretion. Another gift it bestows is that of concentration—the ability to focus the mind and keep it steadily fixed on a single point *(ekaggata,* or one-pointedness), and this is the great secret of success in any undertaking. The mind is hard to tame; it roams here and there restlessly as the wind, or like an untamed horse, but when it is fully under control, it is the most powerful instrument in the whole universe. He who has mastered his own mind is indeed master of the Three Worlds.

In the first place he is without fear. Fear arises because we associate mind and body *(rūpanāma-rūpa)* with "self"; consequently any harm to either is considered to be harm done to oneself. But he who has broken down this illusion, by realizing that the five *khandha* process is merely the manifestation of cause and effect, does not fear death or misfortune. He remains equable alike in success and failure, unaffected by praise or blame. The only thing he fears is demeritorious action, because he knows that no thing or person in the world can harm him except himself, and as his detachment increases, he becomes less and less liable to demeritorious deeds. Unwholesome action comes of an unwholesome mind, and as the mind becomes purified, healed of its disorders, bad kamma ceases to accumulate. He comes to have a horror of wrong action and to take greater and greater delight in those deeds that are rooted in *alobha, adosa,* and *amoha*—generosity, benevolence and wisdom.

Ānāpānasati

One of the most universally-applicable methods of cultivating mental concentration is *ānāpānasati,* attentiveness on the in-going and out-going breath. This, unlike the Yogic systems, does not call for any interference with the normal breathing, the breath being merely used as a point on which to fix the attention at the tip of the nostrils. The attention must not wander, even to follow the breath, but must be kept rigidly on the selected spot. In the initial stages it is advisable to mark the respiration by counting, but as soon as it is possible to keep the mind fixed without this artificial aid, it should be discontinued and only used when it is necessary to recall the attention.

As the state of mental quiescence *(samatha)* is approached, the breath appears to become fainter and fainter, until it is hardly discernible. It is at this stage that certain psychic phenomena appear, which may at first be disconcerting. A stage is reached when the actual sensation of arising and passing away of the physical elements in the body is felt. This is experienced as a disturbance, but it must be remembered that it is an agitation that is always present in the body but we are unaware of it until the mind becomes stabilized. It is the first direct experience of the *dukkha* (suffering) which is inherent in all phenomena—the realization within oneself of the first of the Four Noble Truths, the Noble Truth of Suffering *Dukkha Ariya Sacca.* When that is passed there follows the sensation of *pīti,* rapturous joy associated with the physical body. The teacher of *vipassanā,* however, is careful never to describe to his pupil beforehand what he is likely to experience, for if he does so, there is a strong possibility that the power of suggestion will produce a false reaction, particularly in those cases where the pupil is very suggestible and greatly under the influence of the teacher.

Devices in Meditation

In *kammaṭṭhāna* (mediation exercises), it is permissible to use certain devices, such as an earth or colour *kasiṇa* (disc), as focal points for the attention. A candle flame, a hole in the wall, or some metal object can also be used, and the method of using them is found in the Pali texts and the *Visuddhi-magga*. In the texts themselves it is to be noted that the Buddha gave objects of meditation to disciples in accordance with their individual characteristics, and his unerring knowledge of the right technique for each one came from his insight into their previous births. Similarly with recursive meditation, a subject would be given which was easily comprehensible to the pupil, or which served to counteract some strong, unwholesome tendency in his nature. Thus, to one attracted by sensual indulgence, the Buddha would recommend meditation on the impurity of the body, or the "cemetery meditation." Here the aim is to counterbalance attraction by repulsion, but it is only a "skilful means" to reach the final state, in which both attraction and repulsion cease to exist. In the arahant, there is neither liking nor disliking: he regards all things with perfect equanimity, as did Thera Mahā Moggallāna when he accepted a handful of rice from a leper.

Beads

The use of the rosary in Buddhism is often misunderstood. If it is used for the mechanical repetition of a set formula—the repeating of so many phrases as an act of piety as in other religions—its value is negligible. When it is used as means of holding the attention and purifying the mind, however, it can be a great help. One of the best ways of employing it, because it calls for undivided attention, is to repeat the Pali formula of the qualities of Buddha, Dhamma and Sangha, beginning *"Iti pi so Bhagavā"* with the first bead, starting again with the second and adding the next quality: *"Iti pi so Bhagavā, Arahaṇ"* and so on until with the last bead the entire formula is repeated from beginning to end. This cannot be carried out successfully unless the mind is entirely concentrated on what is being done. At the same time, the recalling of the noble qualities of Buddha, Dhamma and Sangha lifts the mind to a lofty plane, since the words carry with them a meaning that impresses itself on the pattern of the thought-moments as they arise and pass away.

The value of this in terms of Abhidhamma psychology lies in the wholesome nature of the *cittakkhaṇa,* or "consciousness-moment" in its *uppāda* (arising), *ṭhiti* (static) and *bhaṅga* (disappearing) phases. Each of these wholesome *cittakkhaṇa* contributes to the improvement of the *saṅkhāra* or aggregate of tendencies; in other words, it directs the subsequent thought-moments into a higher realm and tends to establish the character on that level.

Samatha Bhāvanā

Samatha bhāvanā, the development of mental tranquillity with concentration, is accompanied by three benefits: happiness in the present life, a favourable rebirth, and the freedom from mental defilements that is a prerequisite for attainment of insight. The mind becomes like a still, clear pool completely free from disturbance and agitation, and ready to mirror on its surface the nature of things as they really are, an aspect which is hidden from ordinary knowledge by the restlessness of craving. It is the peace and fulfilment which is depicted on the features of the Buddha, investing his images with a significance that impresses even those who have no knowledge of what it means. Such an image of the Buddha can itself be a very suitable object of meditation, and is, in fact, the one that most Buddhists instinctively use. The very sight of the tranquil image can calm and pacify a mind distraught with worldly hopes and fears. It is the certain and visible assurance of Nibbāna.

Vipassanā Bhāvanā

Vipassanā bhāvanā is realization of the three signs of being— *anicca, dukkha* and *anattā*—by direct insight. These three characteristics, impermanence, suffering and non-self, can be grasped intellectually, as scientific and philosophical truth, but this is not in itself sufficient to rid the mind of egoism and craving. The final objective lies on a higher level of awareness, the direct "intuitional" plane, where it is actually experienced as psychological fact. Until this personal confirmation is obtained, the sphere of sense perception and sensory-responses remains stronger than the intellectual conviction; the two function side by side on different levels of consciousness, but it is usually the sphere dominated by *avijjā* which continues to determine the course of life by volitional action. The philosopher who fails to live according to his philosophy is the most familiar example of this incompatibility between theory and practice. When the direct perception is obtained, however, what was at its highest intellectual level still merely a theory becomes actual knowledge, in precisely the same way that we "know" when we are hot or cold, hungry or thirsty. The mind that has attained this knowledge is established in the Dhamma, and *paññа,* wisdom, has taken the place of delusion.

Discursive meditation, such as that practised in Christian devotion, is entirely on the mental level, and can be undertaken by anyone at any time. It calls for no special preparation or conditions. For the more advanced exercises of *samatha* and *vipassanā,* however, the strictest observance of *sīla,* the basic moral rules, becomes necessary. These techniques are best followed in seclusion, away from the impurities of worldly life and under the guidance of an accomplished master. Many people have done themselves psychic harm by embarking on them without due care in this respect. It is not advisable for anyone to experiment on his own; those who are unable to place themselves under a trustworthy teacher will do best to confine themselves to discursive meditation. It cannot take them to enlightenment but will benefit them morally and prepare them for the next stage, *mettā bhāvanā* .

The Practice of *Mettā Bhāvanā*

Mettā bhāvanā is the most universally beneficial form of discursive meditation, and can be practised in any conditions. Thoughts of universal, undiscriminating benevolence, like radio waves reaching out in all directions, sublimate the creative energy of the mind. With steady perseverance in *mettā bhāvanā,* a point can be reached at which it becomes impossible even to harbour a thought of ill-will. True peace can only come to the world through minds that are at peace. If people everywhere in the world could be persuaded to devote half an hour daily to the practice of *mettā bhāvanā,* we should see more real advance towards world peace and security than international agreements will ever bring us. It would be a good thing if, in this new era of the Buddha Sāsana, people of all creeds could be invited to take part in a world-wide movement for the practice of *mettā bhāvanā,* and pledge themselves to live in accordance with the highest tenets of their own religion, whatever it may be. In so doing they would be paying homage to the Supreme Buddha and to their own particular religious teacher as well, for on this level all the great religions of the world unite. If there is a common denominator to be found among them, it is surely here, in the teaching of universal loving-kindness which transcends doctrinal differences and draws all beings together by the power of a timeless and all-embracing truth.

The classic formulation of *mettā* as an attitude of mind to be developed by meditation is found in the Karaṇīyametta Sutta [see Appendix]. It is recommended that this sutta be recited before beginning meditation, and again at its close, a practice which is invariably followed in the Buddhist countries. The verses of the sutta embody the highest concept to which the thought of loving-kindness can reach, and it serves both as a means of self-protection against unwholesome mental states and as a subject of contemplation *(kammaṭṭhāna).*

It is taught in Buddhism that the cultivation of benevolence must begin with oneself. There is a profound psychological truth in this, for no one who hates or despises himself consciously or unconsciously can feel true loving-kindness for others. To each of us the self is the nearest object; if one's attitude towards oneself is not a wholesome one, the spring of love is poisoned at its source. This does not mean that we should build up an idealized picture of ourselves as an object of admiration, but that, while being fully aware of our faults and deficiencies, we should not condemn but resolve to improve ourselves and cherish confidence in our ability to do so.

Mettā bhāvanā , therefore, begins with the thought: "May I be free from enmity; may I be free from ill-will; may I be rid of suffering; may I be happy."

This thought having been developed, the next stage is to apply it in exactly the same form and to the same degree, to someone for whom one has naturally a feeling of friendship.

In so doing, two points must be observed: the object should be a living person, and should not be one of the opposite sex. The second prohibition is to guard against the feeling of *mettā* turning into its "near enemy," sensuality. Those whose sensual leanings have a different orientation must vary the rule to suit their own needs.

When the thought of *mettā* has been developed towards a friend, the next object should be someone towards whom one has no marked feelings of like or dislike. Lastly, the thought of *mettā* is to be turned towards someone who is hostile. It is here that difficulties arise. They are to be expected, and the meditator must be prepared to meet and wrestle with them. To this end, several techniques are described in the *Visuddhimagga* and elsewhere. The first is to think of the hostile personality in terms of *anattā*— impersonality. The meditator is advised to analyse the hostile personality into its impersonal components—the body, the feelings, the perceptions, the volitional formations and the consciousness. The body, to begin with, consists of purely material items: hair of the head, hair of the body, skin, nails, teeth and so on. There can be no basis for enmity against these. The feelings, perceptions, volitional formations and consciousness are all transitory phenomena, interdependent, conditioned and bound up with suffering. They are *anicca, dukkha* and *anattā,* impermanent, fraught with suffering and void of selfhood. There is no more individual personality in them than there is in the physical body itself. So towards them, likewise, there can be no real ground for enmity.

If this approach should prove to be not altogether effective, there are others in which emotionally counteractive states of mind are brought into play, as for example regarding the hostile person with compassion. The meditator should reflect: "As he (or she) is, so am I. As I am, so is he. We are both bound to the inexorable Wheel of Life by ignorance and craving. Both of us are subject to the law of cause and effect, and whatever evil we do, for that we must suffer. Why then should I blame or call anyone my enemy? Rather should I purify my mind and wish that he may do the same, so that both of us may be freed from suffering."

If this thought is dwelt upon and fully comprehended, feelings of hostility will be cast out. When the thought of loving-kindness is exactly the same, in quality and degree, for all these four objects—oneself, one's friend, the person toward whom one is neutral, and the enemy—the meditation has been successful.

The next stage is to widen and extend it. This process is a threefold one: suffusing *mettā* without limitation, suffusing it with limitation, and suffusing it in all of the ten directions, east, west, north, south, the intermediate points, above and below.

In suffusing *mettā* without limitation *(anodhiso-pharaṇa),* the meditator thinks of the objects of loving-kindness under five headings: all sentient beings; all things that have life; all beings that have come into existence; all that have personality; all that have assumed individual being. For each of these groups separately he formulates the thought: "May they be free from enmity; may they be free from ill will; may they be rid of suffering; may they be happy." For example, he will specify the particular group which he is suffusing with *mettā* as: "May all sentient beings be free from enmity, etc… May all things that have life be free from enmity, etc." This meditation embraces all without particular reference to locality, and so is called "suffusing without limitation."

In suffusing *mettā* with limitation *(odhiso-pharaṇa),* there are seven groups which form the objects of the meditation. They are: all females; all males; all noble ones (those who have attained any one of the states of sainthood); all imperfect ones; all devas; all human beings; all beings in states of woe. Each of the groups should be meditated upon as described above: "May all females be free from enmity, etc." This method is called "suffusing *mettā* with limitation" because it defines the groups according to their nature and condition.

Suffusing with *mettā* all beings in the ten directions is carried out in the same way. Directing his mind towards the east, the meditator concentrates on the thought: "May all beings in the east be free from enmity; may they be free from ill will; may they be rid of suffering; may they be happy!" And so with the beings in the west, the north, the south, the north-east, south-west, north-west, south-east, above and below.

Lastly, each of the twelve groups belonging to the unlimited and limited suffusions of *mettā* can be dealt with separately for each of the ten directions, using the appropriate formulas.

It is taught that each of these twenty-two modes of practicing *mettā bhāvanā* is capable of being developed up to the stage of *appanā-samādhi,* that is, the concentration which leads to a jhāna, or mental absorption. For this reason it is described as the method for attaining release of the mind through *mettā (mettā cetovimutti).* It is the first of the Four Brahmavihāras, the sublime states of which the Buddha says in the Karaṇīyametta Sutta: *"Brahmaṃ etaṃ vihāram idhamāhu"*—"This is divine abiding here, they say."

Mettā, karuṇā, mudita, upekkhā—loving-kindness, compassion, sympathetic joy and detachment—these four states of mind represent the highest levels of mundane consciousness [see Nyanaponika Thera, *The Four Sublime States,* Wheel No. 6]. One who has attained to them and dwells in them is impervious to the ills of life. Like a god he moves and acts in undisturbed serenity, armoured against the blows of fate and the uncertainty of worldly conditions. And the first of them to be cultivated is *mettā,* because it is through boundless love that the mind gains its first taste of liberation.

Appendix

Loving-Kindness as a Contemplation

Karaṇīyametta Sutta

From the Sutta Nipāta, verses 143-52
(spoken by the Buddha)

What should be done by one skilful in good
So as to gain the State of Peace is this:
Let him be able, and upright, and straight,
Easy to speak to, gentle, and not proud,
Contented, too, supported easily,
With few tasks, and living very lightly;
His faculties serene, prudent, and modest,
Unswayed by the emotions of the clans;
And let him never do the slightest thing
That other wise men might hold blameable.
(And let him think:) "In safety and in bliss
May creatures all be of a blissful heart.
Whatever breathing beings there may be,
No matter whether they are frail or firm,
With none excepted, be they long or big
Or middle sized, or be they short or small
Or thick, as well as those seen or unseen,
Or whether they are dwelling far or near,
Existing or yet seeking to exist,
May creatures all be of a blissful heart.
Let no one work another one's undoing
Or even slight him at all anywhere;
And never let them wish each other ill
Through provocation or resentful thought."
And just as might a mother with her life
Protect the son that was her only child,
So let him then for every living thing

Maintain unbounded consciousness in being;
And let him too with love for all the world
Maintain unbounded consciousness in being
Above, below, and all round in between,
Untroubled, with no enemy or foe.
And while he stands or walks or while he sits
Or while he lies down, free from drowsiness,
Let him resolve upon this mindfulness:
This is Divine Abiding here, they say.
But when he has no trafficking with views,
Is virtuous, and has perfected seeing,
And purges greed for sensual desires.
He surely comes no more to any womb.

Translated from the Pali by Ñāṇamoli Thera

— §§§ —

Comments on the Buddha Word

John D. Ireland

Bodhi Leaves No. 16

First published: 1963

Comments on the Buddha Word

It is the purpose of this article to give a few ideas which may be useful to bear in mind when one is reading the suttas, or discourses, of the Buddha. As practising Buddhists who have placed our trust in the Buddha as the true guide and good friend, we should approach these sayings with a certain attitude of reverence. According to tradition the whole of the Pāli canon is the Buddha-word, and we should treat with caution the views of various Western scholars who assert, "this is genuine and that a later interpolation." In addition, there is no reason why we should not believe that the Pāli language, in which these scriptures have been handed down, was actually the language used by the Buddha, if it helps to arouse faith, despite what these scholars would say to the contrary.

The only sure guide we have to the interpretation of these sayings, outside of our own personal experience, is to be found in the writings of the ancient commentators, such as Buddhaghosa, and other bhikkhus past and present, well versed in the tradition. It is far better to obtain our knowledge of what Buddhism is about from the available translations of these old texts rather than from popular books about Buddhism, of which there are so many. Although this way may appear as slow and difficult it is much more rewarding, and we are less likely to acquire more and more concepts and opinions. Modern authors tend to gloss over, or even miss out completely, things they do not like or misunderstand, and these, although often minor points, could be vital for our own understanding and spiritual development. A quite common attitude of these writers is to uphold the Buddha's teaching as being rational, scientific, or as a mere "philosophy of life." All this is true, up to a point, but when they exclude or explain away the miraculous, devotional and definitely religious aspects, this is surely rather overstepping the mark. It has been said that the Buddha-dhamma is perfectly reasonable and logical up to the moment of attaining the Path, the seeing of the Unconditioned, but after that all such ideas no longer apply:

> "… when all conditions are removed, all grounds for the arising are removed."[55]

There still exists with many people, confusion over *"attā"* and *"anattā."* Does Buddhism teach there is a "self" or "soul" or is it a "soul-less religion?". Concerning this almost classical controversy, if we only obtained our knowledge of the teaching from the Buddha's discourses themselves this apparently perplexing question ought never to arise at all!

The Form of a Discourse

Turning to the suttas themselves, we should first of all note the type of audience addressed and, if possible, their level of understanding or attainment. This may show whether or not the subject matter is helpful to our own immediate situation. But do not hastily reject anything—all has some relevance. Is the Buddha talking to a bhikkhu or bhikkhuṇī, a non-human being (deva, yakkha), a lay-follower, a brahmin, or a follower of another sect (Jain, naked ascetic)? Again, is he talking according to conventional truth—that is to say, about kamma, healthy and unhealthy actions and their results, merit and demerit, generosity, moral conduct, heaven worlds, etc. Or is he discoursing on ultimate things? On the aggregates, sense spheres, elements, the dependent origination, Nibbāna? To make the best use of what we are reading it is good to be perfectly honest with ourselves here, to be quite sure, as far as is possible, where we stand, and what our limitations and capabilities are. Usually, before dealing with the subject proper, a discourse commences with a brief description of where it was uttered, and the circumstances under which it was uttered. If this is not mentioned at the beginning, the commentary supplies the necessary information. There is always a specific reason as to why the Buddha gives forth a discourse. He never wastes words, and nothing is said which would merely fall on deaf ears. A person may come with a question, or he may have a doubt which the Lord knows by understanding the mind of

55 Sutta Nipáta, v. 1076.

that person. Again, there may be a genuine need unknown to the audience, or the Lord may just teach Dhamma out of compassion, knowing there are certain beings present who will benefit.

"... then the Lord, having surveyed the minds of the whole assembly with his mind, thought: 'Who is there here capable of understanding Dhamma?' Then the Lord saw the leper Suppabuddha sitting in the crowd, and having seen him, he thought: `This one is capable of understanding Dhamma.' For the leper Suppabuddha he spoke a graduated talk, that is to say, a talk on generosity, good conduct, the heaven world, the disadvantage of sense-desires, the degradation of the defilements and the advantage in renouncing them ..."[56] The preamble, "Thus have I heard" refers to the venerable Ānanda, who recited the whole of the Buddha-word soon after the Lord's Parinibbāna (not "death," it should be noted):

"All this was only heard by me; it was spoken by the Lord, the Arahant, the fully Awakened One himself." In saying this, the venerable Ānanda effaces himself and points to the Teacher. He puts forward the Conqueror's words, and establishes Dhamma as the (sole) guide. He demonstrates for direct experience the Lord's Dhamma-body by revealing it as it was heard by him. He thereby comforts beings who are disappointed at not seeing the Lord (in person) and tells them: "This is not a doctrine with a teacher who is dead, this (the Dhamma) is your teacher."[57]

At the end of a discourse there is often a tail-piece showing how the teaching was received and what happened to the audience subsequently.

The subject-matter of the discourses appears at first glance to deal with a bewildering array of topics, but it is possible to divide it up, for convenience, into four main groups:[58]

That dealing with defilements.

That dealing with conduct, the various meritorious actions and their results.

56 Udāna, V 3.

57 Khuddakapāṭha Commentary.

58 Nettippakaraṇa, p. 128.

That dealing with penetration, the understanding of the Four Noble Truths.

That dealing with a person who has attained to realisation.

Of course this is somewhat of an oversimplification, and these four groups, more often than not, are combined in a great variety of ways. Something to be noted when reading the Pāli Canon is that, in spite of its bulk, all the material is treated very briefly; in fact, it can be looked upon as merely a summary serving as an outline for a teacher to enlarge upon. The suttas mostly deal with type-situations and it is often difficult to apply the advice contained therein to one's own special problems without a fair amount of insight and introspection. Further, a sutta cannot be studied in isolation. There is an intricate network of cross-references throughout the whole canon and, ideally, when reading one discourse, one should know everything else that has been said on that particular subject.

The Analysis of the Subject-Matter

Concerning the subject-matter, the commentaries analyse it in two ways:

Word for word analysis according to the grammatical construction, and the meaning or meanings of individual words. This is not very useful however, without a knowledge of the original language.

The analysis of the meaning, purport, of the passage in question.

It is quite in accord with the spirit of the Buddha's teaching that the discourses should be investigated in these two ways, for, "… two things conduce to the confusion and disappearance of the true Dhamma. What two? The wrong expression of the letter and wrong interpretation of the meaning …

"… These two things conduce to the establishment … of the true Dhamma. What two? The right expression of the letter and the right interpretation of the meaning …"[59]

59 AN I 58.

In connection with the meaning, careful attention should be paid to the similes and parables used by the Buddha in illustration. These are always completely to the point, and demonstrate subtleties of meaning which could be brought out in no other way. It is interesting to note that the Buddha was the first to use the idea of the parable to illustrate a meaning, long before Christianity made use of it.

A useful method when analysing a passage is that of the Four Noble Truths: Suffering, Origination, Cessation and the Path. In the discourses these will be found, individually and in various combinations, often not evident at first glance. For example, the first verse of the Dhammapada:

"Mind foreruns all states: mind is chief, (they are) made by mind; if with an impure mind one speaks or acts, from that suffering follows, as the wheel the hoof of the draught-ox."

"An impure mind," this is the second Truth; "from that suffering follows," this is the first Truth. So here in this verse there are two Truths: Suffering and the Origin of suffering. The second verse of the Dhammapada contains the third and the fourth Truths: "If with a pure mind one speaks or acts (the Path), from that bliss follows (Cessation) like a never-departing shadow (simile)."

One should bear in mind that the Truth of Suffering is defined as: birth, sickness, old-age (decay), death, sorrow, non-fulfilment of wishes, the five "grasped-at" aggregates, whenever these are mentioned in the first Truth. Thus:

> "Whoever at the outset, young man, stays one night in a womb; having come to birth, he continues, and does not turn back."[60] This is suffering as birth.

> "Just as the clay vessels made by a potter all end up by being broken, in the same way life ends in death."[61] This is suffering as death.

60 J IV 494.
61 DN II 120.

"There are four Dhamma-teachings taught by the Lord who knows, who sees, the Arahant, the fully Awakened One … The world is unstable and goes to destruction …

The world is no refuge, no protection …

The world is not one's own, one must depart leaving everything …

The world is insatiable, enslaved by craving …"[62]

This is suffering as the world.

Under Origination come such states as ignorance, craving, clinging, greed, hate, delusion, and wrongly regarding things as permanent, pleasant, me and mine. The opposite of these is the (Eightfold) Path, referred to as: wisdom, mindfulness, detachment, patience, calm, the perceiving of impermanence, unsatisfactoriness, not-self, etc. Cessation is Nibbāna with all its various synonyms, such as: the supreme happiness, peace, the unborn, the undecaying, the deathless, the refuge, security from bondage, the far shore, etc. The four Truths can be incorporated with the method of dependent origination (*paṭicca-samuppāda-naya*) thus: "Whatever there is of craving and grasping, all that has its source in ignorance and ends in suffering." The dependent origination shows how Suffering is linked to Origination, and Cessation to the Path, and how, by the removal of the cause, the effect collapses.

"The world goes on because of kamma (acts of will, craving); beings are held by kamma as is a chariot wheel by the linchpin."[63]

The world of suffering, the wheel of births and deaths (*saṃsāra*), comes to a halt, and is destroyed by taking out the linchpin, the removal of craving, which is the origin of suffering.

Other methods of analysis are:

Advantage, disadvantage and escape, and,

Injunction (what is to be done), method (how to do it) and fruit (the result obtained).

---

62 MN 82.

63 Sutta Nipāta, v. 654.

"If he in whom there is desire for sensual pleasures is successful, certainly he is thrilled, having obtained what a being desires." This is the advantage.

"But if for a being, who has sensual desire, those pleasures disappear, he is hurt, as if struck by an arrow." This is the disadvantage.

"He who avoids sensual pleasures as with the foot (one would avoid) a snake's head, he mindfully overcomes craving in this world." This is the escape.[64]

"A fool, having fared wrongly in body, speech and thought, at the breaking up of the body after dying arises in the sorrowful ways, the bad bourn, the downfall, Niraya-hell." This is the disadvantage.

"A wise man, having fared rightly in body, speech and thought, at the breaking up of the body after dying arises in a good bourn, a heaven-world."[65] This is the advantage.

"Whoever, having formerly been negligent, afterwards is diligent, he illuminates this world like the moon appearing from behind a cloud."[66] This is the escape.

"Look on the world as empty, Mogharāja (the injunction), continuously mindful (the method); uprooting the view of self you may thus be one who overcomes death (the fruit)."[67]

Another example of the latter method is the Mettā Sutta, too long to be quoted in full, but which should be familiar to most. The first half of the first verse is the injunction, "This should be done by one skilled in good ...," the last verse is the fruit, "Not being involved with views ... undoubtedly one shall not come again to conception in a womb," and the rest of the discourse is concerned with the method.

Perhaps the most famous injunction of all is the last saying of the Buddha as recorded in the Mahāparinibbāna Suttanta:

64 Sutta Nipāta, vv. 766-768.

65 MN 129.

66 Dhp 172.

67 Sn 1119.

> "Come now, bhikkhus, I exhort you. Of a nature to pass away are conditioned things; strive by (means of) diligence to realise (this)." [68]

Finally, with the next quotation, we shall attempt to bring together everything that has been said above, to show how it can be applied in analysing a passage.

> "The burden indeed, is the five aggregates, the burden-bearer the individual. Taking up the burden is suffering in the world, putting it down is happiness. Having put down this heavy burden and not taking up another burden; withdrawing craving with its root, he is one who is desireless, one who has realised final deliverance."[69]

Firstly, this passage deals with penetration of the Truths and the person attained to realisation, by means of the simile of a burden. The "aggregates," regarded as a "heavy burden" are the Truth of Suffering. "Taking up," or grasping, the aggregates is the Truth of Origination. "Putting down," "not taking up another," and "withdrawing craving with its root (ignorance)" is the Truth of the Path. "Happiness," "desirelessness," "final deliverance" are synonyms for the Truth of Cessation.

Further, "taking up the burden" is the disadvantage, because it produces "suffering;" "putting it down" is the advantage because it produces "happiness." "Not taking up another … he is … one who has realised final deliverance" is the escape. There is an implied injunction "to put down" and not take up another burden, by means of "withdrawing craving with its root," resulting in the fruit of being "one who is desireless … has realised final deliverance."

It will be seen that, really, everything converges in the Four Noble Truths, for the disadvantage is merely suffering with its cause; the advantage, injunction and means are different ways of regarding the Path; and the escape and fruit are the cessation of suffering. It may be helpful to the reader to try this approach, for the Four Noble Truths should always be present at the back of

68 DN II 166.

69 SN 26.

one's mind. It is generally understood that the Buddha's teaching is summarised in these four Truths, and it should be realised that they may be bound in their many aspects, like a continuous thread throughout the whole of the Pāli Canon. The Buddha has declared that, "Formerly (i.e. from the time of the first sermon) as well as now, I teach but suffering and the cessation of suffering." [70]

And again, according to a commentary, "Whatever was described and taught by the Lord without restriction, in various phrases, sentences, words, methods of presentation and ways of speech, was for the setting forth, announcing, uncovering, analysing, making clear, the making known of the meaning of just this Noble Truth of Suffering and the other Truths ... From the night of the Lord's complete awakening till the night of the Parinibbāna, whatever the Lord spoke ... all that was the keeping in motion of the Wheel of Dhamma. Nothing the Buddhas, the Lords, teach is external to the teaching of Dhamma, the revolving of theDhamma-wheel. From this, everything that has been learnt concerning the noble dhammas (i.e., the Four Truths) should be investigated." [71]

"Dhamma-wheel," in the above quotation, refers to the Buddha's first sermon, called, "The Discourse on the Setting in Motion of the Wheel of Dhamma," in which the teaching of the Four Noble Truths was first announced to the world.

All this should be sufficient to show the importance of these Four Noble Truths.

It must be pointed out that these ways of analysis, outlined above, are not the invention of the writer of this article, but are an ancient method used by the commentators. They are to be found in two very old books, the Peṭakopadesa and Netti-pakaraṇa,[72] said to have been composed by Kaccāyana Thera, who lived at the time of the Buddha.

70 MN 22.

71 *Peṭakopadesa*, p. 5.

72 See *The Guide* (*Netti-pakaraṇa*), translated by Bhikkhu Ñāṇamoli, Pali Text Society, London 1963. His translation of the *Peṭakopadesa* is likewise issued by the same publishers.

Using the Discourses

The problem we have is to bring these sayings of the Buddha to life, to lift them out of the dry pages of the books, and make them living experiences today: to penetrate deeply into the meaning, with all its implications, by turning it over and over in the mind, and then acting accordingly. This teaching, in contrast to other systems, is called *ehipassika*, a doctrine inviting one to "come and see." It definitely encourages investigation, but this is best done by practice; by testing its ideas in everyday life, rather than theorising about them. The discourses are to be used, but a word of warning is necessary here: they are not to be misused, they are not ends in themselves, but merely a raft "for crossing over, not for retaining." In the end we have to go beyond the words to the experience they point to. There are many short utterances which may be used for meditation—for instance, those contained in the Dhammapada. And there are numerous cryptic passages which are well worth investigating, such as:

> "What is impermanent, you should get rid of desire for that" [73]
>
> "Objects are not worth holding on to" [74]
>
> "If I were not, it would not now be mine" [75]

See also the verses and their explanation in the Majjhima Nikāya, Suttas 131–133. Examples could be quoted indefinitely.

If we could really understand these teachings through our own experience, we would be able to live independent of others, not relying on what they say is or is not Buddhism, or what we should or should not do. Which, after all, is the aim of the Buddha-dhamma!

"If a bhikkhu has learnt, `all objects are not worth holding on to,' he knows every object fully; knowing every object fully he knows every object accurately; knowing every object accurately whatever feeling he feels, whether pleasant or painful or neither painful nor pleasant, he dwells contemplating the impermanence of those feelings, he dwells contemplating dispassion, he dwells

73 SN III 74.

74 SN III 60.

75 SN III 56.

contemplating cessation, he dwells contemplating renunciation ... so dwelling, he does not grasp at anything in the world; not grasping he is unperturbed; being unperturbed he experiences Nibbāna himself and realises: `finished is birth, lived is the divine life, done is what had to be done, there is no more of this or that state.'" [76]

— §§§ —

76 MN 37.

Buddhism and Democracy

Two Essays

Prof. Kurt Leidecker

and

Buddhadasa P. Kirthisinghe

Bodhi Leaves No. 17

First Published: 1963

Buddhism in a Democratic World

Prof. Kurt F. Leidecker

Buddhism is a way of life. It is also an attitude. From these two features stems the uniqueness of Buddhism in the world. What is that way of life and how does it integrate itself in the modern world?

1. Buddhism is not thinkable without the towering figure of the Buddha. Let us consider this first and find some clues there as to the adaptability of the way of life he preached to what we call a democratic outlook.

Though the Buddha was the founder of the way of life we call Buddhism, he never put his own person into the foreground. Instead, he put there the insight he had won in the shape of the Dhamma. He was a teacher, but such a one that will not make the acceptance of the thing he taught dependent on the fact that it was he who taught it. He never asked anyone to follow him personally. He asked people to think with him and, having thought, prove their findings reasonable to themselves. He left the personality of the pupil intact.

Thus we gather from the attitude of the Buddha himself that in Buddhism, personality is respected above all else. Teaching and expounding of the Dhamma is carried on in the most ideal way, with no trace of indoctrination, without coercion. The pupil gives his free assent, if he so decides, with his own mind left in complete integrity.

This is the ideal education we have been striving for all along. Education is a growth of the mind and personality. But just as the garden needs a gardener, so the pupil needs a teacher. The gardener can do no more than to hoe and weed and water. That there shall be flowers and fruits is dependent on the inherent qualities of the plants themselves. In the democratic society we recognize these fundamentals of education.

Of late they have been called progressive. Yet we know they are very ancient. We find them practised by every teacher worthy of the name.

2. The Buddha, thus, in keeping his own person in the background, centered attention on the Dhamma. He set up the Dhamma like a road-sign by the way which may be heeded or not, which is there, whether thousands pass this way or only a few. No wayfarer is compelled to read it and benefit from its message. Of course, he will do so for his own benefit. Likewise the Four Noble Truths are there to accept or reject as man chooses. The Eightfold Noble Path is there, objectively, once it was announced. It is now, as it were, independent of its author.

So thoroughly did the Buddha eschew personality cult, that the first centuries of Buddhist history allude to him only in symbols—in the wheel, the column, the tree, the empty throne, so that the symbol came to stand for the Buddha as well as the idea he preached. The Buddha, thus, was a leader in the sense of an explorer whose discovery anyone may imitate, once given the clues. His leadership continues, but he is a gentle leader, not riding on a prancing horse, but sitting or standing, perchance walking, not with beckoning or threatening gestures, but with gestures that are reminders of his teaching and his way of love, which was gentle and illumined by an inner light.

3. The Orient respects the teacher. It thus shows that knowledge and wisdom are prized above position and wealth. For the sake of knowledge Prince Siddhartha left home; for the sake of expounding the wisdom he had acquired he renounced all. It is a commendable practice of the Thai people to have their sons spend at least three months out of their lives in imitation of the Buddha, renouncing pleasures, wealth and all attachments, by taking the yellow robe. Thus at least once in a lifetime it is brought home to the individual that in humbleness wisdom grows, and insight, if not enlightenment, comes with detachment.

The reverence which is paid to the Buddha in his images is not worship as such. It is respect for the personality of the greatest teacher, who, having explored the highest reaches, did not withdraw to enjoy his salvation, but laboured hard to put his wisdom into simple words, restate it in many ways and phrases, so that all men, intelligent and lacking in intelligence, may understand. This is thinking which is not selfish but is social in the highest sense. Even in the unspeakable bliss of Nibbāna, the Buddha thought of his fellowmen compassionately. It is in this attitude that Buddhists reverence the Buddha, with eyes closed and an ethereal smile on his countenance. The conqueror, Jinā, not of armies but of the baser elements of human nature, draws the Buddhist to the temple. It is not Prince Siddhartha in all his splendor he bows to, but that mature person under the Bo Tree, the receptacle of wisdom. The implications for a life of reason and a peaceful attitude are patent. With this the Buddhist community should make solid contributions to the democratic way of life.

4. Though rank and splendor were not reverenced by the followers of the Buddha to the superlative degree that wisdom was, the Buddhist vocabulary does contain the concept of nobility. Not only are the Fourfold Truths and the Eightfold Path to Nibbāna noble; he is noble, *ariya,* who follows in the Path. In other words, the life you lead, the thoughts you think, ennoble you, not the clothes you wear, or the title and position you hold. The monks are the real *ariya* Sangha, the company of Nobles.

All this goes to show that in Buddhism the real value is shifted from the material and worldly to the spiritual, but without denouncing wealth and prowess as an evil. There is a recognition, therefore, that all these things are necessary so long as we have not reached the highest level of thinking. Kingship and worldly pomp are accepted; however, true nobility is denied them.

The Buddha consorted with the people, the lowliest sometimes, and he felt no compunction to avoid the princely caste. In fact, he recognized caste in the sense that it represented a classification of society according to occupation. He recognized a king, he recognized a Brahman. He did not recommend a false equalization in society, for he knew that true equality could never be in the world of appearance. A true Brahman, a true Prince, was he who, apart from appearance, had that inner worth, that nobility of thought and character.

Buddha, thus, was no reformer, least of all a revolutionary, although he has often been portrayed as such by Western scholars.

He is supposed to have had in view the reconstruction of Hindu society and the elimination of caste. If as a consequence of his teaching, a relaxation of the restrictive forces in Hindu society took place, that was coincidental. To say that the Buddha set out to reform society is a gross mis-statement of the facts. His aim was enlightenment and the elimination of sorrow and suffering, no matter where it occurred, not only the suffering of those who were low in the social scale. The Buddha's problem concerned the very nature and principle of suffering and death itself, not merely the sufferings due to social ills and inequality.

In fact, the Buddha has advanced, unwittingly, in his teachings, the best refutation of the justification of class struggle. His method is peaceful, does not require the conversion by force or otherwise of those who think differently, but implies setting one's own thinking in order. Salvation, *vimukti,* was not to be attained by outward means. It is an inner reformation of the spirit which thereupon is to find its outward expression in ethical activity. One cannot do the good without having an idea or notion of the good.

5. It is one of the basic assumptions of democratic society that it is made up, and should be made up, of a variety of individuals whose individuality is guaranteed. This is also the meaning and intent of Buddhism. In the Milindapañhā it is stated that as the trees differ depending on the nature of the seed, so the character and destiny of man varies with the different deeds whose consequences are earned. This is the doctrine of kamma, action, which is so universal in Indian thinking. A man becomes good by good action, and bad by bad action. The West calls it the doctrine of individual responsibility. There is only this difference: Buddhism carries it beyond the present life span of a man into his past and future.

Essentially, however, there is agreement. An individual must be held fully responsible for his thought and action, for otherwise any action of his can be excused and laws would be futile. Society would disintegrate, just as nature would, were the laws of causality not universal.

Man is by no means regarded perfect in a democratic society. In free association with his fellowmen he practises self-reliance which is allied to belief in kamma. It is the Buddhist view that man can and must perfect himself by shaping his own kamma. Yes, there is a national kamma, and the citizens of free communities believe in it, for no despot is permitted to tamper arbitrarily with justice. We are the heirs of the sins of our forefathers, but also of their virtues.

6. It follows from the kamma theory that man must have freedom to make his own decisions. Whether a man wants to head toward *vimukti* and Nibbāna is his personal concern in the thinking of the Buddha. He, therefore, must imply that society also is such that it provides the necessary conditions for the attainment of Nibbāna. In other words, freedom must be guaranteed in the world.

Freedom, in fact, is the very life-blood of religion, in whatever form it may occur. Any society which believes in strict determinism will eventually ensnare man in a world of thought and action in which he can no longer move about freely. *Vimukti* then becomes impossible through individual effort.

7. It was Emerson, the American, who said, "civilization depends on morality." With this every Buddhist would agree, for *sīla* is basic to human life. Perfect speech, *sammā vācā,* perfect comportment, *sammā kammanta,* and a perfect occupation or livelihood, *sammā ājīva:* these are three important items of the Eightfold Path. If they break down, if, for instance, truth and sincerity are not in the word, which is the very cement of human relationships, for without language man cannot be man, society breaks down and with it civilization goes by the board. The same holds true if we behave asocially by harming our fellowmen bodily, or taking from them what does not belong to us, or engage in activity which does not make them happy and content.

In a democratic society and one that believes in spiritual freedom there is room, then, for those virtues which we prize in the West and which we include in the phrase "the milk of human kindness." In Buddhism, likewise, both bhikkhu and layman are encouraged to move and have their being in the Divine Abodes, the *brahmavihāras*: *mettā, karuṇā, muditā* and *upekkhā*.

Mettā is good will-and friendship. With it the true Buddhist should permeate all quarters. The same with *karuṇā*, compassion with all living creatures, for all are heirs to sorrow and suffering. Scholars have not yet agreed on the meaning of *muditā*. They call it disinterested love, as if love could ever be disinterested. Perhaps sympathy is the English equivalent. *Upekkhā* has been given as "hedonic neutrality or indifference," yet equanimity perhaps is the correct translation.

8. A society which incorporates the concept of freedom rather than repression and suppression, and a religion which permits the unrestricted exercise of the human will to perfect itself, will inevitably be characterized by tolerance. There are two kinds of tolerance, one that just bears with the dissenter, and the other that as a genuine interest in the heterodoxy though it does not subscribe to it. The right to dissent is jealously guarded by all democratic nations. For man must realize that he does not possess the ultimate truth, that he is groping in opinion, however well founded, so long as he has his human limitations.

The same right is implied in Buddhist thinking. For the ultimate reality, Nibbāna, is indefinable and inexpressible. If, thus, either you or I start out in search of it, we do so to the best of our knowledge and intent. It would be illogical if not unethical to fight because of any differences.

9. The conclusion, I think, is now easily drawn as to the place of Buddhism in a democratic world: its place is firmly anchored therein. Buddhism is bound to make a major contribution to the freedom-loving, democratically-governed nations which cannot be otherwise than profound.

The Buddhist's way of life is secure as long as the spirit of the Buddha's words is alive. The overt enemy is easily recognized, but the subversion of thought is subtle indeed. Hence, it is paramount to be grounded not merely in action and know Buddhist philosophy also.

We glibly say "right" action, "right" thought, "right" determination, meaning that they should be perfect, not merely correct. Yet it takes not merely intuition, not merely habit, to do the right or perfect thing. It takes thought, for how can the "right," the *sammā* or perfect, be determined otherwise than in thought? Shall we settle the question by action, shall we use the stick or the gun? Man must be a thinker, and only as a thinker is he man.

Buddhasāsana is based on thought. It stands or falls with the grand and simple ideas that the Buddha has given us and which he has won for us in his profound *dhyāna*. The enemies of Buddhism are enemies of its ideas. While outwardly they fawn on Buddhist ways and practices, they pervert the thought by subtle dialectic. The gravest danger to the Buddhist community consists in that it may not recognize the intellectual attack, and is unprepared by logic and fundamental thinking to repel the onslaught.

Let us, therefore, recapitulate the main ideas on Buddhasāsana which form the sure foundation of a democratic world and a democratic way of life:

True leadership,
Respect for personality,
Teaching without domination,
Nobility of thought and character rather than of wealth or station,
Reconstruction and rehabilitation of the inner man rather than revolutionizing society,
Individual responsibility,
Self-reliance,
Freedom of choice and action,
Morality as the basis of society,
Good will,
Kindness,
Peacefulness, and tolerance.

There is no finer list of virtues than that. All men of high purpose will agree with Buddhists in their aim to perfect the person, in order to make the world a better place to live in.

From *The Golden Lotus*, August, 1960

— §§§ —

The Buddha and Democratic Principles

Buddhadāsa P. Kirthisinghe

The basic principle of a democratic form of government is the freedom and dignity of the individual with equality before the law. No man can be called free unless he is able to pursue his calling unhampered by barriers of caste, class, or special privilege. In a deeper sense no man is truly free until he can without fear or pressure from authoritarian coercion, unfold his innate potentialities and perfect himself by shaping his own *kamma* or destiny. It was the Buddha who for the first time taught and realized these values through his Dhamma. It has led to a flowering of a civilization that, to this day, stands as a marvel in the history of mankind.

Three centuries later it led, for the first time in the annals of mankind, to establish hospitals for both men and animals and organize universal education which culminated in establishing international centers of learning, known today as universities. With the spread of Buddhism in greater Asia from the 3rd century BC it stimulated the formation of new civilizations depending on the national genius of the inhabitants in each State. These civilizations produced a fascinating array of art and dance forms, literature, and social and economic institutions based on the Dhamma.

Democratic Values

> The recognized prerequisites of democratic cultures are:
> A productive economy to raise man above the level of poverty and misery. A progressive society with security and opportunity for all. A literate society with universal education.
> Personal liberty and self-reliance.
> A system of ethics based on moral law.
> Deep-rooted respect for the system of values and institutions that helped each culture to evolve into great civilizations.

These values were respected in the ancient Buddhist civilization of Asia, particularly in the Asokan period from the 3rd Century BC, the golden period of Indian history. These conditions exist today in highly industrialized Japan where there is a predominantly Buddhist civilization, and in the newly emerged Buddhist States of Asia. These technically backward nations are rebuilding their economies to raise the standard of living of their people. Among these, Ceylon has an almost fully literate society with free education from kindergarten up to university.

Buddhism has given each man or woman sturdy independence, rather than dependence on the mercy of a Creator God to better themselves. The Buddha taught man the gospel of self-help in his efforts to lead a noble life. To achieve the highest conditions of mind and heart, the Buddha said man must work out his own way. He asserted that man's own deeds would make him noble and advised him to guard against deeds that would make him low.

Further, the Buddha stated that all beings, including man, are suffering, and through his Noble Eight-fold Path he gave an efficacious prescription how to make an end of that suffering. Since that Path is a road of gradual progress it is intelligible and practicable by all, even on the lowest rungs of human development. None is excluded from reaching final deliverance if only he takes resolutely one step after the other on that road. Thus we see that the Buddha conceded equality to all human beings—a cardinal principle in a democratic society.

Thus, the Buddha founded the clarion-call of human liberty. He said: "Take ye refuge unto yourself; be ye your own salvation. With earnestness and high resolve work out your own salvation."

The Buddha pointed out the absolute folly of artificial distinctions between man and man. At the time of the Buddha there was a rigid caste system in India. It determined and fixed man's place in the social order by the mere fact that one's father was of such and such a descent and had such and such an occupation. The low castes were denied an education and were placed low on the social ladder, and this with such a rigidity that a low caste man could hardly break out of his situation. The Buddha revolted against this injustice and asserted the equality of all men as far as their basic rights are concerned.

The Buddha unhesitatingly admitted to his Order of Monks also people of the so-called low castes—barbers, butchers, sweepers, and the untouchable—along with the members of the noble and priestly castes. He made absolutely no distinctions between them in the ranks of the monks. All received equal homage, reverence and respect. Some members of the nobility were upset by these actions of the Buddha and one of them dared challenge the Buddha to define a nobleman. It was then that he declared:

No man is noble by birth,
No man is ignoble by birth.
Man is noble by his own deeds,
Man is ignoble by his own deeds.

Commenting on the Buddha's discourse, the Sigālovāda Sutta,[77] which is based on social ethics, the world-famous British scholar, Professor Rhys Davids, chairman of the Department of Comparative Religion, Manchester University, England, says: "Happy would have been the village or the clan on the banks of the Ganges, when the people were full of kindly spirit of fellow feelings, the noble spirit of justice, which breathes through these naive and simple sayings." He adds: "Not less happy would be the village on the banks of the Thames, today, of which this could be said."

He continues: "The Buddha's doctrine of love and goodwill between man and man is here set forth in domestic and social ethics with more comprehensive details than elsewhere … And truly we may say even now of this Vinaya or code of discipline, so fundamental are the human interests involved, so sane and wide is the wisdom that envisages them that the utterances are as fresh and practically as binding today as they were then, at Rajagaha (India)."

The Buddha strongly condemned all sacrifices performed in the name of religion, particularly those involving animal sacrifices. It was believed at that time, that sacrifices atoned for sin and protected against evil spirits. The Buddha said that these sacrifices were cruel and useless, as it is only through a noble life that man can elevate himself and be secure against evil.

77 Translated in Wheel No. 14, *Everyman's Ethics.*

The Buddha's compassion extended also to those who were ailing. Once he said to his disciples: "Whoever, monks, nurses the sick, will nurse me." And in that spirit, hospitals for both animals and men were later established during the reign of Asoka in 3rd century BC.

The Buddha condemned slavery in any shape and form. He laid down golden rules for the right manner of earning one's living in a way not harmful to others, and this included also that any trafficking in human beings was out of bounds for a Buddhist.

The temperance movement owes its beginnings to the Buddha who asked his followers to abstain from using or selling liquor and other intoxicants.

Gospel of Tolerance

The Buddha also preached the gospel of tolerance, of compassion, loving-kindness and non-violence. He taught men not to despise other religions and not to belittle them. He further declared that one should not even accept his own teachings unless one found them to be in accord with one's personal reasoning, according to the Kalama Sutta.[78]

During the Buddha's time there were a number of great kingdoms in India such as Magadha and Kosala, and some of them were established on the democratic form of government. The Buddha favoured the democrat form over the oligarchical form of government as it was the best form of government which is conducive to the stability of society.

The Buddha showed great admiration of the Vajjis or Licchavis. In the Mahāparinibbāna Sutta he likened the Licchavis to the Thirty-three Gods *(Tāvatiṃsa-deva).* He also warned Vassakāra, minister of the parricide king Ajātasattu that the Vajjis would remain invincible as long as they adhered to the seven rules of a nation's welfare *(aparihāniya dhamma),* namely:

> Frequent meetings for consultation.
> Concord in action.
> Adherence to injunctions and traditions.

78 Translated in Wheel No. 8.

Respecting elders.
Respecting women, who shall never be molested.
Reverence to places of worship within and outside the territory.
Protection of worthy saints in the territory.

The Buddha continued: "So long as the Vajjis meet frequently in council, assemble and disperse in harmony (and observe the other rules of welfare), their prosperity is to be expected, not their decline."

Asoka's Reign

The Emperor Asoka worked with ceaseless energy for the propagation of Buddhism and transformed it into a world religion. The Asokan period from 325 to 288 BC is of special significance to mankind, as it is one of the most illustrious liberal democratic periods in history.

In his time Asoka established public gardens, medical herbs were cultivated, trees were planted along roads, hospitals were established for both men and animals. He sank wells for public use, and educational and religious institutions grew up all over the country.

The late H. G. Wells writes in his *Outline of World History:* "Amidst the tens of thousands of names of monarchs that crowd the columns of history, their majesties and graciousnesses, and sovereignties and royal highnesses and the like, the name of Asoka shines, and shines almost alone a star. From the Volga to Japan his name is still honoured. China, Tibet and even India, though it has left his doctrine, preserves the traditions of his greatness. More living men cherish his memory today than ever heard the names of Constantino and Charlemagne.

It is claimed that Asoka was one of the first to grant gender equality by sending his own son and daughter to Ceylon for missionary work. In this vast empire, Asoka treated all his subjects with equal justice and admitted no privileges of caste or class.

Formation of democratic thought originated in ancient India by the spread of Buddhism from the 3rd century BC. In an introduction to the book *Legacy of India*, Lord Zetland, former Viceroy of India, states: "And it may come as a surprise to many to learn that in assemblies of Buddhists in India, two thousand or more years ago, are to be found rudiments of our own parliamentary system as practised today."

Professor G. P. Malalasekera says: "The spread of Buddhism from country to country in greater Asia was without bloodshed and it is by itself a great democratic process never witnessed by any other world religion."

From *World Buddhism, Vesak Annual* 1963

— §§§ —

Buddhist Therapy

Ruth Walshe

Bodhi Leaves No. 18

First published: 1963

Buddhist Therapy

Living in the 20th century, the word therapy is quite familiar to us, especially in connection with occupational therapy. Now, let us reflect for a moment, why so many people find occupational therapy so helpful—particularly in mental distress? Is it because it takes our mind off our worry?

According to Buddhism, however, occupational therapy is not a satisfactory solution to our problems. Buddhism is a way of life which helps us to look within—to dig deep inside us—right down to the core of trouble. While to take the mind off our worry is in fact nothing else but an escape, though it might work quite well for the time being, Buddhism is against all escapism. Instead, you must have courage to look at yourself the way a detached stranger might look at you, and face up to your emotions—especially your anxieties—which are bound to come up in the process of your investigation. Only by accepting these at their face-value, can you ever hope to transcend them one day.

This, on the other hand, might give the impression that Buddhism is very closely related to psychology.

To some extent, yes, but with one tremendous difference. While psychology helps you to understand yourself intellectually and, at best emotionally, Buddhism helps you to get beyond the intellect to the actual experience of life itself. That's why applied Buddhism goes so much deeper than any school of psychology can ever claim to do. But how does one achieve this? The only way is through meditation and the practice of mindfulness—*satipaṭṭhāna*.

As I am not in a position to write on meditation, because I have not practised half enough myself, I shall just restrict myself to mindfulness as the cure of most suffering: Buddhist therapy.

In Buddhism we can apply mindfulness at

body,
feelings,
states of mind, and
contents of mind.

But as the actual suffering comes to us through bodily feelings (pain) and states of mind (emotions), I shall only deal with those two, in particular, with our emotions. But of course, great stress in Buddhism is also laid on mindfulness as to the body (watching your breathing, mindful walking) and as to the contents of mind (watching your thoughts and images).

Bodily Feelings

The greatest suffering our body has to endure is through pain. In this case we nearly always look for help from outside: either we call the doctor or we get drugs or both. But what are we to do if we can't get any help from outside? Suppose we have such dreadful toothache that no pills will help at all. And the attack starts in the middle of the night, when no dentist is available. I'm sure many people will have had such an experience in the past. And most of us will have suffered agonies. Why? Because we didn't only have to suffer the pain itself—but also our various emotions round the pain; such as anxiety, self-pity, resentment, etc. But I am afraid it isn't even as simple as that. If we could just accept these things for what they are, our suffering could be greatly reduced, as I will try to explain later when I deal with mental suffering. But alas acceptance is our very weak point. Instead, the ego simply loves spinning cocoons round any-and everything. If the pain becomes too acute, we repress it, and thus we only suffer a double dose. The same happens to our emotions. So we can truthfully say that the real cause of our suffering is not the pain, nor even the accepted fear of the pain—but the repressed fear. To quote Graham Howe: "Neurosis is nothing else but unadmitted fear."

Now let us go back to just the bodily feeling of the pain: in our case, the tooth-ache. How can we help ourselves in the Buddhist way—that is to say, from within? Simply by concentrating wholly on the tooth-ache.

Doesn't this make it worse? Or isn't this too introspective? Too negative?

Yes, in the beginning you might actually increase the pain by concentrating on it, for no escapism is allowed. But when I say, concentrating, I mean watching it with detachment—not wallowing in it with your precious little ego as the centre. Now if you can really concentrate on nothing else but the pain for long enough, it will be greatly reduced, if not completely transcended. Why? Because by the sheer act of concentration you wholly accept your situation, however unhappy it might be. And if there is only the act of watching without a watcher in the centre—surely, this cannot be introspective, nor negative, nor positive.

States of Mind

As I explained before, it is our emotions which cause our main suffering, whether they plague us on their own or in connection with the suffering of our body. Therefore, I want to deal now entirely with the suffering caused by our various states of mind—our various emotions.

When I made myself the guinea-pig of these investigations, I found that six states of mind seem to be responsible for my main suffering. They are:

Greed in general,
Greed for a bigger and better self,
Hurt pride,
Envy,
Hatred, and
Anxiety.

Don't let us feel uneasy about them! Let us remember, they just constitute our ignorance—our Jungian shadow. Nothing more—nothing less. First, we may accept them intellectually without pinning labels to any of them. But perhaps I might be allowed to point out that of these six states of mind, anxiety is by far the most deadly of the lot. That's why I have reserved the last and longest section to anxiety which I will boldly call the core of all our mental suffering.

Greed in General

I feel greed is a very good example to illustrate that it is frustration far more than the greed itself which causes our suffering. Suppose I feel greed for a pretty frock in an Oxford Street shop window. It nearly buys me—but I manage to resist the temptation at the last minute. Now when the greed first occurred in the here-and-now, it was quite a pleasant sensation. But of course it didn't last long; not even as long as eating a cream-pastry, for my reasoning set in and I had to frustrate it. It was no good buying the frock—I simply didn't have the money. This hurt quite a bit. But more pain was to come. For my frustration increased as time went on, as I was still attached to that frock in the window. I just couldn't put it down. Every time the frock tried to appear in my mind accompanied by some feeling of pain, I pushed down my greedy emotion further and further, which only made matters worse. For the longer my greed is frustrated, the longer I have pushed down my longing for the frock by pretending it was not really there—the greater the suffering. This is a sure way of becoming attached to my own attachment.

Now please don't make any mistake. All this is a purely intellectual understanding of the situation and as such it is of no use whatsoever while we are in the grip of the emotion. For the grip is too strong to allow us to think reasonably at all. It will, no doubt, help us a little afterwards. It might even make us be less foolish next time. It might ... but let us be quite clear on one point. This intellectual reasoning is as far removed from mindfulness as I am from the man in the moon!

What is the main difference then? As I can only explain this intellectually, it is a very difficult task indeed. For mindfulness is a direct experience of life—a direct seeing of things as they are—and therefore it cannot really be rendered in concepts.

Through right mindfulness and right concentration, the so-called reality which we usually give to all the objects we desire or hate drops off and just makes them into appearances; here one moment and gone the next. They become valueless phantoms.

Now if we apply mindfulness as to emotions—in our case, greed for the frock—through the absorbing process of watching, the central watcher (I), as well as the object (the frock), will suddenly disappear. In the end there will be just greed and nothing else: no classification, comparison, or judgement, just the seeing of the innocent eye. And this very seeing is the Buddhist therapy—the immediate cure of our suffering. It works even in the smallest instance and the knowledge deep down that it works already makes the usual vicious circle unvicious. It also strengthens our faith in the Buddha, the Dhamma, and the Sangha—which is absolutely essential on the Buddhist path.

Greed for a Bigger and Better Self

This is far more devastating to us than our greed in general—our greed for objects which have no direct bearing on our self-esteem. It stands to reason: if our ignorant belief in the ego constitutes our suffering, then any emotions, thoughts or actions tending to inflate this erroneous belief even more, will have grave consequences for us, not only in the present but also in the future. Imagine life as being like the current of a stream. If we try and swim against this current, it will soon catch up with us. We will exhaust and harm ourselves in the process until, in the end, we shall have learned our lesson the hard way.

Let me give you an example again. Suppose I want to become an actress—a famous actress. This is wrong from the very start. Why? Buddhism teaches us not to look at our action but at our motive behind the action: I want to become famous, "I want" is wrong and the clement of fame is worse still, for it stands for ego-boosting. You might argue here that the "I want" cannot be avoided in life with its main-theme of the survival of the fittest.

But life should not be a game of grabbing and clinging. This is where we go completely wrong. Though its laws can be cruel and murderous, it is our mode of awareness which is the balancing factor in our life. The more we can reduce the centre figure of the self through right awareness, the more we reach the balance of the true centre: the middle way where the karmic laws no longer operate.

Perhaps, I have succeeded a little in showing you not only why my desire to become a famous actress is wrong—but also why any desire to become anything is equally wrong. What is the right motive then? Simply love for acting, without any scheming and machination of the ego. This, of course, is quite impossible for us unenlightened creatures. That is why we still have to cope with this round of endless rebirths. But we need not be disheartened, for we have the power to *purify* our motives bit by bit, as our insight into life as it is increases.

But now let us go back to the I which suffers. The I who wants to become a famous actress: who wants to be in the lime-light and thus have more so-called security in the ego. The I who wants to earn more money in order to satisfy more desires.

Again, as in the case of greed in general, as long as my desire to become a famous actress is not too much frustrated—as long as there is still the element of hope—my suffering is not too acute. But all the same, there is a constant amount of suffering—especially as it is unadmitted, repressed. But the more I fail in achieving this desire, the greater my suffering; and the greater my suffering, the more I repress; and the more I repress, the more acute my suffering. The vicious circle at its worst. When we can't bear this state of affairs any longer, we just go and change our set of desires and hope that this time we might be a little more successful. But what we don't understand is the fact that even the success of our desire is bound to bring suffering in the course of time. For desire—attachment— means running counter to the flow of life.

Suppose I do become a famous actress. My desire doesn't stop there, for I have constantly to prove to myself and others that I really am a famous actress. And there are difficult relationships with my co-workers. The more difficult, the more inflated my ego becomes. And in the end—through illness, old age and maybe all sorts of other circumstances—my desire will be frustrated after all, unless these outside circumstances force me to surrender my desire myself.

But why wait for outside circumstances when you can be your own maker and master from within? Watch your greed for a bigger and better self the way I described before. Turn the light onto the spot which hurts most, instead of pushing it into the dark labyrinth of the unconscious. And the seeing of the situation as it really is—not imagined by an imaginary self—is the one and only cure. The more the ego kicks in all directions and the more it complains bitterly, the more you must turn on the light. For this light shines from within; it is the insight into the true nature of things coupled with compassion for these things, including yourself.

Hurt Pride

Hurt pride is the direct outcome of our erroneous ego-belief. The more inflated our ego, the greater our hurt pride. If we become so attached to this precious little I that we can only see and experience life from the point of view of this I right in the centre of all things, we are asking for trouble. We simply have to get hurt all the time. It isn't only other people's actions or non-action which can hurt our ego, but any little critical remark might give us pain too. Especially if it comes from someone we love—someone we are attached to.

Again let me give you a little example.

One day my husband suddenly complained that I had an aggressive way of arguing. I was quite a bit hurt there and then but soon I seemed to have forgotten all about it.

And then, quite suddenly, a few days later when I was sitting in an armchair resting after lunch, the whole scene presented itself again—practically word for word. I seemed to enter into the same emotions as I did when my husband made this unfortunate remark. My cheeks felt flushed and I suffered. New emotions got hold of me: that of anger—even hatred—for my husband.

Of course, while I have this attack of hurt pride I can't see it this way at all. Everything is distorted by my emotions and my consequent self-pity makes my suffering even worse. Then all of a sudden in a moment's lull, I remember to apply mindfulness. And, as usual, it works. For a few moments I manage to step out of my own shoes—my emotional shoes. And then, for the first time, the scene presents itself with a strange actress who seems to have taken my part. I have no longer anything to do with it. I'm just an onlooker. Everything seems suddenly different, rather absurd, almost funny. Is it really me sitting in the chair wallowing in warmed-up emotions? I burst out laughing. Having detached myself from my own self, I also detached myself from my emotions by going right through them as a neutral watcher.

"That is all very well," it might be argued. "Your husband's criticism was not at all serious and maybe there was a little truth in it too. One shouldn't be so touchy. But what about people who make really serious, wicked accusations which are quite unfounded? Surely, you can't help feeling hurt about it!"

To this I just say: If you have overcome your wrong ego-belief, if you are completely detached from yourself and everything round you, nothing will hurt you any more. After all, hurt pride is only attachment to the so-called virtue of your so-called ego!

Envy

If you go in for either or both kinds of greed—the greed in general and the greed for a bigger and better self—in a big way, you will often find yourself stumbling over people who have got exactly what you desire yourself so ardently. Up will come the emotion of envy. And the more you are attached to things you cannot obtain—the more your greed is frustrated—the more likely it is for envy to arise.

Please, always follow me from the Buddhist angle which, as I pointed out before, is so much deeper than even the psychological. No excuses, nor self-accusations are allowed. Instead, we are just aware of anything and everything which presents itself before our mind. And you will find that the unvicious circle can increase in volume just as much as the vicious. As our insight increases so does our faith in the Dhamma and vice versa. Thus slowly, but surely, our attachment to ourselves and the people and things around us decreases. We are getting healthier in mind and body.

By the way, it might be amusing to see that jealousy is really nothing else but also a kind of envy resulting from greed. I become attached to a person of the opposite sex. I want to possess him—to own him as I own my flat. Now if another woman receives some of his attentions which I desire all for myself, I feel jealous. I envy her this man of mine! It's as simple as that. Actually, if you look at these emotions without labelling them with nasty adjectives, such as sinful or wicked—this can become quite an amusing game. So long as you don't get attached to the game, of course.

If the feeling of envy becomes terribly strong, it might even develop into hatred. Take, for instance, our example of the greed for a bigger and better self. Suppose I don't become the famous actress I desire so much, but instead, my school-friend Susan does. All my ambitions in this direction get frustrated, while Susan seems to climb to the top almost effortlessly. I think, this is a clear case for the arising of hatred. The amount of hatred I repress, though, will only intensify my suffering. But at this point we'd better leave envy and go over to hatred proper.

Hatred

Hatred, we might say, is like a whirlpool in the stream of life. Hatred arises towards any person who stands between my ego and my desire. But in this case the emotion of desire can be felt positively as well as negatively. If my school-teacher makes me do a sum I don't want to, I hate him. I feel, so to speak, desire for not doing the sum. To make things even more complicated, we might say that hatred for a person in itself is a negative attachment. I just can't put him down—in a similar way as I can't put down a person I love; only with much more unpleasant emotion. This might, perhaps, illuminate a little the Buddhist teaching of kamma which claims that we are to meet in our next rebirth those people we are specially attached to by love or hatred in this life. A rather gruesome thought, I always think.

Because hatred makes us suffer severely—for already the emotion itself is completely out of step with the harmony of life— we repress it as much as we can. And if we do accept it, we usually hate ourselves for it, which is nothing else but a negative attachment to our ego.

It is here, I feel, that Buddhism is unique compared with all other religions in its profound wisdom. No Christian self-mortification in any shape or form, as the Buddha had proved on his own mind and body, as both opposites constitute attachment: self-love, as well as self-hatred. Only the complete abandoning of the illusory self in the middle way—only true detachment—is man's liberation from all suffering.

Anxiety

As I said right in the beginning, anxiety is the most deadly of all our emotions. Why? Because it is bred from our feeling of insecurity. And the root-cause of this insecurity is our old friend attachment.

When Dr. Suzuki says so wisely that our trouble starts from the movement of the arising of the consciousness of "this and that," he implies our suffering through attachment. The very moment I artificially place the ego in the centre of the Universe, I start discriminating between this and that. And by so doing I am attached. So we might say: the arising of the consciousness of this and that produces the force of attachment.

The various emotions I have just discussed, spring from various definite attachments—but our constant feeling of insecurity which produces anxiety in general, springs directly from the force of attachment. The second of the Four Noble Truths: the origin of suffering is craving! Once we have established this, we can go further by saying that as we are so strongly attached to this life—to a great extent because we are afraid of the unknown in the state of death and afterwards—a great deal of anxiety can be traced back to the death-fear in us. But, of course, this death-fear too has its roots in the force of attachment.

Now, for me anxiety always shows itself in the form of an emotional cramp. If it is strong enough, it produces a physical cramp as well. And when it's on its way out through the act of watching, it usually leaves me with an intellectual cramp as its farewell present. The remainder of my mental cramp quickly moves into my thoughts until I seem to ride around on them like on a rocking-horse in a merry-go-round. It took me quite a while to find this out—but now I can always trace this as a definite pattern repeating itself again and again. All these various cramps are, of course, part and parcel of the original cramp of attachment, manifesting itself through various channels according to its intensity. This is important to know, for then we don't get sidetracked so easily by the various labels we ourselves seem to stick on to this cramp or attachment.

After this elaborate analysis of the attachment I simply must warn you, or rather encourage you: because I've just put it all down in concepts for our brain to understand it doesn't mean this attachment exists in reality. Its only existence is in our illusory mind—let us make no mistake about this. Thus, we even get cramped about this very cramp. We cling to our own anxiety—we fear our own fear. But once we have broken right through this illusion of the mind—if only for a short time—the cramp will dissolve completely in all its forms for the time being, leaving us wondering what the fuss was all about. But I shall come to this more fully presently.

Now let us go back to our samsāra again, to our vale of tears.

Suppose the force of attachment shows itself first in the form of a general feeling of uneasiness. What do we usually do with this glowing cinder? We immediately start feeding it with thoughts—all sorts of thoughts. Our head gives this general feeling of anxiety a label and thus transforms it into my special anxiety—as distinct from yours. For example: Will I be able to tackle this and that job tomorrow? Now had we not fed the cinder with suitable coals, it might have slowly burnt out by itself, instead of growing into a little fire.

But sometimes, worse still, the fire becomes bigger and bigger until it threatens to get out of hand. What has happened? I have been suffering so much anxiety that suddenly besides all my other fears, I start fearing my very anxiety. I get, in my despair, attached to my own attachment. But this, of course, is so subtle that my consciousness is not aware of it.

Again, mindfulness—detachment is the cure for any anxiety. But I have to realize that, though my anxiety might leave me for the moment, it is liable to come up again—either with the same or with a different label. Due to my *kamma-vipāka* the same pattern of ignorance will present itself to me for a long time to come. But it will continue to decrease in intensity, the deeper my experiences get and, consequently, the more my insight grows. My new *kamma*—my reactions to *vipāka*—will become more and more wholesome, when my particular anxiety becomes just anxiety, and when it disappears altogether for the moment.

Sometimes I even catch anxiety before I put the label on and then it is definitely easier to deal with. But sometimes my cramp of anxiety seems to get worse, instead of better. What went wrong? I am so set on my goal: the goal of freeing myself from suffering, that—besides my cramp of anxiety—I am also cramped with attachment to my goal. The ego wants detachment and thus only adds a new attachment to all the others. What am I to do?

In such a case the answer for me invariably is to have faith.

Faith in the Buddha, the Dhamma, and the Sangha.

Here one might ask: "But what do I do to get this faith?"

I'm afraid this question is wrong from the start, because the ego can never get any faith. The only thing it can do is to humble itself not before other people—but before itself. After all, the ego stands for ignorance and the acceptance of this is humbling. Consequently, there will also be a true acceptance of my suffering and thus my ego will be silenced for a longer spell. This will result in the immediate cessation of suffering for the time being.

Now let us pause here for a moment to consider why true acceptance of suffering is the one and only cure, while repression only makes our suffering very much worse. This is hard to explain conceptually—but I will try.

Repression seems to me nothing else but a continuation of my attachment in the sub-or unconscious level of the mind. Somehow, I always imagine the unconscious as a huge pantry where I store unpleasant things I don't want to face. When the smell gets too bad, however, I hurriedly open the pantry just for a second to take the most rotten piece out—only to lock it up again immediately. But the real trouble lies in the fact that I am still attached to all these emotions in the pantry, in spite of being out of my conscious reach. And in order to keep them locked up there, I need a lot of energy which only increases my state of suffering.

Now acceptance—true Buddhist acceptance—on the other hand, constitutes detachment, for the I is no longer on the scene to be attached to. It is as simple as that, and yet the hardest thing for the ego to bear.

Let us throw the final flash-light once more onto the true acceptance of our suffering through anxiety. As I tried to explain before, the mere act of acceptance already contains the cure: the cessation of suffering. For when the ego is out of the way, volition ceases too. We are no longer attached to: "I want to" or "I don't want to." Therefore true acceptance is detachment.

Now during this cessation all our energy, which is usually needed for our ego-make-believe, becomes released. No longer is our line with the whole Universe blocked. *Mettā* and *karuṇā* can, at last, flow backwards and forwards unhindered. By going right through suffering to non-suffering we find the unspeakable bliss of peace—the peace that passes all understanding. For the time being, we are cured of our cramp of anxiety!

— §§§ —

The Dhamma

And Some Current Misconceptions

Bhikkhu Khema

Bodhi Leaves No. 19

First published: 1963

The Dhamma

And Some Current Misconceptions

The objection is sometimes raised by Westerners that the Dhamma belongs to another cultural pattern altogether, and is therefore unsuited to the Western outlook.

Buddhism arose among the Indo-European people of northern India some 2,500 years ago, while the predominant religion of the West came from the Semitic tradition of the Near East, which has also produced Judaism and Islam. Consequently, it is hard to understand in what respect Semitic culture is nearer to the West than Indo-European culture itself. Nor should one forget that Christianity expanded from the Near East by way of the Roman empire to Western Europe and America, while Islam is established in such dissimilar cultural areas as West Africa, Malaya and Indonesia. If it be objected that there have been changes to suit local conditions, what happens to our original criticism? It is true that the majority of individuals in a culture have to face the same problems and this suggests the conclusion that these problems have been created by the specific life conditions existing in that culture. That they do not represent problems common to human nature seems to be warranted by the fact that the motivating forces and conflicts in other cultures are different from ours.[79] But this does not imply that the basis of the human condition found in, for example, birth, death, the search for the pleasant and the avoidance of pain, is not the context in which all the cultures are bound to function.

In present Western conditions it may be hard to appreciate the Dhamma, and no doubt people are put off when they come in contact with the "cocktail-party Buddhism," which is a by-product of the insistence of looking at life as an intellectual exercise. For

79 K. Homey, *The Neurotic Personality of our Time*, W. W. Norton, New York, p. 34.

similar reasons Jung found occasion to animadvert against those Westerners who practise Eastern yoga.

It is quite true that much, probably most, of the so-called yoga practice indulged in by Westerners is foolish and misguided. That is, however, not because it is "eastern" in origin, but because it is not pursued for the right reason.[80] In both these cases superficiality or crankiness are the root of the trouble.

A distinction should be made between the location in time and place of the Dhamma and the question of its validity. References in the Pali Canon to externals are historical and should be distinguished from the essentials, such as the Four Noble Truths, each person being left to put them to the test for himself. The present international situation should also provide food for thought on *mettā*, or loving-kindness, surely as necessary now as at the time of the Buddha. However it is formulated, the Dhamma remains true to its description as "*ehipassika*," something to come and see for oneself. This should suggest that Buddhism is more than a bundle of notions. The person who is used to intellectual and speculative edifices is not usually in the habit of testing them by the criterion of personal experience. Contrast this with the words of the Buddha: "I teach you a teaching for the rejection of, the getting rid of, any self, a way by which impure conditions can be put away and pure conditions brought to increase. By which one, even in this very life, may attain unto the fulfillment and growth of perfect wisdom, realising it by one's own direct knowledge, and therein to abide. Now it may well be that this thought will occur to you: 'Yes, this may be done but yet one remains sorrowful.' But that is not the way to look at it, for when this is done, there will be as a result joy, zest, calm, mindfulness, self-possession and the happy life. And if others should ask us this question: 'But what is that getting of a physical-body self, a mind-made self, a formless self about which you say all this?' Then we should thus reply: 'It is the same self of which we speak, for at the moment when any one of these three modes of self is going on, it is not reckoned as one of the other two: it is only reckoned by the name of the particular personality which prevails. For all these are merely names, terms, ways of speaking, definitions

80 S. K. Prem, *The Yoga of the Bhagavat Gita*, I. M. Watkins, London, p. xv.

of everyday use. These we use when we speak, but we are not deceived by them.'" [81] This cuts across Western lines of thought. Many scholars, however sympathetic they may have been on the intellectual level, missed the point because they tried to deduce where the Dhamma leads instead of combining intellect with experience. How many of those who indulged in the hair-raising speculations about Nibbāna for instance ever did any meditation?

Another extreme is represented by those who sought to smuggle in esoteric teachings. Since the Buddha explained that he was not holding back anything that was conducive to the welfare and progress of anyone who was interested, in the "closed fist of the teacher," there can be little justification for this. He stated that he knew more than he was prepared to divulge as he was only interested in that which was of practical application. Speculation may be entertaining but it is incompatible with concentrating on the task which can bring beneficent results in the immediate future. The Dhamma is for the individual and not vice versa and this is one reason why it is based on the First Noble Truth, which states that life involves suffering. Everyone has experienced it to some extent in his own life.

So, far from being alien to the Western person, Buddhism can appeal to him on his own ground. Since the Renaissance the best of the European tradition has aimed at a humanistic training, in which the individual is urged to think for himself. Comparable to this is the advice given by the Buddha to the Kālāmas, who complained about the difficulty of assessing the various teachings in circulation: "Do not be led by the authority of religious texts, nor by mere logic or inference, nor by considering appearances, nor by delight in speculative opinions, nor by seeming possibilities, nor by the idea 'this is our teacher.' But when you know for yourselves that certain things are unwholesome then give them up. And when you know for yourselves that certain things are wholesome then accept them and follow them." [82] This resolves the problem of "faith," which has caused so much discussion in the West, particularly when it has been opposed to modern science. Galileo

81 DN 9, Poṭṭhapāda Sutta.

82 Anguttara Nikāya, Pali Text Society, London, vol. I p. 188. Translated by Soma Thera in Wheel No. 8.

suffered for his views, and it was long time before it was admitted in some quarters that this world was not the center of the universe but merely part of a galaxy. It was only in 1950 that the Pope lifted the ban on Darwin's theory of evolution.

Man cannot change the world overnight, but the Dhamma shows the practical possibility of the individual bringing about a healthy change in his attitude and therefore in his actions, which is bound to affect the environment. Whether he does so is his own business, and unless he appreciates the reasons for doing so, it is literally meaningless to try and force him to understand. As the Dhammapada says:

"By oneself, indeed, is evil done; by oneself is one injured. By oneself is evil left undone; by oneself is one purified. Purity and impurity belong to oneself. No one purifies another." [83] Purity is to be understood in the sense of the purity of a chemical substance and not merely according to moral or ritual convention. The Dhammapada explains that just as a water-pot is filled gradually by small drops of water, so a person may be gradually filled by healthy aims, or else by those which lead to painful results. Only those who are not stuck in the mud themselves can pull another out.

A contemporary psychoanalyst remarks: "The East was not burdened with the concept of a transcendent father-saviour in which the monotheistic religions expressed their longings. Taoism and Buddhism had a rationality and realism superior to that of Western religions … Paradoxically, Eastern religious thought turns out to be more congenial to Western religious thought than does Western religious thought itself."[84] He further[85] comments on the cheerful mood of humanistic doctrines, contrasted to the feelings of guilt which arise in theistic religion, in which the devotee is likely to deprive himself of all good qualities by projecting them on to a supernatural agency. In this case it is not surprising that he ends up with the feeling of being a worthless sinner. Nor should the implications of religious masochism be overlooked, in which an apparently acute self-criticism masks arrogance and delusion.

---

83 Dhammapada v. 145, trans. S. Radhakrishnan, Oxford University Press.

84 E. Fromm, *Zen Buddhism and Psychoanalysis*, Harper, New York, p. 80

85 E. Fromm, *Psychoanalysis and Religion*, Yale University Press, p. 50.

Theodor Reik dealt with some of these problems in his *Masochism in Modern Man*. Such mechanisms delude the person into thinking he is getting the best of both worlds, whereas it is hindering him from taking the steps which may be reasonably expected to be conducive to better results.

As far as the West is concerned, the present age is one of science and analysis. How does this affect the Dhamma? Psychologists[86] can tell us how this "self" is gradually built up in the originally "selfless" infant, how it expands and becomes more complex with experience, how strains in the imperfectly integrated experience may sometimes distort and split it into two or more separate "personalities," and how these may be welded into one again by harmonizing the conflicting stresses. Truly do they teach, as the Buddha taught long before, that in all this there is nothing immortal, nothing permanent, no hard changeless centre in the ever-changing flux of experience which could in truth be called a self (conventionally speaking). This self that we prize so dearly and to which we subordinate all is a mere emptiness, the empty heart of a whirlpool, a mathematical point which changes its position, not only from year to year, but even from hour to hour, as a man shifts from his "business integration to that which is manifested at his home or club." This lack of an abiding substance or ego-entity in the ultimate sense (*anattā*), impermanence (*anicca*) and *dukkha* are the three characteristics of life and are so closely related that it is hard to appreciate them as separate concepts. Whether it is the cells of the body, arrangements of atoms or just external events, the element of transitoriness is noticeable in life, and from this it is easier to see the lack of an abiding ego entity and hence the incomplete and sometimes unsatisfactory or painful side of it. Anyone may observe the flux of his thoughts and emotions, but if it is to be of real help to him, these three characteristics of life must be understood or realised more deeply than as purely intellectual concepts. "Dukkha" has no single equivalent in English adequate to the range of all it implies. To call it simply "suffering" is misleading. It is obvious that this is not the whole of life, and it would be an error to assume that the Dhamma is either

86 Prem, op. cit. p. 39.

pessimistic or optimistic. Its aim is to see life as it really is, which does not depend on feelings one way or the other.

This may be compared to the aim of a scientist, and it follows that so far from fearing scientific inquiry the Dhamma welcomes it. But neither science nor logic can "prove" nor disprove the validity of the Dhamma, since it must be personally experienced. The present theory of matter[87] as energy or motion seems near to the Buddhist view of *anicca* or impermanence, but then it is clear that the atomic theory of the last century would not have been so sympathetic. What will science say tomorrow? Physics may be applied to the environment, but for the individual it may be more fruitful to look within, not in the sense of brooding or mulling over the projections of the mind. Until recent years the West has largely neglected this in favour of "conquering nature" but in depth psychology in particular there is a move towards dealing with levels of the mind which are normally unconscious. This does not mean they are inoperative, even if many people ignore them. The works of Fromm already referred to are an interesting bridge between certain aspects of oriental doctrine and depth psychology, but it is especially in meditation that the Dhamma has something of great value to offer to the West.

The struggle between dogmatism and science in Europe has had far-reaching results. For many it has posed the false antithesis of either accepting theistic religion, with its demands of faith, or rejecting all religion for some form of materialism or nihilism. To judge by the increase in neuroses and the number of patients in mental hospitals, and perhaps those who should be there as well, the present trend in Western culture would not appear to be a healthy one. Previously patients complained of specific disorders and suffered from definite symptoms[88] but now the majority complain of "mal de siècle": the sickness[89] of the age, which despite material affluence[90] seems to get into distress. The free-for-all of the present does not provide the pleasure, let alone happiness, that on paper it might lead one to expect.

---

87 See W. Heisenberg, *Physics and Philosophy*, Allen and Unwin, London.

88 See Breuer and Freud, *Studies on Hysteria*, Hogart Press, London.

89 Fromm, *Zen Buddhism and Psychoanalysis*, p. 85.

90 Horney, op. cit.

False antithesis has indeed become part or an ingrained habit of dualistic thinking in the West. Without the comforting labels of good and bad, hot and cold, pleasant and unpleasant, people get lost, but do not consider whether such labels mean anything; in most cases they are highly subjective and the results of past conditioning. "People are so fond of discriminating labels that they even go to the length of putting them on human qualities and emotions common to all. So they talk of different 'brands' of charity, as for example of Buddhist charity or Christian charity, and look down on other 'brands' of charity. But charity cannot be sectarian; it is neither Christian, Buddhist, Hindu nor Moslem." [91] Many of these mistakes could be avoided if the three characteristics of life, especially *anattā*, were borne in mind, but Western thought as a whole is based on the tacit assumption of the ego, which even in its milder forms distorts perception. It may be objected that the Pali Canon abounds in discriminative labeling and that Buddhist analysis is exhaustive in its lists of categories. This is true, but it should be remembered that the texts are the basis of practice, and not a substitute for it. Buddha stated that eventually one has to go beyond suppositions or concepts, and in a well-known sutta of the Majjhima Nikāya it is stressed that the Dhamma is the means to the end. The image used is that of a raft, which one uses for crossing a river and does not, if one is wise, carry on one's back afterwards. A raft on dry land is a burden.

The way out of the discriminative impasses is the Middle Path. It is characteristic of the Dhamma in its avoidance of extremes. It recognises conventional truth (*vohāra-sacca*) and ultimate truth, (*paramattha-sacca*). The former is for everyday use, and life as we are bound to live it would be impossible without it. A "person" for instance is not an ultimate truth according to the Buddhist view, but obviously must be treated as humanity and common sense suggests. The two sorts of truth do not therefore exclude one another, and the Dhamma aims at a healthy balance between them. Each individual is so conditioned that he can see only a little objectively, in the ordinary sense, while in the ultimate sense his mind is so unconcentrated and undisciplined that he mistakes the impermanent for the permanent, the unpleasant for

91 W. Rāhula, *What the Buddha Taught*, Gordon Fraser, Bedford, p. 5.

the pleasant, and is so attached to the idea of the ego that he is rooted in ignorance (*avijjā*). Thus his relation to his own existence and the world is based on a fundamental error, and it is hardly surprising if he runs into difficulties. The Middle Path aims to correct these errors and their results. Man is not the exclusively intellectual creature some writers would have us believe, and the Path is designed to cater for the whole being. It has often been described,[92] but unless it is trodden it can scarcely be expected to produce results. As an analogy one might think of the difference between a thirsty traveler having a drink of water, and the same traveler just discussing the nature of drinking water as an academic proposition. To classify the Dhamma, which is based on Buddha's experience, is superfluous. The goal is Nibbāna and it represents, among other things, a solution to the problem of discriminative thinking: "Just as a rock of one solid mass remains unshaken by the wind, even so neither visible forms, nor sounds, nor odours, nor tastes, nor bodily impressions, neither the desired nor the undesired, can cause such a one to waver. Steadfast is his mind, gained is his deliverance." [93] This does not sound like the nihilism that some critics have reproached Buddhism with, and if anything has been annihilated it is only the bogus ego-feeling. In the Cūḷa-Māluṅkya Sutta[94] the Buddha explains that following the Path does not depend on speculative views as to whether the world is infinite or not, and in this foreshadows the modern approach, which prefers empirical experience and the tangible. This is of relevance to the present situation in the West, where there is a disparity between intellectual achievement and ordinary happiness. Quite rightly the Westerner is not willing to take a leap in the dark, and the Dhamma may be put to a practical test. Eventually even right views have to be put aside, as they are but the means. The Dhamma is not authoritarian, demanding that a person condemn other views, but shows how views arise. Nor is it suggested that liberation can be attained by formal methods: "Better than reciting a hundred verses composed of meaningless words is one text on hearing which one becomes peaceful." [95]

92 Rāhula, op. cit. p. 45.

93 A III 378.

94 MN 63.

95 Dhammapada, v. 102.

Buddha described attachment to rites and rituals as a hindrance. Such attachments are subjective, so that they hinder a clear view of reality and represent craving. Rites and rituals are likely to delude a person and deflect his attention from the effective parts of the Path, such as meditation or mind training.

Misconceptions about meditation abound in the West. Some think it is an artificial induction of esoteric states, and others think it is day-dreaming and a waste of time because the meditator does not appear to be "doing" anything. An English classic remarks: "The tendency of Indian mysticism to regard the Unitive life wholly in its passive aspects, as a total self-annihilation, a disappearance into the substance of the Godhead results, I believe, from a distortion of truth (due to temperament). The Oriental mystic presses on to lose his life upon the heights, but he does not come back and bring to his fellow-men the life-giving news that he has transcended mortality in the interests of the race." [96]

Leaving aside the use of theistic terminology, it would be a grave error to suppose that Buddha became enlightened by purely passive means. His trials in the forest were faced with determination. In the Majjhima Nikāya he frequently advises the monks not to be slothful, but to meditate, in order to avoid regrets later. Finally, it is difficult to ignore his exposition of the Dhamma during the last forty-five years of his life. After this it was transmitted orally, and later written down.[97]

Meditation requires a basis of calm, which results from a certain ethical standard, and it requires effort. One of the factors of enlightenment given in the texts is energy (*viriya*). Those who doubt whether this applies to meditation should not take it on trust, but try it for themselves … the benefits that may be experienced are considerable.

"Ehi-passika" …

Reprinted from *Sangha*, February 1962

— §§§ —

96 E. Underhill, *Mysticism*, Methuen, London, p. 434.

97 It is still common in countries such as Burma to find people who have committed a whole book, or more, to memory.

Guide Posts for Buddhists

Adapted from Theravadin Buddhist Writings

Sita Paulickpulle-Renfrew

Bodhi Leaves No. 20

First published: 1964

Guide Posts for Buddhists

Buddhists and Buddhism

One becomes a Buddhist by free determination; not by birth, nor race, nor by nationality; not by consecration, baptism, nor any other legally binding ceremony. Buddhism does not assume to be a state religion, nor can any hierarchy use it as such, for the Sangha (Monks) are merely more earnest than lay Buddhists in the search for truth and right action in practice.

The Buddhist monk at his best exemplifies the heights of evolution possible by meditation, and practice of the Buddha Path. As such he is worthy of honour and is respected, both as an evolved person and as a teacher of the Buddhist Way of Life. If he is not worthy of such honour he is merely disregarded, but not condemned.

According to Buddhist ethics no person or authority can ever impose upon another any code of conduct lower in morality or humanity than the individual himself desires. Neither can anyone make another act on a higher plane than the individual himself wishes. Each person can act only according to the level of his state of evolution, and has to live by the consequences thereof. Therefore it is the duty of all those who call themselves Buddhists to seek to become progressively more and more evolved by living according to the teachings of the Buddha, whether they belong to any Buddhist congregation or not.

The right to be a Buddhist and to practise the Buddha's way of life is the natural right of all beings. There should never be any compulsion by parents or monks. Hence any one can begin at any time, even discard it if the Way is too difficult for one's state of spiritual evolution. In Buddhism the individual is largely the architect of his spiritual structure ... he may seek instruction, but when he acts it has to be entirely of his own volition, and with the full understanding that he, and he alone can be held accountable for the resulting consequences. No monk or spiritual leader can ever command the conscience of a Buddhist, however humble such may be.

Buddhism when practised even imperfectly, but without hypocrisy, enlightens its adherents as to the real nature of the universe, including laws and forces operating therein. Buddhism discloses to the earnest seeker the essence of his being, showing him the true nature of the higher destiny which extends beyond this fleeting earth-life; by awakening his slumbering moral forces and faculties, it kindles in him a desire for the good and noble and true. Thus he seeks to become humane, patient, unselfish, and enduring, thereby gaining understanding of life's sorrows, confidence in his ultimate destiny, and courage to seek the highest aim of every living being … emancipation, consummation, Nirvana, which is a state of errorlessness. In as far as Buddhism does this, it is truly a religion!

Buddhism is also a philosophy, for it demands of its adherents not blind faith in any Creator-God, or revealed word, but a personal conviction gained and confirmed by one's own investigation, examination, and experimentation in dealing with the facts as they exist, using the Buddha-dhamma as a guide. Thus the precepts of Buddhism can be verified by earnest reflection because they are not based upon the will of an incomprehensible supreme being, nor upon any supernatural revelation of truth, nor upon the pronouncements of any pope, abbot, monk, patriarch, or any religious dignitary. Instead, the natural constitution of the world and of life as we experience it are freely studied and investigated in order to become enlightened as to the true nature of reality, resulting in a life so lived that the least harm results to oneself or fellowman.

Buddhism does not ever frighten the wrongdoer with threats of eternal punishment, nor does it bribe anyone with promises of eternal happiness in the life to come. Instead it seeks to clear up the eye of the erring one, who ensnared by delusion becomes confused and frightened. All Buddhism can do is to lead the honest struggler after right action on the way to further spiritual development and moral perfection until everything transitory becomes known to him as worthless. Therefore every desire for vengeance, all acts of angry rebellion or coercion and idle daydreaming, are recognized as being irrelevant, futile, and not conducive to the understanding of reality. Thus every type of prejudice, illusion, and confusion become known and ultimately disappear in the light of knowledge based on facts.

Accordingly it is the duty of the practising Buddhist to correlate in his own life the highest religio-moral principles known to him with the deepest philosophical-ethical truths discovered by mankind. Thus the true Buddhist seeks to gain wholeness both within himself and in unison with the rest of mankind wherever he may be, but he is ever aware that inner wholeness is more important than outward conformity. To a Buddhist all men are brothers who are born with differing talents and possibilities. Therefore they should be respected regardless of race, colour, creed, or status. Since a Buddhist seeks only to reform himself (though he gladly helps those who seek his aid or advice) he has no other mandate but to live his life without harming fellow beings or himself.

The Buddhist seeks to attain errorlessness[98] in this or in some future state of existence. When errorlessness is attained the life-cycle is ended, hence mere salvation from the consequences of error is not the goal of Buddhism. Instead, it is Enlightenment leading to an errorless life. This is ultimately possible only on an individual basis; any one, being enlightened, may help, but he can not achieve it for another, nor can enlightenment be organized en masse.

Avenues of Enlightenment

1. Through energetic effort—mental, spiritual, physical.
2. Through personal experience and experimentation with truth.
3. Through trials and temptation—mental, emotional, physical.
4. Through close and earnest investigation of facts as they exist.

---

98 "Errorlessness," in the author's terminology, means freedom from ignorance and delusion; and this, again, is identical with the full understanding, the perfect practice of the Ennobling Eightfold Path and the attainment of Nibbāna, which has been called the "errorless state" (*asammosa dhamma*).—Editor.

All these avenues may be explored individually or with the help of others, but whenever personal action is called for it is the individual who has to assume responsibility for resulting consequences. No Buddhist can ever blame another for his acts.

Enlightenment in Action [Righteousness]

1. Self is recognized as not consisting of an everlasting soul, but as an ever-changing flux that can become progressively more controlled.
2. The interdependence and interrelatedness of all life is accepted as natural, but no effort is made to enforce uniformity or conformity.
3. Because the life-flux is an ever-changing manifestation the practice of all-comprehensive kindness toward living beings becomes accepted behaviour.
4. Since good consequences are sought it is necessary to practise virtue and wisdom in thought, word, and deed.
5. The development and achievement of spiritual power within oneself rather than power over others is a goal leading to final emancipation.
6. Compassion toward every suffering being is practised in thought, word, and deed, whenever and wherever possible.
7. No remission of the results of error is expected by prayer or supplication to a Supreme Being, but there is willingness and ability to recognize error and work for its amelioration individually or in cooperation with others.
8. The fires of greed, lust, hatred, and ignorance are understood and conscientiously avoided until they cease to function in one's life.
9. Truth in every aspect is respected and searched for as a basis for making value-judgments.
10. Without self-righteousness or arrogance Nirvana is made the final goal of life.

Nirvana

All-Comprehensive Truth, Compassionately Expressed

The Four Ennobling Truths

1. Sorrow is everywhere, and ever present.
2. Sorrow is the result of uncontrolled desires.
3. Emancipation from sorrow is possible for those ready for self-discipline in every aspect of life.
4. The Path to Emancipation is Eightfold.

The Ennobling Eightfold Path

1. Right comprehension that dissipates delusion.
2. Right aspiration that hurts no one.
3. Right speech that makes for clarity.
4. Right conduct that brings no regret.
5. Right livelihood that causes neither discredit nor hurt to oneself or others.
6. Right endeavour that results in goodness.
7. Right mindfulness that gives controlled action.
8. Right meditation that prepares for Nirvana.

Results of Enlightened Action

1. Neither oneself nor others are harmed.
2. None is forced to act against the dictates of conscience.
3. A sense of inner peace and security is achieved.

Ten Cardinal Errors and Where They Originate

1. Murder, theft, lust: The Body.
2. Lying, slander, abuse, gossip: The Tongue
3. Greed, hatred, misconceptions: The Mind.

By persistent practice of the Ennobling Eightfold Path (in spite of failure and discouragement) the body, tongue, and mind will be progressively controlled, eliminating these errors.

Ten Negatives and Positives of Buddhist Living

1. Kill not, but have regard for life in all its manifestations.
2. Steal not, neither rob, realizing that each is the owner of only the fruits of deeds, good or bad.
3. Abstain from lust and lead a life of self-control, thereby achieving self-respect.
4. Lie not but be truthful, speaking the truth with discretion and kindness.
5. Invent not evil reports nor repeat them, but look for the good qualities of fellowmen, and defend them whenever possible.
6. Swear not, but speak with propriety and dignity, regardless of circumstances.
7. Waste not your time in gossip, but speak to the point or keep silent.
8. Covet not, nor envy, but rejoice at the good that others enjoy, knowing that sorrow is ever-present.
9. Cleanse your mind of malice and cherish no hatred, not even against those who seek to do you evil, because the evil-doer can not escape his own evil deeds, but you can avoid them.
10. Free your mind of ignorance and seek to know the truth in all matters that lead to a good and worthy life, as expounded by the Buddha.

The Four-fold Struggle for Perfection

1. Struggle, without violence, to prevent error from arising.
2. Struggle, without malice, to put away error that has arisen.
3. Struggle, with diligence, to increase the truth that is known.
4. Struggle, with mindfulness, to produce the truth that is not yet known.

This struggle for perfection may be carried on either alone or with the cooperation of others of like mind. Waste not time in idle persuasion.

The Five Moral Powers to be Cultivated

1. Self-reliant practice of the Dhamma by the individual, because no one can live another's life for him.
2. Indefatigable persistence in using the guidance of the Buddha will ensure success.
3. Mindful analysis of conduct to prevent errors from creeping in unobserved.
4. Concentration upon Buddhist goals in order to achieve good results in any endeavour.
5. Wisdom culled from personal experience, analysed in the light of Buddhist precepts. Without this, none can achieve Nirvana.

These moral powers should be carefully cultivated and consistently practised on an individual basis. They may not be forced upon any one by another, however strong. They should be encouraged and fostered at all times and in every circumstance.

The Buddhist Way of Life

Live quietly amid the noise and haste of life, remembering what peace there is in silence. As far as possible, without surrender, be on good terms with all persons, listen to the opinions of others and seek to understand their ideas, yet be unafraid to speak the truth as it is known, quietly and clearly, without arrogance or self-importance.

Whenever possible avoid loud, thoughtless and aggressive people; they are vexatious to the spirit, causing trouble wherever they are.

Never compare yourself with others, lest vanity or bitterness result; ever remember there will always be persons greater and smaller than yourself; such is the working of cause and effect (law of kamma).

Enjoy achievements and plans, being interested in a career however humble; by so doing, happiness is possible in this life of uncertainty and change.

Accept the good with the ill, knowing both are merited; but remember none can be his brother's keeper ... the evolved may seek to help another, never to live the other's life for him.

In all business matters exercise caution and intelligence, for always there are dishonest persons whose words are worthless.

Yet never blind yourself to the virtue there is; it is ever present like springs of water in a dreary desert.

Always be aware of the kindliness and goodwill of others in all dealings, for without these it is possible to become cynical; remember in the face of all disenchantment that kindness and goodwill can still work wonders.

Above all, be honest, feigning neither affection nor learning; hypocrisy is like a cancer that grows and grows.

Do not be disturbed by dark imaginings about yourself or a fellow man, or doubt and despair may result.

It is necessary to view all life dispassionately, for only thus is calmness of spirit attained, and without it life becomes burdensome.

At all times be reasonable with yourself and others, thus developing an understanding of life's difficulties, and making them serve the purposes of truth and goodness.

Never forget that yourself and others all have a right to be here or they would not be; take comfort from this all-pervading truth … be they stars, trees, animals, or human, they each follow their own laws and karmic pattern, and are not misplaced.

In all life's situations seek opportunities for performing good and useful acts, thus helping life to unfold with kindness as it should.

Whatever woe betides you, seek to express all the goodness possible, thus growing in graciousness and wisdom.

Develop the courage and wisdom to take kindly the counsel of the years, and gracefully surrender the attributes and excitements of youth, so that one may be better able to serve the needs of youth.

Above all, keep peace within yourself regardless of the noisy confusion around, because life presents opportunities making fullness of living possible, in spite of its many labours and seeming inconsistencies.

Whatever is experienced … be it shams, drudgery, broken dreams, faded hopes; be it success, fame, wealth, or glory … it is well to ever bear in mind that each life is essentially none other than what the individual makes it. It is still possible to live gloriously and well in spite of life's difficulties or worldly success.

Bear in mind that no one can ever take away the individual's initiative in the field of self-development in search of truth, happiness, and peace; this right can only be voluntarily surrendered by each individually; it can not ever be forcibly taken away from anyone, however weak or humble.

Therefore be of good cheer, and unafraid, continue the search for truth; this is the natural right of every human being that seeks to walk the Buddha Path.

A Buddhist's Reaction to Life

A Buddhist seeks to be ever mindful of the following:

1. No life is permanent; all states of mind and matter are in flux, therefore be undismayed.
2. Since all phenomena are impermanent, vanity and arrogance are meaningless.
3. Since all phenomena are consequential, act mindfully at all times.
4. Evolution depends greatly on the karmic pattern, which is always capable of modification by the individual himself, with or without the co-operation of others.
5. If need arises, dignified and firm opposition to undesirable situations should be expressed by groups or individually, in a spirit of calm good-will and a sense of humour.
6. Whether life is a challenge or a burden depends on the individual's view-point, not on circumstance or the will of others.
7. Sorrow is ever present; it is increased by the heedless, the careless, the arrogant, the knave, and the fool; it is minimized by the intelligently mindful, the conscientious, the humbly good, and the wise.
8. Even "righteous" anger is a stumbling block to one who would follow the Buddha Path.
9. Life cannot be effective if oriented upon the past or the future; it has to be lived in the ever-changing present,

utilizing every opportunity to progress toward the ultimate goal.

10. By observing rites and rituals no one can be absolved from the consequences of erroneous action in thought, word, or deed. Compassion and understanding should be extended toward the erring one, but "forgiveness of sins" is not possible for any god or fellowman to grant, nor can any person achieve it by performing acts of penance or contrition.
11. Delusion is the basic cause of all error and unhappiness; it should be dispelled by understanding the nature of reality, accepted without vain regrets. Error can be counteracted only by investigating facts and acting according to the dictates of truth and goodness.
12. On whatever level the individual seeks to function, careful preparation is necessary for effective living. Those who seek to do this find no disadvantages to achieving the goal of Nirvana.

— §§§ —

Aspects of Buddhism

Piyadassi Thera

Bodhi Leaves No. 21

First published: 1964

Aspects of Buddhism

A Word to the Reader

Today we are living in an age of science—an age where man is inclined to accept the truth of anything by observation and experiment rather than by mere belief. With the recent advances of science, man is becoming more and more rationalistic in his outlook and blind belief is fast disappearing.

Science in general has been somewhat of a threat to religion. This threat has been levelled against religious conceptions of man and the universe from the time of Copernicus, Galileo, and Bruno (17th century) who were instrumental in altering erroneous notions of the universe. The theory of evolution and modern psychology went against the accepted religious conception of man and his mind recorded in 'Sacred Writings.'

Has Buddhism suffered the same fate? Does modern science look unkindly at Buddhism? Whatever the critics of Buddhism may say, the dispassionate reader of early Buddhism will realize that the basic principles of Buddhism are in harmony with the findings of science and not opposed to them in any way.

"Early Buddhism emphasizes the importance of the scientific outlook in dealing with the problems of morality and religion. Its specific 'dogmas' are said to be capable of verification. And its general account of the nature of man and the universe is one that accords with the findings of science rather than being at variance with them.

"There is of course no theory of biological evolution as such mentioned in the Buddhist texts, but man and society as well as worlds are pictured as changing and evolving in accordance with causal laws.

"Then, in psychology, we find early Buddhism regarding man as a psycho-physical unit whose 'psyche' is not a changeless soul but a dynamic continuum, composed of a conscious mind as well as an unconscious in which is stored the residue of emotionally charged memories going back to childhood as well as into past lives. Such a mind is said to be impelled to act under the influence of three types of desires—the desire for sense-gratification (*kāma-taṇhā*), the desire for self-preservation (*bhava-taṇhā*) and the desire for destruction (*vibhava-taṇhā*). Except for the belief in rebirth, this conception of the mind sounds very modern, and one cannot also fail to observe the parallel between the threefold desire in Buddhism and the Freudian conceptions of the *eros, libido,* and *thanatos*." [99]

It must be mentioned that the Buddhist way of life, the Buddhist method of grasping the highest truth, awakening from ignorance to full knowledge, does not depend on mere academic intellectual development—on science—but on the adoption of a practical teaching that leads the follower to enlightenment and final deliverance. The Buddha was more concerned with beings than with inanimate nature. His sole object was to unravel the mystery of existence so far as the being is concerned and thereby to solve the problem of becoming. This he did by comprehending in all their fullness the Four Noble Truths, the eternal verities of life. This knowledge of the truths he tried to impart to those who sought it, and never forced it upon others. He never compelled people to follow him, for compulsion and coercion were alien to his method of teaching. He did not encourage his disciples to believe him blindly, but wished them to investigate his teaching which invited the seeker to 'come and see' (*ehipassiko*). It is seeing and understanding, and not blind believing, that the Buddha approves. To understand the world within, one must develop the inner faculties, one's mind.

Today, there is ceaseless work going on in all directions to improve the world. Scientists are pursuing their methods and experiments with undiminished vigour and determination. Modern discoveries and methods of communications and contact have produced startling results. All these improvements, though they have their benefits and advantages, are entirely material and external in nature. The scientist has brought the external world

---

99 Dr. K. N. Jayatilleke, *Religion and Science*, Wheel No. 3.

under his sway, and seems to promise that he can turn his world into a paradise. But man cannot yet control his mind, despite all the achievements of science. Within this conflux of mind and body of man, however, there are unexplored marvels to occupy men of science for many years.

The students of Buddhism who are not inclined to read large volumes on the Buddha and his teaching, may, perhaps, find this booklet agreeable and useful. Those, however, bent on a comprehensive and detailed study of Buddhism, may read, *The Buddha's Ancient Path*[100] by the present author.

The Buddha

The Buddha, the founder of the great religion called Buddhism, lived in North India in the 6th century before Christ. Siddhattha (Siddhartha in Sanskrit) was his personal name. Gotama or Gautama was his family name. His father, Suddhodana, ruled over the land of the Sakyans at Kapilavatthu in the Nepal frontier. Mahāmāyā, princess of the Koliyas, was Suddhodana's queen. She gave birth to her only child, Siddhattha, in the Lumbini grove. Lumbini or Rummindei, the name by which it is now locally known, is a hundred miles north of Varanasi (Benares) and within sight of the snow-capped Himalayas. At this memorable spot is where the prince, the future Buddha, was born. Emperor Asoka of India, 316 years after the event, erected a mighty pillar which is still to be seen.

According to the custom of the time, at the early age of sixteen, the prince was married to a beautiful princess named Yasodharā who was of the same age as the prince. Lacking none of the good things of life, he lived knowing not of woe. But with the advance of age and maturity, the prince began to glimpse the woes of the world. The more he came into contact with the world outside his palace walls, the more convinced he became that the world was lacking in true happiness.

Then, at the age of 29, in the flower of youthful manhood, on the day Princess Yasodharā gave birth to his only son, Rāhula, he left the palace. Giving up a crown that held the promise of power and

100 Buddhist Publication Society, Kandy, Sri Lanka.

glory, and in the guise of an ascetic, he retreated into forest solitude to seek a solution for the problem of life, in quest of the supreme security from bondage, Nibbāna. This was the great renunciation.

Dedicating his life to the noble task of discovering a remedy for life's universal ills, he sought guidance from famous religious teachers hoping that they, masters of meditation, would show him the way to deliverance. But their range of knowledge, their ambit of spiritual experience, was insufficient to grant him what he earnestly sought. He was not satisfied with anything short of supreme enlightenment. He left them again in search of the still unknown. Five other ascetics who admired his determined effort joined him.

There was, and still is, a belief in India among many of her ascetics that purification and final deliverance from ill could be achieved by rigorous self-mortification, and the ascetic Gotama decided to test the truth of it. He began a determined struggle to subdue his body, in the hope that his mind, set free from the shackles of the body, might be able to soar to the heights of liberation. Most zealous was he in these practices. He lived on leaves and roots, on a steadily reduced pittance of food. The utter paucity of nourishment left him a physical wreck.

"Rigorous have I been in my ascetic discipline. Rigorous have I been beyond all others. Like wasted, withered reeds became all my limbs...." In such words as these, in later years, having attained full enlightenment, did the Buddha give his disciples an awe inspiring description of his early penances.[101]

Struggling thus for six long years, he came to death's very door, but he found himself no nearer to his goal. The utter futility of self-mortification became abundantly clear to him by his own experience; his experiment for enlightenment had failed. But, undeterred, his still active mind searched for new paths to the cherished goal. He gave up self-mortification and extreme fasting and partook of normal food. Now his five companions left him disappointed; for they thought that he had given up the effort to a life of abundance.

101 See Bodhi Leaves, A Series No. 7. *Master's Quest for Light* by R. Abeysekera.

Nevertheless, with firm determination and complete faith in his own purity and strength, unaided by any teacher, accompanied by none, the Bodhisatta (as he is known before he attained enlightenment) resolved to make his final quest in complete solitude. Cross-legged he sat under a tree, which later became known as the Bodhi tree or the 'Tree of Enlightenment,' on the bank of the river Nerañjarā, at Gaya (now known as Buddha-Gaya), 'a pleasant spot soothing to the senses and stimulating to the mind.'

Applying himself to 'mindfulness on in-and out breathing' (*ānāpānasati*), the Bodhisatta Gotama entered upon and dwelt in the four meditative absorptions (*jhāna*, Sanskrit, *dhyāna*) by gradual stages. While thus seated in meditation he understood as it really is the Four Truths: 1. this is suffering or unsatisfactoriness (*dukkha*), 2. this is the arising of suffering, 3. this is the cessation of suffering, 4. this is the path leading to the cessation of suffering. He understood as it really is: these are taints (*āsavas*), this is the arising of the taints, this is the path leading to the cessation of the taints.

Thus did Siddhattha Gotama, on a full moon of May, at the age of 35, attain Supreme Enlightenment by comprehending in all their fullness the Four Noble Truths, the Eternal Verities, and become the Buddha, the Enlightened One.

Two months after his Enlightenment, the Buddha made up his mind to communicate the Dhamma, the truth, he had realized, to his former friends, the five ascetics. Knowing that they were living at Vārānasi (Benares), in the Deer Park at Isipatana (modern Saranath) still steeped in the unmeaning rigours of extreme asceticism, he left Gayā for distant Vārānasi, India's holy city, walking by stages a distance of 150 miles. There at the Deer Park he rejoined them.

Now, on the full moon day of July, the Master addressed the five ascetics: "Monks, these two extremes ought not to be cultivated by the recluse, by one gone forth from the house-life. What two? Sensual indulgence and self-mortification, which lead to no good. The middle way, monks, understood by the Tathāgata, the Perfect One, after he had avoided the extremes, gives vision, knowledge, and leads to calm, realization, enlightenment, Nibbāna. And what, monks, is that middle way? It is this Noble Eightfold Path, namely:

> Right Understanding,
> Right Thought,
> Right Speech,
> Right Action,
> Right Livelihood,
> Right Effort,
> Right Mindfulness,
> Right Concentration." [102]

Thus did the Enlightened One proclaim the Dhamma and set in motion the matchless 'Wheel of Truth' (*anuttaraṃ dhammacakkaṃ*).

When the number of followers increased up to sixty, the Buddha addressed them and said: "Go now and wander for the welfare and happiness of many, out of compassion for the world. Let not two of you proceed in the same direction. Proclaim the Dhamma that is excellent in the beginning, excellent in its progress, excellent in the end, possessed of meaning and the letter and utterly perfect." [103] Thus did the Buddha commence his sublime mission which lasted to the end of his life. With his disciples he walked the highways and by-ways of India enfolding all within the aura of his boundless compassion and wisdom.

The Buddha made no distinction of caste, clan or class when communicating the Dhamma. Men and women from different walks of life—the poor and the needy, the lowliest and the lost, the literate and the illiterate, aristocrats, brahmins, outcasts, princes and paupers, saints and criminals—listened to him who showed the path to peace and enlightenment.

Since he was one who always acted in conformity with what he preached, his acts were always dominated by the four Sublime States *(brahma vihāra)* namely: unbounded loving kindness *(mettā)*, compassion *(karuṇā)*, sympathetic joy *(muditā)*, equanimity *(upekkhā)*.[104]

---

102 Vin I 10, S V 420

103 Vinaya Mahāvagga

104 See *Four Sublime States*, by Nyanaponika Thera. Wheel No. 6.

The Buddha never encouraged animosity and strife. Addressing the disciples he once said: "I quarrel not with the world, monks, it is the world that quarrels with me. An exponent of the Dhamma, doctrine, quarrels not with anyone in the world."[105]

Though the Order of the Sangha, the ordained disciples, began its career with only sixty disciples, it expanded into thousands. As a result of the increasing number of monks, monasteries came into being and in later times, monastic Indian Universities, like Nālandā and Vikramasilā, became cultural centres which gradually influenced the whole of Asia, and through it, the mental life of mankind.

After a successful ministry of 45 years the Buddha passed away at the age of 80 at Kusinārā (in modern Uttara Pradesh about 120 miles north-east of Vārānasi) with a final admonition to his followers:

"Subject to constant change are all conditioned things. Strive on with heedfulness."

Buddhism penetrated into many a land and is today the religion of over 600 million, more than one fifth of the world's population. Today Buddhism is found in Sri Lanka (Ceylon), Burma, Thailand, Cambodia, Laos, Vietnam, Nepal, Tibet, China, Japan, Mongolia, Korea, Taiwan, in some parts of India, Chittagong in Pakistan, Malaya and in some parts of Indonesia. Several Western countries with a Buddhist Sangha are now qualifying themselves to be included in this list.

Buddhism made rapid strides chiefly due to its intrinsic worth and its appeal to the reasoning mind, but there were other factors that accelerated its progress; never did the messengers of the Dhamma (*dhamma-dūta*) use any iniquitous methods in spreading the doctrine. The only weapon they wielded was that of universal love and compassion. Furthermore, Buddhism penetrated to these countries peaceably without disturbing the creeds that were already in existence. Buddhism was thus able to diffuse itself through a great variety of cultures throughout the world.

---

105 S III 138

Some Salient Characteristics of the Buddha

One of the noteworthy characteristics that distinguishes the Buddha from all other religious teachers is that he was a human being with no connection whatsoever with a God or any other 'supernatural' being. He was neither a God, nor an incarnation of God, nor any mythological figure. He was a man, but a superman, an extraordinary man (*acchariya manussa*). He was beyond the human state inwardly, though living the life of a human being outwardly. Just as he is for this reason called a unique being, man par-excellence (*purisuttama*).

Depending on his own unremitting energy, unaided by any teacher, human or divine, he achieved the highest mental and intellectual attainment, reached the acme of purity, and was perfect in the best qualities of human nature. He was an embodiment of compassion and wisdom, which became the guiding principles in his Dispensation (*sāsana*).

Through personal experience, he understood the supremacy of man. The Buddha never claimed to be a saviour who endeavoured to save 'souls' by means of a revealed religion. Through his own perseverance and understanding, he proved that infinite possibilities are latent in man and that it must be man's endeavour to develop and unfold these possibilities. He proved by his own experience that enlightenment and deliverance lie absolutely and entirely in man's hand. Being an exponent of the strenuous life, by precept and example, the Buddha encouraged his disciples to cultivate self-reliance.[106]

It was also the Buddha who, for the first time in the world's history, taught that deliverance could be attained independently of an external agency. That deliverance from suffering, conflicts of life or unsatisfactoriness, must be wrought out and fashioned by each one for himself upon the anvil of his own actions. The Buddha warns his disciples against shifting the burden to an external agency (a saviour, a God or Brahma), directs them to the ways of discrimination and research, and urges them to get busy with the real task of developing their inner forces and qualities. He says: "I

106 Dhp 160

have directed you towards deliverance. The Dhamma, the Truth, is to be self-realized." [107]

The Enlightened Ones, the men who saw truth, are the true helpers, but Buddhists do not pray to them. They only revere the revealers of Truth for having pointed out the path to true happiness and deliverance. Deliverance is what one must secure for oneself. Buddhist monks are not priests who perform rites and sacrifices. They do not administer sacraments and pronounce absolution. A Buddhist monk cannot, and does not, stand as an intermediary between man and 'supernatural' powers. For Buddhism teaches that each individual is solely responsible for his own liberation. Hence there is no need to win the favour of a mediating priest. "You yourselves should strive on; the Buddhas only show the path." [108] The path is the same ancient path trodden and pointed out by the Enlightened Ones of all ages. It is the Noble Eightfold Path leading to Enlightenment and the highest security, Nirvana.

Another distinguishing characteristic is that the Buddha never preserved his supreme knowledge for himself alone. To the Buddha such a wish is utterly inconceivable. Perfect Enlightenment, the discovery and realization of the Four Noble Truths (Buddhahood), is not the prerogative of a single being chosen by Divine Providence, nor is it a unique and unrepeatable event in human history. It is an achievement open to anyone who earnestly strives for perfect purity and true wisdom, and with inflexible will cultivates the Noble Eightfold Path.

When communicating the doctrine (Dhamma) to his disciples, the Buddha made no distinction whatsoever amongst them; for there were not specially chosen favourite disciples. There is not even an indication that the Master entrusted the Dispensation (*sāsana*) to any particular disciple before he passed away. He did not appoint anyone as his successor. In this connection, it is interesting to note that the Buddha made clear to his disciples, before he passed away, that he never thought of controlling the Order of monks, the

---

107 MN 38
108 Dhp 276

Sangha. Addressing the monks who assembled round his death-bed the Master said:

"The Doctrine and the Discipline (*dhamma vinaya*) which I have set forth and laid down for you, let them after I am gone be the teacher to you." [109] Even during his life time it was the Dhamma-vinaya (Doctrine and Discipline) that controlled and guided the monks.

Characteristic, again, is the Buddha's method of teaching the Dhamma. He disapproved of those who professed to have 'secret doctrine' saying, "secrecy is the hallmark of false doctrine." In his own words, "the Dhamma proclaimed by the Tathāgata, the Perfect One, shines when revealed and not when hidden." [110] Addressing the Venerable Ānanda, the personal attendant of the Master, the Buddha said: "I have taught the Dhamma, Ānanda, without making any distinction between exoteric and esoteric doctrine, for in respect of the Truth, Ānanda, the Tathāgata has no such thing as the 'closed fist' of a teacher who hides some essential knowledge from the pupil." [111]

He declared the Dhamma freely and equally to all. He kept nothing back and never wished to extract from his disciples blind and submissive faith in him and his teaching. He insisted on discriminative examination and intelligent inquiry. In no uncertain terms did he urge critical investigation when he addressed the inquiring Kālāmas in a discourse[112] that has been rightly called 'the first charter of free thought.'

Buddhism

What the Buddha taught is popularly known as Buddhism. Some prefer to call it religion, others call it a philosophy, still others think of it as both religion and philosophy. It may, however, be correct to call it a 'Way of Life.' But that does not mean that Buddhism is nothing more than an ethical code. Far from it. It is a way of moral, spiritual and intellectual training leading to complete freedom of

---

109 DN 16
110 AN 1
111 DN 16
112 See Wheel No. 8, *Kālāma Sutta* translated by Soma Thera.

mind. The Buddha himself called his teaching 'Dhamma-vinaya,' the Doctrine and Discipline.

Those who wish to call Buddhism a religion may bear in mind that it is not 'Action or conduct indicating belief in, reverence for, and desire to please, a divine ruling power; the exercise or practice of rites or observances implying this . . . recognition on the part of man of some higher unseen power as having control of his destiny, and as being entitled to obedience, and worship.' [113]

Those who prefer to call Buddhism a philosophy may note that it is not mere, 'love of, nor inducing the search after, wisdom.' Buddhism also advocates the search for truth. But it is no mere speculative reasoning, a theoretical structure, a mere acquiring and storing of knowledge. It is an encouragement of a practical application of the teaching that leads the follower to dispassion, enlightenment and final deliverance.

The Buddha emphasizes the practical aspect of his teaching, the application of knowledge to life—looking into life and not merely at it. Wisdom gained by understanding and development of the qualities of the mind and heart is wisdom par-excellence. It is saving knowledge, and not mere speculation, logic or specious reasoning. It is not mere theoretical understanding that matters. For the Buddha, the entire teaching is just the realization of the unsatisfactory nature of all phenomenal existence or conflicts of life (*dukkha*) and the cultivation of the path leading away from this unsatisfactoriness. This is his philosophy. His sole intention and aim was to explain it all in detail: the problem of suffering or unsatisfactoriness, the universal fact of life, and to make people feel its full force and to convince them of it.

Though we call the teaching of the Buddha 'Buddhism,' thus including it among the 'isms' and 'ologies,' it does not really matter what we label it. Call it religion, philosophy, Buddhism or by any other name you like. These labels are of little significance to one who goes in search of truth and deliverance. The Buddha has definitely told us what he explains and what he does not explain.

113 *The Short Oxford English Dictionary*, 1954, under the word Religion.

What the Buddha Taught

Once the Buddha was living at Kosambi (near Allahabad) in a Siṃsapa Grove. Then, gathering a few siṃsapa leaves in his hand, the Buddha addressed the monks:

"What do you think, monks; which is greater in quantity, the handful of siṃsapa leaves gathered by me, or what is in the forest overhead?"

"Not many, trifling, Venerable Sir, are the leaves in the handful gathered by the Blessed One; many are the leaves in the forest overhead."

"Even so, monks, many are the things I have fully realized, but not declared unto you; few are the things I have declared unto you. And why, monks, have I not declared these? They, monks, are indeed, not useful, are not essential to the life of purity, they do not lead to disgust, to dispassion, to cessation, to tranquillity, to full understanding, to enlightenment, to Nibbāna. That is why, monks, they are not declared by me.

"And what is it, monks, that I have declared? This is suffering—this have I declared. This is the arising of suffering—this have I declared.

"This is the cessation of suffering—this have I declared.

"This is the path leading to the cessation of suffering—this have I declared.

"And why monks, have I declared these truths? They are indeed useful, are essential to the life of purity; they lead to disgust, to dispassion, to cessation, to tranquillity, to full understanding, to enlightenment, to Nibbāna. That is why, monks, they are declared by me." [114] Thus spoke the Buddha.

To understand this unequivocal utterance is to understand the entire teaching of the Buddha. It would appear that what can be called the discovery of a Buddha, is just these Four Truths. The rest are logical developments and more detailed explanations of the Four Noble Truths. This is the typical teaching of the

---

114 S V 437

Buddhas of all ages.[115] The supremacy of the Four Truths in the teaching of the Buddha becomes abundantly clear from the message of the Siṃsapa Grove as from the message of the Deer Park at Benares.

All the Four Truths are associated with the so-called being. They are not to be found in the external world. Referring to these Truths, the Buddha says in another context: "In this very body, a fathom in length, with its consciousness and perception, I declare are the world, its arising, its cessation and the path that leads to the cessation of the world." [116]

Limited space prevents one from discussing the Four Truths in detail. In brief, the first Noble Truth, suffering or unsatisfactoriness, which is known as dukkha in the Pali language, is used in more than one sense in the early Buddhist scriptures. It is used in the psychological sense, physical sense and in the philosophical sense, according to the context.

To those who try to see things as they really are, the concept of dukkha is no insignificant thing. It is the keystone in Buddhist thought. To ignore this essential concept is to ignore the remaining three Truths. The importance of knowing dukkha is seen in these words of the Buddha: "He who sees dukkha sees also the arising, the ceasing, and the path leading to the ceasing of dukkha." To one who denies dukkha, a path leading to deliverance from dukkha is meaningless.

We must also bear in mind that the recognition of dukkha as a universal fact, however, is not a denial of pleasure or happiness. The Buddha, the Lord over dukkha, never denied happiness in life when he spoke of the universality of dukkha. In the text, Aṅguttara Nikāya, there is a long enumeration of the happinesses that beings are capable of enjoying.

To those who view the sentient world from the correct angle, that is with dispassionate discernment, one thing becomes abundantly clear: there is only one problem in the world—that of dukkha, unsatisfactoriness. All other problems, known and unknown, are

---

115 Vinaya Mahāvagga, II 48

116 A II 48

included in this one which is universal. If anything becomes a problem, there is bound to be unsatisfactoriness, or if we like, conflict—conflict between our desires and the facts of life. And naturally man's every endeavour is to solve the problem, in other words, to remove unsatisfactoriness, to control conflict—which is pain, a wretched state of mind.

Can you call this pessimism or label the Buddha as a pessimist? As a matter of fact, Buddhism is neither pessimism nor optimism. Buddhism tries to show the realistic view of life and the world. The Buddha's teaching is a message radiating joy and hope and not a defeatist philosophy of pessimism.

In the second Truth, the Buddha explains the cause of this dukkha, unsatisfactoriness. As there is, in Buddhist thought, no arbitrary creator who controls the destinies of man, Buddhism does not attribute dukkha, or its arising, to an external agency, to a 'supernatural' power, but seeks it in the innermost recesses of man himself. It is craving, backed by ignorance, the crowning corruption of all our madness, that brings about unsatisfactoriness. This most powerful force, craving or thirst, keeps existence going. Life depends on the desires of life. Craving is the propeller of not only the present existence, but past and future existence too. Craving, however, is not regarded as the First Cause with a capital 'F' and 'C.' Craving, like all other things, physical or mental, is also conditioned, interdependent and relative. Hence, it can cease.

The third Truth is cessation of this dukkha. In the words of the Buddha, it is 'the complete cessation of (*nirodha*), giving up (*cāga*), abandoning *(paṭinissagga)*, release (*mutti*), and detachment *(anālayo)* from that very craving.' [117] Complete cessation of craving implies Nibbāna, the *summum bonum* or the highest happiness spoken of in Buddhism. But it is not something merely to be theorised about, but realized. Though the sentient being experiences the unsatisfactory nature of life, and knows first-hand what suffering is, what defilements are, and what it is to crave, he surely knows not what the total extirpation of defilements is, because he has not experienced it. If ever he does, he will know through self-

117 S V 421

realization, what it is to be without defilements, what Nibbāna, or reality is, what true happiness is.

The fourth Truth is the path leading to the cessation of craving. It is the Noble Eightfold Path:

Right Understanding Right Thought	Wisdom Group (paññā)
Right Speech Right Action Right Livelihood	Virtue Group (sīla)
Right Effort Right Mindfulness Right Concentration	Concentration Group (samādhi)

The Eightfold Path is here arranged in accordance with the three groups: virtue, concentration and wisdom. These three are not isolated divisions, but integral parts of the Path. This idea is crystallized in the clear admonition of the Buddhas of all ages:

The giving up of all evil,
The cultivation of the good,
The cleansing of one's mind,
This is the Buddhas' teaching.[118]

Dukkha, suffering, is the dire disease. It is to be known and not ignored. Craving, the cause, is to be removed. The Eightfold Path is to be practised, to be cultivated, for it is the remedy. With the knowledge of suffering, with the removal of craving, through the practice of the Path, Nibbāna's realization is ensured. In this connection the Buddha's reply to Sela, the brahmin, who doubted the Master's enlightenment is interesting:

I know what should be known. What should
Be cultivated I have cultivated.
What should be abandoned that have I let go.
Hence, O brahmin, I am Buddha, the Awakened One.[119]

118 Dhp 183
119 Sn 558.

The Doctrine of Karma

There are two other principal teachings of the Buddha that a student of Buddhism ought to be acquainted with. They are *kamma (karma)* and rebirth or repeated existence. These are two principal tenets of Hinduism too, but there they are permeated with the notion of Self or Soul (Ātman) which Buddhism categorically denies.

Karma is the law of moral causation. Basically it is volition. 'Volition, O monks, I declare is kamma' is Buddha's definition. Volition, which is will, a force, is a factor of the mind. Karma is the action or seed. The effect or fruit is known as *kamma-vipāka*. Volitions may be good or ill, so actions may be wholesome or unwholesome, according to their results. This endless play of action and reaction, cause and effect, seed and fruit, continues in perpetual motion, and this is becoming *(bhava)*, a continually changing process of the psycho-physical phenomena of existence.

Having willed, man acts (through body, speech and mind), and actions bring about reactions. Craving gives rise to deed; deed produces results; results, in turn, bring about new desires, new craving. This process of cause and effect, actions and reactions, is natural law. It is a law in itself, with no need for a law-giver. An eternal agency, or power, or God that punishes the ill deeds, and rewards the good deeds, has no place in Buddhist thought. Man is always changing, either for good or for ill. This changing is unavoidable and depends entirely on his own will, his own action, and on nothing else. This is merely the universal natural law of the conservation of energy extended to the moral domain.

The world seems to be imperfect and ill balanced. Amongst us human beings, let alone the animal kingdom, we see some born in misery, sunk in deep distress and supremely unhappy; others are born into a state of abundance and happiness, enjoy a life of luxury and know nothing of the world's woe. Again, a chosen few are gifted with keen intellect and great mental capacity, while many are steeped in ignorance. How is it that some of us are blessed with health, beauty and friends, while others are pitiful weaklings, destitute and lonely? How is it that some are born to enjoy long life while others pass away in the full bloom of youth?

Why are some blessed with affluence, fame and recognition, while others are utterly neglected? These are intricate problems that demand a solution.

If we inquire we will find that these wide differences are not the work of an external agency, or a superhuman being with understanding and compassion, but are due to our own actions and reactions. We are responsible for our deeds whether good or ill. We make our karma. A Buddhist who understands the operation of the law of karma would say:

According to the seed that's sown
So is the fruit ye reap therefrom.
The doer of good will gather good,
The doer of evil, evil reaps.
Sown is the seed and planted well,
Thou shalt enjoy the fruit thereof.[120]

Here, however, we must understand that the Buddhist doctrine of karma is not fatalism, is not a philosophical doctrine to the effect that human action is not free but necessarily determined by motives which are regarded as external forces acting upon the will or predetermined by God. The Buddha neither subscribed to the theory that all things are unalterably fixed; that all things happen by inevitable necessity, that is, Strict Determinism (*niyati-vāda*); nor did he uphold the theory of Complete Indeterminism (*adhicca-samuppanna*).

The Doctrine of Rebirth

According to Buddhism there is no life after death, or life before birth, independent of karma or volitional actions. Karma is the corollary of rebirth; rebirth, on the other hand, is the corollary of karma.

Man today is the result of millions of repetitions of thoughts and acts. He is not ready-made; he becomes and is still becoming. His character is predetermined by his own choice. The thought, the act, which he chooses—that, by habit, he becomes.

120 S I 227, *The Kindred Sayings*, i. p. 293.

Birth precedes death, and death, on the other hand, precedes birth, and the pair thus accompany each other in bewildering succession. Still, there is no Soul or Self or fixed entity that passes from birth to birth. Though man comprises a psycho-physical unit of mind and matter, the 'psyche' or mind is not a soul or a self, in the sense of an enduring entity, something ready-made and permanent. It is a force, a dynamic continuum capable of storing up memories not only of this life but also past lives. To the scientist, matter is energy in a state of stress, change without real substance. To the psychologist, the 'psyche' is no more a fixed entity. When the Buddha emphatically stressed that the so-called 'being' or 'individual' is but a combination of physical and mental forces or energies, a change with continuity, did he not antedate modern science and modern psychology by twenty-five centuries?

This change of continuity, this psychophysical process, which is patent to us in this life, does not cease at death, but continues incessantly. It is the dynamic mind-flux that is termed as karmic-energy, will, thirst, desire or craving. This mighty force, this will to live, keeps life going. According to Buddhism, it is not only human life, but the entire sentient world that is drawn by this tremendous force—this mind[121] with its mental factors, good or ill.

Man's Deliverance

Man's passions are disturbing. The lust or craving of blinded beings has brought about hatred and all other sufferings. The enemy of the whole world is lust; through which all evils come to living beings. This lust, when obstructed by some cause, is transformed into wrath and man falls into the net which he himself has made of his passion for pleasure, like the spider into its own web.[122]People both in the East and West seem to have become more and more materially-minded, and, as they have almost ignored the mental realm—the world within—they seem to be lop-sided and even ill-disposed. Slogans and political propaganda seem to mould man's mind, and life seems to be mechanical; man has become a puppet controlled by others.

---

121 A II 177

122 Dhp 347

Modern man seems to be enmeshed in all sorts of ideas, views, opinions and ideologies both wise and foolish; he is film-fed, television minded and radio-trained. Today, what is presented by the newspapers, radio, television, some novels and pictures, by certain literature on sex psychology and by sex-ridden films tend to confuse man and turn him from the path of rectitude and understanding. Today, more than at any other time, right understanding, calm and compassion are needed to guide mankind through the turmoil of life, to 'straighten the restless mind as a fletcher straightens his shaft,' [123] and to make it conform to justice and rectitude.

Refraining from intoxicants and becoming heedful, establishing himself in patience and purity, the wise man trains his mind. A calm attitude preserved at all times bespeaks a man of culture. It is not too hard a task for a man to be calm when all things around him are favourable, but to be composed of mind in the midst of unfavourable circumstances is hard. It is this difficult thing that is worth doing. For by such control one builds strength of character. Psychological changes come very slowly. It is through training in quiet contemplation that a quiet mind is achieved. Can we also achieve it? Lord Horder's answer is interesting: . . . "The answer is 'Yes.' But how? Well, not by doing 'some great thing.' 'Why were the saints saints?' someone asked. And the answer came: 'Because they were cheerful when it was difficult to be cheerful and patient when it was difficult to be patient. They pushed on when they wanted to stand still, and kept silent when they wanted to talk.' That was all. So simple, but so difficult. A matter of mental hygiene..." [124]

No amount of logic and argument on the perfecting of life leads us to our desired goal. No amount of speculation brings us near to our aim. We should learn to tame our fickle mind; for control of mind is the key to happiness. It is the force behind all true achievement. The movements of a person void of control are purposeless and unsettled. A certain aloofness, therefore, from the business of life and withdrawal into the silence is helpful in

---

123 Dhp 33

124 *The Hygiene of a Quiet Mind.* Trueman Wood Lecture delivered before the Royal Society of Arts, 1938.

contacting the power within and overcoming the weakness and limitations of ordinary experience.

For an understanding of the world within, science may not be of much help to us. Ultimate truth cannot be found in science. For that we need the guidance, the instruction, of a competent and genuine seer whose clarity of vision and depth of insight penetrate into the deepest recesses of life and cognize the true nature that underlies all appearances. The Buddha is such a seer, and his path to deliverance is open to all genuine followers. It is different from other paths to 'salvation,' for the Buddha teaches that each individual, whether layman or monk, is solely responsible for his own liberation.

The path pointed out by the Buddha for man's moral and mental development is the Noble Eightfold Path which is Buddhism in practice. This when carefully and fully cultivated lifts man from lower to higher levels of mental life; leads him from darkness to light, from passion to dispassion, from turmoil to tranquillity.

Our attempts to reach purity and peace, are at times, not crowned with success. But failure does not matter so long as we are sincere in our attempts, pure in our motives, and strive again and again without stopping. The Buddha says, "Like the skilful smith who blows away the dross in gold bit by bit, man must try to purge his life of impurities."[125] A child learns to stand and walk gradually and with difficulty. So too have all great ones, in the march to perfection, moved from stage to stage through repeated failure to final success.

To put aside each ill of old,
To leave no noble deed undone;
To cleanse the mind, in these behold,
The teachings of the Enlightened One.[126]

May All Living Beings Be Well and Happy!

— §§§ —

---

125 Dhp 239
126 Dhp 183

Great Sayings of Anāgārika Dharmapāla

Collected by

Bhikshu Sangharakshita

with a Life Sketch by

Buddhadāsa P. Kirthisinghe

Bodhi Leaves No. 22

First published: 1964

Publisher's Note

This booklet is published as a tribute to the birth centenary of the late Venerable Anāgārika Dharmapāla (17th September 1964). The sayings reproduced here have been collected by Bhikshu Sangharakshita from Vols. XVI, XIX, XXI, XXIII, XXV and XXVII of *The Mahā Bodhi* journal which the Anāgārika had edited for 40 years. They were first published separately in 1957 by The Mahā Bodhi Society of India, Calcutta, to which we are obliged for permission to reprint them.

It is hoped that these precious sayings of the great Buddhist leader will be an inspiration to many readers.

A life sketch of the Anāgārika, written by Buddhadhāsa P. Kirthisinghe of New York, has been added to this publication.

Buddhist Publication Society

ANĀGĀRIKA DHARMAPĀLA

Venerable Anāgārika Dharmapāla shines in the history of Ceylon— Sri Lanka—for his nobleness, serenity and selfless devotion to the service given to his beloved country, to India, and the rest of humanity. Like Emperor Asoka, his life was guided by a spirit of humanitarianism. While Asoka spread the word of the Buddha throughout India, Ceylon and by his missionaries throughout the world known to him in the third century BC, in our age, Anāgārika Dharmapāla did an equally notable service to humanity by reviving Buddhism and Buddhist culture in India, Ceylon and other lands of decadent Buddhist Asia and carrying the message of Buddhism to the West.

The rise and fall of great civilizations are, perhaps, a pattern in history. The Indo-Ceylon Buddhist period, from third century, BC to 12th century after Christ, is recorded as the golden period in their history. After that these great civilizations began to decay, and when the Portuguese, Dutch and British arrived in Asia from the 16th century onwards, these civilizations were decadent.

These foreign rulers destroyed the traditional culture of the land and Christian missionaries increased like mushrooms in these lands of Asia. Christian schools were opened by every Christian denomination. The Buddhist children were forced to go to these schools and Buddhists were compelled to go to Christian churches, even for the registration of marriages. In addition, economic pressure was used for the conversion of Buddhists to Christianity. It was a sad period when people were afraid to declare themselves Buddhists and when Buddhist culture had degenerated to the lowest ebb.

It was in the midst of this national calamity in Ceylon that a son was born to a wealthy Sinhalese family in Colombo. This boy was destined to lead his people to regain their national pride in their religion and culture. He was born on 17th September, 1864, and died on 29th April, 1933. He was named David Hewavitharne, but later in life bore the name of Anāgārika Dharmapāla.

David Hewavitharne was brought up in the traditional Sinhalese culture, which is based on a Buddhist way of life. His piously religious parents instilled in him the traditional piety which had been the heritage of his people for over 2000 years. Together with his parents, he took refuge daily in the Buddha, Dhamma and Sangha, and adopted the traditional five precepts of good daily conduct taken by the laymen. He was destined by karmic merits to become a saintly man and a selfless servant of the Buddha. In spite of the temptations of modern life he lived a pure and simple life, shunning all evil.

As a custom among the Buddhists, the first lesson in Sinhalese is usually given by a Buddhist monk. It is not surprising, therefore, that that first lesson given to Dharmapāla was by the renowned scholar, Venerable Hikkaduwa Sri Sumaṅgala Mahā Nāyaka Thera, of the famous Vidyodaya Pirivena, now the Vidyodaya University of Ceylon. After studying in a few, minor Christian schools, Dharmapāla attended the missionary Anglican (C.M.S.) School, Kotte, about six miles from Colombo. There he was forced to go to church at 7:30 a.m., and to receive Bible instruction daily. Later, Dharmapāla attended St. Thomas' College, near Colombo, where the elite received their schooling. St. Thomas's had a high standard of English education and discipline. If anything kept him within the Buddhist fold, it was the Buddhist virtues of tolerance and respect for other religions, together with the deep influence of his parents. Today, largely due to the influence of the work of Colonel Olcott and Venerable Dharmapāla, all Buddhist children receive instruction in Sinhalese and Buddhism whichever school they attend.

An important event in the Buddhist revival movement was the arrival of Colonel Olcott and Madame Blavatsky in Colombo, in May, 1880.

They were the founders of the Theosophical movement in New York City. They had previously corresponded with the Venerable Migettuwatte Gunananda, the famous monk-orator who triumphed over his Christian adversaries in public debates held in Panadura, in 1873. The sublime teachings of the Buddha triumphed over Christian dogmatism. It was the study of these debates that influenced the two co-founders of Theosophy in their decision to go to Ceylon.

When the great American Colonel and Madame Blavatsky arrived in Galle, South Ceylon, on 21st May, 1880, they publicly took the three refuges and the five Buddhist precepts in the familiar Pali from a Buddhist monk, profoundly influencing the young Dharmapāla, who was present with his parents on this occasion. It was an historic event—the first time in the history of Ceylon Buddhism that two Western people had come to Ceylon and had openly adopted Buddhism. The conversion of Madame Blavatsky and Colonel Olcott to Buddhism marked the beginning of a new epoch in the history of Ceylon Buddhism.

In 1883 a Catholic mob attacked a Buddhist procession opposite a Catholic church at Kotahena, north of Colombo. This infuriated Hewavitharne's father, and he refused to allow his son to attend any Christian school again.

Young Dharmapāla had to leave St. Thomas' College, and during the first few months he regularly visited the Colombo Public Library, studying European classics. In 1884, young Dharmapāla, at the age of eighteen, joined the Theosophical Society in Ceylon, together with two other bhikkhus. They were initiated personally by Madame Blavatsky and the noble Colonel, and became lifelong members.

The young Dharmapāla spent some time studying with Madame Blavatsky at the headquarters of the Theosophical Movement in India. Although he was interested in the study of occult phenomena, Madame Blavatsky encouraged him to study Pali and master the Tripiṭaka. On his return to Ceylon, Dharmapāla, who was then twenty years of age, believed with the rest of Buddhist intellectuals that the interests of Buddhism and the Theosophical Society were identical. Now Dharmapāla asked his father's permission to take Brahmachariya (celibate) vows and dedicate his life to the service of the Dharma. This request was hesitatingly granted by his father. Thereafter, Dharmapāla lived and worked at the Theosophical Headquarters in Ceylon.

In 1886 Colonel Olcott and the Rev. C. M. Leadbeater came back to Colombo from Adyar, to collect funds for the Ceylon Buddhist educational movement. They intended to tour the whole Island, but they needed an interpreter since they could not speak Sinhalese. Dharmapāla, who was then a clerk in the Ceylon Education Department, readily gave up his post and promptly offered his services to them. His father was dismayed, but his mother readily blessed him.

The three toured Ceylon's villages by bullock cart for several months, and by 1887 had become familiar figures in the national revival movement of Ceylon. The young Dharmapāla spoke as vigorously as the noble Colonel Olcott on social, economic and religious problems of the day.

From 1885 to 1889 Dharmapāla devoted his whole time to the Buddhist revival movement, thereby obtaining for himself the training needed to become the greatest Buddhist missionary of our time. During this period Dharmapāla and Colonel Olcott established the "Sandarasa" a weekly magazine in Sinhalese, and in December, 1888, they issued the first edition of "The Buddha" in English, under the editorship of the Rev. Leadbeater. The latter magazine has become the organ of the Colombo Young Men's Buddhist Association and has a long history of 75 years service to Buddhism.

Colonel Olcott and Venerable Dharmapāla left for Japan in 1889. They had with them a letter of good wishes in Sanskrit from the Buddhists of Ceylon to the people of Buddhist Japan. Japan was one of the few free nations of enslaved Asia, and their visit played a vital role in the Buddhist revival of all Asia.

In January 1891 Venerable Dharmapāla, together with a Japanese Buddhist monk, Kozen Gunaratna, decided to visit Buddhist holy places in India. At Buddha Gaya, Dharmapāla found the place shamefully neglected and the Buddha Gaya temple in the hands of a hostile and mercenary Mahānt. His life-long effort to free this holy place failed, though later it was handed over by the Government of India, to a committee of Hindus and Buddhists for its management, as an act of goodwill to Buddhist Asia. This change was entirely due to the heroic efforts of Venerable Dharmapāla, aided by the cry of millions of Buddhists throughout the world.

The Mahā Bodhi Society, which Venerable Dharmapāla had established at Colombo in 1891, was shifted to Calcutta in 1892. There it remains today as a magnificent monument, not only to his memory but also to the great benefactress of the society, Mrs. Foster, of Hawaii. At Calcutta he started the Mahā Bodhi Journal. This has been published continuously for the last 71 years, and today it is one of the leading journals of Buddhism. From the beginning to this day its motto is the Buddha's great exhortation to his first sixty disciples: "Go ye, O bhikkhus, and wander forth for the gain of the many, the welfare of the many, in compassion for the world, for the good, for the gain, for the welfare of devas and men. Proclaim O bhikkhus, the doctrine glorious, preach ye a life of holiness, perfect and pure." During the World Columbian Exposition of 1893, the World Parliament of Religions was held in the Columbus Hall of the city of Chicago. It was one of the most important events of the late nineteenth century. On this common platform, together with other leaders of great religions, Venerable Dharmapāla addressed a capacity audience three times, with saintly diligence, on the sublime teachings of the Buddha. He did not possess the magnetic oratory of Vivekananda—the exponent of Hinduism—who also addressed these gatherings. Nevertheless, what was said by the saintly Dharmapāla was forceful and lucid, and it caught the ear and the interest of the vast throng of the American public. His paper, "The World's Debt to the Buddha," had a deep influence on his audience at this Parliament of Religions. In this connection, Bhikkhu Sangharakshita states: "So striking was the impression made by the young preacher from Ceylon that when his colleague, Vivekananda, was compared to noble but passionate Othello, Dharmapāla was compared with no less a person than Jesus Christ."

Dharmapāla visited England several times. On his first visit in 1893 he met Sir Edwin Arnold, with whom he called on the Secretary of State for India, Lord Kimberley, regarding the Buddha Gaya temple. On this visit he tried to establish a branch of the Mahā Bodhi Society in London, but failed. Today, however, there stands the London Buddhist Vihara at Chiswick, a monument to his earlier efforts. It is under the management of the Mahā Bodhi Society.

For the first time in the history of modern India, Vesak was celebrated at Calcutta, on May 26, 1896, by Venerable Dharmapāla. This celebration was presided over by the Hon. Narendra Nath Sen. It was believed to be the first organized celebration of Vesak, since the decay of Buddhasāsana in India round the twelfth century AD. He also had the satisfaction of holding the first Vesak celebration in New York City, in 1897, on his second visit to the United States of America, at the invitation of Dr. Paul Carus.

His father, who had given enormous financial help to spread the word of the Buddha, died in 1904. On hearing the news, Mrs. Foster of Hawaii, a great philanthropist and generous benefactor of the Buddhist revival movement, wrote to him to ask him to regard her as his foster-mother. She gave him vast sums of money, without which he could not have carried on his missionary work so intensively, either in India or Ceylon.

In 1913 Venerable Dharmapāla left Ceylon for Honolulu, to thank Mrs. Foster personally for the magnificent and generous help given to the Mahā Bodhi Society. It was with her financial support that the headquarters building now occupied by the Society at Calcutta was purchased. Before Dharmapāla left Hawaii Mrs. Foster gave him Rs. 60,000. With this money he founded the Ayurvedic Hospital in Colombo and named it the Foster Robinson Hospital, in memory of the great benefactress. With still further help from Mrs. Foster, the Sri Dharmarajika Chaitiya Vihara was built in Calcutta. In 1920 Lord Ronaldshay, the British Governor-General of India, presented a sacred body relic of the Buddha, which was found in the Madras district, for enshrinement in the Vihara.

Dharmapāla's crowning achievement was the erection of the Mulagandhakuti Vihara at Saraṇath—where the Buddha preached his first sermon—and the enshrinement in it of the Buddha's relics which he had received from the British Governor of Bengal.

From 1917 Devapriya Valisinha had become Venerable Dharmapāla's chief disciple, who received his personal training from his master (guru). He is a devoted hard-working Sinhalese university graduate, and today he carries heavy responsibility of running the manifold activities of the Mahā Bodhi Society's headquarters at Calcutta, assisted by Venerable Bhikkhu

Jinaratana, and many notable Bengali Buddhists. Mention must also be made of Venerable Bhikkhu Sangharatana, an active worker of the society and a disciple of Venerable Dharmapāla, who has been in charge of the Saraṇath Vihara since 1930.

In January, 1933, Venerable Dharmapāla took the higher ordination of *upasampada*, in spite of recurring ill-health, and received the full name of Bhikkhu Sri Devamitta Dhammapala. He could, however, not live the life of a bhikkhu for long. His health deteriorated rapidly and in April of the same year he passed away. His was a life selflessly lived in the service of humanity.

Great Sayings of Anāgārika Dharmapāla

Without effort progressive development is impossible. Buddha built his religion on the foundations of energetic effort and vigilant activity.

1. Buddhism is a religion of strenuous endeavour. Its mission is to enlighten each human being to cleanse himself from psychical impurities of covetousness, anger, pride, stubbornness, conceit, malice, envy, etc.
2. The uncontaminated mind is radiant. The contaminations are later accretions.
3. The development of consciousness, strengthening the memory, avoiding recollections of associations tinged with sensual desires, resolute effort to generate thoughts of kindness, and renunciation are necessary to realize Nirvana.
4. Anger makes man a demon; fear is caused by ignorance, and ignorance is the cause of all physical and mental suffering.
5. The glory of the Buddha depends not on his own royal birth, but on the supreme wisdom that he obtained by self conquest and his infinite love.
6. Avoid the path of injustice. To please friends or relations, one should never do an unjust act. Never do anything in anger and malice, and show no fear and do no cowardly act, and avoid doing things foolishly.
7. Activity in doing good is the law of progress. Delay and neglect produce suffering and misery.

8. Nothing should be done without thought. Sitting, standing, walking, lying down, every movement of each limb should be associated with consciousness.
9. One should never dogmatise, but always analyse.
10. Inasmuch as all good deeds proceed from the elements of renunciation one should always strive to avoid sensuous pleasures, that are correlated with sin and lust.
11. Exert yourself to realize the unconditioned, infinite, eternal happiness of Nirvana, in full consciousness in this life, on this earth.
12. Freedom is wisdom's highest gift, depending on perfect Brahmacariya.
13. The past is infinite. It has no known beginning. With an infinite past, with the future before you, which you make for good or for evil, with the present under your control, your destiny is in your hands.
14. The Buddha is the embodiment of the Dhamma. The elements that go to make up the personality of the Buddha are identical with the principles that he enunciated. By thought, words and deeds the Buddha does not differentiate from absolute Truth.
15. Renunciation of sense pleasure may cause a temporary painfulness, but it has its reward in the realization of the infinite bliss of Nirvana.
16. Nirvana simply means freedom from ignorance, freedom from anger, freedom from lustful desires. It is a consummation worth striving for. Renunciation therefore from all sense pleasure and from all evil is Nirvana.
17. Pessimism has no place in the dynamic doctrine of the Lord Buddha. The wise man is a potential god. His powers are infinite, but they must be brought into existence by effort. The way to become a god is to practise the Noble Eightfold Path.
18. It was given the lion-hearted Prince of the Sakyas to proclaim the religion of Truth (Dharma) breaking the barriers of caste, creed, race, and territory. Territorialism was vanquished by the sunlight of Truth. An imperial religion was for the first time proclaimed by the Buddha as king of righteousness, whose territory extended to the uttermost limits of the Earth.

19. A progressive evolution with a definite ideal, its realization here and now, making life cheerful, energetic, serene, worth living for the sake of doing good for the welfare of others, this the Tathāgata proclaimed.
20. The innocent bliss is born of perfect purity without attachment to the things of the world, where no question of the *ahaṃkāra* and *mamaṅkāra* ("I-making" and "My-making") arises in the mind, free from covetousness, free from ill will, hatred, anger, and free from foolish superstitions born of fear and delusions.
21. Here is the religion of consciousness, of perfect recollection, of presence of mind, of fearlessness, of freedom, of activity, of loving compassion and of immortality.
22. A co-operative commonwealth working for the welfare of the many and for the happiness of the many is the kind of institution that civilized humanity needs.
23. The doctrine that Buddha taught was an analytical ethico-psychology based on the principles of evolution and causality.
24. There is no permanency but change. From the most minute atom to the highest heaven everything is becoming. It comes into being, stays for a time and passes away, like the volume of water in the flowing stream.
25. It is here that all philanthropic projects are accomplished, it is here that meritorious work is done. It is here human kindness and self sacrifice are appreciated. It is here that man can transcend the gods and save suffering humanity.
26. Morality is the most solid foundation that is needed to build up a lasting society. The Lord Buddha again and again emphasized that the Aryan religion shall only last so long as the disciples would strictly follow the path of purifying morality. When morality disappears society degenerates.
27. The sensual-minded people fond of sense pleasures yearn to be born in the regions of the gods, but the follower of wisdom looks with loathsome disgust on the pleasures of the senses, whether human or divine.
28. Effort is what the Buddha wished that people should make. Effort is all in all. Effort is the basis of karma. Even the effort to think is karma.

29. No truth can come out of the man who is not absolutely free to express his highest convictions. Absolute freedom is a needed factor when we are in search of Truth.
30. Neither the existence of an eternal hell nor of an eternal heaven is acknowledged in Buddhism. Each individual being has to suffer according to the evil karma he has done; it may be for a *kalpa*, but at the end, cessation of suffering is the law.
31. Buddhism is a kind of spiritual athleticism. It teaches you the way to develop your spiritual muscles and to strengthen your spiritual tendons. If another does your work where is the glory of your effort?
32. The passionate sensualist could never comprehend what Nirvana is. Where there is anger there is no Nirvana. Where there is no anger there is Nirvana. Where there is covetousness there is no Nirvana. Where there is no covetousness there is Nirvana. Where there is ignorance, there is no Nirvana. Where there is no ignorance, no ego desires of "this is mine, this is I," there is Nirvana. Absence of evil, development of good, and purification of the heart are what constitutes Nirvana.
33. The desire to destroy all evil desires should be ever active in the mind. When all ego desires are abandoned Nirvana reveals itself to the mind.
34. Absolute peace amidst the clanging of a million bells is only possible when the Nirvana consciousness unfolds itself.
35. Instead of making an effort to cleanse the heart from sin, ignorant man seeks to gain happiness by outward purification.
36. The Blessed One was the embodiment of strenuousness. He adopted as the motto of his religion the two words *appamada* and *viriya* (non-delay and diligent activity).
37. If only the bhikkhus would stir themselves and follow the Holy Master, Buddhism would not be then called a religion of pessimism.
38. The foundations of the Aryan Doctrine were laid not on asceticism, neither on sense perceptions. It is the doctrine founded on joyous cheerfulness, radiant mentality,

strenuousness, aesthetic calm, analytical investigation of truth, contentment and supreme wisdom.

39. Power and pride degenerate man into a demon. The way to Truth is one, the way to power is another. All civilizations that were founded on mere materialism have ceased to exist.
40. This doctrine of "mine" and "thine" is the chief source of all human suffering, enhanced by covetous desire, egoistic pride, and the lack of insight to recognize Truth in the right way.
41. Without *dhyana* there is no way to acquire the wisdom of Nirvana, and without the acquisition of *prajña t*here is no realizing the *dhyana*.
42. As long as the people of ancient India remained true to the wisdom teachings of the Blessed One there was happiness in the land.
43. The *atta* doctrine is injurious to the progressive development of the individual. It makes man arrogant and develops his conceit. Biologically, psychologically, super psychically, sociologically and morally it is destructive to progress and expansion.
44. It is in lonely retreats that spiritual visions always come to the ascetically inclined. Investigate into the history of each religious founder regarding his early religious experiences, and the fact will be revealed that he was a mystic, given to fasting, away from the crowd, and desiring for spiritual unfolding.
45. The Buddha laid great emphasis on the moral progress of the individual. The householder without morality is like a ship without a rudder. When a man is morally conscious of his own progress, he is able to transcend the knowledge of gods.
46. Mere morality is insufficient to realize the wisdom of Nirvana. Nirvana is all wisdom, and only by the strenuousness of earnest effort in the Middle Path can the Brahmachari obtain the realization of Nirvana.
47. When the Brāhmaṇa shall change his haughty spirit and look on the other people with compassion and work for the elevation of the masses, then will India again take the supreme place that she, in ancient times, occupied.

48. We are selfish, and our luxurious lives are the cause of our forgetfulness of our duty to our fellow man.
49. One individual, like the Buddha, gives happiness to countless millions of human beings, and they in their turn give others happiness.
50. The blood of innocent animals slaughtered by man through false religious convictions if measured would make an ocean.
51. The real understanding of Buddhism is an attainment that has to be obtained by gradual spiritual progress; it cannot be obtained by mere reason, nor can it be destroyed by criticism; not because it is a matter of faith but because to those who have tasted its flavour, there is no other flavour that can replace it.
52. Parents, teachers, spiritual and secular, should be examples of the highest virtue so that they will be able to influence the future generations.
53. The more the teachers show the spirit of self-sacrifice, associated with the spirit of compassion, like the mother that takes every care of herself for the love of her unborn child still in the womb, the better it will be for the development of the future generations.
54. If the householder does not see in the spiritual teacher virtue, why should he pay him homage? He must be an example of self abnegation, cultivating the higher life, to receive the homage of the householder.
55. The religion of the Buddha was intended for all castes. He made no distinction between the Brahman and the Sudra. To all he gave the ambrosia of the eternal Dhamma.
56. There is no world-teacher that loved India more than the Lord Buddha. Millions of times he renounced the eternal peace and bliss of Nirvana for the love of humanity.
57. The exclusive teachings of the brahmins can never help cosmopolitan India. If there is any religion that can bring about the consummation of the cherished desires of Indian patriots, it is Buddhism.
58. The essential principle that the Lord Buddha emphasized is ceaseless activity—activity in destroying evil, activity in generating good thoughts, good words, good deeds—thereby achieving the peace and happiness of Nirvana.

59. A very good act done with an unselfish motive and without the association of the ego consciousness is helpful to realize the Nirvana ideal.
60. To save the world from ignorance by means of wisdom and love was the object of the Buddha.
61. The earth, season after season, gives fruits; the sky gives rain, the cow gives milk, and the beggar who visits the door of the householder gets his dole. Charity is the law of life.
62. Those who wish to get at Truth should not be contented with the myths and theories of the mystics and ascetics. They should be daring, courageous and full of intense earnestness.

— §§§ —

The Place of Animals in Buddhism

Francis Story
(Anāgārika Sugatānanda)

Bodhi Leaves No. 23

First published: 1964

The Place of Animals in Buddhism

In an article on evolutionary ethics, Sir John Arthur Thomson, Regius Professor of Natural History, Aberdeen University, makes the striking observation that "Animals may not be ethical, but they are often virtuous."

If this opinion had been expressed by a Buddhist writer, it might have met with scepticism from those who hold "commonsense" practical views on the nature of animals. Perhaps it would have met with even more incredulity from those whose religion teaches them to regard man as a special creation, the only being with a "soul" and therefore the only one capable of noble and disinterested action. Scientific evidence that man differs from the animals in the quality of his faculties, but not in essential kind, has not yet broken down the age-old religious idea of man's god-bestowed uniqueness and superiority. In the minds of most people there is still an unbridgeable gulf between the animal world and the human. It is a view that is both convenient and flattering to *Homo sapiens*, and so will die hard, if it dies at all, in the popular mind. To be quite fair to theistic religious ideas, the anthropocentric bias is just as strong among people who are pleased to call themselves rationalists as it is among the religiously orthodox.

But Prof. Thomson's verdict is that of an unbiased scientific observer and student of behaviour and must command respect. Furthermore, most open-minded people who have been in close contact with animals would endorse it. The full implication of his statement lies in the distinction between the "ethical" and the "virtuous," a distinction that is not always understood. Ethical conduct is that which follows a code of moral rules and is aware, to some extent, of an intelligible principle underlying them. It is the result of a course of training in social values, many of which are artificial in the sense that they have no connection with any standards but the purely relative and adventitious ones that govern communal life. Virtue, on the other hand, is rooted more deeply. It expresses itself in instinctive and unanalysable conduct; its values are personal and seem to flow from levels of awareness that behaviouristic soundings cannot plumb. This is the source from which spring ethically uncalled-for acts of kindness, self-abnegation and heroism, prompted by a primal and spontaneous urge of love.

It is not an ethical sense that makes the female animal defend her young with her life, or a dog remain with its unconscious master in a burning house rather than save itself. When, as Prof. Thomson points out, animals "are devoted to their offspring, sympathetic to their kindred, affectionate to their mates, self-subordinating in their community, courageous beyond praise," it is not because they are morally aware or morally trained, but because they possess another quality, which can only be called virtue. To be ethical is man's prerogative because it requires a developed reasoning faculty; but since virtue of the kind found in animals takes no account of rewards or punishments it is in a certain sense a higher quality than mere morality. Moral conduct may be based on nothing more than fear of society's disapproval and retaliation, or the expectation of reprisals from a punitive god. In morality there may be selfishness, in virtue there is none.

No one is benefited by extravagant claims made for him, and what has been said is not intended to deny that for the most part animals are rapacious and cruel. It cannot be otherwise when they live under the inexorable compulsions of the law of survival. But what of man, who has been called the most dangerous and destructive of animals? Would the majority of human beings be much better than animals if all restraints of fear were removed? Are not most of man's moral rules only devices for holding society together in the interests of mutual security? Is not man the only being who kills unnecessarily, for mere amusement?

But just as there are vast differences between one man and another in nature and conduct, so there are between animals. Anyone who has taken pleasure in feeding monkeys in a wild state will have noticed that there is usually one old male who tyrannizes over the females and their young, greedily snatching more than he needs himself rather than let the weaker members share the food. That does not mean that all monkeys are egoistic bullies; it only shows that they share more characteristics in common with man than do most other animals. A few years ago, it was reported from India that a monkey had jumped into a swollen river and saved a human baby from drowning, at great peril to its own life. The incident is noteworthy because it concerns a wild animal; such actions by domesticated animals are so frequent that they often pass unnoticed. It suggests a special relationship between wild animals and those human beings who live at peace with them; perhaps a rudimentary sense of gratitude or even a dim idea of the need for mutual help against the hostile forces of nature. Monkeys are treated with kindness by the Indian villager, and all the higher animals are well able to distinguish between friendliness and enmity. At least, that is how it used to be in India; but now one wonders sadly whether respect for Hanuman-ji will be able to prevail over the demand for polio vaccine.

Regarding the human-animal relationship, Prof. Thomson also has something to say and his words have a special significance for Buddhists. He writes that although there is no warrant for calling animals moral agents, for the reasons we have seen, "a few highly-endowed types, such as dog and horse, which have become man's partners, may have some glimpse of the practical meaning of responsibility," and that there are cases in which possibly "ideas are beginning to emerge." That there is the possibility of such ideas being formed in the animal mind, and that they can be encouraged and cultivated, is nothing strange to Buddhist thought. The evolution of personality is as much a certainty as the evolution of biological types, and since it is concerned with the mind it is often much more rapid.

Buddhism takes into full account the animal's latent capacity for affection, heroism and self-sacrifice. There is in Buddhism more sense of kinship with the animal world, a more intimate feeling of community with all that lives, than is found in Western religious thought. And this is not a matter of sentiment, but is rooted in the total Buddhist concept of life. It is an essential part of a grand and all-embracing philosophy which neglects no aspect of experience, but extends the concept of personal evolution to all forms of sentient life. The Buddhist does not have to ask despairingly: "Why did God create obnoxious things like cobras, scorpions, tigers and tuberculosis micro-bacterium?" The kitten on the lap and the uninvited cobra in the bed are all part of a world which, while it is not the best of all possible worlds, could not be different, since its creator is craving. The universe was not brought into existence solely for man, his convenience and enjoyment. The place man occupies in it is one he has created for himself, and he has to share it with other beings, all of them motivated by their own laws of being (*dhammatā*) and will to live.

So in the Buddhist texts, animals are always treated with great sympathy and understanding. Some animals indeed, such as the elephant, the horse and the Nāga, the noble serpent, are used as personifications of great qualities. The Buddha himself is *Sākya-sīha,* the Lion of the Sākya clan. His teaching is the lion's roar, which confounds the upholders of false views.

The stories of animals in the canonical books and commentaries are often very faithful to the nature of the beasts they deal with. Thus the noble horse, Kanthaka, pined away and died when its master, Siddhattha, renounced the world to attain Buddhahood. That story has the ring of historical truth. The Canon also records one occasion, at least, when the Buddha himself found brute society more congenial than human. The incident calls to mind Walt Whitman's poem: "Sometimes I think that I could live with animals…." On this occasion an elephant, Pārileyyaka, and an intelligent monkey were the Enlightened One's companions when he retired to the forest to get away from quarrelling bhikkhus. In the story, after the troublesome monks' bad conduct had caused the Teacher to leave them, they found themselves abandoned by their lay supporters, and the lack of food and necessities quickly brought them to their senses. The Buddha, meanwhile, was being kept supplied with all he needed in the way of fruits and drink by the devoted animals. If the reader finds the story hard to believe, he may take it as allegorical. In either way its meaning is clear enough, for bhikkhus as much as for laymen.

Then there was the case of the elephant, Dhanapālaka, which suffered from homesickness in captivity and refused food.

The Buddha immortalized it in the stanza;

> *Dhanapālako nāma kuñjaro*
> *katukappabhedano dunnivārayo*
> *baddho kabalam na bhuñjati*
> *sumarati nāgavanassa kuñjaro.*

"The elephant Dhanapālaka,
in rut and uncontrollable,
eats nothing in captivity,
but longs for the elephant-forest." (Dhammapada, v. 324)

Also from the *Dhammapada Commentary* is the tale of Ghosaka, a child who was laid on the ground to be trampled on successively by elephants and draught-oxen, but was saved by the compassionate beasts walking round instead of over him. The suckling of this child by a she-goat is reminiscent of other stories, such as that of Romulus and Remus, suckled by a wolf, and Orson by a bear. These are accounted legendary, but there have been well-attested cases in recent times of human children being nurtured and raised by animals. It is known to have happened in India and Ceylon.

The good nature of animals is the subject of several *Jātaka* stories, the best known being that of the hare in the moon (*Sasa Jātaka*) and the story of the heroic monkey-leader who saved his tribe by making his own body part of a bridge for them to cross the Ganges (*Mahākapi Jātaka*). In both cases the animal-hero is said to have been the Bodhisatta in a previous birth. Mahāyāna Buddhism in particular emphasises that the Bodhisattvas (the Skt. form of Bodhisatta) manifest themselves in the animal world just as in the human. This is pictorially represented in the Tibetan wheel of life, which has the twelve *nidānas* of dependent origination around its rim, while inside are shown six major divisions of saṃsāric existence: the purgatories, the world of unhappy spirits, of angry spirits (*Asuras*), of radiant spirits (*devas*), of humans and of animals. In each of them a Bodhisattva is depicted teaching the Law.

Among the less well-known of the *Jātaka* tales there are many others that give a prominent place to animals. Among them there is the *Chadanta Jātaka*, in which the Bodhisatta appears as a six-tusked elephant; the *Saccamkira Jātaka*, which contrasts the gratitude shown by a snake, a rat and a parrot with the base ingratitude of a prince; and the curious tale of the *Mahākusala Jātaka*, where a parrot, out of gratitude to the tree that sheltered it, refuses to leave the tree when Sakka causes it to wither as a test of the bird's constancy. There is even an elephantine version of *Androcles and the Lion*, in which a tusker gives itself and its offspring in service to some carpenters out of gratitude for the removal of a thorn from its foot. The theme of animal gratitude runs very strongly through all these tales. They are obviously intended to teach humans the importance of this high virtue, in which men show themselves all too often inferior to the brutes.

Whether we choose to take these last examples literally, as events that occurred in previous world-cycles when animals had more human characteristics than they have now, or as folk-tales of the *Pañcatantra* type, is immaterial. Their function is to teach moral lessons by allegory. But they are also important as illustrating the position that animals occupy side by side with men in the Buddhist world-view. By and large, the *Jātakas* do not exalt animals unduly, for every tale of animal gratitude or affection can be balanced by another, showing less worthy traits that animals and men have in common. There is at least one, however, which satirises a peculiarly human trait—hypocrisy. In the *Vaka Jātaka,* a wolf, having no food, decides to observe the *Uposatha* fast. But on seeing a goat, the pious wolf at once decides to keep the fast on some other occasion.

If the story were not intended to be satirical, it would be an injustice to wolves. Whatever other vices it may have, no animal degrades itself with sham piety, either to impress its fellows or to make spiritual capital out of an involuntary deprivation. For better or worse, animals live true to their own nature. Pretentious sanctimoniousness is not one of their characteristics.

It is worth remarking as a curious fact of history that even in the West, animals have been regarded as morally responsible beings, although this has seldom worked to their advantage. It brought them within the punitive scope of the law without giving them any corresponding rights. For example, Plato, in *The Laws*, prescribed that "If a beast of burden or any other animal shall kill anyone, except while the animal is competing in the public games, the relatives of the deceased shall prosecute it for murder." Moses, too, legislated for animals, as we find in Exodus xxi, 28: "And if an ox gore a man or woman to death, the ox shall be surely stoned." But he was also considerate enough to prohibit the muzzling of an ox that was trampling on the grain. In western Europe there was a legal custom of bringing animals up for trial, which survived until quite recent times. Such proceedings against animal offenders were brought in both the civil and ecclesiastical courts. The animals were provided with counsel, were summoned to appear, and were duly tried with all the formalities of the law. Extenuating circumstances in their favour were solemnly taken into account, and their sentences were sometimes commuted on the grounds of youth, exiguity of body, or previous good character. As late as 1750, a she-ass was condemned to death in France, but was pardoned because of her otherwise good reputation. Some interesting evidence of this European attitude towards animals can be found in *The Criminal Prosecution and Capital Punishment of Animals*, by E. P. Evans (New York, 1906) and in *Proces au Moyen Age contre les Animaux*, by Leon Menabrea (Chambery, 1846). It does not appear, however, that animals were ever given legal right to prosecute human beings. Man's capacity for feeling moral concern has always been limited. Even today there are countries in which the law gives animals no protection, and many others where only a partial recognition is given to their rights.

There is abundant evidence of natural intelligence in animals, as well as of virtue. Research by a group of scientists at Oxford has shown that monkeys have a system of communication by sound which may be classed as a rudimentary language. Many of their "words" have already been listed. It may be that all animals possess a means of sound communication adapted to their limited needs and thought-processes. This appears to be the case even with fish, which rank rather low in the accepted evolutionary scale. A group of workers at the University of Rhode Island Graduate School of Oceanography has obtained proof that fish, although they cannot produce "sound" as we know it, are able to communicate with one another by means of a variety of underwater vibrations which they produce by means of the air-bladders that control their depth in the water, or by the snapping of their fins and movements of the gills. By the use of tape recorders and underwater cameras, the research group has been able to establish definitely that certain sounds produced in this way relate to specific activities and have clearly-defined meanings. The recordings have been collected for further study and already form a quite comprehensive bio-acoustics library.

Since the time when Darwinism reversed the dictum of Pope by suggesting that the proper study of mankind is animals, science has made unlimited use of the subhuman order of beings for research and experiment. It cannot be denied that much knowledge of the origin and treatment of disease has been gained in this way; but all the same, no humane person can feel quite happy about the sufferings undergone by animals in experiments on living organisms. Many of these experiments have to be made with only partial anaesthesia or none at all, in order that neural reactions can be observed; and while in all civilised countries vivisection is carried out under more or less exacting legal requirements, the suffering undergone by animals for the benefit of mankind in the torture chamber of our laboratories still amounts to a man-made hell in our midst. Beside it, the swift death of the slaughterhouse becomes almost humane. The question it poses—whether man is justified in inflicting so much prolonged agony on other creatures for his own advantage—is one that even so conscientious a thinker as Schweitzer has either to by-pass or to bury uneasily under an appeal to the superior claims of humanity. But even if it is held that these claims are ethically valid, the argument still has serious weaknesses. There are no records to show how many animals suffered, or for how long, to perfect the technique of the operation for pre-frontal lobotomy. Now it is a completely discredited operation, one of the dead-ends of science. Years of experiments on various kinds of animals went into the perfecting of penicillin and the sulfa drugs; now they are regarded with distrust, and some have been declared to be actually harmful. Even the use of certain antibiotics has to be approached with extreme caution. And recently the world received a horrifying shock from the effect on human babies of thalidomide, an anti-emetic prescribed to their mothers during pregnancy.

For the Buddhist, the problem is clarified by the knowledge that the innate *dukkha* of sentient life will always prevail over science and that, no matter what remedies are found for specific diseases, new forms of bacteria and virus will emerge by mutation or adaptation, so there can never be an end to the need for experiments on animals, and no ultimate good to be expected from them. Viewed in the light of *kamma* and *vipāka*, there can be only one answer to the question. Morally, man is not justified in subjecting animals to prolonged pain for his own ends. Moreover, it is not in his own best interest to do so, since he is thereby creating the karmic conditions that will eventually nullify whatever temporary benefits he may have gained. It would be far better if science, now that it has succeeded in tracing the biological processes to their physical source, were to seek methods of controlling disease without further recourse to experiments on living creatures. That animals should be compelled to go on paying so heavy a price in order that man may have the privilege of destroying himself by nuclear warfare or commercially contaminated food instead of succumbing to natural sickness, is too illogical a proposition to find support even in a man-centred morality. Perhaps when science is at last satisfied that it cannot eradicate disease by perpetually disturbing the balance of nature[127] but can only bring about fresh tribulations, a higher science may be evolved: one that takes as its field of research the mental and spiritual origins of suffering—the *vipāka* from the past and the unwholesome karma that man in his ignorance is creating in the present. Then it may be found that Pope was right after all: the proper study of mankind is man.

Buddhism shows that both animals and human beings are the products of ignorance conjoined with craving, and that the differences between them are the consequences of past karma. In this sense, though not in any other, "all life is one." It is one in its origin, ignorance-craving, and in its subjection to the universal law of causality. But every being's karma is separate and individual. So long as a man refuses to let himself be submerged in the herd, so long as he resists the pressures that are constantly brought to bear on him to make him share the mass mind and take on the identity of mass-activities, he is the master of his own destiny. Whatever the karma of others around him may be, he need have no share in it. His karma is his own, distinct and individual. In this sense all life is not one, but each life, from lowest to highest in the scale, is a unique current of causal determinants. The special position of the human being rests on the fact that he alone can consciously direct his own personal current of karma to a higher or lower destiny. All beings are their own creators; man is also his own judge and executioner. He is also his own saviour.

127 I refer particularly to the modern passion for artificially sterilizing the system. The best feature of present-day toothpaste is that they do not do what the advertisements claim for them. If they literally did destroy all oral bacteria they would be about the most pernicious products of commercialism.

Then what of the animal? Since animals are devoid of moral sense, argues the rationalist, how can they be agents of karma? How can they raise themselves from their low status and regain human birth?

The answer is that Buddhism views life against the background of infinity. *Saṃsāra* is without beginning, and there has never been a time when the round of rebirths did not exist. Consequently, the karmic history of every living being extends into the infinite past, and each has unexpended potential of karma, good and bad, which is known as *kaṭattā-kamma*. When a human being dies, the nature of the succeeding life-continuum is determined by the morally wholesome or unwholesome mental impulse that arises in his last conscious moment, that which follows it being his *paṭisandhi-viññāṇa*, or rebirth-linking consciousness. But where no such good or bad thought-moment arises, the rebirth-linking consciousness is determined by some unexpended karma from a previous existence. Animals, being without moral discrimination, are more or less passive sufferers of the results of past bad karma. In this respect, they are in the same position as morally irresponsible human beings, such as congenital idiots and imbeciles. But the fact that the animal has been unable to originate any fresh good karma does not exclude it from rebirth on a higher level. When the results of the karma that caused the animal birth are exhausted, some unexpended good karma from a previous state of existence will have an opportunity to take over, and in this way the life-continuum is raised to the human level again.

How this comes about can be understood only when the mind is divested of all belief in a transmigrating "soul." So long as there is clinging, however disguised or unconscious, to the idea of a persisting self-entity, the true nature of the rebirth process cannot be grasped. It is for this reason that many people, although they maintain that "all life is one," fail to understand or accept the Buddhist truth that life-currents oscillate between the human, the animal and many other forms. However comforting it may be to believe that beings can only ascend the spiritual ladder, and that there is no retributive fall for those who fail to make the grade, that is not the teaching of the Buddha.

It is now necessary to introduce a qualification to the statement that the higher rebirth of animals must depend upon unexpended good karma. Within the limitations we have noted, it is certainly possible for animals to originate good karma, notwithstanding their lack of moral sense. As Prof. Thomson suggests, contact with human beings can encourage and develop those qualities which we recognise as virtue in the higher animals, and even bring about in them a dawning consciousness of moral values. When the compulsions of the law of survival are removed, as in the case of animals under the protection of man, we get examples of those endearing and even noble qualities in them which have sometimes put human beings to shame, and have even caused non-Buddhists to ask themselves doubtfully whether man really is a special creation of God, and the only being worthy of salvation

— §§§ —.

The Three Roots of Ill and Our Daily Life

Karel Werner

Bodhi Leaves No. 24

First published: 1965

The Three Roots of Ill and Our Daily Life

We live in a world of great material achievements and we are all fascinated by them. The riches of the world multiplied by modern industrial productivity draw the attention of all people who, then, wish to possess them, and to share the pleasures that can be bestowed upon them by the infinite variety of things invented by the restless mind of modern man, who is never content with what he just possesses and who is always seeking for something new.

This infinite variety of our modern technical civilisation seems to be something peculiar to our present age and it instils into us a sense of unhealthy pride and of being somehow placed above past periods and epochs of mankind's history.

The marvels of technical progress are the outcome of the external inventive activities of Western nations who thus gained an external superiority over the rest of the world. They have gained for themselves whole continents—America and Australia—and, for a long time, were forcing their supremacy upon the peoples of Asia and Africa.

Now that almost all nations of these two continents are free and may shape their destinies according to their wishes, we see that the fascination of the technical civilisation affects them too, and that, to a serious degree, they neglect their own spiritual heritage, and are taking over from the West with its technical achievements even some ideologies and some pseudo cultural features of doubtful value.

But is our fascination by today's multiplicity of material things offered to us for enjoyment justified by their inner value? Is our eager pursuit of material things in ever new shapes something new and different from what, essentially, took place in previous times, in other epochs and civilisations? Is there behind it, something nobler and more worthwhile? Certainly not.

The Real Cause of External Achievements

At the root, or better to say, the very root of this everlasting pursuit of things that fills our life from the moment of birth till the moment of death, is craving and only craving, which manifests itself in manifold ways through our constant struggle to satisfy the desires of our six senses.

It may sound an exaggerated assumption, but it is, notwithstanding, true that all the seemingly marvellous achievements of our present civilisation are nothing but the outcome of our blind urge to satisfy our craving for pleasurable sensations. When one particular craving is satisfied, another one arises. And to produce ever-renewed sensations, we blindly produce ever-new needs that clamour to be satisfied. If all our needs were made subject to a careful analysis, we should find out that the vast majority of them are superfluous and artificially produced.

There are, it is true, a few unavoidable needs which must be satisfied for us to survive. But who of us remains content with mere survival in satisfying his actual needs?

We have to eat. But though we are long past the stage of wild animals who feel only an instinctive urge to fill their stomachs when hungry, it is seldom that we give reasonable consideration to the quantity and constituents of our daily meals. Moreover, we have lost the soundness of the animal instinct. We seek to prolong and repeat more often than necessary the satisfaction we feel when stilling our hunger.

The pleasurable taste sensations connected with eating became important for themselves, no more serving the primeval purpose of testing the suitability of the devoured food. And so we eat more than is necessary for survival and, which is still worse, we eat and drink things which are completely superfluous for, or even harmful to, the purpose of keeping our body and mind healthy and fresh (to say nothing of the completely foolish habit of smoking).

Clothing is, no doubt, one of our fundamental needs as well. It should protect us against cold or heat and various whims of weather and climate, and it may be adjusted to the customs of the country and time and perhaps even be up to a certain degree of elegance. But does this imply the pursuit of all the extravagant caprices of fashion? Here often craving manifests itself very strongly, especially in women (but in many men as well) who thus become the victims of the "law-givers" in fashion to whom the creation of new patterns in clothing serves as a source of considerable income.

Thus we could go on discovering the real needs of man and the manifold ways in which he, out of craving, exaggerates them, seeking to experience the repeated satisfaction of wish-fulfilment and the pleasurable sensation connected therewith. It is the sensual craving that manifests itself in this way—craving for pleasing forms, sounds, flavours, tastes, touches and ideas.

But this craving is never satiated. We usually identify our happiness with acquiring some particular sense-object. Soon after we have acquired it, however, we lose interest in it and another object appears to be desirable to us. Obviously, it is not the object that is desired, but the sensation connected with acquiring or using it. This sensation, lasting for a short time only, we have, in order to repeat it, to struggle to acquire the object again or, when the object has lost the capacity to produce the desired sensation in us, to acquire another object promising to do so; and so on endlessly.

The real cause of our willingly obeying the urge of sensual craving is not—as we presume it to be—an actual, positive state of happiness we should gain thereby. The sensation of pleasure felt in the moment of wish-fulfilment only pretends to be happiness. It is in fact, only an instantaneous relief of a tension caused by craving.

This tension is, in fact, ever present in our mind as a dimly felt unsatisfactoriness of our whole existence, of the ways and possibilities of our entire life in the form we know it. It is sometimes slight, but at other times it becomes almost unbearable and even causes deviations from the so-called normal states of mind and one speaks then of mental diseases.

However, even the so-called normal mind is every moment under the compulsive urge to find every possible means for the relief of tension. This is almost the only source of man's entire activities. Thus we live amidst suffering like a victim on a rack ladder. When the strain is loosened, we feel some ease, but soon the torturing tension is felt again.

The Second Cause of Entanglement

Craving, however, is not the only source of our suffering and entanglement. Seeking for pleasure we instinctively avoid all things unpleasurable, and when we cannot avoid them, we try to remove or destroy them, taking for granted that these obstructing things prevent us from attaining to happiness and thus cause our suffering. That is why we hate them and so we come to the second root of ill which is hate or ill-will in many forms, obvious as well as hidden.

In spite of all the riches the modern world abounds in, in spite of its capacity to provide for the actual needs of everybody on earth, the world is far from the satisfactory state of affairs when there would be no starvation, no lack of clothing and lodging and of medical treatment for everybody. The unavoidable needs of a considerable part of humanity cannot be satisfied, while, on the other hand, another, though smaller, part of it possesses the means thereto in such an abundance as not to be able to make actual use of them.

This state of affairs has been brought about by the exaggerated craving described above which blindly seeks to secure the means for gratification in greatest measure for an endless future without reasonable purpose. The artificial poverty and unnecessary misery created thereby becomes the source of hate which is dividing mankind, nations, natural groups of society and even families. Hence, all class-division appears to be artificial and superfluous, even when proprietary differences might not disappear altogether.

Hate, however, is no outside force. Like craving, it can be experienced by living beings only, by us. And we experience it only too often. Every deed we perform to obtain any privilege at the cost of someone else, every harsh word we pronounce to anybody, any thought condemning another living being is basically motivated by hate which, of course, may be crude or mild, intense or subtle. How often hate is hiding itself behind imagined "righteous indignation" or "well intended criticism," aiming, in fact, only at justifying our pursuit of satisfaction or our effort to avoid discontent.

It is almost universally admitted or, at least, it is felt that hate is an undesirable and unpleasant state of mind, and hence the effort to disguise it by justifying terms. Compared with craving, hate seems to be, in a way, secondary. Out of sensual craving for pleasure comes the craving for the existence of pleasing objects and the craving for the non-existence of unpleasant or obstructing objects and this is, in fact, hate.

Craving causes us to grasp the thing that promises to bestow pleasure upon us, and hate causes us to aim at the destruction of other things which prevent us from gaining the desired object. But to experience craving means, fundamentally, to be suffering, and so with hate. And to obtain the gratification of a particular craving brings about a new craving and a new suffering, and so with hate. Why is this so? Obviously, because both craving and hate are blind, are associated with ignorance.

The Primary Root of Ill

Ignorance is thus the primary root of all ill present in every action in deed, speech or thought, which is connected with craving or hate in pursuing an object of our craving. We take for granted that the acquisition or the possession of it will bring us lasting happiness. But this view proves to be false. Nevertheless, we try again, changing perhaps, the object. In removing a hated obstacle preventing us from acquiring the desired object, we believe we have come nearer to our aim of lasting happiness, but this proves to be a false view as well.

Nevertheless, we still go on and only change, perhaps, the means we used till now. We may even turn to the pursuit of subtler objects, looking, for instance, for gratification in art instead of in the mere pleasures of the flesh, or, perhaps, even in philosophical speculations instead of in art. We may, too, considerably transform our hate—no more killing our enemies, no more destroying the careers of our opponents, but only avoiding or ignoring them; but still we remain caught in the net of craving, hate and delusion.

The subtler forms of craving and hate should become the objects of our circumspect attention; we should always be aware of their occurrence if we earnestly wish to do something about them. They often disguise themselves in very refined ways and even their grosser forms may outwardly look harmless or noble, being in fact, most pernicious for us, because they smuggle through into our subconsciousness almost unnoticed.

Thus, even the most appreciated works of art are often coupled with, or inspired by sex, however hidden the links to it might be and however sublimated it may appear when closely analysed. But the impulses and seeds implanted by such works of art into the unconscious layers of our mind find response there and strengthen the urge in us to act accordingly when adequate conditions arise.

Thus, in such a refined disguise the sexual urge involuntarily gets a footing even where its grosser and more obvious appeals, such as the oversexed films and magazines of today, are purposely avoided as worthless or harmful.

Hate also finds its way into our minds in inconspicuous disguises. A warm love for one's motherland, an enthusiasm for a particular religion or ideology may seem to be harmless at the beginning and may appear to be an outcome of one's sense to adhere to the truth as one sees it. But too often we have seen such attitudes evolve into open hate for enemies or into persecuting religious or political opponents.

Even if such an enthusiasm for certain ideas and philosophies remains limited to the intellectual level, these require to be formulated in opposition to the ideas and philosophies of the others which involves vain polemics, the stressing of the illusory importance of one's opinions, and from this comes separation of oneself from other fellow-beings which is again a disguised form of hate.

All these various forms and degrees of hate that are usually not felt and not realized as such, become possible by one's deeply ingrained illusion of the importance of the things concerned, which are, in fact, unimportant and unsubstantial. Thus the ignorance is perpetuated.

A Way Out

Is there a way out of this maze, and a secure state of lasting happiness that is real and free from any delusion? We all know there is. To reach it, we must overcome and transcend the three roots of ill. But seeking for pleasure and avoiding pain is the natural course of conduct of all living beings which cannot be changed. Our question concerning the state of lasting happiness is likewise only the outcome of the same natural course of things when one grasps the impermanence, basic wretchedness and unsubstantiality of all pleasures connected with the six senses so that a new way out is looked for.

Once more we see that it is ignorance concerning the real, true happiness to be aimed at, that is the primary cause of all our endless and purposeless suffering. We are ignorant of the fact that all pleasures of the six senses are of the phenomenal world and hence unreal. When we encounter them in life, they appear to us to be real, though immediately after they have passed, we may see their basic emptiness and illusory nature. However, we seem to be unable to draw a lesson therefrom and to direct our attention to the true nature of these seeming pleasures, only looking forward to new pleasures in future with an unexpressed and unfounded hope that once, perhaps tomorrow, after some successful revolution or after death in some paradise, these pleasures will be bestowed upon us forever and in some more perfect form.

This expectation of ours, to gain lasting happiness from outside through some sudden change of outer circumstances or by the act of some higher power, is the greatest delusion of ours today. And this is the reason why we must first try to disperse our ignorance, step by step. Can we do it ourselves and unhelped? I do not know. There may be and may have been people who acquired this liberating knowledge by themselves. But we need not bother ourselves about this problem, for we have got a true help. Our Teacher, the Buddha, the Awakened One, has left to us his incomparable Teaching that has been preserved through the ages in a form comprehensible enough for us to gain a kind of initial right understanding necessary for stepping on the path to liberation from all ill.

Thus, we are able to take the first steps in overcoming ignorance if we make use of the help offered to us by the Awakened One. Provided with the first glimpses of right knowledge gained by the instruction in the Teaching, we become able to identify craving as craving in its various modifications and hate as hate in its various disguises. And we realise that we must cope with them everywhere if we wish to gain true happiness. How can we do this in our daily life?

The First Practical Steps

We must take care never to lose our first insight telling us that it is not the desired object that can bestow happiness upon us and that it is not the obstructing thing or being that is the cause of our tension, pain and suffering.

The cause of suffering is craving and only our overcoming or transcending this craving can bring us nearer to freedom and hence to happiness. Whenever craving or hate prevails, it will lead to deluded action in deed, words or thought and hence to further entanglement and prolonged suffering. To prevent the prevailing of both these roots of ill, we must constantly maintain our insight concerning their true nature. In doing so, we are in fact coping with the basic root of all ill, with ignorance.

Practically, we may proceed in the following way:

1. Identifying. First we should identify craving and hate whenever they occur. That requires that we be constantly mindful and watchful as to the real motivations behind our deeds, words and thoughts. Usually we act, speak or judge in thought without actually knowing our real motives in the moment of performing the action. Later on, especially when a performed act has brought some disagreeable consequences upon us, we are more willing to admit that we were overwhelmed by a sudden attack of anger and lost our temper.

Sometimes we cannot even understand how we could have done this or that and we say it was stronger than us. But if we try, we cannot find any subject in us we could identify ourselves with, a subject that would be separate from the emotion or tendency to act in this or that way in the moment we felt driven to act according to it. Our separating ourselves from that emotion or tendency takes place in retrospective analysis only, i.e., when it is over and "we" are able to think again. This separation, which is additionally established, comes from thought that postulates a fictitious subject being in possession of an emotion, but it is, by no means, an outcome of experience in the respective moment.

This proves that in the moment when we were acting out of craving, we just were that craving, and when acting out of hate we just were that hate. Or better expressed, there just was craving or there just was hate—in both cases, of course, connected with ignorance.

If we, however, maintain observant awareness of what is, of what we are experiencing in a moment of a strong feeling of some desire, anger, hate, etc., then "we" are not that desire, anger or hate, but "we" are that observing awareness and we can identify the desire as a kind of craving, the anger as a kind of hate, etc. Such a state of mind is not completely connected with ignorance. The watchful awareness represents here a degree of true knowledge and hence no deluded action can result out of it.

2. Pausing. This brings us to our second task. Whenever we want to perform an act, i.e., to do something, to say some word to anybody or to think, to draw a conclusion, we should first pause to see the motive of the intended act. Such a pause before the performing of an act would be, in fact, a natural result of our attitude of watchful mindfulness aiming at identifying the lustful or hateful state of mind whenever it occurs, if we do succeed in maintaining it. But if we don't, then our preconceived intention to pause before acting to see the true motivation, may still help us to identify craving or hate if it is present.

How often we act, speak or judge under the influence of an immediate reaction to some event or to some deed or word of another person. Seldom can such a deed, utterance or judgement be called wise when examined by an impartial observer or, later on by us when we are in a quiet mood again.

Many problems in our lives could be solved with greater advantage, many families could live a more happy life, many a suffering could be avoided, if people earnestly tried always to pause for a fraction of a second to see the pressing force present in themselves that is driving them to do an unkind act, to say a harsh word, to condemn someone in thoughts.

3. Quick reflection. If we succeed in identifying the real motive of our act just before performing it, we may utilize the gap for a quick reflection whether it is worth being performed at all or not, which is our third task. When we identify one of the two roots of ill as being the motive or driving force urging us to do this or that, we shall most probably leave the act undone, without being obliged to struggle with it very much.

When the desire, repulsion or hate is strong and persistent, even when cognized as such, we may use all our capacity of reflection and imagination to call to mind the evil consequences of acting out of such a deluded state of mind. By constantly observing the desire or hate as an object, and not identifying ourselves with it, we are sure to see how it begins to fade.

In this way we shall, as already mentioned, drop many an intention, leave many a deed undone and many a word unspoken, and shall break many a harmful course of thought. In case we do not find any harmful motive, still a wise reflection may show us the purposelessness or futility of an intended act and we may dismiss it as well. Thus we shall avoid further useless entanglements. And only when our reflection shows us that the act we are going to perform is not only harmless, but useful to us or others as well, we shall accomplish it, making use of our alert mind sharpened through the attitude of watchful mindfulness.

The Safe Guide

We shall, it is true, not be able to decide always according to our own knowledge acquired through our own inner vision. Our insight may be still too narrow or faint. But then we may take refuge in the instructions of the Awakened One who is our incomparable Teacher and a safe guide to the true goal.

There are in the discourses of the Awakened One, directions for both the advanced and the beginners, for monks and lay people; there is a code of discipline for the life in monasteries and a code of behaviour for the life in the world. It is only necessary to read and study them. The beneficial results of applying those bits of advice will be experienceable very soon.

When we gain a certain skill in maintaining the watchful attitude of mindfulness and thus become able to see the frequent occurrence of various forms of craving and hate in association with our consciousness, we shall discover the enormous depth and measure of our entanglement. Realizing the fatal influence of hate, we shall not be willing to tolerate it anywhere, not even in the slightest forms of dislikes or resentments. Though not always able to cope with it perfectly, we shall constantly try to dissociate it from our mind.

The Subtler Forms of Craving

With the subtler forms of craving, however, it will be, for some time, different. We can hardly expect to find ourselves capable of abandoning all desires at once. There are mean desires and there are desires we can, with a certain reservation, call noble.

We may succeed soon in giving up some personal desires, but we shall perhaps not abandon the desire to secure a certain standard of living for our family as long as the welfare of its members is dependent on us. We may succeed in controlling our sensual desires to a considerable degree, but we might not be, all at once, inclined to give up all aesthetic pleasure of music or art. Nor is it always advisable.

Art comes to us through the senses too, so that it must be, no doubt, abandoned as well when the time is ripe to do so, but more "earthly" pleasures should be given up first. In this respect we shall hardly take seriously the proclaimed desire to realize the ultimate truth—which presupposes, first, the abandoning of all worldly tastes and attachments—with those persons who are, for example, smokers or cannot do without two or three cups of coffee a day.

The aesthetic pleasure, if it is free from sex, may accompany us for a long time in our efforts to go along the Path and prove, sometimes, even helpful, especially that inspired by the beauties of nature. We only should not cling to it for its own sake, nor lose the notion of the final necessity of abandoning it. Thus we shall not get lost in a vain or too enthusiastic pursuit of aesthetic pleasure, but on the other hand, will not try to suppress them by force altogether, if our inclination to it was quite strong. In the course of progress and as the result of occasional inner states of happiness connected with it, our interest in aesthetic pleasure will grow weaker until it will fall off as if of itself.

The final necessity of abandoning, or, better to say, the ultimate uselessness or purposelessness of aesthetic pleasures may be the more understandable to us the more we bear in mind the wise utterance of the Awakened One that even his noble Teaching is to be abandoned, not to be clung to when the right moment comes and one is standing on the threshold of the final deliverance; for this Teaching, however noble, however consistent and however dear to us now, is similar to a raft for getting across and not for retaining.

This last step of putting aside the Teaching would be, no doubt, the highest and ultimate act of right mindfulness, the first steps of which we have tried to describe here.

Thus, if we are persistent and do not fall into sluggishness, grosser forms of craving will, one by one, fall from us and this will give us an experience of real relief, as the heavy burden we are carrying becomes somewhat lighter. And also the hateful and malicious states of our mind will grow weaker and less frequent, allowing us to experience, in rare moments of mind-quietude, the foretaste of happiness of a liberal state of mind.

— §§§ —

The Buddha's Practical Teaching

John D. Ireland

Bodhi Leaves No. 25

First published: 1965

THE BUDDHA'S PRACTICAL TEACHING

In a previous Bodhi Leaf, 'Comments on the Buddha Word'[128] there was an attempt to demonstrate the theoretical aspect of the Four Noble Truths of Buddhism and their continuous presentation, in various guises, throughout the Sutta-piṭaka of the Pali Canon. The Four Truths are the essential and characteristic feature of Buddhism and its goal the complete penetration and understanding of them. The Buddha has stated that it is by not understanding and fully comprehending these Four Truths that we wander aimlessly on in this world, caught between birth and death and subject to innumerable sufferings.

Before going any further however we should be quite clear as to what is meant by 'understanding.' Firstly there is the understanding arising from reading and hearing about the teachings.[129] This is, of course, only the very first step, insufficiently by itself, but nevertheless to be done carefully; because a wrong grasp of letter and meaning, at this stage, may affect the following stages of understanding. Then there is the understanding arising from thinking over[130] what one has learnt, drawing out the implications of the words, digesting and relating them to personal experience. Finally there is the understanding arising from actually putting the Teaching into practice,[131] treading the path which culminates in the experiencing for oneself of Nibbāna, the real aim of Buddhism. And this last type of understanding is what is intended here. Then the four stages of sanctitude arise in due order, consisting of an understanding that is irreversible, i.e. can never be lost, and which may be called to mind whenever one wishes to do so. The final stage of sanctitude is complete deliverance of mind from all suffering, but to have actual assurance

---

128 Bodhi Leaf No. 16

129 *Suta-maya-ñāṇa.*

130 *Cintā-maya-ñāṇa.*

131 *Bhāvanā-maya-ñāṇa,* 'understanding derived from mental development', i.e. by meditation and other practical applications.

of this final goal it is imperative to reach the first stage called the 'Path of Stream-entry' or the 'possession of clear seeing' into the Four Noble Truths. Without reaching this stage we have no actual guarantee of making true progress on the Buddha's path to final deliverance, and are liable to be swept away and lose all that has been gained in a single moment if circumstances go against us, as would happen, for instance, if we were to die before reaching this stage. The Buddha teaches that it may be very long indeed before we might become fortunate enough to hear of the Teaching again and be able to put it into practice. Therefore our aim should be to reach this stage of assurance, the Path of Stream-entry.

The question now arises: how are we to produce that kind of understanding leading to sanctitude? The answer lies in the preparedness of the mind for understanding. Many times in the discourses of the Buddha it is told of individuals who on hearing but a few words on the teaching immediately gained a deep understanding and attained the stages of sanctitude, apparently without effort, but these are actually exceptional cases. Most of the Buddha's disciples had to go through a long and laborious training before being ready to attain the goal. Again, in the Buddha's time, and even today if one has an experienced teacher, it was made easier because the Buddha, through his comprehensive vision, understood the minds of his audience and could correct their faults so that they were prepared for understanding. But those who have no teacher in the flesh may still have a teacher in the Buddha through his recorded utterances, and this was recognised after his passing away by his immediate followers. Indeed the Buddha says just this to the elder Ānanda when he was lamenting over the fact that he was soon to lose his beloved Teacher.[132]

In many places an indication is given of this preparation of mind culminating in 'samādhi,' concentration, absorption or one-pointedness, whereby the hindrances which dull and corrupt the mind and act as a block to understanding are set aside.[133] A summary of the process leading up to this state is found, for

---

132 See *Last Days of the Buddha,* Wheel No. 67-69, p. 73.

133 The Pali word *nīvaraṇa,* or hindrance, has the meanings of an obstruction; a covering; something which prevents, shuts out, or keeps back, something else.

example, in the discourse addressed to Suppabuddha the leper (Udāna, v. 3). Here is the relevant passage:

> "Then the Lord saw the leper Suppabuddha sitting in the crowd and having seen him he thought, 'This one is capable of understanding Dhamma.'
>
> For the leper Suppabuddha he spoke a graduated talk, that is to say, a talk on generosity, good behaviour, the heaven world, the disadvantage, inferiority and defilement of sense desires and the advantage in renouncing them. When the Lord knew that the mind of the leper Suppabuddha was prepared, receptive, free from hindrance, joyful and confident, he then made known the Dhamma-teaching discovered by the Awakened Ones (Buddhas): Suffering, Origination, Cessation and the Path. Then, just as a clean cloth without stain would properly take up a dye, so in the leper Suppabuddha, even as he sat on that seat, arose the undefiled and stainless Dhamma-eye (which sees): Whatsoever is of a nature to arise is of a nature to wholly cease."

We will now proceed to expand on this passage. At the very beginning a person has to have a capability of understanding, a certain level of intelligence. This is the result of past reasonable human moral conduct[134] and is called merit or worthiness (*puñña*). This must be present for one even to care to learn of the Teaching or be in a position to learn it. But in Suppabuddha's case the Lord knew he had the capability of reaching sanctitude 'even as he sat on that seat,' so his 'worthiness' was above average. Then the Lord by just talking to him was able to raise his mind to a high level of purity. To begin with the Buddha uses for this purpose a carefully graded method of teaching in five divisions:

1. Generosity or giving (*dāna*) is the fundamental virtue of Buddhism, the foundation-stone upon which the whole edifice is built. Now in the Buddha's teaching the intention or state of mind is most important and generosity produces a broad and open

134 The stress here is on the 'human' state. Neither the divine or god-like state nor a sub-human, e.g. animal state, is a suitable basis for 'the practice of moral conduct and discipline' and this is one of the reasons why a human birth is praised and regarded as valuable in Buddhism.

disposition, weakening the tendency to avarice and egoism. It is the cultivation of the habit to be able to let go of things easily and not hold fast to them.

2. The next step, morality or good behaviour (*sīla*), follows on naturally from generosity, for being well-disposed towards others, one would conduct oneself so as to not deprive them of anything nor harm them in any way. This implies a restraining and guarding of the activities of body, speech and thought. It is an attitude of self-control.

3. The 'heaven world' is a state of mind of pure and blameless happiness. The mention of it is meant to indicate the result of generosity and good behaviour. By it the mind is healed of any ungenerous and perverted behaviour still remaining, and becomes balanced, well and wholesome.

4. Next, seeing the disadvantage of sense-desires is necessary to counterbalance the previous step, for, the heavenly world being such a pleasant state, one is liable to become enamoured by it and unable to progress and discover the true aim of the Buddha's teaching. Heavenly enjoyment is the highest form of sensuality and to break one's attachment to it the Buddha shows it has the disadvantage of not lasting, of being impermanent and mixed with disappointment and distress. He points out that sensual pleasures are really an inferior form of happiness compared with the bliss obtained by the practice of meditation, and even this is of little worth when one has experienced the supreme bliss of Nibbāna. Sensuality is a very real and strong defilement and difficult to get rid of. It dulls and corrupts the mind so that those controlled by it find it hard to believe there could be any condition superior to it, not to mention any happiness outside of it.

5. Finally the Buddha teaches the advantage of being free from sensual desires and the escape from the suffering engendered by them. Whenever we attempt to gratify our desires sooner or later we are bound to experience disappointment and frustration, for the objects of our desires are continually altering and disappearing. The Buddha has said that the average person knows of no escape from suffering other than pleasures of the senses, so it is merely a vicious circle: suffering leading to the search for pleasure and the latter leading back to suffering again. If we could break away

from this circle by disciplining the mind not to automatically run to the distractions of the world, but to face and investigate the causes of our unhappiness, we would then discover the sure deliverance from it. The way of deliverance is by the practice of meditation which withdraws the mind from the senses and turns it upon itself, then *samādhi* arises, a state of great calm and bliss, superior to the dubious pleasures of the world of the senses.

Suppabuddha understood this and turning away from sense-desires his mind became endowed with five qualities: preparedness, receptiveness, freedom from hindrance, joy and confidence.[135] These counteract and replace the five hindrances (*nīvaraṇa*)[136] which prevent the attainment of concentration (*samādhi*) and clarity of mind. The first and foremost of these hindrances is the desire for sensual pleasures; by being rid of this the mind is prepared to clearly comprehend whatever it may turn to. The second is aversion which sets up the barrier of not wanting to understand; by breaking this down the mind becomes sympathetic and receptive. The third is sloth and torpidity of mind and is opposed to alertness and clarity. The fourth is worry and distraction, discarded by a joyful serenity of mind, and the fifth is doubt, overcome by confidence and trust.

The state so attained is called *upacāra-samādhi*, concentration that is approximate or akin to *sammā-samādhi*, perfect concentration of the Noble Eightfold Path.

On careful examination it may be seen that the Four Noble Truths have already been presented here in a disguised manner, for the disadvantage or impermanence of sense-pleasures is the Truth of Suffering, the desire for the sense-pleasures is the Truth of the Cause of Suffering, being free of this desire is the Truth of the Cessation of Suffering and the renouncing of sense-pleasures is the Path. But the understanding arising from this is not a stage of sanctitude: it is unstable because the vision of Nibbāna is not obtained here. It is merely an insight into the nature of sensuality, yet it is a sound foundation, for it gives a glimpse of what might be and may generate an aspiration (*dhamma-chanda*) for the true

135 *Kalla-cittaṃ, mudu-cittaṃ, vinīvaraṇa-cittaṃ, udagga-cittaṃ, pasanna-cittaṃ.*

136 See Wheel No. 27: *The Five Mental Hindrances and their Conquest.*

goal. Furthermore, by anticipating the trend of the actual Four Truths, which come next, the mind will take them in more easily. Being familiar with the 'method' of the Truths they will not be utterly outside one's experience and so will be easier to assimilate.

For those of us less endowed than Suppabuddha, the way to the attainment of this state may be more circuitous, taking a long time, perhaps years, to realise, and for us the Buddha teaches the many meditation exercises and other devices whereby our merit, character and mind are strengthened and purified. For instance, again from the Udāna (4.1), is told a story about the bhikkhu Meghiya who, although he attempted to practise assiduously, was continuously assailed by distracting and impure thoughts. The Buddha when told of this state of affairs instructed him in five things leading to preparedness of mind for understanding or according to the text, for maturing a mind immature for release:

1. Having good friends and companions to encourage and advise one;
2. being scrupulous in observing the rules of moral behaviour;
3. being able to listen to talk that inspires one in the practice—perhaps today we may substitute this with reading the discourses of the Buddha and the life-stories of famous disciples;
4. being firmly resolved to make a continuous effort in getting rid of bad, unwholesome states and cultivating good states; and
5. developing wisdom and discrimination by observing how everything in this world arises only to pass away again is conditioned and impermanent.

After this the Buddha advised Meghiya to practise four more things, four hints we might say, for overcoming four specific negative states of mind:

1. The contemplating of the non-beautiful (*asubha*), unpleasant nature of the body by mentally dissecting it into its various component parts and organs and also its functions such as digestion and excretion. This is for overcoming excessive attachment and love of one's own body and the bodies of others, and gives freedom from worry and concern about the body.
2. The impartial development of an attitude of friendliness (*mettā*); or kindliness, sympathy and identification with others. This overcomes anger, ill will and annoyance and leads to a happy, contented and tolerant state of mind.
3. Mindfulness of breathing, the awareness of the breaths entering and leaving the body by the sense of touch at the nostrils, which overcomes the turmoil of excessive and distracting discursive thoughts. The mind is then able to be controlled and concentrated and to be used more effectively. This last is an important meditational practice in Buddhism, its reputation being enhanced by the tradition of it being the main practice of the Buddha himself.[137]
4. Developing the idea of the impermanence of everything that is called oneself, which removes egotism and pride and leads to an understanding of the teaching that all phenomena are empty and without a permanent core, i.e. are not-self (*anattā*).

Another preparatory practice occurring in the Pali Canon (Aṅguttara-nikāya, iii) consists of five contemplations, their importance stressed by being described as 'five things often to be contemplated by laymen as well as by bhikkhus':

1. 'Old age will come: I have not outstripped old age.'
2. 'Disease will come; I have not outstripped disease.'
3. 'Death will come; I have not outstripped death.'

These three overcome the 'three prides' (*mada*), of youth, health and life respectively, causing people to do evil deeds.

137 See *Mindfulness of Breathing. Buddhist Texts from the Pali Canon and the Commentaries*, by Ñāṇamoli Thera (Buddhist Publication Society, Kandy).

4. 'All things near and dear to me are subject to alteration, subject to separation.'

This overcomes excessive attachment to people and possessions.

5. 'I am the result of my own deeds; whatever deed I do, skilled or unskilled, good or bad, I shall become an heir to it.'

This overcomes wrong acts of body, speech and thought.

The ideas of impermanence, suffering and not-self are at the heart of the Four Noble Truths and produce the experience of Nibbāna. As the Buddha says to Meghiya:

> "By perceiving impermanence, Meghiya, the perception of what is not-self is established. Perceiving not-self means the up-rooting of the 'I am' conceit and one realises Nibbāna in this life."

That the body, feelings, perceptions, activities and mind are actually impermanent and impersonal is highly unsatisfactory and so we experience suffering because we crave to exist and experience the things of the world as if they were really permanent and belonged to us. This disparity between reality and our views and longings concerning it is what is termed suffering. By developing the idea of impermanence we cease to identify ourselves with what is impermanent and so do not crave for it, because if we did we would only experience suffering. If there is no craving, there is no suffering—when this is clearly seen it is called Right View, the first step on the Eightfold Path. According to our View, so we think, speak, act and live (steps 2–5); all our efforts to purify and rid our minds of suffering-producing cravings and the practice of mindfulness and meditation (steps 6–8) are directed by this Right View and lead towards the cessation of all such craving-engendered suffering.

In Suppabuddha, his mind compared with a clean cloth ready to be dipped in the dye of understanding, arose this Right View, 'the undefiled and stainless Dhamma-eye' which sees that suffering arises from craving and can cease by the cessation of craving. This is the Dhamma discovered and taught by the Buddhas and known as the Four Noble Truths: (1) Suffering, (2) its Origination in craving, (3) its Cessation or Nibbāna, and (4) the Path leading to its cessation, composed of eight factors, right view, thought, speech, action, livelihood, effort, mindfulness and concentration.

This 'clear seeing with the purified eye of Dhamma' into the Four Truths is the first stage of sanctitude, the 'entry into the stream' that carries one to the ocean of Nibbāna. From here there is no turning back, one knows where the final goal lies and one sets out on the journey towards it. Previously there was aimless wandering, being pulled first in this direction and then in another by one's desires, opinions and speculations, but now one knows the direction in which to go. One has started out on the path and however long or short the journey one is bound to reach the goal, final deliverance from all suffering.

Suppabuddha's attainment of this state is confirmed in the continuation of the passage from the Udāna quoted above:

"Then the leper Suppabuddha, having seen the Dhamma, realised the Dhamma, understood the Dhamma, penetrated the Dhamma, crossed beyond doubting, being freed from uncertainty, confident, not needing another (to inspire him with faith) in the Teacher's message, arose from his seat and approached the Lord. Having drawn near and prostrated himself before the Lord he sat down at one side. Sitting there the leper Suppabuddha said:

'Excellent, Sir, excellent, Sir. Just as if one should set upright the overturned, or should uncover the hidden, or should show the path to one who is lost, or should bring an oil-lamp into darkness so that those with eyesight could see objects—even so, by various methods has the Dhamma been explained by the Lord. I, Sir, go for refuge to the Lord, to the Dhamma and to the Community of bhikkhus. May the Lord accept me as a lay follower gone for refuge from this moment forth for as long as life lasts.'

Thereupon the leper Suppabuddha having been taught, instigated, roused and gladdened[138] by the Lord's talk on Dhamma, pleased and appreciative of the Lord's words, arose from his seat, prostrated himself before the Lord and keeping his right side

138 The Pali word *sampahaṃsito*, translated as 'gladdened', is also connected with the ideas of 'beaten, refined and wrought' (as with metals by a smith); hence it suggests purification and alteration of character by his attainment.

towards him[139] went away. Now (soon after) a calf attacked the leper Suppabuddha and deprived him of his life.

Then a large number of bhikkhus approached the Lord ...... and said:

'Sir, the leper called Suppabuddha who was taught, instigated, roused and gladdened by the Lord's talk on Dhamma has died. What is his destiny? What is his future state?'

'The leper Suppabuddha, bhikkhus, was a wise man. He practised according to Dhamma and did not trouble me with queries about Dhamma. By destroying three of the fetters, bhikkhus, the leper Suppabuddha is a Stream-enterer, not liable to fall away, assured, bound for complete Enlightenment.'"

The beginning of this passage leaves no doubt on Suppabuddha's assurance as to the nature of Dhamma and his confidence in it and in the Teacher. He then openly makes known his realisation, illustrating it with four similes, and declares that he goes for refuge to the Buddha, Dhamma and Sangha, i.e. that he accepts them as his sole guide and ideal 'for as long as life lasts.'

In the Pali Canon there are listed four characteristics of the Stream-enterer: having unshakable confidence in the Buddha, the Dhamma and the Sangha, and the practice of perfect morality. The simple ceremony of going for refuge to the three 'Jewels' of Buddhism and the undertaking to observe the five precepts of non-killing, non-stealing, etc. before a member of the Buddhist Sangha is the outward token of acceptance into the Buddhist religion. But strictly speaking only on the attainment of Stream-entry does one truly become a follower of the Buddha, for only then does one understand what is really meant by the three refuges and the vital importance of correct moral behaviour. For an ordinary person the Buddha, Dhamma and Sangha are external, whereas for a Stream-enterer they are within his own mind, a part of his being and intimately bound up with his realisation. The definition of a Stream-enterer is a person who has completely destroyed the first three of the ten fetters (*saṃyojana*) so that they can never arise again. They are:

139 This is a mark of respect.

1. The view that the various factors such as the body, feelings, perceptions, etc. are actually permanent, satisfying and constitute or are owned by a personal entity or 'self,' thought of as having existed in the past and continuing into the future.
2. Doubts about the Dhamma and the path to be pursued.
3. Looking externally to the world for purification and deliverance.[140]

The next two fetters, which the Stream-enterer still has intact, are sensual passions and animosity. Their grosser aspects are eliminated on reaching the second stage of sanctitude and completely eradicated at the third stage, where he severs his attachment to the world as we know it. There still remains however attachment to existence of a subtler kind, conceit, restlessness and residual ignorance (about the Four Truths) which are only destroyed on attaining the fourth and final stage of the arahant, the complete deliverance from suffering by the destruction of the last vestiges of craving and attachment.

The fact that Suppabuddha was gored to death may not have been purely accidental. The commentary suggests it was the work of a yakkhinī, a demoness who had taken on the form of a calf, but no concrete reason as to why this should have happened is given. It is recorded of other disciples that they died in similar circumstances after attaining a stage of sanctitude: for instance, Bāhiya, after becoming arahant (Udāna 1.10) and Pukkusāti who had reached the third stage of sanctitude (MN140). A possible explanation could be that in Buddhism what we are is the result of former deeds (*kamma*) and when these are worked off, like a debt, a change must occur in our circumstances. The discourse states that Suppabuddha was a leper, 'a poor, insignificant, wretched person,' maintaining himself by begging. He had only happened to come and hear the Buddha's teaching with the idea he might get something to eat from the other people listening there. His circumstances were the end of a long series of sufferings, the result of an evil deed in a former life. However on the attainment of sanctitude, a powerful source of good, and the simultaneous

140 *Sīlabbataparāmāsa* usually translated as 'dependence upon mere rule and ritual.'

wiping out of his past evil, he could not continue living in his previous miserable state and so died and was reborn, the Buddha says, among the gods (deva) of the Tāvatiṃsa-heaven, 'where he outshines the other gods in beauty and glory.' He is now destined for rebirth seven times at the most, in happy states of existence either among humans or gods, before attaining final deliverance, this being the result of his attainment of Stream-entry.

To summarise what has been indicated above, our aim should be complete deliverance from suffering, or stated positively, the unconditioned and perfect happiness of Nibbāna; to be differentiated from other forms of happiness which are imperfect because 'conditioned' by impermanence, and thus liable to revert to suffering when circumstances or 'the conditions' change. By an understanding of the Four Noble Truths of Buddhism we are set in the right direction to achieve this aim. But to reach this understanding the mind must be carefully prepared by moral discipline and other virtues, released from the grip of worldly pleasures and emotions and reach a state of clarity and purity through meditation and wise discrimination. Then by reflection on the three characteristics of existence, the impermanence, suffering and absence of an underlying entity, this understanding will arise giving assurance and confidence. The practical nature of the Buddha's teaching is that it leads one gradually step by step, like a building raised brick by brick upon secure foundations.

Although what has been said above may appear fairly straightforward, in fact it is very difficult to do and so we must not be disheartened by apparent setbacks and failures. And in case one may be led astray along false paths, it is worthwhile bearing in mind the following distinction from the Aṅguttara-Nikāya (vol. IV) that this Dhamma "leads to dispassion and not to attachment; to release from bondage and not to bondage; to the dispersion of defilements and not to accumulating them; to fewness of wishes and not to wanting much; to contentment and not to discontent; to solitude and not to mixing in crowds; to exertion and not to laziness; to frugality and not to greediness." And by this test one will know whether one is really following the Buddha's teaching or not.

— §§§ —

Our Reactions to Dukkha

Dr. Elizabeth Ashby

Bodhi Leaves No. 26

First published: 1965

Our Reactions to Dukkha

> "Now this, monks, is the Noble Truth about Ill. Birth is Ill, Ageing is Ill, Sickness is Ill, Death is Ill, likewise Sorrow and Grief, Woe, Lamentation and Despair. To be conjoined with things we dislike, to be separated from things which we like — that also is Ill. Not to get what one wants, that also is Ill, In a word, this Body, this fivefold mass which is based on grasping, that is Ill."
>
> — SN 5

Here, bleak and uncompromising, is the First Noble Truth. To understand it "according to reality" is the hard-won privilege of the Stream Winner, the result of earnest contemplation. But it seems possible that we can condition our minds intellectually in such a way that, when the right time comes, the Truth will reveal itself. The more we know about Ill, the more clearly shall we see the unsatisfactory state of "being" in which we find ourselves, and the "dry method" of approach will perhaps enable us to face up to Ill in all its myriad manifestations.

There is no English word that will render all the meanings of the Pali *dukkha.* "Ill" serves the purpose pretty well, so to a certain extent do the terms "suffering" and "anguish." There remains a deeper, more general meaning, given by Evola, as "a state of agitation, of restlessness or commotion rather than suffering…it is the antithesis of unshakable calm."

There are three different angles from which we can consider the way that *dukkha* impinges on the senses.

1. *Generalized dukkha.* The mass suffering due to war, famine, and pestilence that overwhelms large groups of humanity at the same time, and the less appreciated concealed dukkha, common to all, dependent on our underlying restlessness and discontent — the rubs and frustrations of everyday life, and the moods and emotions that interfere with the inner life, which, for want to a better word, we call "spiritual." As St. Paul put it: "We know that the whole creation groaneth and travaileth together in pain until now."

2. *Adventitious dukkha.* By this is meant dukkha that comes under our immediate observation, but which does not primarily involve ourselves; street accidents, the sick neighbour, the live thrush caught in a strawberry net.

3. *Dukkha that is Private and Personal.* This is the ill that affects each and all of us according to our kamma, and as such it is of the first importance to our own poor little egos. It will be dealt with more fully later on, but first let us consider some of the reactions that are evoked by dukkha in general.

Types of Reactions

1. *Blinkers.* Many people find the thought of suffering very unpleasant, and they try to shut it out as far as possible. "I'm so sensitive I can't *bear* to hear about it," or, more callously, "It's not my funeral." Those who are "born lucky" or in fortunate circumstances are prone to wear blinkers. These, when they first contact Buddhism, are repelled by the idea that life is fundamentally unsatisfactory; they think of their pleasures past, present, and future, and ignore the minor frustrations of everyday life. An extension of the "blinkers" is that of the "rose-coloured spectacles," the wearers of which think that "all is for the best in the best of all possible worlds." Voltaire's *Candide* is a bitter satire founded on this theme.

2. *Blind Acceptance.* This is characteristic of animals and some primitive races which accept the miseries of an uncomfortable situation, or the hazards of existence, because such things are part and parcel of their ordinary life.

3. *Prayer.* The reaction of the "faithful" is to look for supernatural aid. This, performed in a somewhat perfunctory fashion, may be a day set apart for nation-wide prayer in the advent of some calamity, or the prayers of an individual in distress. From the Buddhist standpoint this reaction is useless if there be no God, and a gross impertinence if there is one. Psychologically the individual may feel comforted by the thought that he has shifted his responsibility on to a higher power.

4. *Lamentation.* This is very usual when a valued treasure has been lost, or in the case of bereavement ("Where are you, little only son? Where are you, little only son?" —MN 87). A frequent form

of lamentation in the West is "Why should this happen to ME?" When shouldn't it? Have we never heard of kamma?

5. *Grumbling.* A useless proceeding; moreover it is likely to create fresh dukkha. The confirmed grumbler is disliked, and is consequently avoided by his acquaintances who leave him "to stew in his own juice."

6. *Worry and Flurry (Agitation).* This, one of the Five Hindrances, is destructive of calm. Work is badly performed, and the unfortunate sufferer may in time wear himself to a shadow. "We worry because we want to do so." This is a hard saying, but worth some wise reflection.

7. *Look for a Quick Remedy.* "I've got a headache. Where's the aspirin?"

8. *Drink and Drugs.* "He drowned his sorrows in drink, and got a helluva hangover!" "She's taken to chain-smoking, and it ain't 'alf done 'er cough good!" The Welfare State has had sad repercussions in the way of addiction to "tranquillizers" and "pep pills," and the smuggling of cocaine and heroin. "Drugging" may take a mental or intellectual form, such as the incessant use of radio and television. The constant reading of sensational literature, space-fiction or who-dun-its is another example. This sort of thing, especially when read in the small hours, is likely to exacerbate rather than relieve nervous strain.

9. *Hate and Ill-Will.* Another Hindrance, and very liable to crop up when one has suffered a real, or supposed, injury by somebody else. A common example is the "slanging match" that ensues when two motor cars have been in collision. The injured party lets off at the other fool, who immediately retaliates, and so, probably because both are suffering from shock, they increase each other's dukkha. On a lesser scale is the ill-will that is engendered when one encounters a rude shop-assistant, or is pushed about in a queue. The tendency is to shove back, or be sarcastic, and these minor frets linger in the memory for a long time afterwards.

Revenge is a deadly extension of the Hate reaction. "An eye for an eye, and a tooth for a tooth." The worst results are individual murders, and the age-old blood feud, or vendetta. For the Buddha's advice on this subject see "The Parable of the Saw" (MN 21).

10. *Envy.* "I've been ploughed in my finals, but that blighter X has pulled off an honours degree!" And so on, in every walk of life. There is one form of envy which we, as Dhamma farers, must be especially careful to avoid. This arises when our own practice is going badly, and we hear of someone else who has "made gains." If we are not careful we fret, and lose heart, with disastrous results. Does somebody whisper "*Mudita* — sympathetic joy?" That ought to be the reaction.

11. *Hysterical Outbursts.* This type of reaction is very interesting. Floods of tears, outbursts of profanity, and the smashing of crockery are frowned upon by society, but in actual fact they have a cathartic effect; a vast accumulation of emotion is worked off in a very short time, and when the sufferers come to their senses they feel much better for having given way.

12. *Enjoyment of Suffering.* The worst manifestation is sadism, which is fortunately rare. There is, however, a delight in spectacles that involve suffering to others, such as the gladiatorial combats in ancient Rome, the Spanish bullfights, and sports that frequently involve serious accidents. These things provide thrills for the spectators who thereby satisfy their craving for sensation.

The Tragic Drama of ancient Greece was designed for a different purpose, that of arousing pity and terror in the audience. The effect was intended to be cathartic: by witnessing dukkha on an Olympian scale the spectators gained a sense of proportion, and were purged of their own emotions. The effect can be quite terrifying; on one occasion a translation of "The Trojan Women" of Euripides, acted on an English stage, reduced the whole audience to tears. The reaction was a strange mixture of pain and exaltation.

In a more subtle form there is enjoyment of one's personal dukkha — the sensation of being a martyr. And it is possible to feel that, because one is capable of great suffering, this faculty raises one above the insensitive herd. This appears to be a superiority conceit.

13. *Capitalization of Misfortune,* as in the case of midgets, "armless wonders," and Siamese twins who earn their living by exposing their deformities to the public gaze. A degrading example of gain from another's misfortune is the case of the Spanish beggar who displays the distorted legs of his own little boy. A minor example of

this is the desire to make the most of one's own affliction as when a blind man or a cripple hurls himself into a stream of traffic because he knows that everything will give way to him. And have not many of us been tempted to prolong a period of convalescence?

14. *Relapse into Dullness (Moha).* Sometimes it seems that the ego can no longer contend with life; it throws in the sponge, so to speak, and the sufferer becomes mentally deranged. Any form of mental disorder may occur; and the patient has the doubtful blessing of being freed from his responsibilities. Another type of this reaction occurs in people who, tired out with the hardships and monotony of life, refuse to get out of bed after an illness. There they will lie, year after year, content to spend the rest of their lives as social parasites.

15. *Physical.* Dukkha, which is always associated with some kind of emotion, shows out physically in a number of ways. Sudden bad news has the effect of a blow in the stomach, and in times of stress there is a general feeling of weight in the abdomen; continued worry frequently produces gastric troubles of an organic nature. Shock can turn the hair white in the course of a few hours, and fear, now, as in the Buddha's time, can make the hair stand on end (Dig. Nik. I.2.). Sweating is another phenomenon associated with fear and nervousness, so is palpitation. "My heart went into my boots!" is a common expression signifying a state of alarm. When anger arises as a result of some unpleasant happening circulatory changes are very common: the red, or even purple, face; and there is a "white anger" that is still more devastating.

16. *Suicide:* the last resort of the anguished. In the eyes of the Western Church it is a "mortal sin"; the law regards it as a crime, and the public believes that it is due to either cowardice or lunacy. The Stoics thought otherwise: "Remember that the door stands open. Be not more fearful than children; but as they, when weary of the game, cry 'I will play no more,' even so, when thou art in like case, cry 'I will play no more' and depart. But if thou stayest, make no lamentation" (Epictetus). For the Buddhist, suicide is a grievous mistake because it is a kamma-producing act, and on account of its violence will produce some violent form of kamma in a future life.

The only exception is the arahant, a perfected one whose kamma is no longer operative; he may end his life how and when he will.

This is a formidable list, though incomplete; the most obvious reaction has been left out. Can readers supply it for themselves? On looking through this unedifying catalogue the writer was horrified to find how many of our reactions to dukkha stem from the three roots of evil: greed, hate, and delusion. There remain, however, several reactions that are, in the main, healthy.

Positive Reactions

1. *Endurance.* "The Lord gave and the Lord taketh away. Blessed be the Lord." That is the endurance of the "faithful," and it is dangerously near blind acceptance. In Buddhism endurance is a positive virtue which eliminates some of the cankers (*asavas*). Uncomfortable physical conditions, minor pains and injuries, "irritating talk" are things to be taken in one's stride, without complaint and without ill-will, and without even the wish for a more comfortable situation (MN 2).

2. *The Heroic.* "Curse God and Die!" That is defiance of Fate in the person of Omnipotence,

> "Under the bludgeonings of chance My head is bloody,
> but unbowed."

Pride, "stinking pride," but there is nothing craven in it. A very different heroism is that with which the blind and the disabled fight their way back again into a useful existence and the unrecognized courage of the women who cope with the *res angusta domi* — the littleness and bitterness that domestic life so often involves. It can be said that the heroic reaction is needful to all of us; only those disciples who possess the Ariyan, or heroic spirit will be able to remain steadfast.

3. *The Philosophic.* "There are worse things happen at sea!" "It'll be all the same in a hundred years." On a somewhat higher level, Lady Mary Wortley Montague wrote to Pope: "Let us then, which is the only true philosophy, be contented with our chance of being born in this vile planet, where we shall find however, God be thanked, much to laugh at, though little to approve." For "chance" read kamma, but let us keep the laughter (it is one of the "selling

points" of Zen). Humour, because it is aware of the incongruities of existence, is in reality a sense of proportion. It ought to be possible to see oneself as of less importance in the general scheme of things than is a solitary louse, crawling down Piccadilly, compared with the rest of London.

4. *The Creative.* Poets, in company with artists and musicians, often find that their best work is done when they are suffering from some stress. Dukkha is then kept under control, and actually serves a useful purpose. This reaction occurs in less exalted people who, instead of moping, have the will to get up and do something. This is the beginning, in a very modest form, of the virtue of energy.

5. *Compassion.* This age is usually referred to as money-grubbing and self-centred. But when obvious dukkha, of the adventitious order, arises there is a quick response. A bad railway accident or a motor smash brings out the fundamental decency of humanity; help is proffered quite regardless of reward, or even of thanks. The infirm and the blind are surprised by the number of helping hands held out to them. On the contrary, the less obvious signs of ill are overlooked. Who has compassion on the grumblers, the bores, and the poor fools whom we imagine to be inferior to ourselves. These people, for whom we have an aversion, are equally in need of compassion. We are under no obligation to seek them out for the purpose of doing them good, but, when they cross our path, we can at least deal gently with them. Lastly, there are occasions when we should have compassion on ourselves, particularly our body, *rūpa-kkhandha,* "Brother Ass," who has to carry the weight of all the other *khandhas.*

Personal Dukkha

Personal dukkha, "wherein the heart knoweth his own bitterness," is our inescapable heritage. From earliest childhood we have been occupied with "I-making and mine-making" until we have persuaded ourselves that "I" am the pivot around which the whole universe, that is to say the *saṃsara,* revolves; our sense of proportion is completely lost. Does it matter to the beings on Mars, if any, that Miss A. has been jilted? "But it matters to ME!" is the instant reply of poor Miss A. And for practical purpose it does matter to Miss A.'s immediate associates how the unfortunate girl will react. She might, for instance, (a) drown herself, (b) go into a convent, (c) get on with her job and stop lamenting, or (d) take to writing poetry.

There are several aspects of personal "ill" that hit us all sooner or later. The most conspicuous of these are:

1. *Pain and Illness.* "Not death or pain is to be feared, but the *fear* of death and pain" (Epictetus). Pain itself is an extraordinary problem. We know that in many cases it is a danger signal indicating that some part of the body is out of order, and we think that pain is felt at the site of the injury or disease. This is not the case, for pain is an affair of consciousness, and is felt in the *mind* where it produces an emotional reaction. This is so deep-seated that we do not recognize its emotional nature, and consequently do not label it. Personally I think it is a mixture of self-pity, resentment and fear, all of which arise from *dosa,* the evil root of hate. Certainly we know from experience than an agonizing pain produces a mental state of sheer, blind misery.

A strong argument that pain is emotional is to be found by watching the results of an injection of morphia. The patient who has had a "shot" frequently notices a queer phenomenon: the pain is *still there,* but he doesn't care a tinker's curse about it! The morphia has acted on the emotional centre in the brain, and damped it down to such an extent that the self-pity, resentment and fear have vanished.

This emotional element explains the very different way in which people react to pain. An apparently trivial injury can lay out someone of the emotional type, while those whose temperaments are phlegmatic or philosophic merely yelp or swear. The intensity of the pain experienced clearly depends upon the consciousness of each individual. The perfected consciousness of the arahant is above both pain and pleasure; the emotional life is so controlled that he is aware of both feelings, but does not "mind" either of them. This suggests that an objective approach to our own pains will diminish our suffering. The analysis of the whole thing from start to finish helps to draw off the mind from the actual feeling, and thereby lessens the emotional reactions. The odd idea of the soldier "biting on the bullet" is no idle fancy, for if he concentrates on the bullet he cannot at the same time concentrate on the pain. What probably happens is that his mind flickers with incredible rapidity between the two ideas; the pain is still there but may be reduced to bearable dimensions.

The same objective attitude applies to illness. As is also the case with pain, illness impairs the mental functions. The practice of Dhamma is hindered, and the sick man becomes dejected and ashamed. "Wherefore, house-father, thus should you train yourself; 'Though my body is sick, my mind shall not be sick.' Thus, house-father, must you train yourself."). The right reactions, therefore, to both pain and illness are endurance and courage — heroism.

2. *Attachments.* Though attachments to things can constitute a menace, attachment to persons produces greater woe than all the rest of our misfortunes put together. There is a very important sutta "Born of the Affections" (MN 87) that emphasizes the dukkha due to personal relationships. We grow up believing that in human love lies our greatest happiness. And for ordinary people it is so. Then, why all this fuss about grief, sorrow, suffering, lamentation, and despair? The answer brings us up against one of the basic facts of existence: *anicca,* impermanence. Love is a conditioned thing — because it arises it must also cease. It is hard to realize that love, even in its most idealistic form, is in reality a manifestation of *tanha,* craving. We grasp at it hoping for security, for understanding, for fulfilment — for the assuaging of our "primordial anguish." And for a fraction of time we may experience all these, and deludedly believe that the riddle of the Sphinx has been answered. This is not so.

Two things are to be apprehended in respect of all attachments, the first of which is death. The sword of Yama sweeps away pets, children, friends, and lovers, and we are left — left to grow old. That, in human terms, is a tragedy, but it is a *clean* ending. Secondly, disillusion sets in when the glamour of the contact has worn off. We notice "alteration and otherness" in the beloved object, and a blight comes over the relationship. This may be so serious that the attachment may be broken off, leaving in many instances heartache and bitterness, frequently accompanied by a sense of shame. In extreme cases love turns to hate. This arises when the hater thinks he has been cheated or deceived; he hates himself for being a fool, and it is this self-hatred which is projected on to the erstwhile loved one.

Some form of "alteration and otherness" *must* occur in every case because we ourselves are altering all the time. Enduring friendships and life-long loves do occur because the partners consciously or unconsciously adapt their behaviour to the altering circumstances, and by so doing alter themselves in the right direction.

The cynic will ask: Why love at all if the end-result is always dukkha? Because, while we are unenlightened, we are impelled into it by the driving force of our own kamma; it is a necessary experience. We shall never understand what *mettā* really is unless, in this or former lives, we have lived through heights and depths of human love. Mettā, which is love on a self-transcending plane, irradiates the whole world, whereas human love can only glorify two bundles of khandhas for a limited period. "Whenever, wherever, whatever happiness is found it belongs to happiness" (MN 59). The Buddha, though he emphasized dukkha, never forbad nor denied happiness. His teaching noted the happiness of the sensory world, and led on to the happiness to be derived from the practice of Dhamma. Beyond this is a happiness "that is more excellent and exquisite," known only in the transcendental states.

3. *Ageing.* Strictly speaking ageing begins at the very moment of conception. A baby in the throes of teething experiences suffering due to ageing, and so too do teenagers at the time of puberty. But the ills of old age are the most obvious. The bodily changes bear hardest on those who were once good-looking, less hardly on the "homely" or the ugly. There is an irksome slowing down of one's physical activities; one can only move in second gear. There is the boredom of too much leisure occupied by too few interests. These things arouse in many people a wild rebellion — "I hate old age!" This is a useless reaction; it only intensifies the suffering.

Old age is a time of limitation, but it could be, indeed ought to be, a time of opportunity. Late nights, motoring, continental journeys, and even gardening are gone forever. These, and similar pleasures, are material things; they belong to *saṃsaric* existence. They must go, but now we have the chance to let them go willingly, with knowledge, but without repining. This is the time to break old habits, to realize that living is just another habit and prepare ourselves to break with that too. Furthermore, it is an opportunity to notice, and to break up clinging, a time to stop accumulating, and to begin disposing of superfluous possessions.

4. *Death.* It is impossible while we are still alive to react to death itself; we can only react to the thought of it. At the moment of writing it is still a future event that may happen twenty years hence, or it might occur within the next twenty minutes. One's thought leaps to the other side of death: What happens afterwards? Here we encounter ideas that vary according to our upbringing and our later studies.

> Rest after toil,
> Port after stormy seas,
> Death after life
> Do greatly please.

Very pretty; very pretty indeed, but probably wrong. As long as "I" want to be "I" (and a long time after), "I" shall plunge back into the saṃsara, the essentially restless state in which "I" am now living. An animal birth? A birth in one of the purgatories, or in a deva world? We do not know. Nor do we know how long it will be, according to time-as-we-know-it, before that rebirth takes place. Can consciousness, having provided itself with a mental body, or "body of craving," still function in the interval between death and rebirth? The Tibetan *Book of the Dead* has much to say about the Bardo, the Intermediate State, but the Pali Canon gives no hint of it; such speculations were put aside as "wriggling, scuffling and speculative views, the wilds of speculative views." The Buddha would have nothing to do with views.

"Let be the future." Our concern is with the here now. Death is Ill because it puts an end to the opportunities we now have, as human beings, for the study and practice of Dhamma. It behoves us, therefore, to cultivate a sense of urgency with regard to death. Paradoxically, at the age of seventy, death seems as far away or even further than it did at seventeen. The old have the habit of living so strongly developed that they cannot conceive the idea of doing anything else. They dislike being disturbed; death will not only disturb them, it will tear them away from their rightful background. They resent this: the "I" without its conventional attire will feel so naked. The Christian heaven has scant attraction for the average Christian because it equates with the unknown.

Many young people respond to the thought of death in an entirely different fashion: "To die will be a great adventure." That is the heroic reaction of the young — and the young in heart.

Erasmus, the greatest scholar that the Reformation produced, wrote a treatise on *The Art of Good Dying*, or *How to Achieve a Good Death*. He held that a deathbed repentance and the Rite of Holy Church availed nothing. In order to die well a man must live well in the highest sense of the word. That is sound doctrine. For us it means Morality, Concentration, and Intuitive Wisdom coupled with the sense of urgency.

"Now this, monks, is the Noble Truth about the ceasing of Ill. Verily it is this Noble Eightfold Path, that is: Right View… *Right Mindfulness*, Right Contemplation."

Students who are well-trained in mindfulness cope with dukkha in a very different fashion from the rest of us whose minds are still at the "drunken monkey" stage. Our personal "Ills" sizzle around us like virulent mosquitoes. If the suffering is severe, our own mindfulness is completely overwhelmed by *self-pity*, which is both a "muddy" and a muddling reaction. Our sense of proportion is lost, and we make matters worse for ourselves by imagining a host of unpleasant developments that might arise in the future. If, when we are in this state of woe, we pause and sort out our reactions — they are usually mixed — to the situation, naming each in turn, whether they are healthy or otherwise, we shall be practicing Mindfulness with regard to Mental States, a very important branch of Right Mindfulness. This is a very helpful practice because the mind is drawn away from the dukkha itself, and is switched on to something that is really worthwhile.

— §§§ —

Treasures of the Noble

Soma Thera

BODHI LEAVES No. 27

First published: 1965

Treasures of the Noble

The treasures of the noble disciples of the Buddha are not precious stones and pearls, silver and gold, or fields and houses. Nor are the noble treasures connected with the power and glory of earthly sovereignty.

On a certain occasion Ugga, the chief minister of the King of Kosala, came to where the Blessed One was, saluted him, and sat on one side.

And the chief minister, who was seated at one side, said this to the Blessed One: "Wonderful, venerable sir, marvellous, venerable sir, is the amount of riches, wealth, possessions of Migāra Rohaṇeyya."

"What is the extent of his vast treasures, his vast wealth, Ugga?"

"Of gold alone he has a hundred thousand, venerable sir. What should one say of silver?"

"Ugga, I do not deny that there is treasure of that kind. But, Ugga, such treasure is the common booty of fire, water, kings, robbers and unloved heirs. But there are seven kinds of treasure that are not the common booty of fire, water, kings, robbers and unloved ones. What are the seven? The treasure of confidence, of virtue, of the sense of shame and fear, of learning, of bounty, and of right understanding."

These are the seven treasures the noble have.
Confidence, virtue, the sense of shame and fear,
Learning, bounty, and understanding right.
Not poor is the woman or man with this great wealth,

Unlosable in the world of gods and men.
Therefore should he who is in understanding fixed,
Be diligent working to gain confidence,
Virtue, clarity, and vision of the truth,
Mindful of the law of him who understood.

In order to gain these treasures of the noble a man should be devoted to the doctrine of the Buddha. Therefore men of old said this:

Except the doctrine of the Perfect One,
There is no father and no mother here.
The doctrine is your refuge and support
And in the doctrine is your shelter true,
So hear the doctrine, on the doctrine think
And spurning other things live up to it.

1. Confidence (*saddhā*)

A noble disciple is confident, trusts in the Enlightenment of the Perfect One, the Tathāgata: "Thus indeed is the Blessed One: He is an arahant, perfectly enlightened, endowed with knowledge and conduct, sublime, a knower of the worlds, a guide of men, a teacher of divine and human beings, enlightened and blessed."

Confidence, according to a great Buddhist writer, is the entrance to the ocean of the Buddha's law, and knowledge is the ship in which a man travels in that ocean.

Says the Buddha, "In three places, Ānanda, should you establish, fix and make firm, your friends, companions, and kith and kin, who think they ought to hear the doctrine. In what three places? In wise confidence concerning the Buddha, the Dhamma and the Sangha, should you establish them, fix them, and make them firm. There may be change, Ānanda, in the four great elements, earth, water, fire, and air, but the noble disciple who is endowed with wise confidence concerning the Buddha, the Dhamma, and the Sangha, cannot change. That is to say, it is impossible for him to be reborn in hell, or as an animal, or where unhappy spirits dwell."

Confidence of the highest kind is that produced in objects connected with the realisation of Nibbāna, the peace arising out of the final destruction of craving. As the Buddha, the Dhamma, and the Sangha, are the objects most intimately connected with Nibbāna, these best of all jewels in the world inspire the greatest confidence in a Buddhist.

The reason for absence of inner development is primarily lack of confidence in truth. It is said that the bhikkhu who lacks confidence departs from the practice of the virtue. He becomes dead to all good, and is unable to establish himself in the Law of the Buddha and the noble discipline. Confidence is the first of the seven treasures of the noble, and the first of the mental powers, and the controlling faculties of the mind. Around the magnet of confidence cluster energy, the sense of fear and shame, mindfulness, concentration, right understanding, and many other qualities of the noble mind.

When confidence in the Buddha's enlightenment is strong in a person, the hindrances—sensuality, ill will, sloth and torpor, restlessness and anxiety, and uncertainty—are suppressed, the passions are dispersed, and the mind is bright and clear. There is no possibility for a disciple of the Buddha to fall into states of demerit so long as he has confidence in the Master and the truth: it is when uncertainty as regards what is good possess him that a disciple is assailed by influences that lead him away from the right path. The Buddha says that he watches a disciple so long as the disciple fails to produce confidence, but once the disciple produces confidence the Master stops watching the disciple knowing that he is self-warded and incapable of slacking.

Confidence is the hand for gathering the merit of good deeds, wealth for the attainment of happiness, and seed for harvesting the fruit of immortality, the deathless Nibbāna. Therefore it has been extolled by the Buddhas and regarded by them as the indispensable qualification for discipleship in the Dispensation of the Perfect One.

Confidence in the Dhamma begins with temporary conviction or belief in morally wholesome objects and reaches its crest in settled trust in the Perfect One, his teaching, and his noble order.

2. Virtue (*sīla*)

Goodness is the best thing in the world. The man of knowledge is indeed supreme.

> *Amongst deities and human beings,*
> *From good and knowledge springs all victory. (Therīgāthā)*

> *A noble disciple refrains from destroying living beings, from theft, from sexual misconduct, from telling lies, and from drink. This is called the treasure of virtue. (Aṅguttara Nikāya)*

Virtue provides a person with strength to realise the noble path leading to the extinction of ill. Vice is a swamp: who is in it sinks. The factors of enlightenment cannot be developed by one who is involved in vice. As the earth for those who live on it, so is virtue for the yogi; he has to be supported by virtue. Essentially virtue is restraint, non-distraction is concentration, and penetration is wisdom.

If a person does not think, speak, or act in a way harmful to his own and others' welfare, he restrains his mind from ruining itself. One who examines his own thoughts, feelings, perceptions, and volitions, will find the natural, untrained mind inclined to do harmful things: "What the virtuous person does is to gather strength for not letting the mind master him and for mastering the mind."

Virtue is necessary not only for reaching the highest happiness, Nibbāna, the extinction of ill, but for living untroubled in the world too. A virtuous man gathers a great mass of wealth through diligence, his good reputation spreads, he enters an assembly confidently, he meets his end mindfully, and is at death reborn in a happy existence, says the Buddha.

A virtuous life is a life full of excellence as it removes the corruptions of hate. Without virtue, man is not different from an animal. Without a strong and pure character, man decays and becomes useless to himself and others. Greatness in the dispensation of the Buddha is established in compassion through renunciation of the destruction of living beings, in honesty through renunciation of theft, in chastity through renunciation of sexual misconduct, in truthfulness through renunciation of false speech, and in sobriety through renunciation of indulgence in strong drink and mind-confusing drugs.

The virtuous man does not act hurriedly; he is patient in all circumstances; he acts only after careful thought; he acts not as a slave but as a master at all times and everywhere. Having built for himself a strong citadel of noble qualities he lives where he can never be taken by Māra. Through guarding their sense faculties, the virtuous preserve their energies, and use them for proper and useful action.

Virtue cannot thrive in minds that are fanatical, violent, avaricious, dogmatic, and inconsiderate of others' well-being. In fact, one of the reasons for a man becoming virtuous is to give fearlessness to others through kindly, thoughtful, self-denying activities. The fragrance of the most sweet-smelling flowers does not travel against the wind, but the influence of a virtuous life pervades all space, and the memory of such a man continues to sweeten the world for a long time.

3 & 4. Shame and Fear (*hiri-ottappa*)

A noble disciple is endowed with the sense of shame, is ashamed of doing wrong in thought, word, and bodily behaviour, is ashamed of committing evil, bad deeds. This is called the treasure of the sense of shame. A noble disciple is endowed with the sense of fear, is afraid of doing wrong in thought, word and bodily behaviour, is afraid of committing evil, bad deeds. This is called the treasure of the sense of fear. Principally connected with the sense of shame is self-respect, and principally connected with the sense of fear is the censure of the wise.

These two qualities, shame and fear, are also called the protectors of the world. True and good men, with fear and shame, the bright qualities, are said to be those who are god-like in the world. These two qualities have always been praised by the Buddhas, the peerless guides, teachers of the world, because they provide effective stimulus to noble action. The man who has these two qualities will keep himself from slackening and going astray. The man who has these qualities is always on the alert, always awake to a sense of his duties: on the one hand he thinks, "Wrong action, thoughts and words are not suitable for me, because I am a man of good upbringing who follows the Buddha and the Dhamma. Further, I am loyal to my fellows in the noble life, and I do not wish to do wrong when they think I am doing what is right. To do wrong or to be slack in doing what is right is not the way to pay homage to the Buddha and the Dhamma I follow. To act in that manner is definitely to be disrespectful and disregardful of the Teacher and the Law. Only when I, by practising the precepts, develop the qualities of compassion, honesty, chastity, truthfulness, and sobriety, do I serve the world and honour the Master and his teaching, through the giving of the gift of fearlessness to all beings." On the other hand he fears the consequences of evil deeds here and hereafter.

The man with a sense of shame and fear has a lofty standard of conduct. Morally he is very sensitive. He will never be careless of the means he uses to achieve his ends. For him the end cannot justify the means. The means must also be clean, non-violent, truthful, sober and honest. Nothing, not even the doctrine and discipline of the Perfect One, the Supremely Enlightened One, the Blessed One, will he defend dishonestly, violently, and untruthfully. If he is attacked, he will not retaliate. Retaliation is wrong according to the Parable of the Saw taught by the Blessed One. In that instruction he said, "Were villainous dacoits with a two-handled saw to cut off a man's limbs and were he even then tainted in mind, he would not be carrying out my instruction." The sensitive person, he who is endowed with a sense of fear and shame, keeps these words of the Master in mind at all times, especially in times of stress and meets with compassion his opponents who wish to destroy him.

The effective observance of the Buddha's teaching depends on the practice of universal compassion and the true follower of the Buddha will think of those who know not what they do with compassionate mind, grown great, lofty, boundless and free from enmity and ill-will.

5. Learning (*suta*)

The Blessed One said, "A noble disciple is learned, and is one who bears in mind what he his learned. By him is learned, borne in mind, recited, pondered on, and penetrated with right understanding, the meaningful, well expressed doctrines good in the beginning, middle and end, which speak of the absolutely complete, perfectly pure holy life. This is the treasure of learning." With that is stated the highest kind of learning known to humanity—the learning that ends all learning.

Other kinds of learning bring a man not to the cessation of suffering; they lead to further suffering, wants, deficiencies, that is to further birth, disease, decay, unions with the unloved, separations from the loved and disappointments. Such learning is worldly, partial, defective and unsatisfactory from the standpoint of one who has seen that all is impermanent, all is ill, and all is beyond the control of the self, except the renunciation of the whole mass of ill through the renunciation of craving.

The Buddha's teaching of liberation from ill is what the noble disciple learns especially. To hear the doctrine and to master it is the object of the follower of the Buddha who has understood this. What arises ceases; what has an origin has also a cessation. But what does not arise does not cease; what has no origin has also no cessation.

Now the learning in which the noble disciple is a master has to be gained through study of the actual instruction of the Buddha now found in the Pali Canon, which gives the most complete account of the Buddha's teachings without the ambiguities of the Mahāyāna, and which is historically the oldest recorded account of the Buddha's words.

The learning of the scriptures by the noble disciple is different from the learning of the words of the Master by the worldling. The noble disciple learns the doctrine through the intensity of diligent practice as well as through the study of it and so reads Law with the body and the mind; but the worldling knows it in a shallow way, through grasping the teaching intellectually and not applying it diligently to his life. The full profit of learning the Law comes only with the understanding of life that makes a man get rid of the attachment to life, that makes a man renounce the world. "It is impossible," says the Buddha, "that he who is full of sensual aims, enjoying sensual pleasures, devoured by sensual thoughts, consumed with sensual heat, and eager in the sensual quest, should know, see, attain, and realise, what has to be known, seen, attained and realised (that is, the Law), by renunciation."

6. Bounty (*cāga*)

The noble disciple lives in the house with thought freed from the stain of avarice, bounteous, with hand stretched forth to give, delighting in letting go, devoted to giving, and happy in distributing gifts. This is the treasure of bounty.

Through avarice and through negligence,
Thus indeed is an alms not given.
Alms must be given by him who is wise,
And wishes merit to accumulate,
Even when little they have, some do give:
Some do not give who have very much,
A giving of alms from a scanty store is thought
Equal to alms with a thousand pieces bought.
A battle and almsgiving are like it's said;
A few good men can overcome a host.
Who trusting in the good gives though a little,
Will in the world to come be happy through giving.

Renunciation, which is the essence of the Buddhist way of life, begins with the practice of bounty. First, the aspirant for enlightenment learns to give away his external possessions; then he learns to become indifferent to his own body and to follow in the path of the Master, who, in his Bodhisatta days, gave limb, life, and all that he held dear for the sake of perfecting the virtues necessary for the attainment of the highest good. The whole way to enlightenment is adorned with bounty. There is no property the man bent on Nibbāna cannot part with.

Through bounty a man becomes dear to others and finds peaceful and noble-hearted associates. The bounteous man's good reputation spreads far and wide; he enters an assembly without embarrassment, without diffidence and when he dies cannot but find happiness in the thought that he is taking with him the treasure of bounty to the next life. Appreciation of the fact that to give is to be endowed with mental treasure is not confined to the East. Bounty was, as it now too is, held in high esteem in the West. We find recorded in Gibbon's *Decline and Fall of the Roman Empire* this epitaph of Edward Earl of Devon: "What I gave, I have; what I spent, I had; what I left, I lost." The line of great givers of the West continues unimpaired. Although there is no-one who could emulate the Emperor Asoka, whose munificence is without parallel in the records of princes of the earth, there are many great and good men who have impoverished themselves for the good of the world, like the great Anāthapiṇḍika. Unbroken as the tradition of the Dhamma knowledge has been the tradition of the bounty in the East; but it could be made stronger and nobler were we to reduce our personal wants, and cut down our desires. The desire to hold on to money, property, power, and position, regardless of the suffering of others must be destroyed. Under no condition does the Buddha encourage blindness to the suffering of others. The stir of mind (*saṃvega*) necessary for pushing a man to Nibbāna comes from seeing the subjection of the world to suffering, and acting in accordance with that vision by letting go, renouncing.

Not only in the Dhamma, but outside it too the importance of renunciation has been stressed. Meister Eckhart says, "O man, renounce thyself and so with toil-free virtue win the prize or, cleaving to thyself, with toilful virtue lose it… He who both has and is resigned nor ever cast one glance at what he has resigned but remains firm and unshaken and motionless in himself, that man is free." To the attainment of unshakable deliverance of the mind through training in the art of renunciation does the practice of bounty lead him who is bent on transcending evil deeds, evil thoughts, and wrong understanding.

Through renouncing zest for every sensuous thing,
For sake of freedom from the thought of self conceit,
The lust of life in fine-material states,
And states of pure mind, all restlessness,
And every form of darkness, ignorance,
The fires of craving will become extinct.

7. Right Understanding (*sammā-diṭṭhi*)

"The noble disciple has right understanding; he is endowed with right understanding which leads to the knowledge of the rise and fall of phenomena, and with excellent penetration which leads the complete destruction of ill."

The summit of the Buddha's teaching is reached when understanding of the nature of life becomes complete, and everything that helps to that right understanding is included in this treasure which is the most valuable of the treasures of the noble. Without right understanding, it is not possible to reach what is beyond the reach of becoming, of existence. To be able to appreciate the happiness of the cessation of becoming, and to work for reaching that happiness, a man has to grow in understanding the impermanence, subjection to ill, and the absence of any self whatsoever in the components of sentient life. He who knows that only ill arises and ceases when there is arising and ceasing of any kind is firmly established in knowledge founded on direct perception and not on knowledge founded on belief in another's word. One who has such direct perception of the fact of ill and impermanence is a man of right understanding. At this right understanding does a man who trains himself according to the instruction of the Buddha decide to arrive when he takes refuge in the Three Jewels: the Buddha, his Law, and the Order of Purified Ones.

In the Dhamma, men are purified finally and completely, not by virtue and concentration, but by right understanding. Virtue and concentration are requisites for preparing the mind for right understanding. Therefore the Buddha praised the life lived with right understanding as the most excellent. How is that life developed? Through association with those who understand rightly, through receiving right instruction, and through becoming dissatisfied with the personality. The Buddha taught us to compare matter to a foam-ball, feeling to a bubble, perception to a mirage, formation to a plantain trunk, and consciousness to an illusion. If a man sees according to the instruction of the Buddha, he will realise the insubstantiality of all phenomena and develop disenchantment in regard to the things that bind beings to life. With the growth of that disenchantment, he will reach the freedom from all craving, the freedom for the sake of which men of good family go forth.

Saddhā-dhanaṃ sīla-dhanaṃ / hiri-ottappiyaṃ dhanaṃ
suta dhanañ-ca cāgo ca / paññā ve sattamaṃ dhanaṃ.
Yassa ete dhanā atthi / itthiyā purisassa vā
adaliddo'ti tam āhu, / amoghaṃ tassa jīvitaṃ.

These are the seven treasures the noble have:
Confidence, virtue, the sense of shame and fear,
Learning, bounty, and understanding right.
Not poor is the woman or man endowed with these,
Not empty is his life of worthy things.

Aṅguttara Nikāya VII: 5

— §§§ —

Escapism and Escape
and
Buddhism and Mysticism

Two Essays

Y. M. Rao

BODHI LEAVES NO. 28

First published: 1966

Escapism and Escape

How does one really distinguish between these two words? The dictionary meanings are pretty clear—"escape" is the emerging from bondage into freedom, "escapism" is flight from reality. If all of us were agreed on what is reality and what is bondage, the millennium would be here now; but in the world as it is, the materialists sneer at the religious people because they (the materialists) know that everything in this world is conditioned and it is escapist nonsense to talk of "The Unconditioned." The religious people on the other hand look at the materialists with pity as these poor fellows escape into their earthly paradise of "eat, drink and be merry, for tomorrow we die," and they do not have the courage or even the desire to think of the possibility of a hereafter. But the fruitfulness of the materialist doctrine seen in the triumphs of science has made the religious people less sure of themselves—this is seen in their attempts to show how very scientific their own religion is, thus unconsciously accepting the canons of science as the criteria for all reasonable thinking. Every religious philosophy must stand or fall on its own merits as a complete system. It is irrelevant to show, for instance, that both science and Buddhism take their stand on causality and that both find no use for words like "soul" and "substance." For, when it comes to kamma or moral causation, the Buddhist has to part company with the scientist, because the latter finds no use for this word either. The danger of eclecticism is that, ultimately, we may pretend to see in the teachings of the Blessed One fundamental ideas never taught by him.

I am here laying emphasis on the eclectic tendencies shown by the followers of the Dhamma in recent times, because the inroads made by philosophies alien to the spirit of the Dhamma can be seen even in the pages of Buddhist magazines. To take an instance, a certain author writes: "All sublimations, substitutions and repressions are temporary escapes which bring in their train more aches and disease. To control the mind according to a certain pattern or mould is simply to imprison it; there is no freedom in such devices. It is by passive and alert observation of the ways of the mind without condemnation or justification that the mind could experience a stillness and freedom not bound to time." These views are reinforced by another writer in a book review where the writer thinks that the practice of mindfulness of in-breathing and out-breathing is good to start with, but one must rise above it to exercise choiceless awareness in regard to the working of one's own mind. Compare the statements of these two writers with the following extracts from the scriptures.

> "What now is the effort to avoid? There, the disciple incites his will to avoid the arising of evil, unwholesome things that have not yet arisen, and he strives, puts forth his energy, strains his mind and struggles . . . he watches over his senses, restrains his senses" (A IV 13).

> "If those monks, O monks, who are learners, who have not yet attained to that unsurpassed security from bondage, were to dwell developing and making much of the samādhi of inbreathing and out breathing, it will be conducive to the attainment of the destruction of the āsavas" (SN 54:12).

It would be worthwhile to enquire into the philosophy whence these new ideas, so diametrically opposed to those of the Buddha, have been adopted. I am referring to the philosophy of J. Krishnamurti. This is a highly original philosophy, compact and independent, with but a superficial resemblance to the Dhamma. The point I wish to make is that the exercise of choiceless awareness of the workings of one's own mind is an integral part of this new philosophy and it cannot be adopted as a method of meditation practice without admitting by implication that the Dhamma as taught by the Blessed One is either incomplete and therefore capable of improvement, or that it is, like other religions, escapist. If, in anyone's view, it is indeed escapist, the right thing to do is to give it up rather than pay lip sympathy to it.

In the interests of clarity of thought, I shall try to state in brief the substance of Krishnamurti's philosophy and then attempt an analysis. If by any chance I have made any misstatements, I am always open to correction. As I understand it, it is as follows:

"The world is a chaos because of our greed, ambition, ill-will and fear. To make this a better world we either join organizations if we are inclined towards social work or politics, or turn towards gurus if religiously inclined, hoping that by these means we can accomplish our ends. We do not realize that the individual is the world, and if the individual were without greed or ambition there could be no chaos in the world. In our attempts to solve the problem, we create two kinds of hierarchies—the outer, consisting of individuals who are social, political or religious leaders to whom we turn for guidance, and an inner hierarchy of values by which everything is judged and arranged according to values. Neither the outer nor the inner hierarchies are of any use since they merely help to distort our minds' perception of reality.

"The mind depends upon two kinds of memories—one, the factual, which is essential for the purpose of making a living and carrying on our daily routines, and the other, the psychological memory which thinks of things in terms of values and hence of arranging everything according to some pattern. This pattern, which is built on the memories of past experiences, blurs and distorts our vision of reality. But reality is ever new and we interpret the new in terms of the old, and hence we never see reality as it is. By comparing other peoples' possessions or intelligence or status with one's own, one develops envy, ambition, greed etc., and therefore one lives either regretting the past or hoping or fearing for the future, but never living in the living present. Even the future we conjure up is but a projection of the past—thus we either find life dull because we ever see the old, or we are frustrated because we are unable to free ourselves from the bondage of the old. Therefore we set out to attain the real and think we can do it by means of self-discipline and a gradual process of modification of the self. But, in reality, there is no such thing as a self. It is a creation of the thoughts in search of security in a world that can never give security. Psychological memories strengthen this imaginary self, because everything is thought of in terms of "me" and "mine."

"Self-discipline which is meant to transform the self merely ends up by strengthening it still further. Why is reality not attainable through a course of self-discipline? Because reality has no abode, no beginning, no end, it is not related to time and hence cannot be "attained" by a process which is based on the thought "I shall gradually discipline myself and next year or in my next birth I shall attain reality." Reality is to be discovered from moment to moment and there can be no set pattern or way or method of attaining it in time. Meditation can help in this, but meditation is not concentration since concentration is but inverted distraction, an attempt to fit the mind into a pattern.

"True meditation is where the mind watches with attention its own workings without condemnation or justification, because in this way one breaks away from the bonds of psychological memory. One does not even analyse the thoughts, because to analyse is to divide the mind into two compartments—the analyser and the analysed. In the absence of psychological memory, the mind becomes truly integrated because now there is no conflict between unconscious longings and conscious taboos. Such a mind becomes alert, simple, innocent, and in a position to experience the real without the haze of memory to obscure the vision. With such a mind one sees the greed and violence in the world and immediately drops the greed and violence in oneself, not in time but instantaneously. Such a mind does not look for results but thinks rightly because it is the right thing to do. It does not even "practise choiceless awareness" because to practise is to postpone for the morrow something that can be discovered here and now."

In the above philosophy of Krishnamurti, we instantly perceive striking resemblances to the Dhamma. There is recognition of the chaos of the world (*dukkha*); its cause is traced to greed, ill-will etc. (*dukkha samudaya*); that it is possible to make an end of it (*dukkha nirodha*) though there is no set way to its ending. Reality is timeless (*akāliko*), to be discovered from moment to moment (*sandiṭṭhiko*), to be realised by oneself (*paccattaṃ veditabbo*). But the differences are no less striking—any kind of effort or discipline whatsoever leads to strengthening of the self, and that anything other than choiceless awareness is not true meditation.

With so much in common, where exactly do they disagree? Both start by accepting the fact of dukkha and both trace its origin to men's greed, ill-will and stupidity, but they part company when tracing the origin of greed and ill-will. The Dhamma teaches that it is due to not realizing the impermanence of all conditioned things with thoughts of "me" and "mine." Krishnamurti thinks it is due to our habit of comparing, contrasting, judging, condemning and justifying things—in other words, of assigning values to things, this valuation being based on the emotional residue clinging to our memories of events. He says we compare ourselves with others and thus allow envy to be born; we constantly judge things—"this is good, this is bad," "this is better, and this is worse." In the world of facts, as in the world of science, the division is between the true and the false only, and not between the better and the worse. He traces the conflicts in the mind due to the conscious mind judging all longings arising from the unconscious as good or bad, justifying the good and condemning the bad, thus creating "a house divided." But if Krishnamurti's analysis be taken seriously, then the very values with which he starts and on which he founds his philosophy vanish disconcertingly as a result of this analysis.

If we never contrasted chaos with order, greed with benevolence and ill-will with loving-kindness, we could never come to the conclusion that the world is in chaos due to greed and ill-will. What I mean will become clearer if I point out that his error is a semantic one. He appears to think that words like "chaos," "greed," "ill-will" etc. have two kinds of content—a factual content and an emotional content. He appears to think that if we ignore the purely emotional content of these words we shall be able to arrive at the purely factual content—thus making it possible for us to see things as they are. But this is a fallacy. The science of semantics shows us that words like "chaos" in Krishnamurti's sense or words like "greed," "ill-will" etc. have absolutely no factual content. They are all what are known as "coloured" words, the colouring being given by our emotions. Let me illustrate this by analysing our attitude towards the act of killing. When we disapprove of it, we call it "murder," and when we approve of it, we call it "war." But if we remove the emotional content from these words it is impossible to say whether killing should be permitted or not.

That the chaos in this world should be removed, that humanity must be saved, are all decisions that can be arrived at only with reference to what we, as human beings feel, about humanity. Nature, because she has no emotions, saves as well as kills all impartially. Only human beings can be compassionate and loving because of their emotions.

"Chaos," in a scientific sense, is a term to denote the state to which all organized systems tend in time. It has nothing to do with the "chaos" of Krishnamurti. If we remove the emotional contents of the words "greed" and "ill-will," they would turn into empty shells. People behave towards each other in certain ways—when we approve of them we use words like "benevolence" and "kindness," and if we disapprove of them we use the words "greed" and "ill-will"—but this approval as well as disapproval are themselves based on emotional valuation. If all our so-called psychological memories were wiped out we would certainly see things as they are, but not as wise human beings would do, but as cameras and tape-recorders would do. It is impossible to have fellow-feelings with other living beings without having recourse to our emotional nature. In one of his talks, he says that the beauty of the present sunset is spoiled by the memory of past sunsets. If we had no memory of past sunsets, if we had never classified things as beautiful and ugly, if we never had preferred one combination of colours to another, then our talk of the "beauty" of the present sunset would lose all meaning.

Besides, Krishnamurti's attitude towards judgment and comparison cannot be consistently maintained. In every talk purporting to show the ills arising out of analyses and comparisons, one finds detailed analyses and comparisons of the motives of gurus and politicians. If he were not carried away by his theories he would have perceived that not all psychological memories with their judgments and comparisons distort reality—for, if that were so, he must admit that when he speaks of "Hindus, Buddhists, Catholics or some such other silly sect," he is resorting to distortion of reality.

To come to the "piece de resistance" of his philosophy which appeals to so many of our present-day intellectuals—his "choiceless awareness of the working of one's own mind," "the watching of the workings of one's own mind without condemnation, justification or analysis." This is supposed to "integrate the mind" by removing the conflict between the conscious and unconscious states of the mind.

Let us try to understand this with the help of a parable. Suppose an evil faction has taken over reins of government in a state. There is a natural conflict between the rulers and the ruled, and there are sporadic revolts ruthlessly suppressed by the rulers. Then a wise man arises among the people and proposes a solution that is astounding in its simplicity. The conflict, he tells the people, is simply because we sit in judgment over the acts of the rulers; we approve of some of their acts and disapprove of others. But if the people refused to condemn or justify or even to analyse the acts of the rulers, it would create a marvellous integration of the state. There would be no conflict and the people would be in direct touch with reality. I do not know whether this method of integration appealed to the foolish people of the state, but there are many clever people to whom the parallel method for the integration of the mind appeals very strongly. In short, it is the art of resolving a problem by ignoring its existence.

We can judge the worth of this philosophy by applying it to the animal world: there is no conflict here between the conscious and the unconscious, there is no invention here of a self to be the secure centre of an insecure world, nor is there a classification here of "better" and "worse." Has that made the animal world less chaotic? The palpitating heart of a deer as it leaps at the crackle of a twig and the terrible fangs of the tiger sunk in the bloody entrails of its victim give an emphatic "no" to this view. It is not because we judge and compare that we have a distorted view of reality, but because we judge and compare wrongly. It is not because we think of things as good and bad that there is misery in this world, but because we have not worked out the right criteria by which to judge what is good and what is bad.

How does one truly integrate the mind? It is a psychological fact that repression drives the evil down into the unconscious—but repression takes place only when the mind is not alert and allows the wrong sorts of emotion to overwhelm one. But when the mind is alert and steadfast, all the repressed thoughts come up into the conscious, and if these thoughts are one by one calmly analysed, an inner transformation takes place and one finds one's evil tendencies gradually attenuated. Compare the historical parallel of the conflict between Asoka and the Kalingas having been resolved by the spiritual conversion of Asoka. Krishnamurti's criticism of one who undertakes discipline so as to postpone having to give up the violence in his heart now, is valid if the man is capable of understanding in himself the process of the arising of violence and yet refuses to drop the violence instantly. But what of those who are sincerely groping after such an understanding? One of Krishnamurti's listeners once confessed at a meeting in Madras that after years of listening to him, he had seen no change in himself— thus showing that a man may listen sincerely for years without developing the understanding; perhaps a course of disciplined thinking would have helped him.

To say that any kind of effort or discipline leads to the strengthening of the self is distortion of facts. The Blessed One realised that clinging to the five constituents as "this is mine, this am I, this is my self" gave rise to greed, ill-will and stupidity and hence advised the discipline of regarding everything as "this is not mine, this am I not, this is not my self." No amount of analysis can reveal in this discipline any element conducive to the strengthening of the self.

Another catchy little phrase that beguiles is that reality is timeless and "the timeless cannot be attained in time," but instantaneously. But even an instant is an instant in time, and if reality cannot be attained in time, it cannot be attained at all. But if reality can be "discovered," as he himself puts it, then it can certainly be discovered in time, for, conditioning is a process that has arisen in time and therefore can be put an end to in time.

In the end, I wish to say that with all the moral and religious fervour that pervades his talks, the spirit of Krishnamurti's philosophy is essentially alien to the spirit of the Dhamma. All said and done, I must concede that each man accepts what appears to him to be reasonable, but that should not lead to turning the Dhamma into an eclectic religion—or should it? "Whatever was said by the Buddha," they used to say, "is well said." But to alter this statement to "Whatever is well said must have been said by the Buddha" is either a sign of degeneration or a sign of "growth and development"—one of these is certainly a path of escape and the other of escapism. Which one is which I leave to the predilection of the reader.

Buddhism and Mysticism

The word "mysticism" is used here not in the general sense of ineffable religious experience, but in the narrower sense of a special interpretation of it according to which: "The phenomenal world of matter and of individualized consciousness—the world of things and animals and men and even gods—is the manifestation of a divine ground within which all partial realities have their being and apart from which they would be non-existent." [141] The mystic asserts in other words that there is a highest reality called variously the Absolute, the Godhead, Brahman etc., and the world around us is a manifestation of this Absolute; and what the mystic feels during his ecstasy is an awareness of the identity of the individual self with the Absolute or Great Self. Many great scholars, wise in the ways of mystics all the world over, have tried to show that the Buddha also was a mystic in this sense; that though he was silent about Brahman the idea peeps out, they say, in such words as *brahmacariya*, *brahmavihāra*, *brahmacakka*, and *brahmabhūta* (translated by them as god-fearing, god-abiding, the Wheel of God, and become-Brahma). One occidental scholar has even gone so far as to accuse the wicked Theravadin monks of deliberately suppressing all references to Atman and Brahman from their scriptures. Some other scholars have conveniently translated the Pali word *attā* by the words "SELF" or "Self" to suit their theories. Such "higher criticism" by which one can see anywhere what one fondly wishes to see must be a pleasant task. Here I intend to attempt a lower and more humdrum type of criticism, and in the process I may possibly tread on some corns.

To begin with let us read a description of mystic experience, shorn of all interpretations, from the pen of a sceptic: "… it brings an unusually precise and poignant awareness both of my present surroundings and of things remote in space and in time. It seems to be simply a very comprehensive act of attention, an attending to everything at once. And in response to all that this act of attention reveals I feel a very special emotion, which I can describe only as

141 Aldous Huxley at p. 13 of *Bhagavad-Gita* by Swami Prabhavananda and Christopher Isherwood, Mentor Religious Classic.

a tension of fervour and peace." [142] Such a vision is described in the Pali scriptures as "the pure and stainless eye of truth" and invariably the only comment accompanying this vision is:

> "Whatsoever is of an originating nature is subject to cessation."

Compared with this restrained and truly Buddhist statement of facts we have picturesque and glowing accounts by the mystics:

> "For he was then one with God, and retained no difference, either in relation to himself or to others." [143]

> "All at once . . , an astonishing radiance welled up on all the familiar things and in the child herself. They were no longer just themselves, separate objects with edges of their own; they were that radiance." [144]

But the most illuminating of all such statements is by the sceptic Stapledon himself:

> "In spite of all the frustration and horror of the human world, I am at these times perfectly sure that all our suffering and all our baseness is somehow needed, not for our personal salvation, for of this I know nothing, but for the rightness of the universe as a whole." [145]

Here we see clearly the difference between the Buddhist and mystical interpretations of the religious experience. The Buddhist is aware, in the clarity of his vision, only of the impermanence of all component things, while the mystic identifies himself with the life-affirming forces of the universe thought of as concentrated in an Absolute which is the fountainhead of all life. When the Bodhisattva sat under the Bodhi tree, Māra attacked him with all forms of horrors and temptations; and perhaps the mystic

---

142 From Olaf Stapledon's *Saints and Revolutionaries* quoted in *The Physical Basis of Personality* by V. H. Mottram, Pelican Book A 139, p. 163.

143 Plotinos, quoted in *Eastern Religions and Western Thought* by S. Radhakrishnan, p. 50.

144 Lady Acland at p. 154 of *Physical Basis of Personality*, op. cit.

145 Ibid, p. 167.

interpretation was the subtlest and most potent temptation of all and the hardest to reject.

Certain conclusions are inevitable if we accept this mystical interpretation. If the Absolute is the fountainhead of the whole world as well as of all the living things in it, then all the evil in the world also has risen from the same source; and Stapledon's conclusion that all the frustration and horror of the world are "somehow necessary for the rightness of the universe as a whole" is the only proper conclusion. We must love all living beings because all life is one and the same Universal Principle pervades them all, the mystics tell us. If this is so there are other conclusions that can equally well be drawn: for, Krishna tells Arjuna in the Bhagavadgitā—"He who regardeth this (Ātman) as a slayer and he who thinks he is slain, both of them are ignorant. He slayeth not, nor is he slain." (II.19)

The logic is unanswerable. If the Ātman is neither the slayer nor the slain then it does not matter in the least whether you love or slay other beings. As a matter of fact, the main purpose of the Bhagavadgītā was to induce Arjuna to kill his cousins and teachers in warfare. The mystic cannot be consistent—he has no valid answer for the ills of the world since ultimately everything arose out of the Absolute. Aldous Huxley with all his enthusiasm for the Perennial Philosophy is forced to supplement it by adding: "Some actions are intrinsically evil or inexpedient, and no good intentions, no conscious offering of them to God, no renunciation of the fruits can alter their essential character." [146] The appeal to *avijjā* as the cause of the feeling of separateness from each other and from the Absolute is vain since *avijjā* (ignorance) in the form of *māyā* is an essential power of the Godhead, or as the Bhagavadgītā says it: "The lord dwelleth in the hearts of all beings, O Arjuna, by his illusive power (*māyā*) causing all beings to revolve as though mounted on a potter's wheel," (VIII.61) or as Stapledon put it, all the suffering and baseness are needed for the "rightness" of the world as a whole.

If the mystical philosophy were to be made the basis of a philosophy of life, then we shall have to accept the world as it

146 *Bhagavad Gita* by Swami Prabhavananda, op. cit., p. 20.

is, with all its lust, hatred and delusion, and throw overboard all ethical considerations. If we look at all ethical and humanist ideals we see that they are essentially attempts by man to curb his normal life-affirming instincts to kill, to acquire property, to have promiscuous sexual satisfaction, to lie and chatter and to fuddle his brains to escape having to face the hard facts of life, ideas that form the basis of the *Pañca-sīla*. And all ethical systems are failures to the extent they come to terms with the life-affirming forces.

It may be objected that some of the greatest saints of the world have been mystics and they have been the personifications of loving-kindness. But this is the greatest of tragedies—that even those who overcame their life-affirming instincts and were imbued with love for all living beings finally fell victim to Māra's greatest and subtlest of temptations. They are a warning to us of the tragic consequences of renunciation unaccompanied by *paññā* (wisdom). The Buddhist arahant in renouncing everything finds nothing at all with which he can identify himself saying "I am this" and, without attempting to reconcile the good with the bad, sees things as they are; the mystical saint begins by renouncing everything but ends up by identifying himself with the very source of everything saying "I am Brahman" because this alone reconciles him to life and gives him peace of mind. The Pali scriptures contain several examples of warnings against Māra's subtlest trap. The most telling to my mind is at Majjhima Sutta 49 wherein the Buddha pays a visit to Brahmā who says of the world of which he is ruler:

> "Here is the eternal, here is the persistent, here is the everlasting, here is indissolubility and immutability, here there is no birth, nor old age, nor death, nor passing away and reappearance; and another, higher liberation there is not."

And Māra entering into one of the devas says to the Buddha:

> "O monk, beware of him, he is Brahmā, the omnipotent, the invincible, the all-seeing, the sovereign, the lord, the creator, the preserver, the father of all that has been and of all that will be . . . "

The Buddha's reply contains the warning to all would-be mystics:

> "Well I know you, Malign One, abandon your hope: 'He knows me not'; you are Māra the Malign. And this Brahmā here, O Malign One, these gods of Brahmā, these celestial companies of Brahmā, they are all in your hand, they are all in your power. You, O Malign One, certainly think: 'He also must be in my power!' I, however, O Malign One, am not in your hand, I am not in your power."

The conclusion to be drawn from this is clear. Even the Isvara, "the Creator and Preserver," is in the hands of Māra for the simple reason that Avijjā, the basis of lust for life, is the creator and preserver of the world. But *avijjā* in Buddhism is not the causeless cause of saṃsāra; it is a simple ignorance of the Four Noble Truths of Suffering.

Nowhere in the whole of the Pali scriptures do you find Nirvana, the Buddhist Absolute, described as the ground of all existence. On the contrary, it is described as the very negation of all life affirmation; either simply as "the destruction of lust, of hatred, of delusion," or more elaborately:

> "There is, monks, a condition wherein there is neither earth, nor water, nor fire, nor air, nor the sphere of the void, nor the sphere of neither perception nor non-perception: where there is no "this world" and no "world beyond;" where there is no moon and no sun. That condition, monks, do I call neither a coming nor a going nor a standing still nor a falling away nor a rising up: but it is without fixity, without mobility, without basis. That is the end of woe."

If all life is one, this oneness must be most in evidence when many people congregate. It would be interesting to know what it is that is common to all living beings. Jung's analytical psychology tell us it is the collective unconscious with its archetypes; and when people in whom the same archetype is active collect together, it drives them to act in an irrational way. This accounts for the brutal behaviour of large mobs, and even normally quiet and well-behaved people have been known to perpetrate unheard of atrocities while participating in the activities of mobs. " . . even a collection of highly intelligent people will act at a much lower level of intelligence than its individual members, and Jung once said bitingly that a hundred intelligent heads added up to a hydrocephalus." [147] Thus that which is common to all living beings is not so much the Ātman, as the lust for life. It is for this reason that the Buddha showed his greatness as a psychologist when, in the quintessence of the Dhamma given to the nun Gotamī, he said "of whatsoever teaching thou art sure that it leads to . . . the love of society and not to the love of solitude … that is not the Dhamma, that is not the Vinaya, that is not the teaching of the Master."

The Arahant pervades all beings with thoughts of loving-kindness, compassion, sympathetic joy and equanimity not because "all life is one," not because "the Ātman dwells in all beings," but because in him the negatives virtues of Pañca-sīla have fully flowered into the positive virtues of brahmavihāra; and to think such thoughts is as much his nature as it is for the sun to shine—or as the Itivuttaka puts it:

> "Just as, monks, in the last month of the rains, in autumn time, when the sky is opened up and cleared of clouds, the sun, leaping up into the firmament, drives away all darkness from the heavens and shines and burns and flashes forth—even so, monks, whatsoever grounds there be for good works undertaken with a view to rebirth, all of them are not one-sixteenth part of that loving-kindness which is the heart's release; loving-kindness alone, which is the heart's release shines and burns and flashes forth in surpassing them."

— §§§ —

147 *An Introduction to Jung's Psychology* by Freda Fordham. Pelican Book, A 273, p. 118.

A Larger Rationalism

Francis Story

Bodhi Leaves No. 29

First published: 1966

A Larger Rationalism

Writing in *The Humanist*, Mr. Hector Hawton once remarked that he had 'always been puzzled by the fact that Indians should become Christians;' and he adds: 'It is equally surprising to me that Europeans should become Mohammedans or Buddhists.'

Europeans who become Buddhists might well share his surprise at the fact that other Europeans become Muslims, since the basis of all theistic religions is the same, and lays them open to identical objections. What can be argued against one religion claiming divine revelation can be applied with the same force to all. If the choice between religion and non-religion could be settled simply by an appeal to the superiority of empirical knowledge over belief in the supernatural, the decision would not be difficult for anyone. And yet among the religions, the special case of Buddhism would still be left outside that decision. For while Buddhism is certainly not supernatural revelation, it does go far beyond the empirical knowledge with which it begins, while never coming into conflict with what we are able to observe and verify for ourselves. Instead of contradicting knowledge and reason, Buddhism accepts, utilizes and supplements them.

It sometimes happens that people change their religion not because one form of theistic revelation satisfies their reason more than another, but because the emotional appeal of a certain faith, or its associations, or perhaps simply revolt against the dogmas of their childhood, impels them to do so. But that is not always the case. There are some for whom the question of why they have not chosen one of the non-religious attitudes which others find satisfactory cannot be answered in terms of filling an emotional need, or following the attraction of the exotic. The rationalist may believe that it can; but his own case may not be so simple as it appears to him. Behind his rejection of all religion there may lie disguised a deeply-rooted feeling that if the faith of his ancestors and compatriots is outdated, all other creeds must be even more so. There is a kind of loyalty in this, but it is not exactly rational.

Those who have decided that Buddhism has more to offer them than atheistic faith on the one hand and the uncertain ethics of humanism on the other, usually come to that conclusion because they have been seeking a more comprehensive view of human experience in all its enigmatic, paradoxical variety, and a more acceptable explanation of it, than either can give. For obvious reasons, religion which offers a supernatural account of man's being in the world is unsatisfactory; at the same time, it is hard to find any superiority in a system which offers none at all. Whatever view we may choose to take of the universe and man's place in it, there are teleological considerations in the very structure of our thinking which refuse to be ignored; there are problems of purpose and of value which insist upon intruding into our picture. The rationalist who succeeds in treating them as though they did not exist is tricking himself in the same way as the religionist who firmly closes the doors of his mind against the improbabilities of his creed.

Rationalism is believed to be based upon a scientific view of the world. But the popular phrase, 'a scientific view,' calls for more clarification than it usually gets. A view that is rigidly confined to what happens to be scientifically demonstrable at any given time is not the same as a scientific view. If it were, no outstanding scientist could be said to have a 'scientific view,' for every advance in science has been the result of someone taking an imaginative leap beyond the bounds of what is already known. The mind which does not reach out, like a plant thrusting towards the light, is dead. Should we accuse Einstein of not having a scientific view because he divined the general principle of relativity first by a kind of insight, and only verified it scientifically afterwards?

At present, scientific thought is satisfied with tracing and defining the operations of the physical world, and its speculations have to proceed cautiously, step by step. It does not concern itself with why these operations take place. Its interest is limited and selective, and is unfortunately bound to become more and more so as specialized knowledge accumulates. We have come to a stage at which the separate departments of knowledge are as clearly marked out as political territories on a map. And just as the map is concerned with nothing more than these arbitrary divisions as they exist, while the reasons for them come within a different province altogether, that of the historian, so the scientist, as far as the field of his particular research extends, can quite happily dispense with all notions of purpose and design, and he is quite justified in doing so. To take one example, we know biological evolution to be a fact.

We are more or less familiar with its general development, and science does not encourage us to ask ourselves precisely why this complicated process began at all; or, having begun, what guiding impulse it was that by laborious trial and error over aeons of time converted elementary single-cell organisms at last into the highly-complex, though still imperfect, structure of human beings. Once it is seen that no Creator-God is necessary—that such a God is not only redundant, but actually impossible—it is thought that all problems connected with a purpose and a directing principle can be set aside. The layman is inclined to believe that because science disregards such questions they are of no importance, or that they have been answered. In this way a mythology of science has grown up which is not the fault of the scientist, but rather of the ordinary man who confuses science with omniscience. It is of course true that some knowledgeable specialists take the view that because science has not so far disclosed any purpose in the universe, there cannot be one, but they are becoming fewer as the vistas of knowledge extend. By appropriating to itself more and more of the supernatural (or what would have been considered so, not very long ago), science is becoming increasingly metaphysical. But it is only by taking a survey of it that is at once minute and comprehensive, that this fact can be appreciated.

In regard to the origin and development of life on this planet, it may quite reasonably be assumed that some fortuitous combination of chemical elements gave rise to the first emergence of living from non-living matter; there is nothing improbable in this. We now know for a fact that living cells could in the beginning have developed from non-living substance, and that it could quite well have happened accidentally or in the normal course of events. It must in fact be inevitable under the right conditions, and for this reason we are justified in assuming that there are other inhabited worlds besides our own. But, granted that life had this beginning, why did not the process stop at unicellular protoplasm? Or, if it did not stop altogether, why did it not go on repeating the same elementary forms instead of, as it actually did, progressing from one stage to another with an ever-increasing organic and sensory equipment?

The answer usually given is that it was in order to master the environmental conditions. But this in itself is an answer on the teleological level. It prompts the further query, What was it that gave apparently intelligent direction to these developments? Was there a something which was able to discern particular needs, however dimly, and to work through natural selection and other biological principles to produce the required organs? For after all, living structures show a degree of organization, with many details still not understood, which seems unaccountable on the theory that it was reached by the purely negative process of eliminating the inefficient. A positive, active process must be in operation before a negative one can take place. Although we see that there could not have been any omniscient power guiding the series of events (since, had there been such a power the fumbling process of trial and error, with all its ruthless wastage, could have been by-passed), are we altogether justified in dismissing the problem as irrelevant?

Even the earliest forms of life were undoubtedly fitted to survive in their surrounding medium, and many have survived to the present day. If, therefore, the sole objective was to produce living forms that could survive and propagate, they were perfect from the beginning. Even locomotion is not essential to life, for plants exist successfully, and in complete adaptation to their environment, without it. All that is needed for the act of living organically is a mouth, a stomach and an excretory system. There was no real need for the single-cell protozoa to develop more organs; no need for successive appearance of eyes, fins, legs, wings or any other embellishments to the primary forms. We choose to regard these as aids in the struggle for survival, but there is another point of view in which they may be seen as causes of that struggle. From either of these two viewpoints, however, the question of what it was that foresaw each need, and experimented until the need was met, remains unanswered.

It worried no less a person than Darwin, to such an extent that he was compelled to put forward, without evidence, a theory by which every cell in the body was supposed to send its representative to the germ cells, there to debate, in parliamentary fashion, the best course for the next generation. Unlike his more timid followers, Darwin repeatedly emphasised the need for speculation. "How odd it is," he wrote in his autobiography, "that anyone should not see that all observation must be for or against some view if it is to be of any service." So to meet a need he did not hesitate to regard cells as thinking, willing and desiring entities.

To discuss questions of motive without being able to define what it is that experiences the motivating urge is unsatisfactory; but in this instance we have no alternative. It is at all events necessary to assume some connecting principle between one generation of living beings and another which converts each generation into a link between what is desired and its realization. Biological evolution may choose to ignore this, but it cannot dispose of the need, nor close up the gap in our understanding which it leaves, so long as it is treated as an illegitimate field of speculation. Where we see something like intention at work, it is natural to ask from what the intention derives. And when, because it blunders towards its goal and operates extravagantly and amorally, we can no longer believe it to be the activity of an omnipotent and merciful Creator, we are not thereby compelled to reject the possibility of other sources of activation.

If the development of more complex and refined organisms was not absolutely necessary to survival, we have to seek elsewhere for a possible cause. We find then that while the acquisition of higher sensory organs did not contribute materially to the ability to survive, it contributed to the ability to enjoy. A tree lives longer than a man, but a man's life is preferable.

So it becomes apparent that survival is not the sole or chief objective: there is another motivation, that of hedonic satisfaction. And this is not merely ancillary to the survival motive, but is in reality the objective that lies beyond it, and to the realization of which survival is only the first necessity. Biological evolution is subservient to the pleasure principle; its purpose is nothing but the development of organisms that are capable of heightened sensory experience, the pleasures of seeing, hearing, smelling, tasting, touching—and thinking.

It is precisely this desire for sensory pleasure that Buddhism declares to be the life-impulse, the causative principle behind every living form, whatever may be its particular stage of development, and whether it be on this planet or any other. Defined simply as *taṇhā* (literally, thirst or craving), this takes the place in Buddhism of a 'creator.' Since it is self-renewing, the process of creation is perpetual and cyclic, and there is no need for a first cause. Although our universe had a beginning, and will one day come to an end, in the Buddhist view it is only one of a series of universes, and the series had no ultimate beginning. According to Buddhist cosmology, when a world-system comes to an end a long period ensues during which matter remains in an unorganized state; then by degrees it forms into fresh world-systems, or island universes, and gradually life appears once more. When it does so it is the result of the rebirth of beings from the previous world-cycle, whose karmic force acts together with chemical processes in nature to produce the first organic structures. The process is described in a mixture of literal and allegorical language in the Aggañña Sutta of the Dīgha Nikāya and elsewhere. In interpreting the Buddhist account of evolution it is useful to remember that we have no geological record of the very first living organisms that appeared on earth. Being protoplasmic they passed away without leaving any fossilized traces. For all we know, there may have been other, even less substantial beings in existence before them, and the Aggañña account may be more literal than it appears.

Craving is a mental impulse, and Buddhism treats mental energy as a force in some ways analogous to electricity, or perhaps to electromagnetic waves. That thought-impulses do take some such form is supported by the evidence of their action on the Hans Berger encephalogram. We will leave aside any reference to telepathy because, although it has been proved to the satisfaction of most reasonable people, there are still those who refuse to acknowledge its reality. Even leaving aside all arguments that can be drawn from parapsychology, science has shown that the great governing principles of the universe operate by means which are themselves invisible and often indefinable. Electric current under the right conditions is transformed into heat, light, sound and power; yet still its actual nature eludes definition. Gravitational force keeps the galaxies in place and the moon gives us our tides, but we can find no physical connection between the moon as a body in space and the water on our planet. We are not even certain whether gravity is a property of matter or a special function of curved space. It is often necessary to remind ourselves that while science points to causal relationships between events it cannot always explain just what these relationships mean in physical terms. Some philosophers of science are even ready to throw the whole concept of causality to the winds. A great part of the scientist's time is devoted to examining and measuring the tangible effects of forces which themselves cannot be examined, and so remain essentially a mystery. If this is true of physics it is even more true of genetics and biology.

So when Buddhism asserts that it is 'craving' which gives directional impulse and purpose to the processes of physical evolution, through mental energy transmitted by one being to another in successive lives, the materialist may raise his eyebrows but he is unable to point to any established scientific truth that is outraged by the theory. The Buddhist, on the other hand, can offer in support of his view the opinion of several eminent men of science to the effect that something like thought and intention is visible in our universe.

In this world, mind depends upon matter for its manifestation, just as the electrical current depends upon some more ponderable agency to convert it into heat, light or power. This fact has given rise to the very unwarranted assumption that mind is a product of matter. It is unwarrantable because the position could quite well be reversed, without changing the picture of the universe as we know it. But avoiding these two extremes, Buddhism maintains that matter and mentality are interdependent; the living organisms produced in the evolutionary pattern have been the result of a transmitted will-to-live, a current of 'becoming' which is based upon craving, and which can be perceived only through its material manifestations, the various grades of living beings. Mind, or mental energy, operates on and through matter to attain its ends.

There is one truth which science impresses upon us very strongly: that this universe is not a universe of 'things' but of events. It is a complex of dynamic processes in which an everlasting 'becoming,' that never reaches the state of perfect 'being,' is the sole actuality. This is the truth as it was seen and taught by the Buddha from the beginning of his ministry. The much misunderstood doctrine of rebirth in Buddhism does not mean the transmigration of a soul, for the existence of any such persisting entity is completely denied. There is no question of a personal survival or immortality, either partial or complete. Personality is seen as a collection of aggregates, physical and mental, which come together and disintegrate again in obedience to natural law and to the mind-originated causes from the past. Everything that is subject to conditionality is subject to dissolution, and can never attain completeness.

Each state of existence is therefore only a momentary link between past and future states, and what we call life is nothing but a causal continuum. To put the case in simple and concrete terms, an old man is not the same person as the infant he once was; that infant has vanished for ever. The old man is the present result of the infant's having existed in the past. Between these two extreme points in the current of cause and effect that makes up the individual's world-line, there have been innumerable other continuity-links from childhood to maturity, and it is not possible to single out any particular stage and say of it, 'This is the man as he really is—this is his essence and real self.' In the same way, at his death there can be no totality of 'selfhood' to survive and be reborn. Instead of the animistic concept of an unchanging soul-essence there is the transmission of his thought potential, by which his will-to-live produces another being (or a further stage in the causal series) to carry on the tendencies engendered in the past. It was this concept of the *will* manifesting itself afresh in a new individual which Schopenhauer called 'Palingenesis.' If the term can be dissociated from Haeckel's use of it in a biological sense it will serve as well as any other to express the Buddhist idea of rebirth.

It is quite commonly supposed that modern science knows all there is to be known about genetics. This is an exaggeration. Enough is known, certainly, to account for the reproduction of species considered only as a mechanical process, but whether it is sufficient to cover all the phenomena is another matter. The biologist is satisfied to name the chemical DNA as being the carrier of the genes which provide the fundamental units of heredity. It appears that all the necessary information concerning physical structure is somehow packed into this substance and thus transmitted from one generation to another. But the theory does not carry us any further than that. It may be adequate to explain how the blueprint of the unborn being is fed into the genetic machinery, but it leaves little room for variations on the given design. Yet variations of a minor kind are constantly occurring, and without them evolution itself would have been impossible. It does not attempt to explain how individual modes of thinking, specific character-traits and, above all, the complicated patterns of instinctive behaviour found in certain animals, can all be conjured into a chemical which, without doubt, we shall soon be able to produce artificially. It is all rather like the unsophisticated savage's notion that the London Symphony Orchestra is seated inside the radio receiving set. Whether there are such simple aborigines today is questionable—but we still have the scientific theorists. Had Flaubert been living now he would probably have found no reason to alter his dictum that heredity is a true principle misunderstood. The real function of DNA may be just what it is claimed to be, but that does not make it anything more than the physical conductor of an unknown force. According to Buddhism, that unknown factor is kamma, and DNA is just another material auxiliary to the process of rebirth.

Sometimes it is said that the Buddha made no direct pronouncement concerning God, and that his position was agnostic. This is completely false. The Buddha categorically denied the existence of a creator or overlord, and his system of philosophy leaves no room for a 'Supreme Being.' The Buddha's refusal to discuss eschatological questions was not due to the agnostic's lack of knowledge; it came from the fact that the mind in its purely intellectual functioning is not capable of dealing with anything outside the realm of relative concepts, and there is no language to express those areas of experience which lie beyond the temporal and spatial relations. We can think and speak only in terms of comparison and contrast, and our communication of ideas is limited to those things we all know and can name. Of ultimate truth nothing at all can be predicated. On the other hand, our need to think in terms of a beginning and a 'first cause' is conditioned by our habitual use of ideas which involve relationships. Ordinarily, relationships and sequences dominate our thinking as space dominates our physical movements. Yet there is no need to resort to metaphysics in order to understand that the idea of a beginning to time is self-contradictory. Although, like the curved space of Einstein's mathematics, it is a truth with which formal logic and semantics cannot cope, we can discover its necessity by reminding ourselves that space and time are concepts derived from the relationship between things and events. There could not have been any time before objects and their movements existed. Consequently, the idea that the universe could have arisen from nothingness at a particular point of time is a contradiction.

But while the life-process had no point of beginning in time, it can be brought to an end by the individual, for himself. He can put a stop to his own particular current of existence, the 'wearisome round of rebirths,' and Buddhism offers a technique of mental cultivation by which this is possible. It consists in the total elimination of all the craving impulses. This fundamental psychic transformation is accompanied by the development of higher faculties of perception and insight, in which the reality beyond conditioned existence is directly experienced. It was this knowledge that the Buddha possessed, and the evidence for it is in the doctrine he taught—a doctrine so different from any other creed that it is even doubtful whether it should be included under the heading of 'religion.' In this method of approach starting from observed facts, analysing and probing into causes and relationships, the Buddha more nearly resembled a scientist of today than any of the mystical dogmatists who have provided the world with religions. But his area of exploration was the mind, not the physical universe. It may be that the future of our own science will also lie in this direction. To understand the external world is merely knowledge; to understand oneself is wisdom.

The humanist and rationalist viewpoints appear to leave no opening whatever for a continuity of experience beyond that of the one life known to us. The good man and the bad, and the man whose life has been nothing but a chronicle of failure and frustration, alike come to the same end, a dark oblivion. If that is indeed the case, the most outstanding characteristic of life is its enormous inanity, its fatuous meaninglessness. Those who have contributed to human progress have no share in its results;

they die without even any assurance that the progress they worked for is a reality. We who live in the present century can no longer believe in progress in quite the same way that our grandfathers did. The idea that evolution marches in a straight line to perfection has had to be discarded. Science itself, which holds out to us gifts with one hand and swift destruction with the other, is rapidly qualifying for a place among the discarded gods. On what evidence can we believe that science will ever succeed in abolishing disease, congenital mental deficiency or deformity? If it cannot do this, it cannot ever assure happiness to all. Even its very real material contributions, which no one can deny, have not brought the happiness which we take to be the chief goal of existence; instead, they have given us more desires. And for many people those desires can never be satisfied.

Apart from these facts, we are confronted by the disturbing realization that this view of life gives us no rational justification for ethical principles. It is useless to talk of a purer ethic emerging from the multiplication of desires; that is the last fatuity of wishful thinking. If the sole object to living is experience of pleasure—which we must accept if we confine our vision to the goal of biological evolution—the most successful organism, be it a man or an animal, is the one that has experienced most pleasure. The means by which it has done this do not matter; the cardinal rule of life on the biological level is that survival and enjoyment are to be achieved at the expense of other weaker organisms. Therefore, any moral principles that man may import into the system are entirely artificial and unnatural. Let those who use the word 'unnatural' as a rhetorical term of condemnation stop for a moment to consider what is 'natural' and what is not! The plain truth is that Nature is amoral, and in this view man's introduction of morality is a perversion. When the humanist says, truthfully, that he experiences happiness in working for others, he is unconsciously denying the basis of what he understands by a rational philosophy. What his experience really suggests is that the ethical motivations which religion has brought into an amoral world survive in certain types of men even when religion itself has been discarded. How else can we explain this curious phenomenon of happiness arising from a subjugation of self-interest which is contrary to all the principles of survival in nature?

There is in fact another explanation, and it is the one that Buddhism offers. There is a larger rationalism, in which it is reasonable and good to introduce pity into a pitiless world, justice into a world of injustice, unselfishness into a system of survival by selfishness. In the higher types of men this knowledge exists subconsciously; they instinctively follow its promptings, whether it agrees with their philosophy or not. But to make the higher instinct rational we have to cast our vision beyond the limitations we have ourselves imposed. It is necessary to leave the dogmas of both religion and science behind. We may then arrive at the Buddhist truth that while all manifestations of life, from the amoeba to man, are dominated by craving and are therefore doomed to perpetual dissatisfaction, there is a fulfilment of another kind to be sought and striven for, and that the moral principle is an inherent part of the universal law of cause and effect. In place of the endless struggle for existence, with its emphasis on egocentric values, Buddhism puts a perfection to be reached on a higher level, the annihilation of desire and the final extinction of the life-asserting urges. When this becomes the end in view, morality ceases to be a morbid excrescence on the natural lust for life, and becomes a logical necessity. The transitory and incomplete happiness that the humanist finds in labouring for mankind is then enlarged to an all-embracing compassion, in which the individual ego is seen to be an illusion.

Then is the Buddhist goal a merely negative one? To the life-worshipper it may appear so. But when we re-orient ourselves to a view that is neither pessimistic nor optimistic concerning man's portion of happiness, but is realistic in its acceptance of the facts, we find that the oppositions of negative and positive have no significance. Or they take on a different meaning in the new context. If all the life-processes are, as Buddhism teaches and experience confirms, impermanent, subject to suffering and void of ego-substance, it follows that their cessation, the Nibbāna of Buddhism, must be the sole reality.

The real cannot be described in terms of the unreal, and the only possible answer to those who wish to know what it is must lie in the Buddha's own words: 'Come, and see for yourself.' Buddhism does not ask us to take any belief on trust, and the Buddha was the only religious teacher in the world's history who condemned blind faith. The worship of science is after all nothing but another kind of religion. The appeal of Buddhist thought to the Western mind is that it has no 'either/or.' It opens the door to a wider rationalism.

— §§§ —

Detachment

T. H. Perera

Bodhi Leaves No. 30

First published: 1966

DETACHMENT

Consort not with those that are dear,
never with those that are not dear.
Not seeing those that are dear
and seeing those that are not dear,
are both painful.

(Dhammapada, v. 210, tr. by Nārada Thera)

The Māra Saṃyutta of the Saṃyutta Nikāya provides us with superb acting by the three daughters of Māra, whose names are immortalised in temple murals, verse and song as Taṇhā, Rati and Rāga. Taṇhā is personified to represent the thirst to satisfy the senses, Rati represents the clinging or the insatiate thirst to satisfy the senses and Rāga represents the desire or the craving for the senses (*kāma*). They are, thus, the three dimensions of the all-pervading desire present in man eager to drink his fill from the founts of the senses. No wonder, then, that man clings convulsively to life when Death is about to lay his icy hands upon him. It should be noted here that these sense founts are called in Pali *āyatana*, in the sense that they lengthen saṃsāric existence instead of shortening it. *Kāma* or lust stands both for sense desire and the object desired *(kilesa-kāma* and *vatthu-kāma).* In its highly intensified form it is known as clinging to sense-desires *(kāma-upādāna),* the germ of future life or becoming *(bhava).* Man, in his ignorance or inability to see reality, invests it with a self or soul, when it comes to be called clinging to a self or soul *(att'upādāna).* Thus arises the belief in a self or soul *(sakkāya-diṭṭhi).* The deluded "being" called Man goes about saying: "This is my self," or "I have a soul," or "This is mine," or "This belongs to me" and so on.

The Aṅguttara Nikāya (A III 55) gives a graphic description of this poor "soul" running and sweating and demanding, for himself and those near and dear to him, the things of the world; not only demanding, but when frustrated, how he becomes the prime mover in causing untold misery to others and inevitably the cause of his own unhappiness and ruin. "Enraptured with lust, enraged with anger, blinded by delusion, overwhelmed, with mind ensnared, man aims at his own ruin, at others' ruin, at the ruin of both parties, and he experiences mental pain and grief. But, if lust, anger and delusion are given up, man aims neither at his own ruin, nor at others' ruin, nor at the ruin of both parties, and he experiences no mental pain and grief. Thus is Nibbāna immediate, visible in this life, inviting, attractive and comprehensible to the wise."

The three daughters of Māra danced, each one trying to excel the other. Lord Buddha sat beneath the Bodhi-tree and looked on with a mind free from lust (*vītarāgaṃ cittaṃ*), with a mind free from hate (*vītadosaṃ cittaṃ*), with a mind free from delusion (*vītamohaṃ cittaṃ*). The initial step to achieve these three supreme states of mind he had taken six years before when as Prince Siddhattha, he left behind all that the heart of man is attached to. In other words, on that great night he made the unique renunciation—*nekkhamma*, the very opposite of sensual desire (*kāma-raga*)—and left home for homelessness (*pabbajjā*) in quest of Truth—the noble quest (*ariyapariyesanā*). Thus detached from all those that are dear, he strove ceaselessly for six long years, and ultimately gained concentration (*samādhi*), which rewarded him with wisdom (*paññā*), with Enlightenment and Nibbāna.

Permit me, at this point, to digress a little. We often hear the phrase "leaving the world" used to mean that a person has left behind much or little, donned the yellow robe of renunciation and sought the shelter of a sylvan hermitage. Yet, he is in the world, as much as you and I are in the world. Let us hear what the Blessed One tells of his supreme renunciation. The reader is referred to the Ariyapariyesana Sutta, MN 26: "I went from home-life (*āgārasmā*) into homelessness (*anagāriyaṃ*)." What he actually did was to change his environment from the pleasures of Kapilavatthu to the rigours of a solitary life on the banks of Nerañjarā. It was here that he developed his mind (*bhāvitaya*) to the highest peak of perfection and understood the world as it really is. Let me quote his words as recorded in the Rohitassa Sutta: "In this very one-fathom-long body along with its perceptions and thoughts, I proclaim the world, the origin of the world, the cessation of the world and the path leading to the cessation of the world." In other words, the Buddha, as well as arahants, have discovered the world (suffering) in this one-fathom-long body, namely the Four Noble Truths, the re-discovery of which by any one of us, in the manner taught by the Buddha, brings to an end the turmoils, the tribulations, the tortures, the tyrannies and the sorrows of saṃsāric existence. Hence, "to leave the world" really means to endeavour with determined zeal to achieve total abandonment of craving, the cosmic energy present in every being carrying in it the germ of suffering. And this supreme consummation, according to the Buddha-dhamma, can only be achieved as a human being, born in the cycle of a Buddha, while sojourning on this physical plane conventionally called the world— be it in a forest glade, a mountain cave or in a cloistered sanctuary.

"In the world" according to the Buddha has only one meaning. It means in this very body. To the Buddha the body is synonymous with the world because of its breaking up and crumbling away. The "world," also, stands for the five groups of clinging (*pañcupadānakkhandhā*), namely: matter or form, feelings, perceptions, mental tendencies and consciousness. Each of these is void, is empty, is insubstantial. It is the self-realisation of the voidness of each of the factors of the five groups of clinging that demolishes the belief: "This is mine," "This am I," "This is myself." Thus Right Understanding of oneself as he really is leads to Right Intention or thoughts of non-covetousness or non-hankering (*anabhijjhā*) for this "world." Thus the Path is paved to rid oneself of sense-desires which keep on feeding craving constantly and thus give rise to fresh rebirth or becoming (*bhava*). Therefore, one does not "leave the world," but makes the best use of the "world" to put an end to the recurrent cycle of births and deaths.

I feel happy in the thought that I have diverted the digression into a channel in which flows the crystal-clear water leading to liberation. The more one contemplates on this "world" of the five groups of clinging the more does the urge to detach himself from all family ties, to leave behind much or little property, to forsake one's friends—be they a small or a large circle—the more does this urge prompt him to go forth (*pabbajjā*) from home to homelessness. To the wandering ascetic Vacchagotta the Buddha said: "There has never been a householder, Vaccha, who without forsaking household ties, has, at the dissolution of the body, made an end of suffering."

Lord Buddha has succinctly formulated the arising and passing away of each of the constituents of the five groups of clinging in this wise:-

> *Thus is form, thus it arises, thus it passes away;*
> *Thus is feeling, thus it arises, thus it passes away;*
> *Thus is perception, thus it arises, thus it passes away;*
> *Thus are the mental formations, thus they arise, thus they pass away; Thus is consciousness, thus it arises, thus it passes away.*

One who in his leisure moments of relaxation contemplates each of these items, and experiences the truth residing in each of them, is drawn closer and closer to the one reality of existence, which is impermanence. But, because of the callings of the domestic life, the continuity of his contemplation is disturbed and interrupted. However, one who has experienced such moments of the impermanency of existence concludes that, bound by the demands of the household life, it is not possible to gain the perfect realisation of the truth of impermanency inherent in existence, its unsatisfactoriness and its impersonality. Then, there arises in him the irresistible urge to leave home for homelessness. This urge and its consummation are considered as selfish by those who are victims to the deluded belief in a self.

Permit me to support my submission from a passage of the Ariyapariyesana Sutta of the Majjhima Nikāya (No. 26) where Lord Buddha tells his disciples the reason for his Great Renunciation: "Now I, O disciples, before my Enlightenment, being not yet fully enlightened, while I was a Bodhisatta myself, still subject to birth, decay, disease, death, sorrow and impurities, there came to me the thought, 'Why do I, being subject to birth, decay, disease, death, sorrow and impurities, thus search after things of like nature? What if I, who am subject to things of such nature, realise their disadvantages and seek after the unattained, unsurpassed, perfect security which is Nibbāna?'

"Then disciples, after some time while I was still young, a black haired stripling, endowed with happy youth, in the prime of manhood, against the wishes of my father and mother who lamented with tearful eyes, I had my head and beard shaved, and, wearing yellow garments, went forth from home to the homeless state."

As I mentioned earlier, when one's mind is intellectually agitated in regard to the evanescence, the unsatisfactoriness and insubstantiality of all existence, then there arises in him the inner urge to detach himself from all those near and dear to him in order to realise by his own efforts the utter voidness of life, and reach the goal taught by the Buddha. The mind is now engaged in a tug-of-war. On one side is the pull towards the domestic hearth, on the opposite is the pull towards faring forth (*pabbajjā*). The pull towards homelessness triumphs over the domestic life. This victory seals all attachment towards possessions, father and mother, wife and children, friends and relations. He now goes forth with a mind freed from worldly affection, and redolent with the will for deliverance (*muñcita-kamyatā*). Wherefore the Blessed One says in the Dhammapada: "Clearly perceiving one's own welfare, let one be intent on one's own welfare" (v. 166).

In this Buddha-statement welfare means one's ultimate goal, that is Nibbāna. This statement must not be given a selfish twist. What it does mean is that like a man whose head is on fire, one should first of all try to extinguish the fire of craving which is consuming the entirety of his being. The Buddha highly commends selfless service.

In certain quarters, this breaking away from one's kith and kin is stigmatized as a heartless act, as a betrayal of the trust and love divinely bestowed upon man by his Maker. Let me hoist these kind friends on their own petard. In the Gospel of St. Matthew at x. 37 it is clearly stated: "He that loveth father and mother more than me is not worthy of me, and he that loveth son and daughter is not worthy of me."

Detachment or the total giving up of attachment is, indeed, a supreme achievement, the result of a supreme effort of self-abnegation, which is the initial step, to the realisation by wisdom of the non-existence of a self or soul on which theists stumble and introduce a "Supreme Being" invested with the highest soul. There is no Being, but actually there is a Becoming—a mighty flow of efficient energy, with its characteristic of arising and passing away from moment to moment with no abiding eternal entity in it.

Detachment is an exceedingly rare commodity. It is because of its rareness that the Buddha says that only a few reach the further shore (Nibbāna) while the majority of beings run up and down on this shore. Detachment is the final flowering of the plant of life, the seed of which had been planted in the past, and through many a life in saṃsāra; the plant that grew from it had been instinctively tended to by weeding out greed and hate that grew around it, and assiduously cultivating it with many a meritorious act of letting go.

These were the people who felt that true freedom of mind lay in giving up everything, who came to feel the urge of the ascetic life, and to whom a few words from the Buddha or his arahants were sufficient to bring about enlightenment and the end of suffering. But many were the people who heard the Buddha word, but their hearts were not properly tuned to receive it.

After the demise of the Buddha there were people who heard the Dhamma from the arahants—people who had given up everything without the least regret—and gained illumination of mind to see things as they really are. To some people detachment, that is to give up one's material possessions, leave behind parents, wife and children, friends and relations, appears as immoral, as unnatural, as moral cowardice, as a mental aberration and as the act of a fool. They say that they perform their duties by their parents, wife and children, they associate with their friends and relations, and, on the whole, they are quite satisfied with the snug comfort of the domestic hearth. We do not want to dispute what they say. We would refer them to verse 214 of the Dhammapada:

> "From attachment springs grief, from attachment springs fear; for him who is wholly free from attachment there is no grief, much less fear."
>
> (Tr. by Nārada Thera)

There are, also, a few people who in their heart of hearts yearn for the ascetic life, but do not possess the moral courage to break themselves away from family ties and associations. To such people the Buddha says:

> "Wise people do not call that a strong fetter which is made of iron, wood or hemp; passionately strong is the care for precious stones and gold rings, for sons and a wife.
> That fetter wise people call strong, which drags down, yields, but is difficult to undo; after having cut this at last,

wise people take to the ascetic life, free from cares; and leaving the pleasures of sense behind."

Dhammapada v. 345–346 (Tr. by Max Muller)

There are, also, some people who have detached themselves from all that belongs to them, from their kith and kin, and having taken to the ascetic life, for some reason or other, best known to them, return to the lay life, from the free life of solitude to bondage. These are the people about whom the Dhammapada says:

"He who, having got rid of the jungle of lust, gives himself over to lust, and who, when free from the jungle, runs to the jungle, look at that man—though free, he runs into bondage!"

v. 344 (Tr. by Max Muller)

We now come to those very few people who, being really stirred by the misery of existence—the recurrent misery of being born, of decaying and of dying—whatever may be their ages, young, middle-aged or old, are overwhelmed by the urge to leave home for homelessness in order to walk the Path which the Buddha trod. Each one of them goes forth, chanting to himself:

May faith awaken my wisdom,
May faith awaken my insight
To see things as they really are:
Their arising and their vanishing,
And reach the goal which the Buddha taught:
The end of birth, old age and death.

These noble sons of the Buddha, having left father and mother, wife and children, relations and friends, wealth and sensual desires, roam at will in forest glades, reflecting on the many facets of the Dhamma, sorrowless, secure and alone like the rhinoceros. To them the Dhammapada pays this handsome tribute:

"He who dwells in the Law, delights in the Law, meditates on the Law, recollects the Law; that bhikkhu will never fall away from the true Law."

v. 364 (Tr. by Max Muller)

Thus a genuine disciple of the Buddha should conduct himself in accordance with the second factor of the Noble Eightfold Path, namely: Right Thought or Right Aspiration (*sammā saṅkappa*) to which are conjoined as auxiliary steps Right Understanding (the first factor of the Path), Right Effort (the sixth factor) and Right Mindfulness (the seventh factor). According to Dīgha Nikāya (No. 22) Right Thought is defined as follows:

1. Thoughts free from lust (*nekkhamma-saṅkappa*)
2. Thoughts free from ill-will (*avyāpāda-saṅkappa*)
3. Thoughts free from cruelty (*avihiṃsā-saṅkappa*).

Right Thought is again subdivided into: 1. mundane Right Thought (*lokiya-sammā-saṅkappa*) the fruits of which are visible in this world and produce good results in the next, and 2. supramundane Right Thought (*lokuttara-sammā-saṅkappa*) which is extra-sensory and extra-worldly and which occurs simultaneously along with the other seven factors of the Noble Path at the moment of Path consciousness (*maggacitta*). This thought originates in a highly developed and purified mind being the direct result of detachment, and it does not embrace "I," "me," or "mine."

Man's thoughts and actions are fundamentally dependent on three forces that lie dormant in his mind. Given the least provocation they prompt him to act in a manner detrimental to his own welfare, as well as to the welfare of others. These forces are: greed, hatred (aversion) and delusion. Greed or craving is attraction, while hatred is repulsion and delusion is one's inability to see the real nature of things, and, therefore, it is the parent of both attraction and repulsion. Thus man with deluded mind regards what he desires or craves as pleasant and lovable, and what he hates as painful and unlovable. It is this delusion that is the cause of the eternal conflict (*dukkha*) in man to be associated with the loved and to be parted from the unloved. Separation from the loved is suffering (*piyehi vippayogo dukkho*) and union with the unloved is suffering (*appiyehi sampayogo dukkho*).

Now, Lord Buddha saw that not only the five groups of existence, which put together is called a being, but also everything, animate and inanimate, in the cosmos is in a constant state of arising and passing away, everything is a constant change (*anicca*), and, that nothing is static (*nicca*) even for a split second. It is because of one's inability to see this real nature in the cosmos that man craves, and is greedy (*lobha*) to possess the loved or the pleasant which is in a constant state of change; and then he weeps, laments and grieves (*dosa*) when he loses the loved and the pleasant or is united with the unloved. In short, the cosmos is indifferent to human suffering, and it is sheer folly to expect security or eternal happiness while one sojourns in a cosmos subject to constant change. All along it is dukkha. Therefore, detachment is the only way to put an end to dukkha.

How can there exist a self or soul in a cosmos 'subject to constant change'? Yet, poor souls who are unable to see this true state in nature cling to a self or soul. The Buddha-dhamma alone, of all religious beliefs, categorically denies the existence of a soul or self. This denial is not a dogma. You and I can see it, if we totally detach ourselves from sense-desires and unwholesome things in the full glare of wisdom. Follow the Noble Eightfold Path in its triple division of morality, concentration and wisdom and you will be rewarded with the full comprehension of not-self (*anattā*).

This is the reward which crowns the ceaseless effort of the worldling (*puthujjana*) who has gone forth and first followed the Noble Eightfold Path in its mundane aspect. He is now no more a worldling. He is elevated to the sphere of a noble one (*ariya-puggala*). It is at this precious moment that he perceives and realises the supramundane Noble Eightfold Path, or, in other words, he enters the Stream (*sotāpatti*). As a Stream-winner (*sotāpanna*), he is entitled to rank as a first samaṇa. A sotāpanna realises that nowhere is there to be found a self or soul. The ego-belief (*sakkāya-diṭṭhi*) in him is shattered. However, he has not yet totally eradicated the concept of a self. He eradicates it completely while standing on the threshold of arahanthood.

You will admit that it is purely due to selfishness that man craves and is bound up with lust and pleasure, which give rise to fresh rebirth. It is only when be becomes fully aware of not-self through his own efforts at gaining wisdom that he transcends the world of desires to the extra-sensory world, and graduating through the four stages and their immediate fruits (*phala*), he cuts across the cosmic ocean of births and deaths to arrive at the further shore— Nibbāna. Detachment is the preliminary step to gain the knowledge of not-self. However, those who love the world, and its so-called pleasures, will not be enamored of leaving behind all that man holds as dear. May they also arrive at wisdom, one day, to see reality.

> *How sweet the peaceful solitude of him*
> *Who has both learned and then perceived the Truth!*
> *Happy to be hate free—kind to all*
> *Happily rid of passion and desire*
> *And Self delusion—that is Supreme Joy.*

Udāna 2. 1

— §§§ —

ABOUT PARIYATTI

Pariyatti is dedicated to providing affordable access to authentic teachings of the Buddha about the Dhamma theory (*pariyatti*) and practice (*paṭipatti*) of Vipassana meditation. A 501(c)(3) non-profit charitable organization since 2002, Pariyatti is sustained by contributions from individuals who appreciate and want to share the incalculable value of the Dhamma teachings. We invite you to visit www.pariyatti.org to learn about our programs, services, and ways to support publishing and other undertakings.

Pariyatti Publishing Imprints

Vipassana Research Publications (focus on Vipassana as taught by S.N. Goenka in the tradition of Sayagyi U Ba Khin)
BPS Pariyatti Editions (selected titles from the Buddhist Publication Society, co-published by Pariyatti)
MPA Pariyatti Editions (selected titles from the Myanmar Pitaka Association, co-published by Pariyatti)
Pariyatti Digital Editions (audio and video titles, including discourses)
Pariyatti Press (classic titles returned to print and inspirational writing by contemporary authors)

Pariyatti enriches the world by

- disseminating the words of the Buddha,
- providing sustenance for the seeker's journey,
- illuminating the meditator's path.

Made in the USA
Columbia, SC
01 August 2024

3821e084-ab48-414d-b305-89a6eb9c8d0bR01